Mussolini

Martin Clark

PEARSON

Longman

Harlow, England • London • New York • Boston • San Francisco • Toronto
Sydney • Tokyo • Singapore • Hong Kong • Seoul • Taipei • New Delhi
Cape Town • Madrid • Mexico City • Amsterdam • Munich • Paris • Milan

PEARSON EDUCATION LIMITED

Edinburgh Gate
Harlow CM20 2JE
United Kingdom
Tel: +44 (0)1279 623623
Fax: +44 (0)1279 431059
Website: www.pearsoned.co.uk

First edition published in Great Britain in 2005

© Pearson Education Limited 2005

The right of Martin Clark to be identified as author
of this work has been asserted by him in accordance
with the Copyright, Designs and Patents Act 1988.

ISBN 978-0-582-06595-6

British Library Cataloguing in Publication Data
A CIP catalogue record for this book can be obtained from the British Library

Library of Congress Cataloging in Publication Data
A CIP catalog record for this book can be obtained from the Library of Congress

10   9   8   7   6   5   4   3
08   07

Set by 35 in 9.5/12pt Celeste
Printed in Malaysia

The Publisher's policy is to use paper manufactured from sustainable forests.

Contents

Acknowledgements

Many people have helped me write this book. In particular, I should like to thank all the helpful staff of the Central State Archives and of the Foreign Ministry archives in Rome, the National Libraries in Florence and Rome, the British Library and the Public Record Office in London, and the National Library of Scotland and the University Library in Edinburgh. I am also extremely grateful to the series editor, Professor Keith Robbins, and to successive editors at Longmans, Andrew MacLennan and Heather McCallum, not least for their patience and forbearance over far too long a time. I owe a special word of thanks to the actor Steven Berkoff, whose marvellous performance some years ago as Coriolanus inspired one of the sub-themes of this book. Above all, I should like to thank my wife Ruth, who has managed to tolerate both *Mussolini* and myself.

Glossary and Abbreviations

A few non-English terms are used in the text:

Anschluss, 'annexation' (of Austria by Germany)

carabinieri, military police

cheka (*chrezvychainaya kommissiya*), 'extraordinary commission' of secret police

dopolavoro ('afterwork'), Fascist leisure organisation

gerarchi (hierarchs), senior members of the Fascist movement or government

listone, long list (of candidates)

Negus, Emperor of Ethiopia

Popolari, members of (Catholic) Popular Party

Prefects, provincial governors

Quadrumviri, the four men (Italo Balbo, Michele Bianchi, Emilio De Bono and Cesare Maria De Vecchi) placed in charge of military operations and political liaison during the Fascist 'March on Rome' in 1922

ras (Ethiopian chief), local Fascist boss or squad leader

spregiudicatezza, open-mindedness, lack of prejudice or of principle

squadrismo, activities and values of local Fascist squads

squadrista, member of a squad

syndicalists, advocates of revolutionary activity by workers themselves, organised in trade unions (*sindacati*) rather than in political parties

Ustasha ('insurgence'), Croatian Fascist movement

Abbreviations

ACS   *Archivio Centrale dello Stato*, Central State Archives, Rome

ASAE   *Archivio Storico del Ministero degli Affari Esteri*, Foreign Ministry Archives, Rome

CLN   *Comitato di Liberazione Nazionale*, Committee of National Liberation

CLNAI   *Comitato di Liberazione Nazionale Alta Italia*, Committee of National Liberation of Upper Italy

DBFP	Documents on British Foreign Policy 1919–39 (HMSO, London)
DDI	*Documenti Diplomatici Italiani*, Italian Diplomatic Documents (Rome)
DGFP	Documents on German Foreign Policy 1918–45 (London and Washington)
FO	Foreign Office, London
IMI	*Istituto Mobiliare Italiano*, State finance house
IRI	*Istituto per la Ricostruzione Industriale*, Institute for Industrial Reconstruction
MVSN	*Milizia Volontaria per la Sicurezza Nazionale*, Voluntary Militia for National Security; Fascist Militia
OO	B. Mussolini, *Opera Omnia* (Collected Works); vols 1–36 published Florence, 1951–63; vols 37–44 published Rome, 1978–81
OVRA	Meaning of initials unknown; secret police
PFR	*Partito Fascista Repubblicano*, Fascist Republican Party
PNF	*Partito Nazionale Fascista*, Fascist National Party
PRO	Public Record Office, London
RSI	*Repubblica Sociale Italiana*, Italian Social Republic ('Republic of Salò')
SPD	*Segreteria Particolare del Duce*, The *Duce*'s Private Secretariat
SS	*Schutzstaffel*, security police

Mussolini: Personality and Power

Benito Mussolini was head of the Italian Fascist government from October 1922 until his death at the hands of anti-Fascist partisans in April 1945. For over 20 years the story of his life can barely be distinguished from that of his regime, or of his country. This presents his biographer with a problem. If the writer is an academic historian by training, his study of Mussolini will be essentially a history of Italy; Mussolini himself is likely to appear relatively insignificant, a puppet of deep structures of power and values well beyond his control or understanding. If, however, the biographer is an amateur psychologist by inclination, as most biographers are, he will be tempted to explain even the most cataclysmic events – economic crises, world wars – in terms of Mussolini's aberrant personality or unhappy early life, and to ignore much of the historical context. Clearly a good biography should avoid both these pitfalls, but no doubt I have succumbed to each. At any rate, I have tried to keep Mussolini in context, but also in the foreground – not too difficult, in his case.

However, 'personality' is a field where evidence is limited, prejudices are strong, and ambiguities are many. Like 'power', it tends to vanish under close analysis. Certainly Mussolini's personality had many contradictions. It seems to me, as it has to many others, that he was essentially a superb ham actor of the old actor-manager school. He loved melodrama, and melodrama loved him. Not for nothing do most people associate Mussolini with his balcony at palazzo Venezia, a true stage on which he could strut and fret his hour to the huge acclaim of the mass audience below. He appeared in public as an exuberant character, colourful and larger than life: fighting duels, racing around in fast cars, piloting dodgy aircraft, hyperactive sexually, a man contemptuous of convention and of lesser mortals. He enjoyed playing the Stern Dictator, but could switch instantly to other roles – the Fiery Socialist, the Sensitive Intellectual, the Far-Sighted Statesman or even the Respectable Family Man. For many years he put on a great show, and his public loved it. Indeed, he pioneered the modern concept of politics as show business, mixed adroitly with 'spin'. Even in one-to-one conversations the play-acting continued: his more perceptive visitors noticed that Mussolini changed his attitudes to fit in with theirs, so they went away happy that he agreed with them, even that he was similar to them, deep down.[1]

Acting ability is a huge advantage to aspiring politicians, but the self-dramatising 'histrionic personality' is a well-known type in the psychology textbooks.[2] The urge always to be the centre of attention and the constant need to win the approval of others indicate deep-seated insecurity. In children, it is sometimes explained as the result of intermittent and/or conditional parental affection, forcing the child to win approval by his own efforts. As adults, such people are introverted, self-absorbed, and very ambitious. Restless and doubt-ridden, they need always to prove themselves. They choose careers – politics, the stage, the media – where they can soon become widely known and admired, and they are often obsessed by their own physical appearance. They are very active sexually but need to dominate their partners, and they do not commit themselves in relationships. They have few friends and even fewer fixed beliefs. They court innovation, danger and adventure of all kinds, not an ideal trait in a political leader. They pose, constantly. This 'histrionic personality' is of course an archetype and there are obvious dangers in psychological stereotyping, especially when done by amateurs in the field. Furthermore, much depends on the observer's perspective ('I am a born leader; you have ideas above your station; he is a megalomaniac'). Even so, this stereotype may be a useful way of understanding Mussolini's contradictory personality. Note that I am not suggesting for one moment that Mussolini was mentally disturbed, nor that he was not fully responsible for his actions. In most ways he was remarkably sane for a politician, but he was a driven, insecure loner, and as dictator he became more lonely still.

Naturally this was not the whole story. Mussolini undeniably had a very attractive side too, at least until the late 1930s. He had real charm – his famous *fascino*, an untamed, unpredictable sensitivity – and he had real political gifts, including caution, lack of conventional prejudices (*spregiudicatezza*) and the greatest political gift of all, ambiguity. He was brilliant at synthesis, grasping the essence of arguments and situations very rapidly, and he was also bold and imaginative. He worked hard, and liked order: his desk was clear of paper, and all his documents were systematically filed. He had curiosity, good humour and a superb memory, and in his early years was good at assessing other people and picking the right ones for his purposes. He admired Churchill, liked Dollfuss and

Austen Chamberlain, despised Neville Chamberlain and all French politicians except Laval, distrusted Franco, respected Stalin, feared Hitler and detested Eden; not a bad record. Like most people, he was far more interested in power, adventure, sport and sex than in money; indeed, he had no interest in money at all, despising it and all those who sought it, and as Prime Minister did not draw his pay. He was a compelling speaker and a superb journalist, in both arts using clear, simple language and communicating a clear, simple message. It was through journalism that he made his name, and it was mostly through journalism that he came to power. He remained a great journalist and editor throughout his life, writing regular articles in his own newspaper and in the foreign press. Like all serious journalists, he was sarcastic, omniscient and omni-competent. He knew he could do everything far better than those currently in charge, and it was his agreeable duty to tell them so. But he was not a fanatic – despite the hard-line rhetoric, he was willing to compromise; and he was not vindictive, as dictators go. Above all, he was a 'Big Man' in the anthropological sense: he had style and a natural authority that imposed itself on the tribe.

But the 'histrionic personality' has its darker side too. Mussolini was often quarrelsome and violent. He was erratic, and liable to betray any cause or colleague. In his early years as a Romagna hothead he was often called *e matto* ('the madman'). Later on, some – including a Milan police inspector in June 1919 – supposed he suffered from the effects of syphilis, wrongly: Mussolini never had that, although he did have gonorrhoea as a young man.[3] A more plausible medical guess, looking at his famously bulging eyes and his volatile behaviour, is to suspect hyperthyroidism, as Enrico Ferri apparently did.[4] Mussolini's real problem was insecurity. It made him very susceptible to flattery but unable to abide criticism, let alone disparagement. He distrusted virtually everybody, perhaps a necessary condition for political success but also a handicap once in office. He was willing to listen to technical experts, but he treated his 'generalist' colleagues contemptuously and allowed very little discussion of political issues: he decided, they implemented. And he was impatient. Like most born journalists, he over-simplified complex issues rather than analysing them fully or reflecting seriously upon them. His published works run to 44 volumes but consist almost entirely of short articles or speeches; only youthful studies of Jan Hus and of the Trentino go deeper, and even they are partisan. This mind-set helped him win power and impress others, but it was a big handicap when it came to running a country. Mussolini's decision-making typically consisted of sudden individual initiatives, 'battles' to achieve loudly proclaimed goals (see Chapter 5). Although he claimed always to be a revolutionary, he lacked the inner self-confidence to tackle the economic, religious, bureaucratic or military elites; so he compromised with them instead, and then complained (rightly) that they had betrayed him. For the same reason he found it difficult to take big decisions, and was often pushed into them by others, or by events – arguably this was true at the onset of both World Wars.

Mussolini's most obvious fault was his pride. He despised most institutions, most countries and most people, especially his own followers – whom he termed disparagingly 'the Fascists', as if he were not one of them. Moreover, he did not mellow with age. He remained a natural bully but lost his streetwise sharpness of the 1920s, and forgot the need for caution. Indeed, he grew out of his job, to a spectacular degree. Power corrupted, in the original sense of the word: it rotted his mind. By the late 1930s, secure in his tenure and flattered by all, he had become an irascible old bore, convinced of his own infallibility and unwilling to take advice or heed information. He had no long-term perspective, knowing little history and having no religious beliefs. He also knew virtually nothing about economics, science, military power or naval strategy, and could no longer be bothered to learn. Instead, he began ranting against his own countrymen, unworthy to be ruled by a genius like himself, and he determined to change their daily habits and their peaceable character. Moreover, he knew even less about foreign countries than he did about Italy. In his youth he had travelled little, and that little only to Switzerland, south-east France and southern Austria, all within easy reach of Italy; and even there he had spent most of his time with other Italians. He still needed the crowd's applause, but after a dozen years of Fascism the audience was growing bored, and so was Mussolini. The only way to win more adulation was war, or rather conquest. So Italy embarked on a series of wars. In 1935–6 Mussolini conquered Ethiopia and founded an 'Italian Empire'. But even that was not enough.

The perceptive reader will have noticed that I have already fallen into my own trap, explaining away wars purely by reference to 'personality'. Well, character is destiny; but clearly the history mattered too. Mussolini was not that unusual; on the contrary, he was a child of his times. Born in 1883, he was brought up in the Republican/Socialist and anti-clerical traditions of his native Romagna, and was imbued with the heroic, manly values of Garibaldi and Mazzini. His education and reading was mostly on semi-contemporary history and literature – Socialist tracts, Romantic French novelists, later on the syndicalists and a touch of Nietzsche. But in 1896, when he was 12, the Ethiopians defeated the Italian army at Adowa – one of the first occasions when Africans defeated substantial European forces in a set-piece battle. While other European powers scrambled for Africa, Italy had to scramble out, at least of Ethiopia. It was a huge national humiliation, and it demanded to be avenged. However, the Liberal politicians of Mussolini's youth showed little interest in such matters. Italy was a poor country, a unified state only since 1861, with immense regional differences and a very limited suffrage. Giovanni Giolitti, Prime Minister for most of the pre-1914 decade, knew he had to win popular support for the weak constitutional regime, so he pursued conciliatory policies at home and (until 1911) cautious ones abroad. He introduced more modern labour legislation, welfare and public works, tolerated strikes and trade unions, and wooed the 'reformist' wing of the Socialist party. In 1912 he brought in almost universal manhood suffrage. However, his opponents denounced him for corruption and for rigging elections, and the radical young came to loathe the whole Liberal political Establishment. Many of the themes of Mussolini's political career – his anticapitalist sentiment, his need to regain Ethiopia and found an Empire, his thirst for revenge, his sensitivity to slights on Italian honour and on the Italian army – were fully shared by the most articulate members of his generation.

The First World War identified Mussolini even more fully with his contemporaries. When it began, he was already the successful editor of the Socialist party newspaper and very prominent in left-wing politics. But in 1914 he broke with the neutralist Socialist party and became a leading spokesman for war. He fought in the trenches, was badly wounded in 1917 and resumed his pro-war journalism, particularly effective in the dark days after the defeat of Caporetto. In short, he made himself the leading spokesman for the 'generation of 1914' in Italy. The Fascist movement he founded in 1919 consisted essentially of returned ex-soldiers. It expressed their patriotic demands and their quest for reward, their hatred of peaceful routine and their acceptance of hierarchy and discipline harnessed to the national cause.

By then Mussolini had grasped, earlier than most, that the old Liberal, parliamentary regime was weak. Now the masses had the vote and the gun, and governments would have to buy them off. He did not think they could manage it. The resulting conflicts would force men to give up liberal democracy, along with its associated 'rights' of free speech, free press, etc., for the sake of security and social cohesion. Only an authoritarian government, with a firm patriotic appeal, could provide internal order and external defence. Mussolini rejected all existing modes of thought – conservative, liberal, Catholic, reformist Socialist, revolutionary Socialist – and invented a new one of impatient patriotic heroism and radical social reform. His argument was, as always, simplistic but it was certainly plausible in the uncertain years after the First World War. It appealed to, and was shared by, a whole generation. Mussolini's success in winning power in October 1922 seemed to prove him right. Like all great politicians, he had spotted what was happening already, had advocated it strongly, and had then claimed the credit. Naturally, he had to compromise, especially early on. Political power always depends on others, and the others are not reliable. Mussolini's power, like everybody else's, rested on constant hard-nosed bargaining and face-saving concessions. For many years he was a charismatic dictator for show, and a cautious mediator for real. Still, the show was what mattered most. Mussolini may have been, in the Italian phrase, a *venditore di fumo* ('smoke salesman'; Americans would say 'snake-oil'), but his patter was convincing, and it was *fumo* that people were very anxious to buy.

One way of understanding Mussolini is to compare him with other politicians, or with well-known literary figures. He seems to me closest not to other twentieth-century dictators but to those other dynamic mountebanks and unscrupulous troublemakers of genius, David Lloyd George and Theodore Roosevelt, both similarly determined not to allow people a quiet life. He also shared many characteristics with General de Gaulle, a man of even greater literary gifts, even greater haughty isolation, even greater sensitivity to slights personal or national, even greater cynicism (*Français, je vous ai compris*) and even greater absurdity. Both de Gaulle and Lloyd George, like Mussolini, ruled autocratically but preserved the constitutional proprieties, as long as it suited them. Certainly the streetwise Mussolini, brought up on Roman ideals of rational h eroism and State authority, had little in common with the 'tragic buffoon' Hitler, wrapt in the old miasmal mist of Nibelungian paganism. Mussolini was human, but not sentimental; Hitler was the reverse.

As for literary figures, there is something of Don Quixote in Mussolini. Mussolini, too, had read too many bad romances, was devoted to remarkably old-fashioned views of 'honour' and was anxious to set the world to rights. He, too, tried to live his own myth, and to make his dreams real. What is Mussolini's slogan 'Believe, Obey, Fight' if not a duller version of Quixote's deluded demands? Moreover, a nation of Sancho Panzas, earthy realists to a man, did believe in him: everyone needs illusions to live by. But Don Quixote is too attractive a figure, and too idealistic, for a good comparison. There is even more of Malvolio in Mussolini. Malvolio is another insecure, lonely figure who despises others and is easily tricked into ridiculous posturing. True, Mussolini did not wear yellow stockings, but he had a distinctly erratic dress sense, and he wore spats and bowler hats long after the fashion had changed. Malvolio, when humiliated, cries out 'I'll be reveng'd on the whole pack of you'[5]: Mussolini's sentiments entirely, throughout his life.

However, the prime literary comparison must surely be with another Shakespearian character. Mussolini would have been chosen from a thousand applicants to play the part of Coriolanus. A valiant, solitary hero, full of contempt for the greedy plebs, a man who despises comfort, cannot control his pride and anger, will not tolerate humiliation, thirsts for revenge and ends up ruining his country; Shakespeare described all this 400 years ago. Mussolini, of course, was not as impolitic as Coriolanus, nor as good at war. He had more self-awareness and irony, and more sensitivity to others, than Coriolanus ever shows. Even so, Volumnia's famous speech to Coriolanus is all too appropriate, as a summary of Mussolini's life and achievements:

The end of war's uncertain; but this certain
That, if thou conquer Rome, the benefit
Which thou shalt thereby reap is such a name
Whose repetition will be dogg'd with curses;
Whose chronicle thus writ: 'The man was noble,
But with his last attempt he wip'd it out,
Destroy'd his country, and his name remains
To th' ensuing age abhorr'd.'[6]

Notes

1 C. Rossi, *Trenta Tre Vicende Mussoliniane* (Milan, 1958), pp. 411–15; L. Frassati, *Il Destino Passa per Varsavia* (Bologna, 1949), pp. 112ff. On Mussolini as actor, see esp. C. Berneri, *Mussolini Grande Attore* (Barcelona, 1934; 2nd edn, Pistoia, 1983).

2 Cf. D.L. Rosenhahn and M. Seligman, *Abnormal Psychology* (New York, 1984), pp. 450–2; R.H. Woody (ed.), *Encyclopedia of Clinical Assessment* (San Francisco, 1980), i, pp. 181–3.

3 R. De Felice, *Mussolini il Rivoluzionario* (Turin, 1965), pp. 462–4 and 730–7.

4 L. Longanesi, *In Piedi e Seduti* (Milan, 1948), p. 57.

5 W. Shakespeare, *Twelfth Night*, V i 364.

6 W. Shakespeare, *Coriolanus*, V iii 141–8.

Chapter 1

Early Years and the Great War 1883–1918

The Rise to Fame

Benito Mussolini was born on 29 July 1883 near Dovia (now Predappio Nuova), a village a couple of miles from Predappio (now Predappio Alta) in the Romagna region of central Italy. His father, Alessandro, was the local blacksmith, a self-educated, forceful character who had been imprisoned as a revolutionary anarchist in his early years, still took a keen idealistic interest in politics, sat on the local council as a Socialist, and knew personally many of Italy's left-wing leaders. He was a man of firm opinions firmly expressed, generous to his friends and implacable to his foes. He could be quick-tempered and he liked both women and drink, but he was not a caricature drunken bully. He used his belt on Benito quite often, but he also encouraged his son's reading and helped him become aware of the wider world.[1] In short, he was an overbearing and rather unpredictable man, just the kind to make a child feel insecure. Benito admired him, resembled him physically and adopted many of his values. Benito's mother, Rosa Maltoni, was a very different character. She was the local primary school teacher, a serious, responsible woman and a devout Catholic, but she suffered from 'nerves' and she never really understood her eldest son. Soon the family grew, although it remained small by nineteenth-century standards. In January 1885, 18 months after Benito, his brother Arnaldo was born – another big blow to Benito's security if we believe the psychiatrists, especially as Arnaldo soon had to be sent away for wet-nursing (the two boys got on extremely well later on). In November 1888 his sister Edvige appeared.

With two such different parents, whatever the young Benito did was unlikely to please both of them. The contrast became evident very early on. His mother insisted on him being baptised, but his father chose the names: Benito, after Benito Juárez who had led the Mexican revolution against France in the 1860s; Amilcare, after Amilcare Cipriani the radical hero of the Italian Risorgimento; and Andrea, after Andrea Costa the famous Romagna anarchist turned Socialist. With names like that, poor little Benito Amilcare Andrea Mussolini could hardly help growing up a 'subversive', like his father. To ensure this happy outcome, his father would cheer everybody up by reading *Les Misérables* to the family in the evenings, and even Machiavelli's *The Prince* as well. One wonders how much fun and laughter there was in the Mussolini household. Furthermore, Benito was the 'son of the teacher', expected to behave well but liable to mockery from fellow-pupils. Romagna in the late nineteenth century had a reputation as an unruly society, where children's arguments were settled by fists or knives, and adult disputes could lead to lengthy family vendettas. In reality, the region was a provincial backwater, although enlivened by occasional crimes of passion. But it had a romantic image, and the *Romagnoli* pretended to live up to it. So the young Benito learned to look after himself, a trait he never lost.

The Mussolinis were a relatively prosperous and well-educated family, with two incomes and only three children. A blacksmith had a skilled job, always in demand; a teacher had a secure one, with high social status. Money was short at times and food was plain, but both Benito and his brother went to school until the age of 18, and this was very unusual in rural areas. At home, the family spoke Italian, not dialect. Benito's grandfather had been a landowner, and in 1903 Alessandro bought some land himself with a legacy and rented it out to a local peasant – and was expelled briefly from the local Socialist party as a result. The property was worth 9,000 lire when Alessandro died in 1910, so Benito and his two siblings inherited 3,000 lire each, quite a substantial sum.[2]

Benito learned to speak late but was soon reading avidly, a life-long trait. He was a lonely child, shy and introverted, but fond of animals. At the age of nine his parents – or rather his mother, overriding his anti-clerical father's objections – sent him away to a boarding school run by Salesian friars in the nearby town of Faenza. This was a miserable experience for the young Benito. Discipline was strict, and he was homesick and lonely. The other boys were not peasants but came from prosperous middle-class families. Hitherto he had been the teacher's son, and the outstanding pupil; now he was at the bottom of the social ladder, and had to eat at the poor boys' table. Furthermore, his teachers (laymen, in the primary classes) disliked him as the son of a notorious left-wing agitator, and by his own account persecuted him unjustly.[3] Benito was not one to take humiliation lying down. Aware of his own merits, he reacted very strongly indeed. Eventually he was expelled for twice pulling a knife on a fellow-pupil. All this naturally boosted his insecurity and sense of grievance against an uncaring world. Perhaps the Salesians have a lot to answer for, although in all probability the real psychological damage had already been done, at home. At any rate, the young Mussolini was consumed by resentment, and by a need to show the world what he was worth. He hated the middle classes, he hated the Church, he hated authority and he hated humiliation.

His next school, the *Istituto Magistrale* at Forlimpopoli, trained future primary teachers and was more suitable socially, if not educationally. The other pupils were lower middle class like himself, and the teachers soon realised that Benito had outstanding ability. Mussolini's education there was traditional, but perhaps not traditional enough. He studied nineteenth-century Italian history, geography, literature, French and basic mathematics, but he learned very little about science, technical subjects, economics, art or classics – anything that might have given him a training in logical thought or a wider perspective. Still, it was a far better education than most Italians received. Benito was much happier at this school, although here, too, he caused trouble: he organised a successful strike against the food, and was eventually expelled from the boarding wing, again for threatening a fellow-pupil with a knife. He was allowed to continue at school, but had to live in lodgings nearby. At age 16 he learned something about sex, losing his virginity in a Forlì brothel in a scene worthy of Fellini: it cost him half a lira, and the woman 'oozed fat from every pore'.[4] He also discovered a natural talent for oratory, and was chosen to give the commemorative address on the death of Giuseppe Verdi in 1901. The same year he qualified as a primary teacher, following in his mother's footsteps, with 132 marks out of 150: he was particularly good at pedagogy and at Italian language and literature, but weaker at maths and agronomy.[5]

When he went home, his father tried to get him a job at the local council as assistant secretary, but in vain. Then he applied for a teaching post in Piedmont, but was turned down. He consoled himself with a local girl, Virginia E. His own later account of this episode is revealing: 'I grabbed her on the stairway, pushed her into a corner behind a door and made her mine. She got up crying, and insulted me through her tears. She said I had "stolen her honour". Perhaps so. But what honour was there? Virginia was not angry with me for long. For three months we loved each other, emotionally very little but physically a great deal.'[6] This idyllic affair ended early in 1902 when Benito found his first job, as replacement teacher at Gualtieri in Emilia. He was paid 56 lire a month, of which 40 went on board and lodging. He found the work dull and the life duller, although made more bearable by music – it was here that he took up the fiddle – and by Giulia, the wife of a local soldier stationed elsewhere.

When the summer term ended, it was time for adventure. He borrowed 50 lire from his mother and caught the train to Switzerland – a strange choice for a 19-year-old seeking adventure, particularly as he already detested both democracy and the bourgeoisie. For the next seven years, apart from his military service in 1905–6, his life consisted of temporary teaching jobs in Italy – it is noticeable that he was never reappointed anywhere – and foreign travel, although the travel was always to nearby countries, where foreign revolutionaries were tolerated and the Italian community was large. He stayed in Switzerland, or just over the border in France, until November 1904, apart from a visit back home in late 1903 to see his mother who was seriously ill. He found work as a building labourer or errand boy/shop assistant (but only for a few weeks in all, at various times) and slept in cheap boarding houses or, on one occasion, under a bridge (but only one night, and it was July). However, he soon found his true vocation, as journalist and agitator. Within a month of arriving he was writing for the Italian-language *L'Avvenire del Lavoratore* in Lausanne, and making (paid) fiery speeches to the thousands of Italian immigrant workers, particularly during strikes or protest demonstrations. He became a brilliant and daring orator, specialising in anticlerical themes. Occasionally he was arrested for sedition or threatening behaviour, fingerprinted and photographed, given a few nights in the cells and then expelled to another canton. This was all much more fun than teaching. Mussolini soon became well known in Socialist circles and found influential friends and supporters, including the Russian Marxist Angelica Balabanova who became both his mistress and his mentor in Socialist politics and in the correct interpretation of Marx.

Mussolini was always a wonderful self-dramatist, and he played the part of angry young agitator to perfection. Thin, pale, scowling, with wide, staring eyes, he wore 'revolutionary' clothing (e.g. a red cravat) and demonstrated a revolutionary temperament. He was a caricature village Marat, a romantic symbol of uncompromising zeal. Once, debating the existence of God with a Protestant pastor in a crowded hall, he challenged God to strike him down dead within 10 minutes, to prove He existed. But God failed His test. Yet despite later myths, Mussolini's youthful bohemian period was not all that uncomfortable. He did not go far – no transatlantic steerage trips for him – and so learned little of the outside world. He was, in any case, a voluntary emigrant. He had a teaching certificate, and could have found work in Italy. His period abroad was really an extended and not very adventurous 'gap year': time out to have affairs and find his vocation. He had plenty of affairs, particularly a serious one with a married Russian medical student, Eleonora H. As for his vocation, he rarely needed to do manual labour. Instead, he worked as a journalist and lecturer, or as a union organiser in the Lausanne building trade, or as translator or language teacher; his mother sent him money when he needed it. So he was fairly privileged, as penniless emigrants go. Indeed, in the summer of 1904 he enrolled at the University of Lausanne's summer course, and attended lectures by the university's most eminent professor, Vilfredo Pareto. He had plenty of time to read, although what he read – Nietzsche, Carlyle, Stirner, Blanqui, the wilder anarchists – served mostly to reinforce his egoism. Like most people, he read books that confirmed his prejudices, not ones that might challenge them. He certainly did not read difficult books on complex subjects: the *Communist Manifesto* yes, *Das Kapital* definitely no. His own ideas were romantic tosh, and at least 30 years out of date at that. Mussolini was and remained a very old-fashioned revolutionary.

All this was enjoyable and gave him some influence in exile politics, but of course if he wanted a real political role he would have to go back to Italy. However, back in Italy he would have to do his military service – indeed, he had already been posted as a deserter for not reporting to the army in 1903. He could return only because the government issued a general amnesty in 1904 to mark the birth of Prince Humbert. In January 1905 Mussolini joined the 10th Regiment of *bersaglieri*, stationed at Verona. Much to his surprise, he liked the army. There was plenty of physical exercise, always good for him, and there were opportunities to meet people from all over Italy. Perhaps the army taught him patriotism, although it seems unlikely: after his military service ended in September 1906 he was as anti-militarist and anti-monarchist as ever, and in 1911 was imprisoned for his part in demonstrations against the Libyan war. More probably, Mussolini was a good soldier just as he was a good journalist, or a good orator, or a good politician. He could grasp quickly what was needed, and knew how to fit in. One lesson he certainly did learn. The *bersaglieri* were crack infantrymen, and they marched at a trotting pace. Years later, Mussolini imposed this on his Fascist movement. He thus became the first jogging politician, one of his more dreadful legacies to posterity.

After military service, Mussolini went back to Romagna briefly, but it was now a gloomy place for him as his mother had died during his military service. He resumed schoolteaching, this time at Caneva di Tolmezzo, in north-east Italy. His stay there in 1906–7 was a period of excessive drinking and womanising, the latter including his married landlady, to great local scandal. Nor could the future dictator manage to keep order in class. But he read continually, and even studied Latin and Greek with the local priest. In November 1907 he also took and passed the exams at Bologna University to qualify as a secondary school teacher of French. Thenceforth he could, and did, call himself *professore*, and might hope for more attractive teaching jobs. In March 1908 he found one, at Oneglia in Liguria. Oneglia was a pleasant Socialist town, and Mussolini began writing for the local Socialist journal, *La Lima*. Soon he became its editor, and showed a natural gift for the job. He took the decisions, laid down the political line, and wrote most of the paper. Here, aged 25, he had found his true *métier*. And the local police had found a true 'subversive'. Mussolini's teaching post was not renewed, and he never taught again. In July 1908 he had to go back again to Romagna, where he was soon involved in the agricultural labourers' strikes over the use of threshing machines, and was imprisoned briefly for threatening behaviour. In November he took more exams at Bologna, this time in German, but not surprisingly he failed. His spoken and written German were never good, although he could read the language well enough and even translated books from German throughout his life.

In February 1909 he went abroad again, but not as a teacher. He moved to Trent, then under Austrian rule, where his anti-clerical reputation and his knowledge of German secured him the posts of secretary of the local labour union and editor of *L'Avvenire del Lavoratore*. The office job bored him but he was, as usual, extremely effective as editor and journalist. He worked with the leader of the Trent Socialists, Cesare Battisti, who edited the daily newspaper *Il Popolo* and in August made Mussolini his deputy editor. Trent was a frontier zone and Battisti was a convinced 'irredentist', anxious for the region to become part of united Italy, but most of the local Socialists favoured some form of 'autonomy' within Austria-Hungary, and Mussolini agreed with them.[7] On the other hand, Mussolini was far more 'revolutionary' and anti-clerical than they were, and with his speeches and above all his journalism he shook up the sleepy world of Trent Socialism. He became a well-known 'personality', and he also learned a great deal about the politics of nationalism in Austria-Hungary. Trent had a good public library, where Mussolini could really study and even write: his essay on the region, *Il Trentino Visto da un Socialista*, later published by *La Voce* in Florence, is undoubtedly Mussolini's most serious and well-documented work, particularly in its discussion of pan-Germanism.[8] He also, of course, found time for love affairs, particularly a serious one with Ida Dalser, by whom he later had a son. As elsewhere, it could not last. The Trent 'clerical' party, which included the future Italian Prime Minister Alcide De Gasperi, soon came to loathe Mussolini as a bullying *mangiaprete* (priest-baiter) preaching violence. They put pressure on the local police, and had him run out of town. Mussolini had already been expelled from several of the Swiss cantons, and briefly imprisoned both there and in Italy. In September 1909 he enjoyed the hospitality of an Austrian prison too (much better than the Italian ones, he had to admit) and was later expelled from Austria as a notorious troublemaker. He had lasted about seven months, about par for the course.

After September 1909 Mussolini's *Wanderjahre* were over: by this time few neighbouring countries would let him in. So he went back to Romagna, where his widowed father Alessandro had moved 10 miles to the provincial capital, Forlì, and had set up a restaurant (*la Trattoria del Bersagliere*) and a new household, both with his former mistress Anna Guidi. Benito also settled in Forlì, and began his real career as journalist, polemicist and political agitator. Eloquent and well informed, he was very good at it. Soon he was running the local branch of the Socialist party, and also editing (and writing) a new 'revolutionary' journal, *La Lotta di Classe*. He also wrote an anti-clerical romantic novel, *Claudia Particella, the Cardinal's Mistress*, set in seventeenth-century Trent and serialised in Battisti's *Il Popolo* in order to boost sales (an English translation appeared in London in 1929). It was not a great work of literature but it was very popular, and curiously prophetic about the future *Duce*'s own mistress, Claretta Petacci. He wrote other pot-boilers too, mostly on Austrian history, e.g. *The Tragedy of Mayerling*; as well as quite a serious work on the Czech medieval reformer Jan Hus, strongly anti-religious in tone and published in a series entitled 'Masters of Free Thought'. It is worth stressing that Mussolini's anti-clericalism was important to him, and the real key to his public appeal. He despised Christ for teaching nothing but cowardice and submission. In his preface to the Hus book, he hoped that 'it would arouse in the reader's mind hatred for any form of spiritual or secular tyranny, either theocratic or Jacobin'.[9] Perhaps it did in the reader's mind, but not in the writer's. Like many others, Mussolini rejected God but then had to find another ideal: first Socialism, then the nation. In both cases he tried to impose it on others, and force people to worship it.

Mussolini needed the money from these publications, because his Socialist work at Forlì brought in only 125 lire a month, because his father was seriously ill and because in January 1910 he himself had set up house with the 20-year-old Rachele Guidi. Rachele was already one of the family, being the daughter of Alessandro's mistress, and no doubt any psychiatrist worth his couch would see this union as conclusive proof of Benito's need to emulate his father. It had not been a romantic courtship, but it was a characteristically melodramatic one. Before he went off to Trent, Benito had brusquely told Rachele that he intended to marry her. While there, he did not even send her a postcard, and had a serious affair with Ida Dalser. On his return to Forlì, he took her off one night, and next day produced a revolver and told his father and her mother (who opposed the match) that they would have to agree, or else he would shoot Rachele and himself.[10] So Mussolini acquired a permanent partner, but without official recognition by Church or state – they married only in 1915 (see below). After many affairs, including some with well-educated women who could provide intellectual companionship, he had chosen a local girl, poor and ill-educated. He obviously thought he could dominate her, but he miscalculated. Rachele turned out to be a strong-minded woman of firm views and simple tastes, supportive of her man but unimpressed by his later success. In September 1910 their eldest child, Edda, was born, presumably named after Ibsen's *Hedda Gabler* (and she turned out rather like her); two months later Alessandro died.

Forlì was a combative province. Local politics meant disputes between Republicans, mostly small landowners or share-croppers, and Socialists, mostly landless labourers, often over control of threshing machines. It was an ideal environment for the young Mussolini, who attracted large crowds to his meetings, and soon became undisputed leader (*duce*) of the Socialists. He campaigned not only against the Republicans, but against the 'reformists' who dominated his own party at national level. They were charlatans, he proclaimed, and should be expelled from the party. He called for violent revolution, for an end to the monarchy, and for international solidarity. The national flag, he proclaimed, was 'a rag to be planted on a dunghill'.[11] In October 1910 he went to the Socialist party national congress and made an anti-militarist speech, but it had little impact; indeed he was laughed at for his provincial crudity. Perhaps because of this humiliation, but more immediately because the reformist deputy Bissolati visited the king for consultations during a government reshuffle, Mussolini decided to expel the party.[12] In 1911 he persuaded the Forlì federation to declare its autonomy from the rest of the party, hoping that other branches would join him; none did.

In September 1911 strikes broke out in Romagna over threshing machines, but they soon collapsed. Then Mussolini had a real stroke of luck. Italy went to war with Turkey over Libya, and protest demonstrations began again, this time nationally. In Forlì, they were serious and lasted two days, during which railway lines and telegraph wires were sabotaged. Both Mussolini and the local Republican leader, Pietro Nenni, were arrested as instigators to violence. After a showpiece trial where Mussolini inveighed splendidly against his 'bourgeois' judges ('if you acquit me, you will please me; but if you condemn me, you will honour me'[13]) he was sentenced to 12 months' imprisonment, later reduced to five on appeal. So he spent the winter of 1911–12 in cell no. 39 at Forlì prison. It was not too bad: Mussolini liked being alone, and prison gave him plenty of time for reading more French and German classics, and for finishing his book on Hus. Above all, it made him a martyr and gave him a splendid opportunity for more self-publicity. It takes a real egoist to write an autobiography at the age of 28, but Mussolini proved equal to the task. His 'La Mia Vita' was not a political blueprint like *Mein Kampf*; it was just a reflection on Mussolini himself, on his schooldays and early manhood. His father figured prominently, but there was very little on his mother except on her deathbed, and even less about his brother or sister. But there was a great deal about his sexual triumphs, recounted with much self-satisfaction and no sign of any affection for his former girl-friends: 'she obeyed me blindly. I disposed of her at my pleasure' – a euphemism his readers would have easily understood.[14]

By the time Mussolini was released in mid-March, he had become an anti-war hero as well as a Socialist one, and he was known well beyond Forlì. Two days later came another stroke of luck. In Rome, an anarchist tried to kill the king, and three leading Socialist deputies, including Bissolati again, visited the royal palace to congratulate him on his escape. Now Mussolini could denounce not only the Libyan war but the 'royal toadies', and demand that they be expelled from the party. But he was not in the party himself, so first of all he had to take the 2,000-odd Forlì Socialists (out of a national total of about 28,000) back in, to ensure his own personal 'block vote' at the next national congress. At that congress, at Reggio Emilia in July, Mussolini secured a personal triumph. Pale, thin, fierce and still radiant in the halo of his prison martyrdom, he spoke passionately against the war, against militarism and against the treacherous reformists. The congress roared its approval. Not only were the reformists expelled, but the 'revolutionary' faction, including Musso-lini himself, took over the party Directorate. It was his first success at national level. Rather characteristically, it consisted of expelling people who disagreed with him, including the very prestigious Leonida Bissolati, one of the party's founders and a former editor of the party newspaper. Again characteristically, Mussolini had simply been swimming with the tide. The 'royal reformists' were deeply unpopular in Socialist circles and would probably have been thrown out anyway, even if Mussolini had not put the boot into them. Still, he had done so very effectively, and now he could claim his reward.

His reward was to be made editor of the party newspaper *Avanti!*. This was in the gift of the Directorate, on which Mussolini now sat, and he was the only one with journalistic experience. A stopgap editor was appointed for a few months, but by November 1912 the job was his. This was just as well, for in September he had failed yet again to win a teaching post.[15] Mussolini, still only 29, now controlled the Socialist party's main propaganda outlet, and had become a key figure in national politics. He had got the foreman's job at last. He could express his views on all the issues of the day, and in Socialist politics journalism was the route to the top. He could look forward to a long, successful career as undisputed Socialist leader and tribune of the people, perhaps even as leader of the Italian Socialist revolution.

Mussolini's rise from provincial obscurity to Socialist power was rapid but explicable. He was a very striking figure. No other Socialist leader had an image like his: the proud *Romagnolo*, the blacksmith's son, the half-starved Bohemian emigrant who had known hard manual work and travelled the world, the heroic leader unjustly imprisoned, the passionate lover, above all the self-educated intellectual fluent in foreign tongues. It was a carefully cultivated image; much of it – especially the manual labour and the travel – was fairly bogus, but it rang true and it had huge appeal.[16] Sex and violence always sells. And some of it *was* true. He was very able, and genuinely dedicated to achieving social revolution. He was also a great polemical campaigner, and campaigning was what the party did. Yet his Socialism was an uncertain plant, derived essentially from Romagna's anti-clerical, Republican traditions and from his father's quasi-anarchism, from the insurrectionist legacy of Blanqui and Bakunin and from the fashionable – and very influential – 'syndicalism' of his day. The syndicalists advocated workers' direct revolutionary action to be carried out not by a party but by the workers themselves, organised in trade unions (*sindacati*). Mussolini admired this resolute approach, and admired too the syndicalists' advocacy of rousing myths and violence. He also had close links with the *Voce* group of radical activists in Florence. As for Marxism, Mussolini preached the class struggle and the need for revolution, but he totally rejected 'scientific Socialism' and determinism, and he had no industrial or economic perspective. He detested a large section of his own party, the 'reformists' and the deputies; and he soon realised that the 'revolutionary Socialists' were revolutionary only in name. So Mussolini was left preaching 'revolution' inside a party that had no intention of attempting one, while admiring people outside the party who had. It was an untenable position. Even in 1912 people thought he would soon walk out.[17] Yet Mussolini was not really an untypical Italian Socialist. The party had always been a mixture of differing traditions, with anti-clericalism, anti-parliamentarianism and village Jacobinism prominent among them. Nor was he quite a syndicalist. He thought political parties, and political organisation, were essential if revolution were to be successful. The workers and peasants might overthrow the despised bourgeois order, but only if inspired and led by a resolute leader like himself.

The *Duce* of Socialism

In November 1912 Mussolini moved to Milan, to edit *Avanti!*. He soon got rid of the previous editor, the reformist Claudio Treves, and even refused to accept any articles by him – quite right too, as Treves was an execrably tedious writer. But he took Angelica Balabanova with him, to keep him right on points of Marxist doctrine; she, too, was eased out after a few months, as Mussolini grew more confident in the job. Mussolini proved as successful a journalist in Milan as he had at Oneglia and at Forlì. He wrote with biting force and passion, but also with clarity and precision of fact and detail. Always polemical, particularly against his reformist opponents in the party, he soon attracted a talented group of Bohemian reporters and columnists, many of them syndicalists or 'Southernists' who focused on the problems of Italy's neglected southern regions. *Avanti!*, previously a dull official paper with a circulation of below 28,000, became the lively focus of Italian revolutionary Socialism, with strong syndicalist overtones. Within a year it was selling nearly 40,000 copies, and by mid-1914 between 60,000 and 70,000.[18] Mussolini also gave speeches, as usual, throughout northern Italy, but journalism mattered most. It was creating 'mass politics' for the new age of mass suffrage, introduced to Italy at exactly this time. Mussolini was probably the best journalist in the country; and journalism and political activism were one.

Yet Mussolini had problems in Milan. He had a stipend of 500 lire a month – he deliberately took less than the 700 lire that had been paid to Treves, and even refused to pay Treves his redundancy money[19] – but Milan was an expensive place, and he had a wife and child to support. He had left Rachele behind in Forlì, but after a month or two she insisted angrily on moving up to Milan, found a flat and brought her mother with her. The real problem was that Milan was a big, sophisticated city, and

Mussolini was seen there as a provincial hick, indeed as a rather comic figure with his permanent scowl and his three days' growth of beard. The leading Socialist reformists, men like Treves and Filippo Turati who were still in the party despite the expulsions of the previous July, lived in Milan and were horrified by Mussolini and by Mussolini's *Avanti!*. They snubbed the new editor, and he cordially detested them. The syndicalists, on the other hand, thought Mussolini was not revolutionary enough. In May 1913 they called an engineering strike, opposed by the reformist Socialist unions. Mussolini's dilemma was acute: should *Avanti!* support it or not? In fact, he did support it, but without enthusiasm; and some members of the party Directorate criticised him very sharply. Indeed, he had to offer a tactical resignation, soon rejected. *Avanti!* was the official Socialist newspaper. Mussolini was the editor, but not the boss. He had some leeway, but he could not write what he liked. He had to toe the party line, as laid down by the Directorate. Mussolini, always impatient of constraints, found this irksome, particularly as he was on the Directorate himself and so knew what the other members were like. In November 1913 he founded his own fortnightly journal, *Utopia*, where he could write freely and where he could challenge the reformists' fortnightly *Critica Sociale*. *Utopia* proclaimed his activist, 'voluntarist' beliefs: revolution by energetic elites. He invited syndicalist writers – Panunzio, Lanzillo, Arturo Labriola – to write for it, and the *Voce* group was prominent too. It discussed the key question of 1914, the increasing threat of war; and whether Socialists could, or should, prevent it.

He still had some striking success with women. Both Balabanova and *Avanti!*'s art critic Margherita Sarfatti – upper middle-class radical chic – were his mistresses. He also had a surprisingly emotional but apparently non-sexual relationship with a curious Muslim anarchist Leda Rafanelli, who later wrote a thinly disguised novel about it.[20] These women, particularly Sarfatti, helped him acquire some Milanese sophistication, but he remained an outsider. Still, he did become genuinely interested in cultural matters, especially literature and the theatre; and he still had his violin.

At the general election of autumn 1913 he stood as Socialist candidate in Forlì, but held only one meeting in the constituency, made a rather dull speech there and was easily beaten, although he did become a councillor in Milan the next year. But parliament and elections never interested Mussolini much. His route to power lay elsewhere. He soon became particularly famous for denouncing official repression of popular demonstrations, especially in southern Italy. In January 1913, at Rocca Gorga in Frosinone province, the police killed seven people, including a woman and a child of five. Mussolini lambasted the police and the government in *Avanti!*.[21] For this he and other colleagues were put on trial yet again, in Milan, for incitement to violence and slandering the army. Yet again he defended himself brilliantly. He brought eyewitnesses up from Rocca Gorga, so that the Milanese jury could see for themselves how poor and oppressed they were. His articles, he argued, had been a duty of solidarity with his fellow-citizens. If any such massacres occurred again, he would write them not with ink but with blood.[22] The accused were all acquitted, amidst great enthusiasm. 'Massacres' were good news for Mussolini, and not only because they helped him to become a popular hero. He thought that only they might rouse the masses and the Socialist party from their torpor, and trigger revolution at last.

In April 1914 came another Socialist congress at Ancona, and another triumph for Mussolini. Freshly acquitted, he was once again the hero of the hour. Once again he expelled his opponents from the party. This time it was the Freemasons who aroused his ire, for being too democratic, too humanitarian and not proletarian enough. The party, he proclaimed, must be a disciplined class army, ready for revolution when the masses were aroused. The congress approved, and so many members (perhaps 10 per cent of the party) were invited, although not forced, to choose between freemasonry and Socialism. Most chose Socialism while remaining Masons clandestinely, as usual. It was, if Mussolini had realised it, a classic lesson on the nature of political power. Still, he had his public triumph, and that was what really mattered.

Soon he had more serious preoccupations. On 7 June troops fired on anti-military demonstrators at Ancona, killing three people. Once more popular protests spread throughout northern and central Italy, this time on a far greater scale. The party Directorate called a national general strike, supported even by the reformist unions. In Romagna and the Marches the movement was not so much a strike as a series of local insurrections. Tax records were burned, churches sacked, shops looted, railway lines blocked and mayors taken hostage. Here, at last, was the revolution or the opportunity for revolution, and it had indeed been triggered by a massacre. Mussolini encouraged the movement enthusiastically in *Avanti!*. On 9 June he made a fiery speech in Milan and urged the crowd to march on piazza del Duomo; but the police were there in force, and the crowd dispersed. Mussolini and his few supporters were left on their own, at the head of a non-existent crowd; so the police naturally beat them up. On 11 June the Socialist union confederation called the strike off, to Mussolini's fury, although the riots continued in some places for a few more days until more troops were sent in to suppress them.

'Red Week', as the movement was soon called, certainly had its comic-opera aspects but it was an important episode in Mussolini's career, and in twentieth-century Italian history. It greatly frightened the landowners and middle classes, who formed vigilante groups to defend their property. Yet in reality it was a political disaster for the revolutionaries, who had shown no sign of coordinating the risings or of attempting a real take-over. Mussolini himself had noticeably stayed in Milan throughout the agitation in his native Romagna. He later claimed some of the credit for the rising – 'we observe it with the legitimate pride of an artist looking at his own creation'[23] – but he had not thought revolution likely, nor had he called for one. Many of the revolutionaries blamed him for not giving an effective lead, but Mussolini realised that revolutionary sentiment, however strong, was just that: sentiment. It might trigger revolt for a day or two, but the army and *carabinieri* would not stay in their barracks, nor would the middle classes lie down without fighting back.

Mussolini was now 31 years old. He was already an important national figure, but he had no influence on political manoeuvres in Rome and no plausible strategy for achieving power. Like millions of others, he was about to face the first big crisis of his life. On 28 June at Sarajevo the Austrian Archduke Francis Ferdinand was assassinated, and Europe began its slide into the First World War. *Avanti!* took very little notice of the war danger until 26 July, when Mussolini, on his own initiative – characteristically, the party Directorate had not met – proclaimed the party's absolute neutrality: 'not a man; not a penny'.[24] On 29 July he spoke against the war at the Milan *Casa del Popolo*. At this time Italy was generally assumed to be bound by the Triple Alliance with Germany and Austria-Hungary, so the 'war' that he spoke against was war on the German side, against Russia and France. In fact, the Italian government decided to stay out, arguing that Italy was not obliged to join as she had not been consulted. In early August 1914, as war broke out elsewhere in Europe and the Socialist International failed to prevent it, Italy stayed neutral. The terms of debate rapidly changed. The issue was no longer whether to join Austria-Hungary and Germany, but whether to join the war at all, and if so on which side. Many of the leading Republicans and syndicalists, including those close to Mussolini like Pietro Nenni, Filippo Corridoni and Alceste De Ambris, were campaigning vigorously for entry on the Franco-British side. So were the Futurists, and Mussolini's friends in Florence. By early October these men had founded a *Fascio Rivoluzionario di Azione Internazionalista* (Revolutionary Group of International Action), and issued a public manifesto. In Milan, popular agitation *against* the war was noticeably absent; the city was, as always, anti-Austrian. So was

Mussolini. On 3 August the Directorate had finally laid down party policy: strict neutrality. *Avanti!* had to conform formally, but Mussolini published pro-war articles in *Utopia* and even occasionally in *Avanti!.* Mussolini's *Avanti!* was, in fact, manifestly not neutral at all. It reported the first few weeks of the war in terms of Teutonic hordes invading poor little Belgium. German atrocities featured regularly, and the Austrian Emperor Francis Joseph was usually termed *l'Impiccatore* (the hangman). Throughout September the syndicalist campaign for war increased, and Socialist unease grew.

Mussolini, forced to stay 'neutral' and support the government for once, was sidelined during all this agitation. This did not suit him at all. He was an active, impatient man and he did not like being upstaged by the syndicalists, nor being isolated from his political friends. Neutralism was not for him; he had never been neutral on anything in his life. His doubts grew. How could a 'revolutionary' party refuse the chance of overthrowing odious despotisms like those of Germany and Austria-Hungary? What influence would a neutral Italy have post-war? Might not war be the only possible midwife of revolution at home? – this last argument, a familiar syndicalist refrain, had great appeal to Mussolini (and turned out to be true in Russia, Germany and Turkey). Moreover, if the Italian government decided to join the war after all, on the Franco-British side, could the Socialist party refuse to support it? Would not an anti-war general strike simply leave the country exposed to her enemies? And could the Socialists refuse to help repel a German invasion? Thus the 'revolutionary' Mussolini wrestled with the usual spurious justifications for war. On 20 August he told Massimo Rocca that Italy was bound to join eventually on the French side,[25] and in September the battle of the Marne confirmed that the British and French would probably win. To an ambitious politician like Mussolini it made sense to join the winning side, and claim some of the credit later. He had other concerns too. Although he was not an irredentist, he had spent some time in Trent and worked closely with Cesare Battisti, who was now in Italy and agitating for war; and he was named after Amilcare Cipriani, who was actively pro-war in Paris. Above all, Mussolini had been unhappy with the feeble Socialist leaders for some time, particularly since 'Red Week'. He was tired of having to kowtow to the tedious bletherers of the Socialist Directorate, men whose policy on all issues was inertia and who would never make a revolution in a thousand years. Now was the time to seize the party and make it patriotic, like its European counterparts. If that meant a split, so be it: Mussolini was never afraid of splits. He had taken the Forlì federation out of the party in 1911, and had ensured that the 'royal reformists' were expelled in 1912.[26]

However, in September 1914 Mussolini was still cautious. He did not know what ordinary party members thought, nor how many might follow him. On 25 September he organised a 'Socialist referendum' via *Avanti!*. All Socialist bodies should meet, canvass their members and send in their decision on the war: for or against? They voted overwhelmingly for neutrality. Mussolini's plan had backfired. His 'referendum' in fact committed the party to staying out, and silenced the party's pro-war voices. It also made his own doubts obvious to all. On 4 October Giuseppe Lombardo Radice, writing in the *Giornale d' Italia*, revealed that an 'authoritative and militant Socialist leader', clearly Mussolini, had written to him saying the Socialists would not react against an Italian mobilisation ('no revolts, no strikes'), and would even support a war against Austria.[27] Three days later the anarchist journalist 'Libero Tancredi' (real name Massimo Rocca) attacked Mussolini in the Bologna newspaper *Il Resto del Carlino*: 'The Editor of *Avanti!* Unmasked. A Man of Straw'. Mussolini clearly had to reply. On 18 October he defended himself in a long article, 'For an Active and Functioning Neutrality', in *Avanti!*. He argued that the Socialists were formally neutral but in reality Francophile; they naturally sympathised with the 'Italian' inhabitants of Trentino and Trieste; they would certainly not try to prevent a war against Austria, and even if there were a revolution a successful new revolutionary government would probably make war on Austria too. They could not stand and watch this immense drama as inert spectators; they had to take part, and 'national defence' was as important to Socialists as to anyone else.[28] This article made a huge impression. Gaetano Salvemini, in Florence, congratulated Mussolini enthusiastically; the young Antonio Gramsci, in Turin, was also much impressed. Mussolini had come out at last, without any ambiguity.

The party Directorate met at Bologna on 19-20 October. Mussolini put a motion for 'conditional neutrality', but he was the only one who voted for it. He promptly resigned as editor of *Avanti!* and from the Directorate, although not from the party, and went back to Milan to clear his desk. Seven months earlier, at Ancona, he had been the party's anointed saviour; now he was the lost leader. But he was still much respected in Socialist circles, and despite the 'referendum' perhaps he still hoped to win over many party members. On 21 October he spoke to the Milan party branch, and was warmly applauded. But the party rallied round its other leaders, against the war. Mussolini had plenty of supporters in Milan but few elsewhere, and even in Milan most of them were not Socialists: it was the syndicalists, Futurists and students, not the party stalwarts, who backed his call. However, Mussolini was not a man to give in without a fight. Late in October he decided to found his own daily newspaper. Although other Socialists had done so before him, and although Mussolini himself already had his own fortnightly journal, the publication of his *Popolo d'Italia* on 15 November was seen as unforgivable disloyalty. Clearly Mussolini was going to campaign against what was now the Socialist party's main policy, peace. Overnight the lost leader became the arch-traitor, the Judas of Socialism. And, like Judas, he must have acted for pieces of silver. How could a notoriously penniless man like Mussolini found a newspaper? Who was paying?

On 24 November, at a stormy meeting of the Socialist party branch in Milan, he was expelled from the party for 'moral unworthiness', i.e. for taking industrialists' money to fund an anti-Socialist campaign. Mussolini, who had twice been expelled from school, who had later been expelled from both Switzerland and Austria, was now expelled from the Socialist party too, amid much abuse and curses – and all this while he still regarded himself as a Socialist, and long before Italy joined the war or the Fascist movement began. He reacted splendidly, in true Coriolanus style. Just as Shakespeare's hero told the mob 'I banish *you* . . . there is a world elsewhere',[29] so Mussolini shouted out 'you think you are getting rid of me, but I tell you that you are fooling yourselves. You hate me, only because you still love me.'[30] But they still threw him out. Mussolini had not expected this. Even after he resigned from *Avanti!*, he had hoped to convert the party to his cause. Henceforth he saw *himself* as the one who had been betrayed. As usual, he never forgave or forgot his humiliation. Soon he would be revenged on the whole pack of them.[31]

In October 1914, therefore, Mussolini threw away his Socialist career and all his prestige and influence over the masses, apparently all in one reckless gamble. However, in reality it had not been an impulsive act, nor a deliberate one. He had clearly hesitated for two months or more, and he went public only when forced to do so by Libero Tancredi. Even then, on 18 October, he tried to hedge his bets, and he wrote not of war but of 'active, functioning neutrality'. Nor did he choose to leave the Socialist party. It was the party, or rather its Milan branch, that ejected him; and for founding a newspaper, not for favouring war, although perhaps the latter was his real offence. This hesitation, and this effort to leave options open as long as possible, were typical of Mussolini. Throughout his life, when faced with major decisions, Mussolini hesitated. Often he was pushed into action by other people or by circumstances, usually after trying to find a compromise. Only when he was quite sure of the outcome was Mussolini resolute; only in retrospect did he appear resolute to others.

A Voice Prophesying War

In fact, the *Popolo d'Italia* was initially financed by Italian industrialists via Filippo Naldi, a born fixer and director of the *Resto del Carlino* in Bologna. It is probable that Naldi promised Mussolini the money for a newspaper at some time between Tancredi's denunciation on 7 October and Mussolini's public response on 18 October. They certainly negotiated a deal in Milan a week or two later.[32] The *Resto del Carlino* provided paper, printing presses and even a few journalists, although some of Mussolini's former colleagues at *Avanti!*, including the chief reporter Alessandro Giuliani, came over to him as well. For finance, the newspaper relied on cash advances from a newly founded advertising agency, which in turn secured advertisements from Edison, Ansaldo, Fiat, etc., and from the Bologna sugar interests. The paper was produced in Mussolini's famous, and well-defended, 'lair' in via Paolo da Connobio in Milan, and it was distributed by the *Messaggerie Italiane*, a subsidiary of the French firm Hachette. The *Messaggerie's* director, Manlio Morgagni, became Mussolini's invaluable close collaborator and manager right up until 1943. But the paper's finances were always precarious, like those of Mussolini himself. Naldi soon backed off when he realised that Mussolini was still 'revolutionary', although some industrialist support continued. From February 1915 until at least mid-1916 the paper was financed mostly by French Socialist party and French government subsidies, since it was clearly in French interests that Italy should join the war. Later on, subsidies also came from Britain, Russia and the occasional maverick labour boss like Captain Giulietti of the Seamen's Union. So it was true that Mussolini relied partly on 'foreign gold'. Still, most Italian newspapers relied on outside funding, and despite all the accusations that he had sold out, he had certainly not acted in October 1914 for financial reasons. Mussolini had plenty of faults but he was never mercenary. He was after power, not money. And he was genuinely committed to the war, like many other highly respectable and intelligent men.[33]

Moreover, Mussolini was not alone in campaigning for war. He was still a hero to some Socialists, mostly youthful activists in Milan and the Romagna. He could also now ally openly with the pro-war syndicalists like Corridoni, with his old prison comrade the Republican Nenni, with the irredentists and with the radical intellectuals. He could even ally temporarily with the non-revolutionary 'democratic interventionists' like his old antagonist Bissolati. True, these groups were disparate and unreliable. They were not much of a base in normal times. But these were not normal times. These men were vociferous, they had useful contacts, and they were very good at organising mass demonstrations. The syndicalists among them had a tenuous organisation, now renamed the *Fascio di Azione Rivoluzionaria*. They claimed an improbable 9,000 members by February 1915. These youthful enthusiasts were just the people Mussolini needed to help rouse public opinion to favour the war. Indeed, they were the true precursors of the later 'Fascist' movement. So Mussolini's personal and political crisis of October 1914 had a happy outcome. It forced him to break with people he despised and enabled him to work among people he liked and respected, for a cause in which he passionately believed.

For the next few months Mussolini addressed mass meetings and was active in the *Fascio*. It was a stormy time, and meetings often ended in violence. Indeed, the war had already begun – the war to control the *piazza*, the main square in Italy's towns and cities. The Socialists regarded Mussolini as a venal renegade, and greeted him with shouts of 'Who's paying?' or 'he who has betrayed once will betray again' (*chi ha tradito tradirà*). In the press, he had bitter personal quarrels with the Socialist leader Giacinto Serrati, one of his former protectors in Switzerland. In February 1915 Mussolini fought his first duel, against Libero Tancredi, whose jibe about the 'man of straw' he had not forgotten. In March he fought again, against Claudio Treves his predecessor at *Avanti!*. The two men had loathed each other for years, and after the duel there was no reconciliation. Mussolini was a good fencer, and he usually won his duels. The 'interventionists' won their duels too, and in northern Italy gradually took over the *piazza*, or at least denied it to the neutralists. Slowly the pro-war crowds grew bigger and more enthusiastic, although they were never large by Italian standards: even in May 1915 the vast crowds of later myth were only 30,000–40,000 people, and only then in a handful of cities.[34] In some ways these months were the most exciting and enjoyable period of Mussolini's life. It was a wonderful melodramatic role he had chosen to play: the tormented patriot, rejected but unbowed. There was a Garibaldine recklessness about him, a spirit of sacrifice as well as combat; he had, after all, given up his Socialist career. His personal life was reckless too. Leda Rafanelli had finally rejected him, but he resumed sexual relations with Ida Dalser, who was now living in Milan. In November 1915 she had a son by Benito, and named him, too, Benito. Benito senior had to recognise the child legally and pay maintenance, but otherwise he ignored his new son. He was still formally single but now there were two women, each the mother of his child, each claiming to be his wife and each liable to turn up at the office and make embarrassing scenes. Rather typically, he did not choose between them, until forced to by events.

I should stress, however, that the 'interventionist' campaign was not really a resounding success. It did not make war or Mussolini popular in the country, nor was it likely to influence respectable middle-class opinion. The 'interventionist' campaign was noisy, but it was not taken seriously by the government. Moderate pro-war apologists like Albertini of the *Corriere della Sera* regarded Mussolini as a ranting demagogue, discrediting the cause. Furthermore, Mussolini was by no means the leader of 'interventionism'. Corridoni and De Ambris had advocated war very stridently in autumn 1914, while Mussolini had still been hesitating; men like Battisti, Marinetti and above all the poet Gabriele D'Annunzio could pack the *piazza* by themselves, and needed no support from Mussolini. D'Annunzio was by far the most famous and flamboyant figure on the 'interventionist' side, and drew the biggest crowds. But Mussolini had something the other radicals did not – a newspaper. There he could argue the case for war day in, day out, and make himself spokesman for the cause. Most of his energy went into his furious, vibrant editorials. His first, on the newspaper's first day, was entitled 'Audacity',[35] and this set the tone. The *Popolo d'Italia* attracted 30,000 core readers, rising to 80,000 on occasions, nearly all in Milan and the north-central cities. He welcomed contributions from favoured non-Socialists – Prezzolini was its Rome correspondent – but its title page proclaimed the *Popolo d'Italia* to be a 'Socialist daily'. He still justified war as a 'people's war' that would transform Italy, rather than as one that would bring territorial gains, although he naturally made an exception for Trent and Trieste (not, as yet, for the South Tyrol, nor Istria).[36] He denounced the forces of conservatism and parliamentarianism – the Catholics, the Liberal supporters of Giovanni Giolitti, above all the cowardly official Socialists – who kept Italy neutral. He denounced the Nationalists as well even though they favoured war, because they were right-wing authoritarians who wanted to acquire Adriatic territory. He threatened the king and the government with dire revolutionary consequences if they did not take Italy into war (although, if they did, the war would itself bring about revolution).

However, paradoxically for a revolutionary, he did not really attack the government. He knew that the government of Prime Minister Salandra and Foreign Minister Sonnino was actually the interventionists' best hope. Salandra disliked his neutralist rival Giolitti and was far more likely than any other leading politician to be tempted by war, perhaps because he had little support in parliament. On 26 April 1915 the government, after months of negotiating with both sides, signed the secret Treaty of London with the *entente* powers Britain, France and Russia, committing Italy to joining the war a month later. After victory, she would acquire

Trent, Trieste, South Tyrol, Istria and half of Dalmatia. But on 10 May Austria made another territorial offer. Giolitti went to Rome hoping to persuade the government to accept it, and so avoid war. Salandra refused and on 13 May resigned; whereupon the king asked Giolitti, who had the public backing of most deputies, to form the new government. The 'interventionists' despaired, and took to the streets. Mass meetings, calling for war, took place in every Italian city. Mussolini had sensed what was going on, and on 11 May had denounced parliament:

I am more firmly convinced than ever that for the salvation of Italy we need to shoot, I say *shoot*, in the back, a few dozen deputies and send at least a couple of ex-ministers to life imprisonment. Not only that, but I believe even more strongly that parliament in Italy is a bubonic plague poisoning the blood of the nation. We must extirpate it.[37]

He continued in this vein for the next few days, threatening to unleash the masses against any Giolitti government, or against the king if he did not declare war. He need not have worried. Giolitti, once he found out about the Treaty of London, could not form a government: Italy had already, in August 1914, refused to join her Triple Alliance partners; she could not betray *both* sides. So Salandra came back to office, and Italy declared war – on Austria-Hungary, not Germany until August 1916, and for quick territorial gains, not for 'revolution'.

The decision for war was, in fact, a 'normal' diplomatic move, the result of secret negotiations among the powers. It owed nothing to the 'interventionists' clamour: they were outsiders, with no influence on events. The government had taken no notice of the demonstrations, except to try to suppress them. However, the parliamentary manoeuvres of May 1915 *did* matter. Italy joined the war with little popular support and also a manifestly reluctant parliament. Giolitti, and the deputies, became symbols of opposition to the war, even – in 'interventionist' eyes – of sabotage and treason. Mussolini naturally seized the propaganda opportunity, and denounced the guilty men. He argued, quite wrongly, that it was the healthy, active, youthful 'interventionists' who had imposed a glorious 'people's war' on the cowardly, peacemongering Establishment. They had made a revolution, and they alone deserved the credit.[38] Of course, they would now need to be vigilant against the enemy within – an enemy that included most of parliament, as well as the Socialists. Thus the myths of 'interventionism' were born: myths that Mussolini himself always firmly believed in, myths that were the real seeds of the Fascist regime.

So the 'intervention crisis' reflected, and influenced, Mussolini's whole view of 'power'. Political power, it seemed, grew out of the barrel of a pen. It was journalism, allied to spectacular demonstrations and control of the *piazza*, that enabled a robust elite to impose its will. Official institutions meant little, and could easily be by-passed. Parliament could be ignored. Governments could be threatened, until they delivered. The king, too, was there to be bullied. All political opponents were cowards or traitors who deserved no mercy. The ultimate aim of political activity at home should be to overthrow this corrupt regime and replace it by an activist, 'revolutionary' system that would transform society. But only war would truly mobilise the people and create a true 'Italian nation' at long last. These were the ideas, or rather the assumptions, that the interventionist Mussolini wove together in 1914–15; and now he was convinced they had succeeded. These were the ideas, or rather the assumptions, of Fascism.

A Good War

Once Italy was in the war, Mussolini expected to be called up into his old regiment. But there was a lengthy and embarrassing delay. Throughout the summer of 1915 Mussolini stayed in Milan and edited his paper, complaining that Italy should declare war on Germany as well, and that the British should stop going on strike. Meanwhile his fellow-interventionists went off to the front, and his many enemies denounced him for cowardice and hypocrisy. In fact, Mussolini was anxious to join up, and tried three times to volunteer. Each time he was ordered to wait until his age-group (he was 32 that summer) was needed. By July he was asking a government minister to pull strings, and threatening to 'desert' and volunteer in France.[39] Finally, at the end of August, his turn came. He was sent again to the *bersaglieri*, where he had served 10 years earlier. By mid-September he was in the war zone above the upper Isonzo river, with the 11th Regiment.

For the next 18 months, apart from occasional leave, Mussolini lived through the usual appalling experiences of a First World War infantryman, and endured the usual privations: lice, damp, mud, boredom, the stench of corpses, sniper fire, shelling, and, above all, the cold. Italy's war was fought in the Alpine hills, 5,000–6,000 feet above sea level. After the glamour and excitement of the 'interventionist' campaign, the war itself turned out to be extremely dull. This was not what he had expected. For long periods he had nothing to do except play cards, while every day men died around him from shells or snipers. In November he contracted paratyphoid and was treated in military hospitals at Cividale, where the king visited him, and at Treviglio, where he married Rachele at last so that she, rather than Ida Dalser, would receive a widow's pension if he were killed. He then had some convalescent leave in Milan over the New Year, and used it to advantage: his eldest legitimate son, Vittorio, was born the following September. But at the end of January 1916 he went back to his regiment, which had moved to the Carnia front, and he stayed there until his next leave in November. This was a long period, and included a dangerous offensive in July when he came under direct fire. But the greatest danger, as usual, came from his own side, and not just from incompetent generals. His fellow-soldiers knew who he was, and blamed him for the war. It was a miracle he survived. Still, he was a keen and courageous soldier. In March 1916 he was promoted to corporal for showing 'true *bersagliere* spirit', and at the end of August he became a senior corporal (*caporal maggiore*). It was unusual for someone like Mussolini to serve in the ranks and he did briefly attend an officer-training course; but the high command were suspicious of this known revolutionary and sent him back as clearly not officer material. Later on his colonel offered him the cushy job of writing the regiment's history, well away from the front line, but Mussolini could not accept: he would certainly have been accused of 'shirking'. By the autumn of 1916 he was obviously exhausted. He suggested that his newspaper should campaign to have all men over the age of 30 transferred from the front line, but nothing came of it.[40] His friends became worried, and Bissolati tried to have him posted away from the front line;[41] nothing came of that either.

He continued to write, keeping a diary and writing dispatches back to the *Popolo d'Italia* for publication. He wrote of how brave and stoical the soldiers were, of their good morale and close comradeship, and of their contempt for the 'shirkers' (*imboscati*) back home. His diary was fairly reticent about his own feelings, except that like many introverted people he responded very strongly to the mountains' beauty. He admired his fellow-soldiers' courage but had little in common with them and certainly did not like living with them at close quarters. He complained about them being given grappa, and said their intellectual level was low; nonetheless it was worth 'trying often to descend towards these simple, primitive souls, who despite everything make up a splendid human material'.[42] He had to admit that patriotic feeling was rare in the trenches. Most of Mussolini's friends at the front were officers, and even they were not all that patriotic. At the end of 1916 the anti-clerical Mussolini praised an army chaplain for his sermon, 'the first truly enthusiastic patriotic speech that I have heard in 16 months of war'.[43]

After his leave in November 1916 he was sent to a new post near Lake Doberdò. On 23 February 1917 Corporal Mussolini was in a group training to fire mortar shells when the trench mortar exploded, killing five soldiers and shaving off much of Mussolini's right leg down to the bone. The explosion left him full of shrapnel, and with open wounds all over the right side of his body. He was rushed to a field hospital at Ronchi with a high fever and some incipient gangrene, and underwent several operations.[44] One day the king visited the hospital and met Mussolini again. The future *Duce* was lucky to survive and even luckier not to lose his leg. He was always grateful to his surgeon, Dr Piccagnoni – 'a first-rate professional and a very patriotic Italian' – and once in power made sure that he was promoted.[45] By early April Mussolini was fit enough to be moved to the military hospital in Milan, where Rachele came to help out, disguised as a Red Cross volunteer. By August most of the wounds had healed and the hospital sent him home with a year's convalescent leave, but he remained on crutches for several more months. Indeed, he never recovered full standing and walking functions: ironically, given his later image, he always had difficulty putting his boots on. Nor was all the shrapnel ever extracted. Fortunately his other functions were still intact, and Rachele's third child Bruno was born in late April 1918.

In the late summer of 1917, therefore, Mussolini limped back to his office at the *Popolo d'Italia*. The war was not going well. The Russian armies were collapsing, and the French were mutinous. There was no sign of the Americans as yet. Italian army morale was not good either, as Mussolini well knew, and morale at home was even worse. The Socialist party was still as anti-war as ever, and parliament still had a Giolittian majority. In August there were bread riots, backed by the Socialists, in Italy's main munitions centre, Turin. In August, too, Pope Benedict XV issued a public call for peace negotiations to end the 'useless slaughter', a phrase that had a huge impact on Italian morale. The Salandra government had fallen a year earlier, and had been replaced by one led by the undynamic Paolo Boselli. Sonnino was still Foreign Minister but the Interior Ministry was now in the hands of Vittorio Orlando, a man regarded by the 'interventionists' as far too soft on Italy's numerous defeatists.

Here was an ideal situation for Mussolini's talents. His tasks were clear: to denounce the traitors, to stir the government into action at home, to boost morale, to 'sabotage the saboteurs'. In short, to make himself once more the spokesman for radical 'interventionism'. To show his anti-clericalism was as vigorous as ever, he not only denounced the papal note but thenceforth referred to 'Pope Pilate XV', and he was just as scathing about the Turin rioters and the parliamentary deputies. By this time the war, for Mussolini, was less against Austria-Hungary and

Germany than against the corrupt Establishment, Giolitti, parliament, the bourgeoisie, the Pope, the 'shirkers' and above all the Socialist party, which he termed the 'PUS' (Partito Ufficiale Socialista). In 1914–15 Mussolini had proclaimed Panunzio's syndicalist creed: only war could bring about revolution. Now he switched to a Lloyd Georgian line: only revolution, his revolution, could win the war. Indeed, he specifically praised Lloyd George and demanded an Italian equivalent, in one of his first post-accident articles.[46] On 11 October *Popolo d'Italia* began issuing a Rome edition, to fight defeatism in its heartland.

Within a fortnight its task had been transformed. On 24 October the Austrians suddenly broke through the Italian 2nd Army lines above Caporetto (Kobarid), mainly by pushing troops through the valleys and ignoring the hills, which were covered in fog. So the Italian artillery was firing blindly, and the Italians had to retreat. Their defences behind the lines were weak and soon morale collapsed. Hundreds of thousands of Italian troops streamed down from the hills, and either managed to cross the river Piave – which became the new front line – or were taken prisoner. It was not just a defeat but a humiliation. In a few days Italy not only lost all the gains made in two-and-a-half years, but much of Venetia as well. Thousands of refugees, including Mussolini's brother Arnaldo, had to flee south. Thenceforth Italy had to fight, not for Trent or Trieste, but to defend her own soil.

Mussolini was, of course, furious at this outcome. He had battled so hard for war, and it had led only to disaster. But the crisis showed Mussolini at his best. He kept cool, put the blame elsewhere, *praised* the soldiers and made practical suggestions.[47] By early November he had come up with a 'Manifesto to the Nation'. He soon realised that Caporetto had given him an even greater opportunity. He had been denouncing the defeatists and traitors for months, but now the guilty men were even more manifestly guilty, and people began to take notice. He embarked on a rerun of the glorious 'interventionist' campaign of three years earlier, this time to *keep* Italy in the war and to rouse her people to win it. But this time it was more serious, and more official. In 1914–15 Mussolini had still been a revolutionary outsider, less significant than Corridoni or D'Annunzio and distrusted by nearly all. Now he was ideally placed. He was a wounded ex-serviceman himself, he had proved his valour on the battlefield and he was a brilliant journalist with his own newspaper in Italy's major industrial centre. No one like him existed in any other belligerent country. He was now welcome in official circles and in Allied ones. He was flown around in military aircraft; in May he had a chat with the Prime Minister. On 26 March he provided General Sir Charles

Delmé-Radcliffe, the head of the British Military Mission – a man who met the Italian king frequently, and corresponded regularly with Lloyd George – with a résumé of the Italian political situation, and urged the British to use their influence to ensure that the troops were paid more and that there was a crackdown on the defeatists.[48] Mussolini was no longer a corporal in the trenches, but a general in what was now the front line, the 'moral trench'. His views, previously extreme, had become mainstream. He was just the man to revive Italy's hopes, when they desperately needed reviving. He could plausibly argue that victory or defeat might depend not merely on better leadership or patriotic discipline but on improved institutions and a radical new social structure.

So the *Popolo d'Italia* became a weapon of war, and the changed circumstances helped. Once Italy had been invaded national sentiment became stronger, even among the neutralists. Furthermore, new army commanders took over. The troops' rations and leave were increased, and better welfare schemes were brought in for ex-soldiers. Morale improved, helped by propaganda units in each regiment. The special volunteer commando troops, the *Arditi*, who had been set up in spring 1917, were expanded: soon there were 40,000–50,000 lightly armed and highly trained men whose exploits became widely celebrated. Aircraft and torpedo-boats began to play a bigger role. The war became rather more mobile, more in line with 'interventionist' hopes; above all, it became more 'national'. In summer 1918 the army successfully repelled further Austrian attacks on the Piave, and Mussolini could plausibly portray this success as a major victory, achieved by high morale. He concluded, disastrously for the future, that patriotic zeal would always triumph over mere numbers or mere weaponry.[49] Italian propaganda against the enemy also became far more effective. Partly because of pressure from Mussolini and his fellow-editor in Milan, Albertini, it now became unofficial Italian policy to dismember Austria-Hungary, although Foreign Minister Sonnino never approved. At any rate, a 'Congress of Oppressed Nationalities' was held in Rome in April, to convince the various peoples of east-central Europe not to fight for the Austrians: a victorious Italy would ensure their liberation. This propaganda was remarkably successful, particularly among the Czechs.[50]

But the essence of Mussolini's propaganda was domestic. He urged that all the national energies should be mobilised in a 'national union', for the common end. Many people agreed with him. In December 1917 the pro-war deputies and senators set up a *Fascio Parlamentare di Difesa Nazionale*, or Parliamentary National Defence Group, a coalition of Nationalists, right-wing Liberals (followers of Salandra) and 'democratic interventionists' (Republicans and reformist Socialists) aimed initially at countering any effort at a comeback by Giolitti. By April 156 deputies had joined, and 92 senators. At local level, too, a host of *Fasci* sprang up to fight the enemy within. They took a tough line against 'subversives' and the neutralist press. These local vigilante groups were often the nuclei of later 'Fascist' bodies, uniting men of varied persuasions in a common patriotic cause, and they became more strident as time went on. However, the 'democratic interventionists', committed to social justice, parliamentary government and to high Wilsonian (or Mazzinian) principles of national self-determination, had little in common with the Salandrians and even less with the Nationalists. The Nationalists were tough-minded authoritarians at home and acquisitive abroad, demanding that Italy obtain, at the very least, the territory promised by the Treaty of London in 1915. Mussolini, seeking 'national union', had to manoeuvre among these groups. In 1918 he moved cautiously towards the Nationalist position, at least in domestic policy, but he gave it more populist, 'social' overtones. He argued that the people's war required a coordinated, 'national' economy geared to higher production. The industrial workers, now commendably patriotic again, had a vital contribution to make, but needed to be disciplined within national unions, or 'syndicates'. The whole economy should be organised along 'productivist' lines, i.e. centrally planned, subsidised cartels should replace the market economy.[51] The peasants should be given land, a reward for their sacrifices in war. As for politics, Mussolini supported the new Orlando government formed after Caporetto, but he also argued that in wartime a dictatorship was necessary. Italy could no longer afford anti-patriotic parties and a neutralist parliament. She should be ruled, instead, by a 'trenchocracy', by ex-servicemen bold and imaginative enough to bring in a new authoritarian regime that would crack down hard on the dissenters and defeatists.

Mussolini's shift towards populist nationalism was symbolised on 1 August 1918, when the *Popolo d'Italia* changed its subtitle: no longer a 'Socialist daily', it became the 'servicemen's and producers' daily'. 'Socialism', Mussolini explained, was an idea whose time had gone, and he was a man of the future. The 'servicemen' included everybody from Marshal Diaz down to the humblest infantry recruit; the 'producers' were everyone except the 'parasites' and 'shirkers'. So 'productivism' now overtly replaced 'Socialism'. Perhaps Mussolini had realised where his support lay – not among the industrial workers but among the army's officers, who were former (and future) middle-class civilians very contemptuous of the politicians. Certainly he was not thinking just of winning the war. He was aiming higher. 'Trenchocracy' was a claim to post-war rule, indeed to rule on quite different lines. Cautiously but unmistakably, Mussolini took over much of the Nationalist programme, and also preached it regularly to mass meetings all over Italy. It was still important to control the *piazza*. It was, in fact, easier to control the *piazza* now than it had been before the war, because there were a large number of wounded ex-servicemen around – wounded, but not so badly that they could not fight against civilians. Mussolini, a wounded ex-serviceman himself, mobilised these men very successfully in Milan, drove the defeatists off the streets, and earned gratitude and financial rewards from a delighted British government.[52] Arguably 'proto-Fascism' already existed by mid-1918. The key ideas had been formulated, and the supporters were already active locally. Mussolini had shifted well away from the Socialist left towards productivism, admittedly still with syndicalist overtones. He now had high status, and few rivals. Corridoni had been killed in the war, D'Annunzio and Marinetti were amusing but preposterous, Salandra was too Liberal and Establishment-minded, Bissolati and the 'democratic interventionists' were too tender-hearted – particularly when it came to Italy's claims on the Adriatic.

By the autumn of 1918 Austria-Hungary was visibly collapsing and the 'interventionists' were clamouring for war yet again, i.e. urging that the Italian army should go on the attack. On 24 October, the anniversary of Caporetto, the army began to advance near Monte Grappa, and on the 26th came the real thrust, over the Piave. The Austrians retreated hastily, in disorder. By the 30th Vittorio Veneto had been captured. On 3 November Trent itself was taken, and troops were landed at Trieste. The next day an armistice was signed, a week before that on the western front. The war was over, and Caporetto was avenged. Italy had lost 570,000 men killed. Mussolini exulted in the *Popolo d'Italia*, as always with more than a touch of menace: it had been a people's war, a people's victory, won 'despite the miserable propaganda of those to whom we do not wish to be cruel, at this time, but against whom we stay very alert'.[53]

He was entitled to rejoice. Italy had won, and that was something few had expected a year earlier. He himself had been remarkably lucky. He had served in an elite corps, the *bersaglieri*, where discipline was effective; he might not have lasted long elsewhere. He had served on relatively quiet fronts and he had got out in time, before the collapse of morale and the disaster of Caporetto. He had seen plenty of suffering and brutality but no defeats, no mutinies and no summary executions of deserters. He had even had a good injury: serious enough to command respect and to end his days in the trenches, but not too crippling. Above all, he had been able to continue his journalism and propaganda just when it mattered most. He had served, as his military record stated, with loyalty and honour. In short, he had had a good war. He had excellent credentials for the battles ahead.

Notes

1 R. Alessi, *Il Giovane Mussolini* (Milan, 1970); Y. De Begnac, *Vita di Benito Mussolini* (Milan, 1936), i, p. 111.

2 P. Monelli, *Mussolini Piccolo Borghese* (2nd edn, Milan, 1968), pp. 9–10; Edvige Mussolini, *Il Mio Fratello Benito* (Florence, 1957), p. 16.

3 Y. De Begnac, *Palazzo Venezia* (Rome, 1950), p. 134.

4 'La Mia Vita', in *OO* xxxiii, p. 239.

5 ACS, De Bono papers, b. unica, f. 2.

6 'La Mia Vita', in *OO* xxxiii, p. 245.

7 Letter to G. Prezzolini, 2 May 1909, in *OO* xxxviii, pp. 7–8; G. Megaro, *Mussolini in the Making* (London, 1938), pp. 152–6.

8 *OO* xxxiii, pp.151–213.

9 *OO* xxxiii, p. 273.

10 Rachele Mussolini, *My Life with Mussolini* (London, 1959), p. 21.

11 *Lotta di Classe*, 2 July 1910; Megaro, *Mussolini in the Making* cit., p. 253.

12 'Tradimento', in *Lotta di Classe*, 1 April 1911; *OO* iii, pp. 336–40.

13 *Lotta di Classe*, 25 November 1913; *OO* iv, pp. 104–7.

14 'La Mia Vita', in *OO* xxxiii, p. 246.

15 ACS, SPD, c. ris., b. 104, sottof. 3; his application is in *OO* xxxvii, p. 189.

16 L. Passerini, 'Mussolini', in M. Isnenghi (ed.), *I Luoghi della Memoria* (Bari, 1997), pp. 167–85; also Passerini, *Mussolini l'Immaginario* (Bari, 1991).

17 Letter to Prezzolini, 20 July 1912; *OO* xxxviii, p. 23.

18 G. Pini and D. Susmel, *Mussolini: l'Uomo e l'Opera* (4 vols, Florence, 1953–4), i, p. 193.

19 *La Folla*, 11 August and 8 September 1912; *OO* iv, pp. 182–3 and 209–11.

20 'Sahra', *Incantamento* (Milan, 1918). Cf. also L. Rafanelli, *Una Donna e Mussolini* (Milan, 1946).

21 'Assassinio di Stato', in *Avanti!*, 7 January 1913; *OO* v, pp. 52–3.

22 His defence speech is in *OO* vi, pp. 128–31; cf. G. Bozzetti, *Mussolini Direttore dell' Avanti!* (Milan, 1979), p. 97.

23 'Tregua d'Armi', in *Avanti!*, 12 June 1914; *OO* vi, pp. 218–21.

24 'Abbasso la Guerra!', in *Avanti!*, 16 July 1914; *OO* vi, p. 288.

25 Letter to Rocca, 20 August 1914; *OO* vi, pp. 439–40.

26 R. De Felice, *Mussolini il Rivoluzionario* (Turin, 1965), pp. 220–87; F. Perfetti, 'La conversione di Mussolini all' interventismo nel suo carteggio con Sergio Panunzio', in *Storia Contemporanea* xvii (Feb. 1986), pp. 139–70.

27 'I Socialisti e la guerra'; *OO* vi, pp. 497–500; Bozzetti, *Mussolini Direttore* cit., pp. 214–16.

28 *OO* vi, pp. 393–403.

29 W. Shakespeare, *Coriolanus*, III iii 125–7.

30 *OO* vii, p. 40.

31 De Felice, *Mussolini il Rivoluzionario* cit., pp. 273–6; A. Lepre, *Mussolini l'Italiano* (Milan, 1995), pp. 58–65.

32 Bozzetti, *Mussolini Direttore* cit., pp. 237–42.

33 De Felice, *Mussolini il Rivoluzionario* cit., pp. xxiii, 280; P. Milza, *Mussolini* (Paris, 1999), pp. 176 ff.

34 De Felice, *Mussolini il Rivoluzionario* cit., p. 298.

35 'Audacia', in *Popolo d'Italia*, 15 November 1914; *OO* vii, pp. 5–7.

36 'L'Adunata', in *Popolo d'Italia*, 24 January 1915; *OO* vii, pp. 139–41; Alessi, *Il Giovane Mussolini* cit., p. 169.

37 'Abbasso il Parlamento!', in *Popolo d'Italia*, 11 May 1915; *OO* vii, p. 376.

38 'Vittoria', in *Popolo d'Italia*, 17 May 1915; *OO* vii, pp. 396–7.

39 Mussolini to Barzilai, 26 July 1915, in ACS, SPD, c. ris., b. 104.

40 Mussolini to Francesco Paolini, 1 October 1916; *OO* xxxviii, pp. 97–8.

41 ACS, SPD, c. ris., 'Bissolati', f. 292; De Felice, *Mussolini il Rivoluzionario* cit., pp. 323–4; Alessi, *Il Giovane Mussolini* cit., p. 203.

42 'Diario di Guerra', in *OO* xxxiv, pp. 3–113. The quotation is from entry of 12 December 1916.

43 Ibid., 31 December 1916.

44 ACS, SPD, c. ris., b. 104. The exact location was unknown, so no monument could be erected later. In 1938 the Ministry of War laid down that officially Mussolini had been wounded at hill 144, eight miles north-east of Monfalcone. By then there were only two surviving witnesses, one of them an anti-Fascist exile in Paris.

45 Mussolini to Prefect of Udine, 29 June 1923, in *OO* xxxviii, p. 382.

46 'Acta non Verba', in *Popolo d'Italia*, 15 June 1917; *OO* viii, pp. 280–2.

47 'L'Offerta', in *Popolo d'Italia*, 2 November 1917; *OO* x, pp. 14–16; 'I Postulati', ibid., 8–10 November 1917, in *OO* x, pp. 33–40.

48 Imperial War Museum, London: Delmé-Radcliffe Papers box 3 (66/80/1–4); M. Cornwall, *The Undermining of Austria-Hungary* (London, 2000), p. 111.

49 'Il Morale', in *Popolo d'Italia*, 18 June 1918; *OO* xi, pp. 132–4.

50 ACS, Fondo Primo Aiutante il Re, filza 24, 'Marina' sez. spec.; Cornwall, *The Undermining* cit., pp. 433–44.

51 'Trincerocrazia', in *Popolo d' Italia*, 15 December 1917; *OO* x, pp. 140–2; 'Orientamenti e problemi', in *Popolo d'Italia*, 18 August 1918; *OO* xi, pp. 282–4. Cf. also M. Clark, *Antonio Gramsci and the Revolution that Failed* (London, 1977), pp. 18–19; De Felice, *Mussolini il Rivoluzionario* cit., pp. 411–12, 492ff.

52 S. Hoare (Viscount Templewood), *Nine Troubled Years* (London, 1954), p. 154.

53 'La guerra è vinta', in *Popolo d'Italia*, 5 November 1918; *OO* xi, p. 460.

Chapter 2

Manoeuvres to Power 1918–22

Peace and Adversity

Mussolini rejoiced at victory, but peace brought him serious problems. He no longer mattered to the powerful, and nor did the *Popolo d'Italia*. There were no more subsidies from foreign governments, and the ones from arms manufacturers at home grew much smaller. Somehow he and his brother Arnaldo kept the paper going with help from steel and ship-building interests, but it was not easy. People wanted to forget the war and all its hardships. Mussolini found himself in the political wilderness. He was still a respected patriot and a stimulating journalist, but he needed to show that the 'interventionist' message was still relevant even after the war, and he needed supporters. His first initiative, calling for a 'Constituent Assembly of Interventionism' to plan post-war reforms ('if in a sense the war was ours, the post-war should be ours too'), was ignored, and the assembly never met.[1] He tried to mobilise the ex-servicemen, and in mid-December went off to Trieste and Fiume and urged his *bersaglieri* to fight against the 'shirkers' when they came home. But most of the ex-soldiers were peasants. They were too rural, too southern, too anxious to get home and too ignorant of politics for Mussolini's purposes. He addressed their rallies, but there was little enthusiasm there. Far more promising were the former *Arditi*, the commandos. These were tough characters and had had a tough training; many were ex-criminals who were good with knives and enjoyed fighting. As always happens, they came back from the war and found the civilians soft, cowardly and ungrateful. They thought they had won the war, but they received no recognition after it, not even a victory parade. Mussolini took their side: 'I feel there is something of me in you, and perhaps you can recognise something of yourselves in me. You represent the wonderful warlike youth of Italy.'[2] They certainly did. In their black shirts and singing their 'Giovinezza' anthem, the *Arditi* were raring to go. In January 1919 they founded an association. The Milan branch was run by Ferruccio Vecchi, and for the next two years Mussolini used *Arditi* as armed guards for his newspaper. They were useful men to have on your side, particularly if you were as unpopular as Mussolini.[3]

This was an exciting time for Mussolini. He was virtually on his own politically, no longer the spokesman for any party nor even any recognisable set of policies. His many enemies were out for his blood, and his Establishment support had vanished. He kept a revolver and a few hand grenades in his office desk. So did Rachele at home, in case the mob attacked the house. Her memoirs tell of an assassin who came round in 1921 to kill Mussolini, found that the Mussolini family lived in modest circumstances, and so gave the idea up and went round to Mussolini's office to apologise.[4] In fact, the Mussolini circumstances were not modest at all. He was, after all, a successful newspaper proprietor. The family moved to a large flat in fashionable Foro Bonaparte, and went to the seaside in the summer. He had a fast car and he travelled round the country in a private plane, one of the first people in Europe to do so. Flying soon became a passion. He loved to be literally on top, dominating the world, and soon he began taking regular flying lessons himself. However, Mussolini may have been prosperous but he never became bourgeois, and he continued to dislike the snobbish conformity of the Milanese middle classes. His personal life was as complex as ever. Ida Dalser still called herself Mussolini's wife, and made scenes occasionally. Eventually (in 1926) she was put away in a mental hospital, and her son was brought up by foster-parents. Mussolini paid maintenance, but totally ignored his child. At home with Rachele he now had three legitimate children, but little understanding. In 1918–19 he was in love for the first time in years, perhaps for the first time in his life. His affair with Margherita Sarfatti had begun before the war, but in the summer of 1918 it became really serious. She had lost her 17-year-old son Roberto in the war, and needed emotional support; so did Mussolini, politically and emotionally isolated as he was. Margherita wrote for the *Popolo d'Italia* and acted as Mussolini's cultural and even political adviser, as well as his mistress. She had a real influence on him during the next few key years, and helped him win respectable backing.[5]

In January 1919 Mussolini's political isolation worsened further. At the end of December the most eminent 'democratic interventionist', Leonida Bissolati, resigned from the government and told the *Morning Post* he was in favour of giving up Italy's claims to Dalmatia and even the South Tyrol, in order to ensure friendly relations with post-war Austria and the newly formed 'Kingdom of the Serbs, Croats and Slovenes', later known as Yugoslavia. Mussolini and his *Arditi* friends were not having that. On 11 January they heckled Bissolati down when he tried to make a speech at La Scala. Mussolini himself had no particular wish for Italy to take over Dalmatia, but he did care about Fiume (now Rijeka), and his few supporters wanted both; he could not afford to appear 'renunciatory' on the eve of the Versailles peace conference. So overnight Bissolati and the other 'democratic interventionists' became traitors to the Italian cause.[6] It was a dramatic dispute within the 'interventionist' camp over the spoils of war, and for Mussolini it had far-reaching consequences, almost as important as his breach with the Socialist party in 1914.

[Worse, the dispute foretold events at Versailles. Italy's wartime allies conceded Trent, Trieste and (more surprisingly) South Tyrol to Italy, but despite the pleas of Prime Minister Orlando and Foreign Minister Sonnino, and despite the Treaty of London, they refused to give her Dalmatia, Fiume or any African colonies. The dispute rumbled on for a couple of months, and then the United States of America's President, Woodrow Wilson, appealed to the Italian people over the heads of their government. This was a foolish move: the Italian people, or Mussolini's part of it, screamed all the louder for Fiume. In June the Orlando government resigned.] The new Prime Minister, Nitti, had to accept the situation. On the Adriatic, Italy gained Trieste and Istria, but not Fiume or Dalmatia. The Nationalists and the *Arditi* were furious, and D'Annunzio inveighed against the 'mutilated victory'. Mussolini, too, railed against the Allies' betrayal of Italy and against the feeble Italian government.[7] He realised that the Allies thought Italy had not made a decisive contribution to the war, and therefore deserved no favours. He was particularly incensed that the Croats in Dalmatia had been rewarded, since they had stayed loyal to Austria-Hungary almost to the end of the war. He never trusted or respected France or Britain again, and he now truly loathed the cowardly Italian government and its ineffable 'democratic' supporters.

In September 1919 the flamboyant poet Gabriele D'Annunzio decided to resolve the Adriatic question himself. He gathered a few thousand 'legionaries' together and seized the city of Fiume, with support from some army and navy units and from the military governor of Dalmatia. For the next 15 months he remained there as *Comandante*, denouncing the feeble Italian governments and proclaiming a syndicalist constitution. Nitti could not dislodge him, for the army was clearly unwilling to drive him out. It was a daring seizure of power, by a man who had always been a far more prominent spokesman for patriotic zeal than Mussolini, and who had had a far more adventurous war – one cannot imagine D'Annunzio doing nothing in Milan for four months and then being trench-bound, as Mussolini had been. D'Annunzio's new adventure in Fiume attracted *Arditi* and radical patriots from all over Italy. He invented, or at least popularised, many of the trappings of later dictatorships, including lengthy speeches from the balcony and meaningless, rousing cries like 'Eia, eia, alalà'.[8] He controlled Fiume and he might easily march on Trieste, or even Rome. He attracted all the limelight, and of course Mussolini had to support him in public. The *Popolo d'Italia* became spokesman for the cause, organised a public subscription for Fiume, and raised 3 million lire (although some of the money was used to pay those 'legionaries' who came to Italy in autumn 1919 to guard Mussolini and other Fascist candidates at the elections).[9] On the other hand, Mussolini knew the adventure might go disastrously wrong if D'Annunzio tried it on in Italy, and he had no intention of being merely D'Annunzio's representative on earth. He could see that D'Annunzio was an even more self-obsessed *poseur* than he was, and incapable of neutralising opposition. So he offered verbal support but little else, and visited Fiume rarely. To D'Annunzio, he played the wise counsellor, sympathetic but responsible, a man who would act in the *Comandante*'s interests but would also take the longer view. This did not go down well, and the correspondence between the two men became distinctly cool. From Mussolini's viewpoint, the best thing about the Fiume expedition was that it left D'Annunzio stranded there, while Mussolini became the only prominent 'non-renunciatory' politician in Italy. As time went on, people became bored by D'Annunzio's tiresome megalomania and indeed with Adriatic issues generally. Mussolini began to take his distance. In September 1920 the *Comandante* tried to persuade Mussolini to join him in a 'March on Rome', but in vain.[10] The road to Rome did not lead through Fiume.

On the contrary, it led from Milan, via journalism. Mussolini remained a superb journalist. He was well informed, he was a master of sarcasm, and he wrote with conviction and clarity. He spoke up for ex-servicemen, denounced the feeble Nitti government and knew how to surprise his readers. When the 'renunciatory' Leonida Bissolati died in May 1920, for example, Mussolini wrote a generous obituary, full of praise.[11] Occasionally, too, he revealed another, more anarchical and perhaps truer, side to his personality, denouncing *all* politicians as charlatans: 'enough, you ridiculous Saviours of Mankind which cares nothing for your infallible devices for human happiness. Out of the way, and let basic individual strength prevail, for apart from the individual no other human force exists!'[12] However, Mussolini always attacked his real enemies, the Socialists. 'I maintain the promise I made on the tempestuous evening I was expelled: I said I would be implacable, and for five years I have not given a moment's peace to the so-called Italian, so-called Socialist party.'[13] The Socialists were a good enemy to have, and not just because of their war record. In 1919 they had joined the Third International, and so were now committed to setting up the 'dictatorship of the proletariat'. They expected revolution to break out any minute, and organised countless strikes and demonstrations. It was easy to portray them as tools of the Bolsheviks and as utter incompetents who would lead the naive workers to destruction. But Mussolini did not just denounce, he inspired. His down-to-earth, disinterested patriotism was compelling. His followers – mostly tough, resolute men, highly suspicious of politicians – revered him. To them, he and D'Annunzio were the only leaders worthy of the name. He did not try to control them too much. The *Arditi*, in particular, took their own initiatives, confident of Mussolini's backing.

Soon Mussolini decided to found his own political movement, to attract the ex-servicemen and undermine the Socialists. On 23 March 1919 the inaugural meeting of the '*Fasci di Combattimento*' was held at the Industrial and Commercial Association hall on piazza San Sepolcro in Milan. The name *Fasci* deliberately had overtones of the interventionist *Fascio di Azione Rivoluzionaria* of 1914–15, and of the more respectable *Fascio Parlamentare di Difesa Nazionale* of 1917–18; but '*combattimento*' (combat) was what the movement was all about. The meeting was chaired by Captain Vecchi of the *Arditi* and was attended mostly by *Arditi* and interventionist syndicalists, with a handful of Futurists and Republicans. It has never been clear how many people attended: Mussolini himself said 'perhaps a hundred' in 1921, although by 1923 he had reduced it to 52.[14] Later on, to have been a *sansepolcrista*, one of the founders of Fascism, became a title of honour and a claim to reward, and so many people claimed to have been there who were not; conversely, those who had left the movement had to be expunged hastily from the roll of honour. At any rate, it was clearly not a large assembly and in any case 'Fascism' had really been born four or five years earlier, as Mussolini had recognised when he summoned the meeting: 'we are the only people in Italy who have the right to talk of revolution . . . we have already made a revolution. In May 1915.'[15] At the meeting, Mussolini made a rousing speech denouncing the Socialists, celebrating the victorious war and promising an Italian empire.[16] But few people took much notice, and Mussolini himself was none too proud of his offspring. The infant Fascist movement was a sickly child, and seemed unlikely to survive. It was not a party, and it was much less important to Mussolini than his newspaper. For the first few months it had no official programme. When one was produced, largely written by the syndicalist Alceste De Ambris, it was the standard Republican-syndicalist package: republic, constituent assembly, proportional representation, votes for women, abolition of the Senate, direct representation by 'syndicates', confiscation of war profits, the eight-hour working day and a 'dynamic' foreign policy.[17] This had little appeal outside the patriotic or syndicalist centres – Milan, Trieste, Bologna and Parma. But the movement could soon claim one achievement. On 15 April a big Socialist demonstration in Milan led to clashes with *Arditi* and 'Fascists'. A handful of *Arditi*, led by Vecchi, then went on to storm the offices and presses of the Socialist paper *Avanti!*. The assault seems to have been unpremeditated and Mussolini took no part, although he applauded warmly later. It was the first real clash between Socialists and 'Fascists', and the 'Fascists' won hands down against far greater numbers while the police stood by. Here was a real sign of things to come. In 1919 the Socialists nearly always controlled the *piazza*, but they might not do so for ever.

The police were not always totally passive. In June 1919 Inspector Gasti of Milan sent a report to his superiors in Rome about *professore* Mussolini. Mussolini, he said, is 'very intelligent, shrewd, moderate, thoughtful, and is a good judge of men, their good qualities and their defects. He is quick to like and to dislike, is capable of making sacrifices for his friends but is resolute in his enmities and hatreds. He is brave and bold; he is a good organiser; he can make up his mind quickly, but he is not consistent in his convictions and aims. He is extremely ambitious. He is inspired by a belief that he represents a real force in the destinies of Italy, and he is determined to make that force count. He is not a man to resign himself to a subordinate position; he wants to be first, and to dominate.'[18] This was perceptive and also cautious: watch out, Gasti was saying, this man is going to get to the top, and we had better not alienate him.

Yet in 1919 Mussolini seemed unlikely to get anywhere. He could not find a political niche. The 'interventionists' had split on the Adriatic question, and D'Annunzio dominated the foreign policy headlines. Mussolini led an anti-Socialist movement and managed to form a coalition against the 'international' protest strike of 20–21 July (called to protest against Allied intervention in Russia, although Italy had not joined it), but the coalition did not last long after the strike. In any case, he aroused non-Socialist suspicions by proclaiming the need for radical social reforms and by supporting a 'work-in' at the Dalmine factory near Bergamo. He courted the reformist Socialist trade unions, knowing that in practice they had helped the war effort and that they detested their more revolutionary colleagues, but he had nothing to offer them and his own syndicalist supporters soon turned restive. The Republicans took a soft line on the Adriatic question, and therefore distrusted Mussolini and campaigned against him. So he was as isolated as ever. There was simply no room on the left for Mussolini, and he had failed to rally the ex-servicemen. His followers were *Arditi*, Futurists and syndicalists, and there were not many of them. In November 1919 came a general election, held under a list system of proportional representation, and the Fascist vote was derisory. In Milan, even with Toscanini and Marinetti on the list, the Fascists secured 4,657 votes, 1.7 per cent of the total. The Socialists organised a mock funeral procession for Mussolini. The coffin was carried past Mussolini's flat and greatly frightened Rachele. The next day the Socialist paper *Avanti!* reported that 'a corpse in a state of putrefaction was fished out of the Naviglio this morning. It seems that the body is that of Benito Mussolini.'[19] Even two of Mussolini's top journalist colleagues deserted him. Elsewhere the Fascist movement virtually collapsed. At the end of 1919 there were only 870 members, in 31 *Fasci*. The police felt brave enough to raid the *Popolo d'Italia* offices, and on 18 November Mussolini spent a night in the cells for illegally holding arms. It was the last of his 11 prison experiences, before 1943. But Mussolini was not the only political corpse. The Socialists won 156 seats in the new Chamber, and the new (Catholic) Popular party 100, out of the total 508. The traditional ruling Liberals won only 216 seats, mostly in the south, and lost control of parliament. In effect, the whole Liberal regime had collapsed, and no stable government could be formed.[20]

So for Mussolini the result was certainly disheartening, but it had its compensations. His brief imprisonment had made him a martyr again. Furthermore, he knew the Socialists' triumph would be short-lived. They would never carry out a revolution, but their constant threats and agitations would soon alienate the public. Moreover, the Nitti government was in real trouble. It no longer had a majority in the Chamber and it could not cope with the constant public sector strikes. It would not last long, and a future government might be grateful for Fascist support against the strikers, provided the Fascists were not too extreme. Mussolini decided to 'navigate', as he put it on 1 January, through the stormy political seas.[21] 'Trenchocracy' had not worked, and the elections had shown that there was no room for him on the left. So, just out of prison, he became a man of order. But he was careful not to go too far right. He supported reasonable wage claims and encouraged moderate trade unionism. In May, at the Fascists' 2nd Congress, he praised productivism but also accepted the market economy and even qualified both his republicanism and his hatred of the Vatican. The next month the Nitti government fell at last and the arch-neutralist Giolitti became Prime Minister, with Popular party support. Mussolini saw his chance to navigate. To general astonishment, he welcomed the new government's reform agenda: 'we are disposed to cooperate with all our forces to help implement this programme'.[22] Marinetti and the Futurists soon left the movement in disgust. Fascism was changing. The radical revolutionaries were departing; the restorers of law and order were moving in, or thinking of doing so. It still had a fairly radical economic and social reform programme, including a high inheritance tax and the confiscation of war profits, but it was no longer revolutionary. On the other hand, it was not too reactionary either. Mussolini was making himself available. He would fight the Bolsheviks, but he would do so as a moderate, patriotic citizen, and he would woo the unions at the same time.

In September 1920 came the most spectacular economic conflict of all, when a normal wage dispute escalated into the 'Occupation of the Factories', a 'work-in' by over 400,000 engineering workers in northern and central Italy. As it was an 'economic', not political, dispute Mussolini initially supported it. After a month Giolitti, with the aid of the reformist-Socialist unions, persuaded the workers to come out of the factories by offering to pass a law on 'trade union control' of industry, i.e. a say in management decisions; Mussolini approved. The 'Occupation' was over, but the leading industrialists were furious with the government. Why had it allowed private property to be seized for a month, and not used the police? Why on earth had it conceded 'control' of industry to rabble-rousing trade unionists? Giolitti had been virtually the last hope of the Liberal Establishment, but he had let them down and appeared to be in league with the unions, indeed with the 'Bolsheviks'. So, forgetting that Mussolini had backed both 'Occupation' and 'control', some industrialists turned to the Fascists. This was very significant. Previously, if respectable opinion had supported Mussolini at all, it was as someone who might help mobilise public enthusiasm for war (in 1914–15 and 1917–18) or public opposition to Socialism (in 1919–20). Now some people began wondering whether he might be useful in opposing the government, and furthermore a government led by the archetype Liberal, Giolitti.

However, Mussolini was still navigating with Giolitti, who had decided to resolve the Fiume issue. In November Italy and 'Yugoslavia' agreed the Treaty of Rapallo, whereby virtually all Dalmatia went to the Yugoslavs and Fiume became an independent state. D'Annunzio, the Nationalists and many right-wing Liberals were outraged, but Mussolini was greatly relieved. He had never cared about Dalmatia and he realised that few Italians did either. The deal gave him a superb opportunity to come out of the wilderness. Indeed, he had met Foreign Minister Sforza in

October, to reassure him that the Fascists would not cause trouble.[23] When the deal was announced, he welcomed the agreement on Italy's north-eastern frontier and accepted the Fiume solution as a regrettable necessity.[24] This was a big political risk for Mussolini, and his supporters were very unhappy. He had to speak three times at the Fascist executive committee on 15 November, and even then it accepted the treaty only in part. But by 19 November Mussolini could claim his reward. He proclaimed, so that everyone would know, that he alone had prevented an uprising against the treaty with 'a gesture of supreme wisdom that without false modesty I am proud to have been the first to make'.[25] A month later he had to make another one. D'Annunzio refused to leave Fiume, so Giolitti sent in the navy and forced him out. This time Mussolini did denounce Giolitti's fratricidal infamy, but the Fascists did not rise. Mussolini had shown real political courage and realism on Fiume. He had controlled his own zealots and helped Giolitti settle the issue without fear of insurrection. This was an important contribution, and it deserved a reward.

By autumn 1920 the war had been over for two years. Mussolini was becoming more respectable and was even backing a Giolitti government, knowing it needed him. Over Fiume, he had passed the first test of a serious politician: he had betrayed his friends. He had also proved right about the Socialists, and nobody now believed a revolution was likely. His 'navigation' had so far been fairly successful and the wind was blowing his way, but he was still an outsider. His political significance depended on his newspaper, not his party. But media bosses matter in Italy, and he was a great journalist. He continued to campaign against the demoralised Socialists and the ineffective Liberals. Now was the time to rout his unpatriotic opponents once and for all. 'A million sheep', he proclaimed, 'will always be dispersed by the roar of a single lion.'[26] This message was just what people wanted to hear. In the next six months Mussolini acquired a real following in the country and became a major political figure, courted by governments and with a sizeable group of deputies behind him. This transformation took everyone by surprise, including Mussolini. It may be explained in one word: *squadrismo*.

Vigilantes and Violence

Armed vigilante groups and paramilitary 'squads' of local *Arditi* or Fascists were nothing new. As I have shown, they had wrecked the *Avanti!* offices in Milan in April 1919, and unofficial citizen defence groups existed in Florence and most other major Italian cities by summer 1919. Mussolini himself had a defence squad of D'Annunzio's 'legionaries' both at the *Popolo d'Italia* and at election meetings in the autumn. But the squads were usually ad hoc, spontaneous groups formed to sort out a particular strike or demonstration, rather than anything more sustained. It was in ethnically tense Trieste that Fascist *squadrismo* really took off. Early in 1920 Mussolini sent Francesco Giunta to the city to organise volunteers to help the army and police deal with strikers and rioters. These men worked closely with the army, and so of course had access to guns and military lorries. They could also rely on enthusiastic support from Mussolini, publicly in the *Popolo d'Italia* and clandestinely by industrialists' money passed on via the newspaper. By the summer of 1920 Fascist groups dominated the *piazza* and the streets of Trieste and of the other towns in Venezia Giulia. When Mussolini visited Trieste on 20 September the whole city was bedecked with flags to meet him. In his speech, he stressed that Fascism was a fighting movement – *Fasci di Combattimento*. Trieste was exceptional, but its lesson was clear. Even in March the *Arditi* leader Ferruccio Vecchi had called for regular *arditismo civile*, i.e. well-trained, permanent vigilante groups all over Italy, and Mussolini had welcomed the idea enthusiastically.[27]

In late 1920 *squadrismo* became most significant in the rural areas of the centre-north. Labour militancy in these zones had been far more intense than in the cities. In some areas, the Socialist labourers' unions had tried to prevent land being allocated to ex-servicemen, and had set up very effective closed shops: no labourer could get a job except through the union, and employers were forced to hire labourers at union rates even in winter when there was no work to be done. In spring and at harvest time overtime was banned, strikes were frequent, and crops were sometimes left to rot. In Catholic areas, the Popular party's unions occupied land directly and founded monopoly cooperatives to market the produce. The party controlled the Ministry of Agriculture in Giolitti's government, which legitimised land seizures and guaranteed all agricultural jobs. Above all, in autumn 1920 local elections resulted in sweeping Socialist victories in Emilia-Romagna and Tuscany, and similar Popular ones in much of Venetia, Lombardy and Piedmont. In Bologna province, the Socialists won 54 of the 61 *comuni*; in Mantua, 59 out of 68. In these areas municipal jobs would go only to Socialists, public works schemes would be carried out only by the appropriate cooperative, and land taxes would rise sharply. Tenant farmers and landowners – including many new landowners who had bought land cheaply during the war – would be bankrupted, or worse. Unless, of course, they fought back. But if they fought back, they would have to do so unofficially, on their own. Giolitti's government would not support them, although local policemen and judges were usually very willing to turn a blind eye.

In autumn 1920 the fightback began. The local elections, the decrees on land, the public debate about 'trade union control' and the Treaty of Rapallo all contributed. So, above all, did events in Bologna on 21 November, when a riot took place at the first meeting of the newly elected Socialist council; 11 people were killed, including one right-wing councillor. The council was soon hounded out of office by *Arditi* and students, an event that attracted great publicity throughout Italy. In the next few months 'squads' of *Arditi*, ex-officers, tenant farmers and students carried out regular punitive expeditions throughout Emilia and Tuscany. They were armed, they were well financed by local landowners, they had transport – usually lorries supplied by the military – and they easily defeated a cowed population of unarmed labourers. They beat up prominent local 'subversives' and/or administered castor oil 'purgations' to them, they wrecked and looted party branches and union offices, they pulled down the Red Flag and ran up the national *Tricolore* over town halls, they made Socialist mayors salute it and shout '*Viva l'Italia!*' in front of the crowd, and they forced Socialist and Popular councils to resign. The squads dealt particularly robustly with strikers, cutting off their beards and making sure they never got another job. Soon the labourers' unions collapsed. The labourers, or at least the ex-servicemen among them, were then offered leases or small plots of land, and were sometimes enrolled into new Fascist-led syndicates or cooperatives. Many ordinary peasants had loathed the union bosses, who had also been violent men, and were happy to accept.

The squads won the propaganda battle too. Public opinion saw them not as violent thugs, but as youthful patriots fighting to save their country from petty local tyrants and from economic collapse. They could even claim to be the heirs of Mazzini's Young Italy and of Garibaldi's Red Shirts. The essence of *squadrismo* was not violence, but ritual. It was the symbolic assertion of authority in the *piazza*. Armed though they were, the squads preferred to beat up their opponents with cudgels (*manganello*) rather than to kill them. The ideal weapon was castor oil; after a dose, union leaders lost all prestige, and their power vanished. As one squad leader remarked, 'ridicule kills more easily than lead'[28] – and it certainly meant the police were less likely to intervene. So the Socialists' pretend revolution triggered a pretend counter-revolution, not a civil war so much as a series of student escapades (the average age of the 'Fascist martyrs' was 21). In Ferrara, for example, Italo Balbo took over the whole province in a few weeks at the cost of about a dozen dead on each side. Interior Ministry figures indicate 278 people were killed at the height of the squad campaigns between January and May 1921, a figure that includes 66 Fascists, 36 bystanders and 24 policemen.[29]

Squadrismo was, of course, a marvellous opportunity for Mussolini. Although he had helped organise the first squads in Trieste he had had very little to do with those in central Italy, which were essentially local and spontaneous and were run by local 'warlords', soon called by the Ethiopian title *ras*: Balbo in Ferrara, Farinacci in Cremona, Arpinati and Grandi in Bologna. Mussolini had not appointed these men and had usually never met them; certainly he could not control them. Many of them disliked him as a self-seeking politician who had just betrayed D'Annunzio. But he was determined to climb on to their bandwagon. He did so by flattering them, by acting as their eloquent national spokesman, and by rewarding brave squad exploits with mentions in dispatches, i.e. with laudatory articles in the *Popolo d'Italia*. As the movement spread he turned up in *squadrista* zones, made rousing speeches of support, and was assiduous in commemorating the Fascist dead. He also helped new squad leaders elsewhere with money and army contacts, and asked existing squads to help out their neighbours.[30] *Squadrismo* may not have been his baby, but he intended to be the godfather. On 20 October 1920 he published an 'Appeal to the Nation', urging all ex-servicemen to join the patriotic struggle against the Bolsheviks.[31] He was clearly trying to assert some sort of leadership over a very undisciplined set of local bosses, but they owed him little and remained distinctly suspicious. On the other hand, they were even more suspicious and jealous of each other. If they were going to have a political spokesman at all, then Mussolini, with his brilliant journalism, his newspaper, his theatrical gifts, his talk of restoring Italy's greatness and above all his remoteness in Milan, was the best bet. In any case, they had no option: there was no one else. Most of them admired the colourful D'Annunzio far more than Mussolini, but D'Annunzio was too radical on socio-economic issues and was said to have called *squadrismo* 'agrarian slavery' – a real stroke of luck for Mussolini.

Squadrismo was, however, a two-edged sword, and it reveals much about Mussolini's ambiguous nature. He welcomed it and supported it, because it destroyed his opponents, distracted attention from Fiume and boosted his own influence; but he had not founded it, nor did he control it. He had no objection in principle to violence and occasionally he would urge his men to attack a particularly obnoxious 'subversive' like the Socialist deputy Cagnoni, who had praised those who planted a bomb in a crowded theatre in Milan and killed 20 people: 'We recommend the hon. Cagnoni to the attention of every Fascist in Italy. His criminal face should become the national spittoon no. 2. It is not admissible that a morally monstrous character like the PUS deputy should be able to move round Italy with impunity.'[32] But he could not allow the Fascist hard men to take total control. He insisted in his speeches and articles that although violence was necessary it had to be 'surgical', 'aristocratic', carried out only as a 'legitimate reprisal', i.e. essentially retaliatory and disciplined, not just mindless thuggery or local vendetta.[33] He portrayed *squadrismo* as a patriotic crusade, and this image was vital if it were to remain politically useful. He did not want the agricultural labourers to be slaughtered – after all, they were more likely to be ex-servicemen than were the young *squadristi*. In practice, he cheered the *squadristi* on but he also urged restraint, often in vain. He also tried to make it clear to respectable opinion that he was a vital figure, the man who could control the squads. This is a familiar posture among all leaders of violent movements, and in this case it was far from true: Mussolini rarely gave the squads advice, let alone orders. Inasmuch as the squads had a national leader and coordinator it was not Mussolini but the intransigent young *ras* of Ferrara, Italo Balbo, who organised major expeditions to nearby provinces and who claimed to have invented the castor oil 'purgation'.

Squadrismo did not succeed everywhere. It was a local movement, and local conditions varied. It triumphed in Emilia-Romagna, in lower Lombardy, in most of Tuscany and in Apulia, but it was weak, absent or soon defeated elsewhere, even in much of the centre-north like Friuli, Piedmont, Venetia, Umbria and the rural zones near Milan, to say nothing of the big cities (except Trieste) and most of the south. Even Bologna province was conquered slowly (only by summer 1922), partly because the local share-croppers sided with the labourers' unions. Some squads were not 'Fascist' at all, but freelance, monarchist or Nationalist – the Nationalists' *Sempre Pronti!* (Always Ready) squads had been founded as early as February 1919, and were far more active in Rome and the south than were the Fascists. Occasionally, too, the police obeyed orders and fought against the squads, e.g. at Sarzana in July 1921 where 18 local Fascists were killed. Many local Fascist associations did not form squads, and lived peaceably enough with their rivals. By mid-1921, too, there were signs of an anti-squad backlash. Republicans and anti-Fascist syndicalists, with Socialist backing, founded *Arditi del Popolo*, People's *Arditi*, to fight back, although the movement soon collapsed for lack of money, guns or lorries, leaving the left more demoralised than ever.[34] But despite all these caveats, Mussolini won the propaganda war, and that was what mattered most. He ensured that in the popular mind *squadrismo* meant Fascism, and Fascism meant *squadrismo* – youthful, dynamic, patriotic and victorious. Mussolini was never one to underplay his hand. 'His' movement had won, and he was going to take full advantage. He proclaimed that it was Fascism, and Fascism alone, that had defeated the Bolsheviks, and would now go on to restore Italy's greatness[35] He was already the man who had won the war; now he intended to be the man who won the peace as well.

A Man of Peace

By spring 1921 *squadrismo* had transformed Italian politics. Mussolini now led, or rather acted as national spokesman for, a mass movement that was radiating out from its central Italian base. It was founding unions for the ex-Socialist labourers, and it now ran many local councils. The Socialist party was completely demoralised, and in January 1921 it split. Henceforth Italy had a real Communist party, too small to be a threat but providing more good propaganda for the Fascists. Giolitti decided on new parliamentary elections, to capitalise on the left's defeat. Hoping, as always, to absorb potential supporters into the Liberal embrace, he offered the Fascists a place on the government parties' electoral list, the National Bloc. Here was real national recognition at last. Mussolini, who as a trainee pilot had been badly injured in March near Milan, became a deputy in the Italian parliament in May with 172,491 votes in the constituency of Emilia-Romagna. Thirty-four other Fascist deputies were elected, although four were disqualified as too young (below 30 years old). But from Giolitti's point of view the election was a disastrous mistake. The Socialist vote did not collapse after all, nor did the Popular party's: there were now 123 Socialist deputies, 15 Communists and 107 *Popolari*, i.e. 245 'subversives' instead of the previous 256, still virtually half the Chamber, and now there were 30-odd Fascists as well. Clearly the various Liberal groups would only be able to form a government with Popular party support. Giolitti promptly resigned. He was succeeded by the reformist Socialist Ivanoe Bonomi, Prime Minister from June 1921 until February 1922, and later by one of Giolitti's supporters Luigi Facta, who headed two governments from February to July and from July to October 1922. These were weak, ineffective governments. Neither Bonomi nor Facta was a particularly prominent politician, and neither was capable of winning police or army loyalty.

Mussolini had little time for parliament, of course, and rarely went there, although often enough to grasp how weak the government and the various parliamentary groups really were – including his own, for despite his efforts he could not stop nearly half the new Fascist deputies going to hear the king's speech. He knew perfectly well that his newspaper was what mattered, and told his colleagues, 'when I am in Rome I feel like a soldier without a rifle. When I am away [from Milan] the *Popolo d'Italia* is just another newspaper like all the others, not a weapon and a spiritual force as it should be.'[36] Still, parliamentary debates were widely reported and it was therefore a useful place for making speeches designed to win over key groups or institutions. Mussolini's maiden speech, on 21 June, unexpectedly praised the historic role of the Church as a truly 'Roman' body, and this had a major long-term effect. Parliament also gave him and his movement greater legitimacy and greater potential for influence in political manoeuvres. But Fascism had no intention of being tamed. There was still room for *squadrismo*, and indeed virtually the first act of the Fascist deputies was to eject the Communist deputy Misiano forcibly out of the Chamber, claiming he had been a deserter in the war. The problem was, however, that in some zones *squadrismo* was running out of legitimate targets. The Socialist and Communist organisations had already been crushed, and so the *squadristi* turned on the Catholic *Popolari*. They, too, ran peasant cooperatives and unions which had secured major concessions; they, too, had done well in the local elections and controlled many local councils; they, too, had been neutralist or at best lukewarm in the war. And they were even less likely to fight back than the Socialists. Furthermore, at national level their support was vital to any government. So in the summer of 1921 the *Popolari* became Mussolini's main target. That was why he praised the Church in parliament and why, with splendid *spregiudicatezza* (political flexibility), he publicly favoured Church schools and condemned both freemasonry and divorce. He was wooing the Vatican in order to isolate and neutralise the Popular party. It was a brilliant political manoeuvre, and in due course it succeeded.

The Liberal governments had no idea what to do about the endemic rural conflict. Or rather, they had a simple policeman's view, but it did not work. Both Giolitti and Bonomi issued the usual brusque instructions to Prefects (provincial governors) and police to crack down on violence and even – in December 1921 – to dissolve all armed organisations on pain of transfer or dismissal, but their orders were usually ignored. The police, like the judiciary and most of the army, sympathised strongly with the Fascists, as did the local middle classes. Prefects could not alienate these natural supporters, and in any case had not Giolitti himself brought the Fascists into parliament as part of the National Bloc? So

Liberal governments were helpless. They regarded *squadrismo* as simple mob violence, but they could not prevent it and they had no intention of trying. With characteristic moral and political cowardice, they therefore turned to Mussolini to do it for them. They believed, or affected to believe, his soothing words, and ignored his belligerent outbursts. In desperation, they called on the man who could control the squads.

Surprisingly, Mussolini did his best to oblige. Like everybody else, he knew that the Socialist menace was no more, that the reformist Socialist unions were anxious for compromise, that *squadrismo* now risked appearing as pointless thuggery, and that D'Annunzio might yet prove a rival peacemaker. It was time to rein the squads in. In July 1921 he took the greatest gamble of his political career, greater even than that of October 1914: he denounced his own followers for indiscipline.[37] A few days later a 'Pact of Pacification' was signed in Rome between the Fascists and the Socialist party and unions. The ceasefire held, more or less, for a couple of months. Only 15 Fascists were killed between 5 August and 5 September. But the *ras* were furious, and so were many ordinary Fascists. To them, Fascism *was squadrismo*; to repudiate *squadrismo* was to repudiate Fascism. The pact was a real threat to their local power. It was also a threat to the agricultural employers, who did not want the Socialist unions back, particularly at harvest time, and to the Fascist syndicalists who were hoping to replace those unions. The familiar graffiti appeared again on the walls of northern towns: 'he who has betrayed once will betray again'. Farinacci and Pietro Marsich of Venice resigned from the Fascist central committee; the Fascists of Emilia-Romagna demanded a national congress to settle the issue. A group of very prominent *squadristi* and syndicalists, led by Dino Grandi of Bologna, even approached D'Annunzio and asked him to lead the Fascist movement, but the poet refused on the grounds that Fascism had become far too reactionary.

That was just what Mussolini thought too. He had a real revolt on his hands, and he reacted very angrily:

I am *duce* only in a manner of speaking . . . a *duce* devoted to the most scrupulous constitutionalism. I have never imposed anything on anybody . . . Fascism is no longer liberation, but tyranny; no longer the nation's safeguard, but the defence of private interests and of the most opaque, mean-spirited, miserable castes in Italy. If Fascism becomes like this it may still call itself Fascism, but it is not the movement in which a handful of us faced the fury and the bullets of the masses, it is no longer Fascism as I conceived it, in one of the darkest moments of recent Italian history . . . Fascism can do without me? Certainly, but I can do without Fascism.[38]

He resigned dramatically from the executive committee, a theatrical move that forced his 'supporters' to ask him back. But the *ras* won, in the short term. On 12 September Balbo and Grandi organised a 'march on Ravenna' by 3,000 black-shirted Fascists, an open snub to Mussolini. He belatedly realised that his gamble had failed. Fascism was no longer just Mussolinism. The *squadristi* were not going to give up. They had their own local bases, their own supporters and their own sources of money. He needed them more than they needed him. It was a salutary lesson. Despite all his prestige and bombast, Mussolini's power was limited. He was, indeed, '*duce* only in a manner of speaking'. He could not control the squads, and he could not deliver peace. So he blamed the Socialists and the government for the continuing violence, and he backtracked. On 26 September eight Fascists were killed at Modena, and Mussolini's oration at their funeral celebrated *squadrismo* very fulsomely again. In November, at the Fascist congress in Rome, he tacitly abandoned the pact and had a public reconciliation with Grandi. The 'peace process' had failed, as such efforts often do, and *squadrismo* resumed.

However, there were compensations. Mussolini had obviously tried to act the peacemaker, and a 'peace process' always boosts the status of the participants. Liberal politicians and journalists persuaded themselves that he might be more successful next time. He encouraged them in this inane belief. Moreover, at the Fascist congress he managed, against some opposition, to turn the movement into a normal political party, with membership cards, a central administrative secretariat and an official programme. He denounced violence, but with wit ('you must cure yourselves of *my* illness'), and he won the congress round.[39] He and the *ras* remained mutually suspicious, but the *ras* accepted his leadership as he was the only man who might win them national benefits. They did it from calculation not loyalty, as he well knew;[40] but they did it. By the end of 1921 the new party had 200,000 members, mostly ex-servicemen and students; by May 1922, as the other parties collapsed, it had 300,000. Mussolini now had a priceless asset: a supposedly disciplined mass party from which troublemakers might be expelled, and which might recruit thousands of respectable middle-class people and members of key elites. But it was a party with a military wing, like Sinn Fein. The National Fascist Party (PNF) remained essentially *squadrista*. At least half of its executive were squad leaders, and the ordinary members were usually loyal to their local boss, not to Mussolini. At the end of 1921 all PNF members were ordered to join their local squad, a characteristically ambiguous move that implied the virtual fusion of the two organisations. It militarised the party, but it also 'partified' the squads. Early in 1922

Balbo and General Gandolfo gave the squads a national structure and titles – cohorts, legions and so forth – that were a foretaste of the later centralised Militia.[41]

The party was not alone. The Fascists, with their genuine syndicalist traditions, also founded trade unions (*sindacati*), initially in the public sector: the first was a Railwaymen's Union, set up in February 1920 to oppose strikes. As the squads wrecked Socialist and Catholic unions in central Italy, the Fascist syndicates moved in, took over the members and negotiated with employers. Often they were a mere fig leaf for land-owner power, but in some places they *distributed* small plots of land to the peasants and became quite popular as a result. The syndicates were the conscience of the counter-revolution. They showed that *squadrismo* was not just violence: it provided the means of overcoming the class war and the constant disruption. Early in 1922 the various syndicates were united into a National Confederation of Syndical Corporations, led by Edmondo Rossoni; by the summer of 1922 it claimed nearly half a million members, over half of them in agriculture. The syndicates, like the party, helped to create a mass, relatively non-violent Fascist movement and to win over many non-Fascists. Mussolini naturally approved, but again his attitude was necessarily ambiguous. The syndicates were run by local bosses too, often by the same men who ran the squads. More-over, Mussolini was still fitfully trying to win over the reformist Socialist unions; and he still needed industrialists' financial support. In 1921–2 Fascist economic policy turned markedly towards a liberal free market, and became therefore anti-syndicalist. Mussolini proclaimed that all state-run economic enterprises were a disaster: 'the state today is tobacconist, postman, railwayman, baker, insurer, sailor, café-owner, biscuit-maker and beach attendant'.[42] He even promised to privatise the railways, al-though fortunately for his later reputation he soon changed his mind.

But the squads were still the key. In spring and summer 1922, while the feeble Facta governments relied on Fascist votes in parliament, squad 'expeditions' took over public works and local government in most of north-central Italy. These ventures were no longer student escapades. They were large-scale and professional, needing more arms and more logistical planning, mostly done by General Gandolfo or Balbo. The rheto-ric was still anti-Socialist and anti-*Popolare*, but increasingly the Fascists' real target was the Liberal state and its institutions. In January 1922 Mussolini founded a new intellectual journal, revealingly called *Gerarchia* (Hierarchy), to stress the values of national discipline needed now that egalitarian democracy was dying: 'new aristocracies are arising, now it has been demonstrated that the masses cannot be the protagonists of history, but only its instrument'.[43] In May–June 1922 a mass occupation of Bologna forced the government to transfer the Prefect, the very emblem of state authority, away from the city. This was highly significant. *Squadrismo* was proving how weak central authority was in Liberal Italy. Authority rested, as ever, on 'opinion'; and opinion had decided what it would accept. It would accept Mussolini. By this time he knew he was safe. He had won enough support where it mattered, and no government would dare to crack down on Fascism. Even so, he needed to retain this respectable support – no easy matter while he was advocating, and even helping to organise, armed risings against state institutions. In 1921 he had tried to resolve this dilemma by the Pact of Pacification; by 1922 a far more self-confident *Duce* could offer other inducements. Early in June he even told Balbo and Grandi to suspend activities in Emilia: 'If you obey me today you will acquire the right to command tomorrow, for the greater good of the country.'[44] They knew he would soon be Prime Minister, distributing government jobs; and obeyed.

Mussolini's problem by 1922 was that the squads were still rampant, but the red threat was no longer plausible. However, there were still local strikes and occasional national stoppages like 1 May, which the Fascists could defeat. By this time there were 20,000 Fascist railwaymen. During strikes they literally made the trains run on time, to great public applause. In the summer Mussolini had a great stroke of luck. The moderate Socialist-led unions, allied to Republicans and radicals in an 'Alliance of Labour', called a 24-hour general strike on 31 July. Their aim was to put pressure on the Facta government, or to secure a tougher government willing to tackle Fascist violence. But few workers responded – at Fiat, only 800 out of 10,000 – and where stoppages occurred at all they were easily defeated by Fascist-led volunteers. The strike's failure discredited the whole left, even its most moderate groups; it guaranteed that there would be no more organised resistance to Fascism; and it ensured that no tougher government would be formed. It also gave Mussolini a wonderful opportunity to proclaim how Socialist treachery and government cowardice alike had been vanquished by Fascist resolution. Once again, his men had proved the only patriotic heroes, keeping public services going despite violence and abuse. They had saved the country from insurrection, and only they could restore national discipline.[45] This was clearly an exaggerated claim, but it seemed plausible in the febrile atmosphere of a failed general strike. It enabled the Fascists to dare even more spectacular ventures. In the next few days they took over the city councils of both Milan and Genoa, and wrecked the *Avanti!* offices in Milan again. The squads became a genuine militia, under unified command,

and took over all the major centres of northern and central Italy. Even more significantly, once it became widely believed that the Fascists really were the only people who could restore order, Mussolini could hold out for power. The failed strike of 31 July 1922 marked the beginning of the Fascist takeover. It was the first step on the 'March on Rome'.

The March on Rome

By autumn 1922 the Fascists had already taken over most of the country north of Rome. They ran local government, they could exact unofficial taxes, and their syndicates controlled the labour market. Once again Mussolini was not too directly involved, although Balbo and others kept him well informed, while he provided money and publicity.[46] He also continued his political manoeuvres, aiming at nothing less than national power. He now had a militia and this was a useful threat to keep in reserve, but he did not intend to use force. To use force might mean having to fight the army, obviously a catastrophic outcome. The key actor now was not the government, which no longer mattered, but King Victor Emmanuel III. Only the king could order the army to fight against the Fascists; conversely, only the king could bring Mussolini to power by constitutional means. Mussolini had to conciliate the king, so he hastily retracted his previous republican beliefs. At Udine, on 20 September, he spoke of how Italy might be transformed while keeping the Crown and other major institutions. The monarchy had no reason to obstruct the Fascists, and would be very foolish to try.[47] This was typical of Mussolini's tactics: an olive branch to the king, but also a warning. Other characteristic moves followed. Two of his more royalist supporters were sent off to Bordighera to win over the Queen Mother, successfully; and the king's cousin took up conspicuous residence near Fascist headquarters in Perugia – clearly available as an alternative monarch or else as a regent for the king's son, if the king were to do something foolish and be forced to abdicate.

It was evident that the Fascists would have to be given a major role in a 'government of national renewal', but how major? Throughout September and October Mussolini negotiated with the leading politicians, including Orlando, Salandra and Giolitti. Giolitti offered four Cabinet posts; Mussolini pressed Salandra for five. But a few seats in someone else's Cabinet were not the issue. He and his men wanted something more visible and spectacular, and the negotiations were a feint. On 16 October Mussolini met his top 'military advisers' in Milan to plan an insurrection and they made their military plans, such as they were. The plans were, in fact, extremely amateurish. Mussolini knew that Facta would always give in, and rightly assumed there would be no resistance.[48] So the 'March on Rome' was a feint too, designed to put pressure on the king and on the politicians. But it had to put real, credible pressure on, or it would be a disaster. Furthermore, Mussolini knew he had to act quickly, because 4 November was the Italians' Armistice Day: Rome would be full of loyal troops brought in for the parades, and D'Annunzio was due to make a speech in the capital. So on 24 October Mussolini addressed a mass rally of 'Blackshirts' in Naples, proclaiming his willingness to lead a government and to accept the monarchy.[49] He also squared D'Annunzio by recognising Captain Giulietti's Seamen's Union and ditching the Fascist syndicates in Genoa.[50] He then went back to Milan and continued to negotiate meaninglessly via the Prefect. He had appointed four *Quadrumviri*, carefully selected from various wings of the Fascist movement, to exercise power when the insurrection started from their base in Perugia – although Balbo kept moving around, and Cesare Maria De Vecchi, a close associate of the king, stayed in Rome to keep in touch with the court. De Vecchi and another of the four, General De Bono, had second thoughts about the 'March' by this time, as did Grandi and Costanzo Ciano, but Mussolini stayed calm. Meanwhile three columns of armed Fascists – two of them carefully placed under army generals, who would do nothing rash – took up positions north of Rome and awaited orders. And Fascist squads took over those few towns and cities in north-central Italy that they did not already control.

The threat was enough. Early on 28 October Prime Minister Facta asked the king to sign a decree bringing in martial law. Initially the king seems to have agreed, or possibly the decree was issued without his knowledge, but soon he refused. His top generals told him that the army might not be willing to fire on Fascists, just as it had not fired on D'Annunzio when he took Fiume in September 1919; after all, many of the insurgents were ex-servicemen led by ex-officers, with several generals among them. True, the army *had* fired on D'Annunzio in December 1920, but that was when Giolitti was Prime Minister. If Giolitti had been in office in October 1922, Mussolini would never have dared stage his 'March', and he had said as much to his military advisers on 16 October.[51] A Prime Minister who had defused the Adriatic crisis in late 1920 would certainly have sorted out the Fascists fairly quickly. Indeed, one reason for pressing ahead quickly with the scheme had been that otherwise Giolitti might resume power. But Giolitti was not in power yet, and the army was unlikely to obey a Facta government. In any case, the king knew that if he issued orders to the army and they were disobeyed, he would have to abdicate. Moreover, he did not want to preside over a civil war. The Fascists had virtually won already. They controlled railways, post offices, prefectures and barracks all over northern and central Italy, and it would have been very difficult to dislodge them. They had massive support in elite and middle-class circles, and their three columns were rumoured to be moving on Rome. So the king refused martial law, and the Facta government resigned. The same evening the king asked Salandra to form a government. But Mussolini, still in Milan, knew that the king would not grant to Salandra or to anyone else what he had refused to Facta. No government now, not even one led by Giolitti, could use force against the Fascists. So there was no need to serve under Salandra, who had to refuse the Prime Ministership. The next day, 29 October, the king reluctantly asked his secretary to summon Mussolini instead. Suspicious as ever, Mussolini refused to come until he received a royal telegram.

The 'March on Rome' was just that: a march, with lots of flags and *evvivas* but almost no actual fighting. It was a bluff, but a daring and successful one that deceived most of the Fascists themselves. They thought they had made a revolution and they were right, in the sense that Mussolini would never have secured the prime ministership otherwise. He himself had stayed in Milan on 28 October. He had gone to the theatre with his wife, and he had tactfully promised the Prefect of Milan a job in his new government, just in case the Prefect felt like having him arrested. Far from marching on Rome at the head of his men, he went there on the overnight sleeper on the evening of 29 October, leaving Milan at 8.30 p.m. and arriving in Rome at 10.50 a.m. the next morning. This, the first train of the Fascist era, did not run on time, because it had to keep stopping to allow Mussolini to address the cheering crowds.[52] He then went to the Quirinal palace, and was appointed by the king in the usual constitutional manner. Many people had reservations about him, but the political and military Establishments knew what they were doing, or thought they did. Mussolini had collaborated with them seriously since at least 1917. Many of them admired him, and now he was indispensable to them. They invited him fully into the political system in order to avoid real bloodshed and in order to 'recover' the centre-north for the official state. They expected that as Prime Minister he would be better able to control his followers, and they expected him to rule constitutionally and not for long. But Mussolini knew he owed his victory to the squads. His first act was to bring his men up to Rome for a victory celebration, particularly symbolic because there had been no victory parade by Italian troops in November 1918. He then ordered all 40,000 of them to go home within

24 hours, and this triumph of railway logistics was actually achieved. Perhaps there had been a revolution after all.

The ambiguous nature of Mussolini's coming to power – both constitutional and revolutionary – tells us a great deal about the man, and indeed about power. Mussolini had to reassure the respectable patriots and be appointed by the king, but he also needed the high drama and the trappings of Cromwellian glory. The respectable approved of Mussolini, manifestly unrespectable though he was, because he had helped secure Italy's entry into war in 1915, because he had fought bravely in the war and been wounded, because he had rallied the country after Caporetto in 1917, and because they thought he had saved Italy from Bolshevism in 1921–2. This last claim was, of course, dubious: Mussolini had simply climbed on to the squads' bandwagon, and the squads, like Mrs Thatcher later, had not defeated Bolshevism but only wet liberalism and militant trade unionism. Even so, that was quite an achievement, and the respectable middle classes had reason to be grateful. Now Mussolini could promise order and the efficient harnessing of national energies on the First World War model. The victorious war was vital to his success. He and his men had become symbols of wartime heroism and triumph, and the country was proud of them.

Yet Mussolini *was* revolutionary too. It was simply that he made his revolution the easy way. His real weapon was his newspaper, which made him the national spokesman for anti-Versailles sentiment and later for *squadrismo*. He showed, not for the last time, that if all power is founded on opinion, then in the age of mass politics the media entrepreneur is king. His men won power at local level first; he then talked, and bluffed, his way into national control. He did not need to storm the Bastille or the Winter Palace. He took a sleeping car instead. However, he had his armed men in position, and the politicians had reason to be nervous. Mussolini *imposed* himself on parliament and king. The roar of a single lion had indeed put to flight a million sheep. Furthermore, he even managed to impose himself on his own supporters, a rather more impressive achievement. Moreover, Mussolini was 'revolutionary' in another sense. He wanted power in order to transform the whole political, economic, diplomatic and constitutional structure of the country, from above. Italy would be run once more on wartime lines, as his wartime articles on 'trenchocracy' had promised. The constitutional democracy of neutralists and defeatists would be replaced by a new regime, the 'rule of war'.

In the Introduction I described Mussolini as a great actor-manager. 'The March on Rome' was one of his finest productions. It was highly dramatic, with lots of unexpected twists and turns, a cast of thousands, plenty of good parts to keep the star actors happy, and an outcome that sent most of the audience home feeling satisfied that justice had been done. The leading man remained offstage until late in the day, but triumphed at the end over his pusillanimous rivals by shrewdness, courage and force of personality. People thought of him as they had of Coriolanus:

He'll be to Rome
As is the osprey to the fish, who takes it
By sovereignty of nature.[53]

Notes

1 'La nostra costituente', *Popolo d'Italia*, 14 November 1918; *OO* xii, pp. 3–5.

2 Speech to *Arditi*, 10 November; *Popolo d'Italia*, 11 November 1918; *OO* xi, p. 477.

3 F. Cordova, *Arditi e Legionari Dannunziani* (Padua, 1969); G. Rochat, *Gli Arditi della Grande Guerra* (Milan, 1981).

4 Rachele Mussolini, *My Life with Mussolini* (London, 1959), pp. 40–1.

5 P. Cannistraro and B. Sullivan, *Il Duce's Other Woman* (New York, 1993), pp. 175–81.

6 'Il nuovo "parecchio" di Bissolati', *Popolo d'Italia*, 10 January 1919; *OO* xii, pp. 125–30; R. De Felice, *Mussolini il Rivoluzionario* (Turin, 1965), pp. 482–4.

7 For example, speech at Fiume, 22 May 1919; *OO* xiii, pp. 142–6. Cf. H. Nicolson, *Peacemaking 1919* (London, 1933; 1964 edn), p. 165. The phrase 'mutilated victory' was first used by D'Annunzio in *Corriere della Sera*, 24 October 1918, before the war ended.

8 J. Woodhouse, *Gabriele D'Annunzio: the Defiant Archangel* (Oxford, 1998); M. Ledeen, *The First Duce* (Baltimore, 1977); F. Gerra, *L'Impresa di Fiume* (Milan, 1974–5).

9 De Felice, *Mussolini il Rivoluzionario* cit., pp. 583–7; Mussolini to D'Annunzio, 30 October 1919, in *OO* xiv, p. 478.

10 Mussolini to D'Annunzio, 25 September 1920; *OO* xv, pp. 313–18.

11 *Popolo d'Italia*, 7 May 1920; *OO* xiv, pp. 436–8.

12 *Popolo d'Italia*, 12 December 1919; *OO* xiv, pp. 193–4.

13 'Il piatto e il resto', *Popolo d'Italia*, 5 May 1920; *OO* xiv, p. 434.

14 'Dopo due anni', *Popolo d'Italia*, 23 March 1921; *OO* xvi, pp. 211–13; speech at Perugia, 30 October 1923, in *OO* xx, p. 71; cf. also ACS, SPD, c. ris., b. 126; G. Pini and D. Susmel, *Mussolini: l'Uomo e l'Opera* (Florence, 1953–4), vol. i, p. 389; M. Sarfatti, *Dux* (Milan, 1926), p. 215; P. Milza, *Mussolini* (Paris, 1999), pp. 237–8, 265.

15 '23 marzo', *Popolo d'Italia*, 18 March 1919; *OO* xii, pp. 309–11.

16 Mussolini's speech at the meeting is in *OO* xii, pp. 321–4.

17 Published in *Popolo d'Italia*, 6 June 1919; *OO* xiii, pp. 218–20.

18 De Felice, *Mussolini il Rivoluzionario* cit., pp. 462–4 and 725–37 (Appendix 18).

19 *Avanti!*, 18 November 1919.

20 R. Vivarelli, *Il Fallimento del Liberalismo* (Bologna, 1981), p. 126; A. Lyttelton, *The Seizure of Power* (London, 1973), pp. 32–5.

21 'Navigare necesse', *Popolo d'Italia*, 1 January 1920; *OO* xiv, pp. 230–2.

22 'Problemi e soluzioni', *Popolo d'Italia*, 25 June 1920; *OO* xv, pp. 55–6.

23 De Felice, *Mussolini il Rivoluzionario* cit., pp. 640–4.

24 'L'accordo di Rapallo', *Popolo d'Italia*, 12 November 1920; *OO* xv, pp. 306–8.

25 'Suprema grandezza', *Popolo d'Italia*, 19 November 1920; *OO* xvi, pp. 17–19.

26 Speech at Cremona, 5 September 1920; *OO* xv, pp. 182–9, at p. 183.

27 *Popolo d'Italia*, 14 March 1920; *OO* xiv, pp. 371–3. His speech at Trieste in September is in *OO* xv, pp. 214–23.

28 R. Riccardi, *Pagine Squadriste* (Rome, 1939), p. 187.

29 E. Gentile, *Storia del Partito Fascista 1919–22* (Bari, 1989), pp. 493–4; J. Petersen, 'Violence in Italian Fascism 1919–25', in W. Mommsen and G. Hirschfeld (eds), *Social Protest, Violence and Terror in 19th and 20th Century Europe* (London, 1982), pp. 275–99, at pp. 287–9.

30 On 18 April 1921 he asked Balbo to help out the Rimini Fascists 'who are fighting in a very difficult environment'; *OO* xxxviii, p. 129. Cf. Lyttelton, *The Seizure of Power* cit., pp. 52–3.

31 *Popolo d'Italia*, 20 October 1920; *OO* xv, p. 274.

32 'Tregua', in *Popolo d'Italia*, 29 March 1921; *OO* xvi, p. 228. National spittoon no. 1 was, of course, Nitti.

33 'Intervento chirurgico', in *Popolo d'Italia*, 25 May 1921; *OO* xvi, pp. 370–2; 'Disciplina', in *Popolo d'Italia*, 24 July 1921; *OO* xvii, pp. 67–8.

34 F. Cordova, *Arditi e Legionari* cit., pp. 83–111.

35 'Dopo due anni', in *Popolo d'Italia*, 23 March 1921; *OO* xvi, pp. 211–13; speech at Bologna, 3 April 1921, in *OO* xvi, pp. 239–46.

36 Speech to Fascist deputies, 3 May 1922; *OO* xxxviii, pp. 138–41.

37 'Disciplina', in *Popolo d'Italia*, 24 July 1921; *OO* xvii, pp. 67–8.

38 'La culla e il resto', in *Popolo d'Italia*, 7 August 1921; *OO* xvii, pp. 89–91.

39 His speech is in *OO* xvii, pp. 216–22.

40 Y. De Begnac, *Taccuini Mussoliniani* (Bologna, 1990), pp. 159 ff.

41 Gentile, *Storia del Partito Fascista* cit., p. 466; Lyttelton, *The Seizure of Power* cit., pp. 52–4.

42 R. De Felice, *Mussolini il Fascista* (Turin, 1966), i, pp. 330–2; A. Lepre, *Mussolini l'Italiano* (Milan, 1995), pp. 90–1.

43 'Da che parte va il mondo?', in *Gerarchia*, 25 February 1922; *OO* xviii, pp. 66–72.

44 Mussolini to Grandi and Balbo, 2 June 1922; *OO* xviii, p. 483.

45 'Continuando', in *Popolo d'Italia*, 7 August 1922; *OO* xviii, pp. 339–40.

46 Balbo to Mussolini, 9 October 1922, in ACS, SPD, c. ris., b. 61 'Balbo', sottof. 4.

47 Speech at Udine, in *OO* xviii, pp. 411–21.

48 *OO* xviii, pp. 581–2; L. Longanesi, *In Piedi e Seduti* (Milan, 1948), p. 95. Cf. A. Repaci, *La Marcia su Roma* (Rome, 1963), pp. 407–13; I. Balbo, *Diario* (Milan, 1932), pp. 179–83; De Felice, *Mussolini il Fascista* cit., i, p. 364.

49 Speech at Naples, in *OO* xviii, pp. 453–60.

50 Lyttelton, *The Seizure of Power* cit., p. 82; R. De Felice, *D'Annunzio Politico* (Bari, 1978), p. 176; *OO* xviii, pp. 565–6.

51 *OO* xviii, pp. 581–2.

52 G. Pini and D. Susmel, *Mussolini* cit., ii, p. 251; Gentile, *Storia del Partito Fascista* cit., p. 680.

53 W. Shakespeare, *Coriolanus*, IV vii 33–5.

Chapter 3

Precarious Tenure 1922–4

The Honeymoon Period

In the afternoon of 30 October 1922 Mussolini sat in the Hotel Savoia in Rome and formed his 'national government'. It was not a radical Fascist government, and it had no radical Fascist programme. Like all other governments it was a coalition, including three Fascists but also two 'Democrats', one 'Social-Democrat', one Liberal, one Nationalist (Federzoni at the Colonial Ministry) and even two *Popolari*, at the Treasury and at the Ministry of Labour. It also included several eminent Establishment figures beyond suspicion, to add much-needed respectability: the philosopher Giovanni Gentile at Education, Marshal Diaz at War and Admiral Thaon di Revel at the Admiralty. It was not exactly a Ministry of All the Talents but some of its members, especially Gentile and also De' Stefani at Finance, *were* talented, independent-minded men who were not likely to bow to pressure from the rough upstart Fascists in the provinces. Mussolini encouraged them, and supported them when need arose. Initially he offered the Labour Ministry to his favourite reformist Socialist trade unionist, Gino Baldesi, but his syndicalist supporters and the Nationalists objected so strongly that he had to give up the idea, although he continued to make overtures to the reformists and clearly still wanted some credentials on the centre left. So even in his hour of triumph Mussolini's hands were tied. His own followers vetoed Baldesi and thus closed off one of Mussolini's options, by shifting the whole balance of the new government to the right.[1]

He himself, as well as being Prime Minister, took both the Foreign and Interior Ministries, and this was no fiction: he did the work, especially at the Foreign Ministry as he had long been obsessed by foreign policy issues. And the key domestic ministry, that of the Interior, was placed firmly in Fascist hands. Mussolini was minister, Aldo Finzi was under-secretary, and two of the *Quadrumviri* were given key posts: Michele Bianchi became secretary-general, and General De Bono became Chief of Police. In an ironic touch, another of the *Quadrumviri*, Cesare Maria De Vecchi – whom Mussolini strongly suspected of having been willing to betray Fascism on 28 October and take the job of Minister of War under Salandra – was given the exalted job of under-secretary at the Ministry of Pensions, although he did not last long even there. He aroused Mussolini's fury by claiming to have thought up the 'March on Rome', and was firmly rebuffed: 'The March on Rome was thought up by myself, willed by myself and eventually imposed by myself. In Milan I was on the barricades ready to risk my life, not engaging in last-minute parliamentary intrigues which would have sabotaged and mutilated our victory.'[2] In May 1923 Mussolini sacked him, partly for turning some rooms at the ministry into a private apartment, and a few months later sent him off to govern Somalia. What was striking in Mussolini's 'national government' was how few prominent Fascists were given important posts, or indeed any posts at all. This was partly because Mussolini had always been a loner with few close colleagues and no cronies. But it was also because Mussolini had grasped that the really important posts were not in government itself. His closest advisers at this time were his brother Arnaldo, the ex-syndicalist Cesare Rossi, and the party treasurer Giovanni Marinelli. Arnaldo became editor of the family firm, the *Popolo d'Italia*, to ensure that Mussolini would have a mouthpiece while in office and a bolt-hole later; Rossi was put in charge of Mussolini's Press Office, arguably the key post in any truly modern government; and Marinelli stayed in charge of party administration and fundraising, since he knew too much to be moved.

During this initial honeymoon period Mussolini was almost the model Prime Minister. He was energetic, sensible, in control and, unusually for a newly elected politician, apparently without manifestly daft ideas. The talk was all of 'normalisation', 'national reconciliation' and 'inclusion', although this last looked suspiciously like the old 'transformism', i.e. turning opponents into supporters by handing out government favours. In fact, he had little choice: there were only 31 Fascist deputies, and few of them would have made reliable ministers. Besides, he had political debts to pay and promises to keep. So he had to include others, although he noticeably *excluded* those who had tried to keep him out of office, e.g. Salandra. Soon he won a vote of confidence in the Chamber, by 306 to 116, and secured 'full powers' to legislate and impose taxes for a year. Mussolini visited the king twice a week, in rigorous morning dress and top hat, and took care to flatter court circles and the Senate. Italians breathed a sigh of relief. Perhaps things had turned out for the best after all. It looked as if the dramatic 'March on Rome', the much-vaunted 'Fascist revolution', had resulted only in reassuringly normal parliamentary government. Even sceptical observers like Gaetano Salvemini and Giovanni Amendola welcomed the new government.[3]

Mussolini in autumn 1922 was like a medieval monarch who had just overthrown his predecessor and had little title to rule. He enjoyed the plaudits of the crowd but he was surrounded by squabbling barons, and he needed legitimacy. So he naturally wooed the Church. He allowed pupils from Catholic schools to sit state examinations, he gave funds to war-damaged churches, he placed crucifixes in schools and law-courts, and he even introduced religious instruction into state primary schools. The Catholic *Banco di Roma* was rescued with public money, and freemasonry was discouraged. In 1923 Mussolini's three children were baptised, rather late in the day (the eldest, Edda, was 12 years old) by Arnaldo's brother-in-law. Mussolini himself met the Vatican Secretary of State, Cardinal Gasparri, in January 1923 and put out feelers towards settling the 'Roman Question', in dispute since 1870. He let the Church know that he – unlike the Popular party – could deliver real benefits, and the Church grasped the point. Even so, the Vatican was typically cautious. Its inhabitants distrusted Mussolini and disapproved of his personal morality. Neither his sexual adventures nor his taste for beating up opponents was reassuring, and his youthful anti-clericalism and *Claudia Particella* had not been forgotten. Mussolini could get away with browbeating the Popular party but he could not yet rely on Vatican support on wider issues, and nobody yet thought of him as a prodigal son.

Yet Mussolini could not afford to be *too* respectable. He owed his victory to the *squadristi*, and he knew it. It was vital to keep them fairly happy, although in fact most of them soon became very disgruntled at the meagre result of all their heroic efforts. 'Normalisation' may have pleased the elites, but it was not what the 'intransigents' in the country had risked their lives for. 'Normalisation' in 1923 was always liable to the same fate as 'pacification' in 1921, and at the same hands. The 'intransigents' wanted a real Fascist regime, with jobs for themselves and no nonsense from the civil service, the Liberals or the Popular party; instead, the hated *Popolari* were in government for Mussolini's first six months, the Prefects were still in charge of local government, and the opposition press and parties still operated normally. Even economic policy was distressingly 'liberal' and made no concessions to the syndicalists. So Mussolini had to conciliate the hard men, and in his first speech to the Chamber as Prime Minister he recognised his debt to them:

With 300,000 well-armed young men, prepared for anything and almost mystic-ally ready for my orders, I could have punished all those who have defamed Fascism and tried to drag it into the mud. I could have made this grey, toneless Chamber a bivouac for my troops. I could have barred up parliament and formed an exclusively Fascist government. I could have done; but, at least for the moment, I did not wish to.[4]

He repeated this threat several times in 1922–3, and on the anniversary of the 'March' in October 1923 he spoke of the need for a 'second wave' of the Fascist revolution. But speeches were not enough. He had thousands of angry supporters to satisfy, and other right-wing groups – e.g. the Nationalists – had them too, in a range of variously coloured shirts. He could hardly tell these men to go home and live peacefully ever after. Apart from the ingratitude, it would have been far too dangerous, as a serious outbreak of Fascist squad violence at Turin in December 1922 proved. What was he to do?

What he did was to dissolve the squads and incorporate the *squadristi* into a new body, the Militia (*Milizia Volontaria per la Sicurezza Nazionale, MVSN*), organised by De Bono at the Interior. The Militia would 'defend the Fascist revolution', would protect the Fascist regime from its enemies, would give the *squadristi* status, pay and some local power, and would also discipline them: the ordinary ex-*squadristi* would supposedly find themselves serving under the command of ex-army officers. It was, there-fore, an ambiguous body, part reward, part constraint; it was also part Fascist, part state, and it had ambiguous functions, part military, part police. However, it soon became clear that neither the army nor any of the various police forces was willing to let the MVSN muscle into its territory. Army officers regarded the MVSN with great suspicion and also jealousy, since MVSN commanders above the rank of *console* received considerably higher pay than they did. Furthermore, Militia members took an oath of loyalty to Mussolini alone, not to the king, and indeed many of them were republicans. The army, soon helped by De Bono – himself a former general – constantly tried to bring the MVSN under full army control. Mussolini sometimes backed this verbally but he could not alienate his supporters, nor deprive himself of a personal armed force and a potential 'parallel' enforcement agency.[5] As for policing, that became very complicated in 1923. Setting up the Militia gave Mussolini an excuse to dissolve the hated 'Royal Guard', which had been founded by Nitti in 1919 and was regarded by the Fascists as a deliberately anti-Fascist police force, and furthermore as a refuge for war 'shirkers' and defeatists. Most of its members were sent off to join the *carabinieri* (military police) to enjoy a spot of military discipline, much needed as the Royal Guard in Naples had burned down the Fascist headquarters; the rest were dismissed without a pension. The demise of the Royal Guard left a policing void, which the Militia tried to fill in competition with both the *carabinieri* and the urban 'Public Security' forces. This complex situation was rendered more complex still by the fact that De Bono, as Chief of Police, was formally in charge of the 'Public Security' forces as well as the Militia. The 'Public Security' police therefore tried to show Mussolini that *they* were the most loyal and useful policemen around. So they arrested large numbers of anti-Fascists, thus proving that the MVSN was no use at protecting the regime. But they had missed the point: the MVSN was designed to contain the Fascists, not the anti-Fascists.

In fact, it failed in this task. De Bono's central control of the Militia was distinctly tenuous. In north-central Italy most of the Militia branches were simply the old squads, consisting of the same people and run by the same locally chosen commanders as previously, although now paid by public funds instead of (or as well as) by local landowners. Mussolini might proclaim that *squadrismo* was now 'anachronistic' in a Fascist state, but it still flourished at local level and it might still have national importance, as events were to prove. Indeed, it was still the essence of the Fascist movement. In many provinces the old squad bosses – Farinacci in Cremona, Scorza in Lucca, Arrivabene in Mantua, etc. – ruled unchecked, since police and Prefects knew where local power lay, and knew that central government would give them little backing if they tried to curb the *ras*. A shrewd Prefect, for example Arturo Bocchini, would even ally with a prominent squad leader like Farinacci in order to further his own career. Some of the bosses, including Balbo and Farinacci, had their own newspapers, and Farinacci's *Cremona Nuova* soon replaced Mussolini's *Popolo d'Italia* as the mouthpiece of Fascist intransigence. These men accepted the MVSN but they expected to run it locally, and also to run local government and much of the local economy. They were a rough crew of parvenus and adventurers, enriching themselves with protection rackets, and they horrified the old Liberal elite. They horrified Mussolini too, but he could do little about them. He might be Prime Minister, but he was still '*duce* only in a manner of speaking', the man who had surrendered to the *ras* in 1921. Balbo, Farinacci or Acerbo regarded themselves as his equals, addressed him with the familiar '*tu*', were extremely outspoken and critical to him in private and regarded him with well-founded suspicion as a man who would betray the cause without hesitation if he saw any advantage in doing so: *chi ha tradito tradirà*. He could influence them and bribe them with rewards for good behaviour, but he had no *power* over them. In reality, they had made a tacit bargain: they would back Mussolini's government and behave not too outrageously in public, in return for a free hand at local level and some national status. So there was no Night of the Long Knives in Italy, and equally no SS. The Militia was not Mussolini's private police force or praetorian guard, although he did soon have his *cheka*, a small group of bodyguards loosely attached to his Press Office, who were used to beat up opponents and dissident Fascists alike.

Mussolini also founded another institution to gratify, and discipline, his turbulent followers. The 'Grand Council', initially with 24 members, was a new body at the head of the party, designed to discuss party and also broader political issues under the watchful eye of the *Duce*. Its first meeting, at the Grand Hotel in Rome in mid-December, approved the Militia; for much of 1923 it debated constitutional and syndicate issues. It was a genuine debating forum – indeed it later became virtually the only place where policy issues *were* debated fairly freely – but it rarely voted and had no formal powers. It was purely consultative; it met irregularly, only when Mussolini convened it; he alone fixed the agenda; he opened the meetings, often with a lengthy speech; he drafted the resolutions, although others might submit amendments; he summed up; and he decided the outcome. Any detailed legislative or administrative proposals had of course to go to the ministers in Cabinet and to parliament. Mussolini used the Grand Council to win broad party approval for his policy on major issues, and he usually succeeded. On 15 February 1923, for example, the Grand Council proclaimed that Fascists could not be Freemasons. This pleased the Vatican and the Nationalists, but horrified civil servants, army officers and the many Fascist Masons, who included Balbo, Farinacci and Cesare Rossi. But these leading Fascists could hardly ignore a decision of the Grand Council.

The Fascist National Party (PNF) needed a strong decision-making body at the top, for it was very divided in 1923. Ambitious careerists – 'last-minute Fascists', *'fascisti dell' ultima ora'* – flooded into the party after the 'March on Rome', and were greeted coolly by the party veterans. Membership rose from about 300,000 in October 1922 to 783,000 by the end of 1923, but the party lost its coherence and enthusiasm.[6] Early in 1923 Mussolini made one of the most unexpected and *spregiudicato* decisions of his life, apparently, as in October 1914, at the suggestion of Sergio Panunzio.[7] To the fury of most Fascists, he decided that the PNF should merge with the conservative, monarchist Nationalist Association. The Nationalists favoured an aggressive foreign policy and colonies in Africa but otherwise had little in common with the semi-republican

Fascists. Furthermore, they had advocated a Salandra government in October 1922; indeed, they had had their own *Sempre Pronti!* squads at the ready, who would have cheerfully fought the Fascists if the king had given the word. Mussolini knew all this, but he needed the Nationalists. They were strong in the south where the Fascists were weak, and above all they were respectable and experienced whereas the Fascists were not. They reassured the king, they had close ties with business and the military, and they would give his movement a conservative right wing. Moreover, by merging with the Nationalists he could absorb the *Sempre Pronti!* into the Militia, thus removing a potential threat.[8]

In the long run, the merger with the Nationalists transformed the Fascist party and indeed the whole Fascist movement. The Nationalist leaders were well-educated men who would make competent ministers, unlike the Fascists. They also had more coherent ideas than any Fascist, including Mussolini, about how Italy should be run. They were tough-minded authoritarian believers in a strong state. This state would 'incorporate' producers into state-controlled syndicates, and political decisions would be made essentially not by a decadent parliament but by a modernised bureaucracy and technocratic experts. It would include the 'masses' but it would not need the old mass parties, and it would not tolerate dissent or permit obsolete 'civil liberties' to hamper progress. Mussolini, now in control of the state machinery but not of parliament, was impressed. Perhaps here was a way to combine 'normalisation' with a real transformation of the economic and political system. He had long held that it was the Fascists' task to create a true 'nation-state' that would unite the people with its rulers, as had briefly happened in the Great War.[9] The Nationalists would help him to achieve this glorious goal.

In the short run, however, the influx of careerists and Nationalists split the already disunited PNF into strongly opposing factions: the suspicious, intransigent old guard from north-central Italy plus the syndicalists and the few southern Fascists, against the Nationalists and the 'normalisers'. Some top leaders, including the radical Aurelio Padovani in Naples, hated the corrupt old Liberal bosses and the dictatorial Nationalists alike, refused to admit them into the party, and had to be purged as a result. The local Prefect there was ordered to carry out mass arrests of Fascist leaders.[10] But in Cremona Farinacci, with his newspaper and his great popularity among *squadristi*, railwaymen and Po valley landowners, was too powerful to be touched. He became surprisingly influential in 1923, at the centre of a web of alliances designed to prevent any back sliding by the *Duce*.[11] The overt 'normalisers' or 'revisionists' like Alfredo Misuri or Massimo Rocca were even more troublesome. These men detested the *ras* and wanted a more effective state, but one where basic civil liberties still prevailed. This, in Fascist terms, was heresy. Mussolini's policy might be 'normalisation', but he could not afford to sound too liberal. The arch-revisionist Misuri, conservative and monarchist, made a speech in parliament in May urging that the party be purged if not dissolved, that it should have no influence on policy, and that the Militia should be merged into the army. He was beaten up as a result, probably on Mussolini's orders, and expelled from the party. But in autumn 1923, as elections approached, Mussolini became rather more sympathetic to the revisionists, who were after all exalting his status above that of party, Militia or *ras*. When the intransigents on the party executive expelled Rocca, the man who had triggered Mussolini's great switch away from Socialism in October 1914, Mussolini sacked the entire executive including the party secretary, Michele Bianchi. Rocca's punishment was reduced to suspension, although he was expelled again a few months later.

In short, Mussolini in 1923 was still having to manoeuvre among the Fascist factions. The revisionists were useful at election time as a counterweight to the uncouth *ras*, but they were too outspoken and Mussolini could not be seen to be influenced by them. Certainly the interminable squabbling in the party was a real disaster for him. It meant he had no reliable power base. On the contrary, he had to cope with a varied host of dissatisfied and mistrustful men who felt betrayed and whom he could not discipline. He was disgusted by his own creation. As he told the Prefect of Cremona in September, 'the party is a vast pitiable panorama of interminable, imbecile squabbles, the object of daily scorn and laughter to all our opponents. For months Fascism has been the only source of unrest in the nation, which has otherwise rallied almost unanimously behind the government.'[12]

Nevertheless, these were perhaps Mussolini's best years, the most successful and fulfilling period of his life. For some months he could hardly believe in his own success: a cat with cream, Dinale called him.[13] Being Prime Minister was a stimulating challenge, and it suited him. He was far brighter and more energetic than his rivals, could grasp the essence of complicated issues quickly, and was clearly respected by his expert colleagues. And Rome was much more welcoming than Milan had been. He was a star, and everyone wanted to meet him. He had a stream of visitors and flattered them by being unexpectedly courteous and apparently knowing something of their interests. Initially shy with ambassadors and Rome aristocrats, he was taken in hand by a diplomat versed in etiquette, Mario Pansa, who instructed him in what to wear and how to behave in polite society. Mussolini owed a great deal to this man, and gained much in self-confidence. For recreation he took up riding in the villa Borghese park early in the morning, so becoming literally the man on horseback. He continued to fence and to fly, although he could no longer take flying lessons at Arcore airfield and so did not receive a pilot's licence until many years later. Best of all, he had left his wife and children behind in Milan. Although they moved later to villa Carpena near Forlì, he still saw them only on occasional visits north or during family holidays in the summer. In Rome he stayed initially in the Grand Hotel, moving in April 1923 to a flat in palazzo Tittoni in via Rasella, where a middle-aged housekeeper, Cesira Carocci, looked after him and where he could receive his lovers. He also briefly kept a lion cub there; when it grew too big it was moved to the zoo, which gave Mussolini the ultimate photo-opportunity, entering the lion's cage. But there were some disadvantages to these happy arrangements. As Prime Minister, he could not walk round Rome freely, or get away from his police bodyguards. He was also cut off from his brother Arnaldo, his only real confidant. Being on his own, he worked too hard. Spending 10 or 12 hours a day behind a desk was no good for an energetic man who needed hard physical exercise, and it made him even more obsessional.

Mussolini, like Oxbridge tutors, governed essentially by interview and interrogation. He was in the office by 8.00 a.m., and every morning he saw his under-secretaries at the Foreign and Interior Ministries and the Prime Minister's Office, the Chief of Police, the heads of the *carabinieri* and the Press Office, and the secretary of the party. Once they had made their reports and departed, he received the lobbyists and postulants. He deliberately ruled through the normal bureaucratic machinery, i.e. the Prefects and the police, not the party; and he tried to impose *state* authority on his own recalcitrant followers. In June 1923 he told the Senate that 'the Prefect and the *questore* [local police chief] are the only legitimate, authorised representatives of state authority in the provinces'; a theme often repeated in future years, but rarely believed. To the Chamber of Deputies, he put it more bluntly: 'The state, what is it? It is the *carabiniere*.'[14] But it was also the banker and the railwayman, and these were Mussolini's major domestic policy preoccupations in his first year. Faced with large budget deficits, he reduced the number of ministries from 15 to 11. He himself knew little and cared less about financial matters, but his Finance Minister De' Stefani was competent and tough, and the budget laws of 1923 and 1924 remained the basis of Italian public finance for over 70 years. He privatised the telephones and life insurance, made big cuts in spending elsewhere, and abolished many price controls and wartime taxes. By 1924–5 the budget deficit had been eliminated and there was even a small surplus, although this was mainly because wartime expenses had ceased at last and also because of a real economic revival from 1922 onwards. Even so, it was a real achievement and Mussolini made the most of it. It was the first of his many domestic 'battles', soon a characteristic feature of his approach to government. He laid down a target ('balance the budget'), appointed the best expert he could find to achieve it, backed him fully,[15] proclaimed a victory – and then dismissed the expert and moved on to the next triumph.

Mussolini took a similar line on the railways, where the political rewards were even greater. It was, after all, the age of the train; he himself had taken one to march on Rome. Many prominent Fascists, including the former stationmaster Farinacci, were railway officials. They knew how to run a railway, and they were not going to let anyone stop them. The (non-Fascist) Railwaymen's Union, which had joined the 'Alliance of Labour' strike in July 1922, was to the Fascists what the National Union of Mineworkers would later be to Mrs Thatcher: the greatest domestic threat, and one that had to be defeated. In January 1924, when a passenger train in Tuscany stopped in open countryside for a few minutes, Mussolini dismissed the sub-Prefect of Pistoia and ordered those responsible to be tried.[16] He tackled the railways in characteristic fashion. He appointed an Extraordinary Commissioner, Edoardo Torre, to be in charge and gave him every support, but not for long. In May 1923 he even sacked the Director General of the State Railways at Torre's request, in words that any user of the contemporary British rail system will find prescient: 'I realise that the railways cannot be run by three different people. To restore the railways or any other business to health a single management structure is strictly necessary.'[17] In 18 months at least 46,000 railwaymen were dismissed, out of about 226,000; when the union complained, Mussolini cheerfully told them that if any of their members actually had any technical competence, they would be kept on.[18] But in 1924 Torre himself was dismissed. Mussolini had already won his 'battle' and established his historical reputation as the man who made the trains run on time.

Creating a Majority

Ever the journalist, Mussolini still wrote occasional articles for the *Popolo d'Italia* and he rang his brother in Milan every evening to pass on titbits of political news and to discuss the next day's editorial content. He also now controlled the Interior Ministry's secret funds, traditionally used to

bribe the press and slant their stories. In fact, Mussolini used this re-
source rather sparingly. In 1923–4 only about 14 or 15 daily newspapers,
out of the hundreds in the country, received a regular subsidy. These
included the Nationalists' *L'Idea Nazionale*, the Catholic *Corriere d'Italia*,
his old friend the *Resto del Carlino*, and three in Sardinia where Mussolini was particularly anxious to win some support. *La Voce di Mantova*
was so heavily subsidised it was virtually the voice of the Ministry.[19]
There was nothing new about all this nor anything specifically 'Fascist',
and most of the press remained independent. But what was new was that
Mussolini, even as Prime Minister, took journalism very seriously. He
realised that influencing the media was vital to his continued power;
indeed, he thought that newspapers, and the way news was presented in
newspapers, were far more important than parliamentary debates, and
he told both journalists and parliamentarians so.[20] But he did not yet
control the press, even the Fascist press.

Regular subsidies were also given out to a few lucky individuals. They
included worthy old Senators fallen on hard times like Senator Massarucci
(300 lire a month), potential troublemakers like General Ricciotti Garibaldi,
and above all Gabriele D'Annunzio, still a potential rival and still supported by his legionaries and by the *Arditi*. D'Annunzio was in contact
with the reformist Socialist trade unionists and with Captain Giulietti of
the Seamen's Union at Genoa, and was posing as national peacemaker.
He had to be flattered regularly, and bought off. Unfortunately he had
expensive tastes. He was given an extremely large pension (over 5 million lire in three years), a magnificent villa on Lake Garda, and the title of
'Prince of Monte Nevoso'.[21] For the next decade and a half he remained a
national monument, maintained at considerable public expense.

But Mussolini did not rely on propaganda alone, nor on flattering and
neutralising his rivals. He offered the carrot, but he also used the stick.
Over 2,000 Communists were arrested in his first three months in office,
although most were soon released. Opposition and dissident Fascist newspapers still appeared, but they were often seized and their editors might
well receive a castor oil 'purgation' or worse. Squads still beat up individual Socialist or *Popolari* activists and sometimes they went too far and
killed their victim, as happened to Father Giovanni Minzoni, priest at
Argenta near Ferrara, in August 1923. In November the house of the
former Prime Minister Nitti was wrecked, and he moved hastily to France;
in December the constitutional Liberal deputy Giovanni Amendola was
beaten up. Fascist dissidents fared just as badly, often worse. Even so,
this was no reign of terror. Mussolini was, after all, pursuing 'normalisation'. There was surprisingly little conflict in most regions in 1923, and

no mass reprisals against whole groups except perhaps the Communists, whom all respectable people feared.

Mussolini's biggest problem in 1923, apart from the disputes in his own party, was that he had no parliamentary majority. So he had to make himself secure. He did so with two brilliantly successful manoeuvres that eliminated his main rivals, the Catholic Popular party and the left Liberals, although one other startling manoeuvre failed. The Popular party was the only mass party left with any influence, and it had 107 deputies. In April 1923 its congress in Turin reluctantly approved of the party remaining in the government coalition, but insisted on rapid 'normalisation' and on keeping proportional representation. Mussolini was not going to accept orders from a party congress, and told his *Popolari* ministers to resign. He knew that the party was disliked in the Vatican. Church leaders had long thought that the *Popolari* leader, Father Luigi Sturzo, was too left-wing, particularly because he had refused to join anti-Socialist coalitions in the 1920 municipal elections. Now that Mussolini was wooing the Church, Sturzo had become a real obstacle. In summer 1923 Vatican pressure forced him to resign. Henceforth the Popular party supported the government in parliament, despite having no ministers and no influence. This was no mean achievement for such an anti-clerical politician as Mussolini.

His second manoeuvre also affected the *Popolari*, but it affected the Liberals more. It was clear that Mussolini would soon call new elections, hoping for a stable majority in the Chamber of Deputies. The one topic that nearly all Liberals and conservatives agreed on was that proportional representation, introduced in 1919 and used again in 1921, had been a disaster. It had resulted only in an unmanageable Chamber, unable to express any stable executive and dominated by two 'subversive' mass parties. Expelling the *Popolari* from government made it essential to give up proportional representation before the next elections, to prevent all their deputies being elected again. But Mussolini had no intention of going back to the former single-member constituencies, as favoured by the Liberals and by some local *ras*, e.g. Farinacci. That would have meant a Chamber dominated by local bosses – corrupt Liberals in the south, warlords in the north. Instead, his party secretary Michele Bianchi proposed a modified form of proportional representation, by which the party list which won the largest number of votes nationally would receive two-thirds of the seats, provided always that it had secured one-quarter of the votes cast. The winning party, or rather the winning coalition, would therefore have a stable majority. The under-secretary at the Prime Minister's office, Giacomo Acerbo, put a bill along these lines to parliament, and the Vatican newspaper *L'Osservatore Romano* welcomed it – a sure sign that the Church had abandoned the Popular party. In fact, everyone realised that Mussolini would win an election whichever system was used. What the bill really meant was that the right-wing Liberals and conservatives – the 'flankers', to use the term common at the time – would have to join the government list if they wished to be elected. A huge Mussolinian 'bloc' would swallow up Salandra's followers and would control the Chamber indefinitely. Mussolini had already absorbed the Nationalists; now he would dominate the entire right, and ditch the *Popolari* as well. After Mussolini had pointedly addressed mass rallies in the provinces, the bill passed its second reading in the Chamber by 235 votes to 139. Most of the *Popolari* deputies abstained because of Vatican pressure. The Liberal old guard – Salandra, Orlando, even Giolitti – backed the bill, supposing that it would make Fascism 'constitutional' and parliamentary, and that the government list would have plenty of room for experienced old hands like themselves. The turkeys, thinking that they were being invited to the feast, voted for Christmas.

In fact, Mussolini was a good enough politician to make sure these men were, in Lyndon Johnson's delicate phrase, inside the tent pissing out rather than outside it pissing in. A 'pentarchy' of five leading Fascists drew up the list on which the fate of so many politicians depended. The *listone* ('big list') of 356 pro-government candidates eventually included 135 non-Fascists, including Salandra, Orlando and even some former right-wing *Popolari*. Most of them were southern Liberals, government supporters by definition, men who needed access to government patronage for their clients and electors. Even the secretary of the Liberal party was allowed in, as were at least half a dozen leading industrialists. If they were prestigious enough they received a personal invitation from Mussolini himself, as the Speaker of the Chamber De Nicola did in Naples: 'Dear and illustrious friend, I pray you to consider me as present among the audience to your speech. There is no doubt that it will be an exalted expression of faith in the greatness of the country, and a loyal recognition of what the National Government, amid a thousand difficulties, has been able to achieve.'[22] All this was good politics, and good 'normalisation'. However, it soon became clear that the list contained *too many* non-Fascists for comfort. The 'pentarchy' had given seats to Liberals instead of to Fascists, and the Fascists were not at all pleased. Moreover, even many of the 220-odd 'Fascists' on the list were latecomers to the party, and some of course were ex-Nationalists. In any case 220 deputies, even if all united, were not going to be a majority in a Chamber of 535 seats. The new government would still depend on the southern Liberals and 'flankers', who were not reliable, and on the ex-Nationalists, who were not reliable either. Perhaps Mussolini's second brilliant manoeuvre had not been so brilliant after all, and the turkeys had been right?

And his third manoeuvre, the one that failed? This was Mussolini's long-standing effort to bring the reformist Socialist trade union leaders – and hence the industrial workers, the one fairly powerful hostile group left – into his fold. He had tried this in October 1922; he turned to them again in July 1923. But, once again, the Fascist syndicates would not permit it. In June 1924 he tried once more, perhaps with disastrous results.

In April 1924 Mussolini called a parliamentary election under the new system. The pro-government *listone*, backed by a 'parallel list' of Giolittians and other Liberals, won 66.3 per cent of the vote, and so won two-thirds of the seats, i.e. 374 out of 535, in any case. Around 60 per cent of the 374 were 'Fascists', including ex-Nationalists; the rest were 'flankers'. The *listone* swept the south, with the aid of the usual fraud and 'management' by Prefects, guided when necessary by the *Duce*. On 20 March he told the southern Prefects that Colonna Di Cesarò's 'Social-Democrat' list was 'one of underhand, demagogic opposition to the Government. This list should therefore be considered as an enemy and fought with the maximum energy.'[23] There is not much doubt that intimidation was more common than usual: beatings-up were frequent, and at the polling stations the presiding officials were often Fascist. Public meetings were strictly controlled, and one Socialist candidate was murdered. However, Mussolini disapproved of violence except against dissident Fascists.[24] The opposition press was left more or less free in the larger towns, and both in Palermo (where Orlando remained supreme) and north of Emilia the opposition groups actually won more votes than the government list. They were of course as divided as ever, ranging from Communists (3.8 per cent of the vote) to constitutional Liberals, via two Socialist parties, a few Republicans and the *Popolari* (9.1 per cent). Even faced by triumphant Fascism, the opposition had failed to unite.

Mussolini did not need to concern himself with these squabbling groups. The days of Socialist and Catholic dominance in the Chamber were over. He had won, at least on the surface, a huge majority in parliament. He had merged with the Nationalists. He had forced the right-wing Liberals and the southern 'notables' to join him. He had his own mass party, which dominated much of the country. He had managed to keep the *ras* fairly quiet, while holding them in reserve as a useful threat. He had pacified the country, on his own patriotic terms. He enjoyed the overt support of Church, army and king, and the tacit support of the reformist Socialist trade unions. The civil servants admired him, as did most of the people and many foreigners. He was manifestly not tyrannical. He had maintained the constitution and civil liberties. The press was still free-ish, despite restrictions on Communist and Socialist papers. He had even restored public finances, and made the trains run on time. It was, indisputably, a brilliant political achievement. What more could anyone ask? What could go wrong?

What went wrong, essentially, was that his commitment to 'constitutional government' was only a half-truth, and the wrong half. Neither Mussolini nor most of his Fascist supporters really believed in 'normalisation'; those few who did were beaten up and hounded out of the party. Too many Fascists were unhappy, and too many basic issues were unresolved: army control of the Militia, excess Nationalist influence, Mussolini's flirting with the reformist unions, non-Fascist ministers in key posts, indeed the whole nature of 'Fascist power' and of the 'Fascist revolution'. Could a Fascist regime really rest on the subtle reciprocal favours and constant bargaining so long familiar, and so often denounced, before October 1922? Even Mussolini did not think so. He had set up the Grand Council as an alternative Cabinet and the Militia as an apparent alternative police force, and he had no intention of dismantling them to please the 'normalisers'. He knew it was the tough ex-servicemen of the World War and the crude *squadristi* after it who had brought him to power, and he remembered how he had been forced to give up 'pacification' in 1921. So he talked of a 'second wave', and he promised that Fascism would 'trample on the more or less decomposed body of the Goddess of Liberty'.[25] He ordered the Prefects to make life difficult for his opponents, even harmless ones like the journalist Piero Gobetti in Turin.[26] His semi-official *cheka* of bodyguards, run by the Italo-American Amerigo Dumini and by Albino Volpi, was as active as ever, beating up dissidents and opposition leaders including Amendola, and even going on a special mission to France to kill anti-Fascist assassins there.[27] Meanwhile the Militia strutted round the streets on their interminable parades, the 'Roman salute', with outstretched right arm, was coming into obligatory party use, and the regime marked the Fascist anniversaries (23 March, 28 October) with great ceremony and public speech-making.

In short, 'normalisation' was a slogan, not a programme. Mussolini and the Fascists in general were too dynamic, too volatile, too rancorous and too vengeful to be satisfied by 'normal' parliamentary routines. He, and they, believed they had a virtual monopoly of true patriotism, that 'audacious minorities' had a right to impose their views, and that opponents always needed to be taught a lesson. Mussolini was an exceptionally shrewd politician with a gift for persuasion and mediation, but he was also intolerant and authoritarian. As the British ambassador commented in June 1924, 'his outlook on public affairs and upon the conduct of government is distinctly medieval, and he makes no secret of the fact'.[28] Clearly he could not be the great national reconciler and the charismatic Fascist *Duce* at the same time. Now that he had a secure parliamentary majority, he was going to have to choose.

The Matteotti Crisis

In the event, he had choice thrust upon him. The atmosphere was very tense when the new Chamber convened. The opposition parties did not want 'normalisation' either. They wanted to denounce Fascism, and some of them were already planning to make a dramatic gesture by walking out of parliament.[29] On 30 May the leader of the reformist Socialist party, Giacomo Matteotti, attacked the government very forcibly. The elections, he claimed, had been a farce, marked by massive intimidation and fraud; Mussolini had trampled on the people's liberty, and his government had no legitimacy. Matteotti was quite a dangerous opponent. He had just been abroad in Britain and Austria, denouncing Fascism and making a big impression on the new Labour government in Britain. Furthermore, he clearly had information about financial scandals involving concessions made by Fascist leaders to the American firm Sinclair Oil, and he published an article on this theme in the British journal the *Statist* on 7 June. Above all, his speech could be understood as a rejection of Mussolini's continuing efforts to bring the reformist Socialists, and the trade unions linked to them, into government – and Mussolini, fresh from an electoral triumph, was at least toying with this project.[30] At any rate, Matteotti's speech infuriated the *Duce*, who allegedly asked the head of his Press Office, Cesare Rossi, 'What is Dumini doing? That man, after that speech, should no longer be around' ('*non dovrebbe più circolare*').[31] Mussolini often talked like this to close colleagues without necessarily meaning what he said, but this time it was not just talk: on 1 June an unsigned article (but clearly by Mussolini) in the *Popolo d'Italia* argued that Matteotti had made 'a monstrously provocative speech, which deserved something more tangible than the epithet of "bandit" shouted out by the hon. Giunta'.[32] Clearly another 'salutary lesson' was needed, and the *cheka* were the men to give it. Nonetheless, by 7 June Mussolini had calmed down enough to make an important conciliatory speech in parliament.

He defended the elections, commemorated the 18 Fascists killed during the campaign, and stressed that the government had always tried to contain violence by forcing the riotous *squadristi* into the disciplined Militia. He also declared that parliament would function normally as a legislature and that the government would no longer issue decree laws. Once again, he wooed the reformist Socialists and the trade unions.[33] The government won its vote of confidence by 361 votes to 107, and tension diminished.

But not for long. Three days later Matteotti left his house on his way to the Chamber, was seized by armed men and bundled into a car. He did not return. Two months later his body was found near the via Flaminia outside Rome. There was naturally a huge outcry, both in Italy and abroad. For a few days Mussolini's stream of visitors dried up, and he sat alone in his office while the opposition press denounced the government as kidnappers and assassins. Even his civil servants failed to show up. An anti-Fascist coup at this time would almost certainly have succeeded, as Mussolini later recognised.[34] But the anti-Fascists had no mettle for a coup. Instead, on 12 June nearly all the opposition parties, except for Giolitti and his followers, walked out of the Chamber – 'went to the Aventine hill', to use the old Roman term – in an extraordinary gesture designed to force the king's hand and make him dismiss the Prime Minister. Worse, passers-by had unexpectedly noted the registration number of the car used to abduct Matteotti, so it soon became clear that Dumini and the *cheka* really were responsible. But this 'punishment squad' had existed for some time, had been organised by the Fascist party's administrative secretary Marinelli, and was closely in touch with Cesare Rossi at Mussolini's Press Office. In other words, this was no 'routine' act of squad violence, perpetrated by provincial thugs; these men were virtually government officials, part of Mussolini's personal entourage. They were at the heart of the Fascist machine and were very unlikely to have acted on their own initiative. So who had given the orders? Had Mussolini himself given them instructions, or 'tacit instructions'?[35]

Matteotti's murder was a 'crisis' because Fascism in 1924 was not yet a 'regime'. Italy still had opposition parties, a fairly free press, a monarch with some discretionary powers in a crisis, and an independent judiciary. Matteotti had been seized while on his way to parliament, and parliamentary privilege still mattered. Moreover, he had been kidnapped in broad daylight, in a middle-class residential area of Rome. Perhaps his assailants had intended only to seize his documents and beat him up, but even that was completely unacceptable if the orders had come from on high. There would have to be an embarrassing investigation and a public trial, revealing far too much about the workings of government. It was a political disaster for Mussolini. He had a big majority in parliament, but it was now morally tainted and fragile. The *listone* had been heterogeneous: his majority might easily collapse, particularly if the Nationalists defected. Even the Cabinet was shaky. Four ministers offered to resign, and indeed only one, Costanzo Ciano, was fully reliable – it was at this time that he became one of Mussolini's very few trusted advisers.[36] Mussolini was virtually isolated, and it was difficult to see how he could survive.

He survived by keeping calm and waiting for the outcry to die down. He did not have to wait that long. The Chamber was now completely docile because all the opposition deputies had walked out – an astonishing stroke of luck for Mussolini. The Senate accepted Mussolini's reassurances and in a vital vote on 26 June voted for continuing government 'pacification' by 225 votes to 21; even Benedetto Croce voted in favour. The great and the good had backed the *Duce*, much to his relief – he later wrote that the Senate vote had been 'extremely important, I venture to say decisive'.[37] D'Annunzio was also clearly unwilling to intervene, although Mussolini made sure by writing him several letters explaining his innocence. The king – the only man who could dismiss a Prime Minister constitutionally and therefore the key actor in the crisis – made no move. Mussolini had, after all, just won a large parliamentary majority and now had virtually unanimous backing in the Chamber. In any case, there was no alternative government except a military one. Victor Emmanuel III had backed Mussolini in October 1922 for fear of civil war. He backed him again in June 1924 with even greater reason, particularly as he knew that Mussolini had summoned three Militia legions down to Rome from Emilia and Tuscany. Moreover, despite the press campaign the country remained remarkably quiet. Matteotti had not been particularly popular and there were few protests or demonstrations at his death, except for one 10-minute work stoppage on the day of his funeral, in which the Fascists themselves joined. The anti-Fascist backlash conspicuously failed to appear. Perhaps people were too frightened; more probably, they were well used to political violence by this time, and one more murder made little difference. The 'Aventine' parties may have held the moral high ground, but few people wished to join them up there. The Vatican described the 'Aventinian secession' as 'a grave error', which it clearly was. Meanwhile the police continued their investigations without hindrance, and the judiciary soon arrested the presumed murderers and the presumed instigators, Cesare Rossi and Giovanni Marinelli. The summer vacation was imminent. Mussolini hung on, careful to avoid giving the impression of a cover-up, or of an apology, or of a retreat.

He did, however, make political concessions. He deplored Matteotti's murder, both privately and very strongly in parliament, and rather plaintively claimed it was directed against Fascism and against himself personally: 'If there is anyone in this hall who has the right to grieve and, I would add, to be exasperated, it is I . . . only an enemy of mine, who for long nights had been thinking up some diabolical scheme, could have carried out this crime which strikes us today with horror and makes us cry out with indignation.'[38] He sacked De Bono and appointed a career Prefect, Crispo Moncada, as Chief of Police. Rossi was, of course, dismissed from the Press Office, and Mussolini gave up the Ministry of the Interior where the under-secretary Finzi also resigned. The new minister was the monarchist ex-Nationalist Federzoni, a sign that Mussolini needed to keep the Nationalists, and the king, contented; Dino Grandi, ex-*ras* of Bologna but gentrifying rapidly, became under-secretary. General Clerici, one of the king's former adjutants, became under-secretary of War. Two right-wing Liberals, friends of Salandra, were given government posts at Education and Public Works, the latter being the lynchpin of the government patronage network; the *ex-Popolare* Cesare Nava, a close friend of the Pope, became Minister of the Economy. In other words, Mussolini carried out a real government reshuffle, to placate king, Pope, Nationalists, *Salandrini*, Catholics and the military. He also dissolved the *cheka*. Mussolini's bodyguards henceforth were normal security policemen, which may explain why there were four attempts on his life in the next two years or so. And he reorganised the Militia, dismissing De Bono from his Militia command as well as from the police, replacing him with Balbo and promising that the Militia would soon take an oath of loyalty to the king as well as to himself.

These measures were effective, for a time. Federzoni was a tough Interior Minister and cracked down hard on Communists and Fascists alike. The opposition parties, isolated on the 'Aventine', played their cards badly. They failed to link Mussolini convincingly to the murder, but nonetheless tried to use it as an excuse for overthrowing the government. All Mussolini needed to do was to deny any complicity, and this was all the more credible since the murder had obviously been a disastrous blow to his position. He also argued that Fascism was an upright movement of selfless patriots, perhaps with a few bad apples who were now being discarded, but nonetheless far more moral and dedicated than the hypocritical opposition which had murdered plenty of Fascists in the past and had now even abandoned its parliamentary duties. He himself intended to remain at his post and carry on the work of national regeneration, including restraining potential Fascist violence. The Fascists, he claimed, should be proud of 'arriving naked at our goal',[39] a much-mocked phrase by which he meant not that the Fascists were classical athletes but that they should not be corrupt – a hint of Mussolini's own view about the possible motives of Matteotti's murderers. At any rate, it is clear that Mussolini did not feel responsible for Matteotti's death. On the contrary, he was furious that it was his own close associates who had dealt him this blow. He saw no reason to give up power for no fault of his own, and he loathed the opposition's moralising: 'the regime is not on trial'. Years later he remarked to De Begnac that if people had thrown a corpse between his feet to make him give up power, they had been mistaken.[40]

Even so, many doubts remained, and remain. It seems to me probable (but by no means certain) that Matteotti's assailants did not intend to murder him; but they were thugs and murder him they did, intentionally or not. The real doubts concern Mussolini's role. Mussolini was certainly shrewd enough to know that it would be a disaster for him if Matteotti were murdered, but he was impulsive and, in early June 1924, very over-confident. It was, after all, Mussolini who had set up the *cheka* in the first place, specifically in order to punish opponents. He had encouraged previous 'lessons', e.g. against the Fascist dissident Forni, and against Nitti. Furthermore, in the days before the murder he had inveighed against Matteotti both privately and publicly in his *Popolo d'Italia*; and that in itself, in the heated atmosphere of the time, was tantamount to an in-struction to beat up Matteotti, at the very least. It may not have been enough to bring him to trial as an instigator – Rossi and particularly Marinelli were clearly the organisers of the venture – but he could hardly escape political and moral responsibility, and he knew it. Mussolini's closest collaborators, men who saw the *Duce* every day, would hardly have arranged for a major opposition leader like Matteotti to be seized unless they had believed, rightly or wrongly, that this was what the boss wanted. By July Mussolini may have been fairly safe politically, but the 'moral issue' continued to split the country.[41]

However, it was the 'Mason issue' and the 'Militia issue' that split the political classes. The *squadristi* had grumbled enough about 'normalisa-tion' in 1923; they were certainly not willing to allow a strident anti-Fascist press campaign in 1924. They thought there were now far too few Fascists left in government, they hated seeing a Nationalist in the Interior Ministry controlling the police, and they were not impressed by appeals to their discipline. Many had their own local 'Matteotti' cases, and they did not want any troublesome police investigations. Thousands of them held rallies in Bologna and other big cities in late June, and there was much talk of a 'second wave'. Squad violence revived in much of central Italy, most furiously when a Fascist deputy from the Romagna, Armando Casalini, was murdered in Rome on 12 September. The squads were not going to stand idly by while their own men were murdered with impunity. Mussolini, now more than ever, had to conciliate the *ras*. He knew it was only the Militia and the threat of *squadrismo* that had saved his government in June. So he gave the party a new executive, including Farinacci who was spokesman for the *ras* and was rapidly becoming unofficial party leader. In August, at the party's national council, Mussolini praised the extraordinary discipline showed by the provincial Fascists and promised to crack down on the Freemasons, who were now overtly 'Aventinian'. All Fascist Masons were to leave their lodges immediately and all Fascists were asked to denounce Masons in high places. Above all, Mussolini now promised, for the first time, to set up a 'Fascist state'. This all went down very well, and Mussolini temporarily regained his grasp of the movement. Furthermore, he meant it. The denunciations started flowing in, and in September he set up investigations all over Italy into real or presumed anti-Fascists in state jobs – a headmaster at Macerata, an admiral at La Maddalena ('he talks too much and too badly'), a 'ferocious anti-Fascist' commanding the port at Castellamare di Stabia.[42] In September, too, he went round central Italy to rally the faithful, and to show he was still in command. It was a successful tour. He made some fine speeches, full of appeals for national reconciliation, and large crowds turned out to hear him. It was a psychological boost both for Fascism and for himself – as a born actor, he had found the absence of an audience for the previous few months very trying – but it did not altogether convince the moderate middle classes. The squads might have been tolerable in 1921–2 when it was a matter of defeating the Bolsheviks and the unions; they were far less tolerable in 1924, when there was no obvious domestic enemy. Nor did Mussolini convince the *ras*, who regarded him by now as a weakling, completely dominated by the Rome Establishment.

The key issue was, as usual, the Militia, and who was to control it. Balbo and his fellow *ras* had no intention of allowing the army to take it over, nor of becoming subject to military discipline. The new oath to the king, eventually taken in solemn public ceremonies on 28 October, was distinctly unpopular with many squad commanders. On 27 November came a further blow. Balbo was unexpectedly forced to resign as Militia commander because of revelations in a court case about the murder of Father Minzoni in 1923, and Mussolini appointed General Gandolfo to replace him. Gandolfo was, on the face of it, a good choice. He had joined the Fascist movement early on, had helped organise some major expeditions and had worked closely with Balbo in 1921–2. Moreover, he had just been a successful Prefect of Cagliari, managing to absorb most of the Sardinian Party of Action into what had been a very small Fascist organisation. However, he was essentially an army general, and the army generals were anxious to bring the Militia under control. It was a great opportunity for them: Mussolini desperately needed army, and royal, support. But he also desperately needed Militia support, and the Militia could not easily be disciplined. It was, after all, voluntary, and its 139,000 members might simply go home, or worse. On 20 December Gandolfo showed his true nature. He sacked all the regional commanders, unless they had risen in the army to the rank of brigadier or above. Clearly the *consoli*, in charge of local legions, would be next to go. This was a real threat to their power, and they could not ignore it. Top Militia men from all over central Italy began meeting clandestinely, almost certainly with Balbo's tacit support.[43]

Mussolini was now in real trouble, much worse than in June. The *ras* were in revolt and the respectable were having doubts, both about the 'moral question' and about Mussolini's continued ability to restrain the hard men. Nor did his campaign against freemasonry endear him to the Establishment. On Armistice Day, 4 November, the ex-servicemen had insisted on holding their own separate parades, and there were clashes between them and the Fascists. The Liberal ex-Prime Ministers – Giolitti, Orlando, Salandra – had grown restive, and they all had the ear of the king. When the Chamber of Deputies reconvened, they began to make gestures of dissent. The Giolittians voted against clauses in the budget, and Orlando abstained. The government still had a majority, but it lacked the backing of respectable opinion, and even the majority was fragile. A third of it consisted of right-wing Liberals and ex-servicemen, now hostile; and many of the so-called 'Fascists' were recent adherents of uncertain loyalty. The Senate was even more uncertain, and more significant. It was full of retired Establishment figures with nothing to lose, and it was far more outspoken. On 5 December the Senators voted only by 206 to 54 in favour of the Ministry of Interior budget, with 35 abstentions including the Minister of the Royal Household, very close to the king. On 20 December 44 'moderate' Fascists, mostly southerners, met in the house of Raffaele Paolucci (a war hero, and therefore fairly safe from reprisal), and called for conciliation, constitutional normality, a purge of the party and a return to single-member constituencies. Paolucci also wrote to the king suggesting a new government including all former Prime Ministers, 'including Mussolini if he accepted, without him if he showed himself intransigent'.[44] Meanwhile the deputy Speaker of the Chamber, Francesco

Giunta, was forced to resign, despite Mussolini's initial backing, for his part in the attack on the Fascist dissident Forni. The respectable were horrified that Mussolini had backed him; the *ras* were horrified that Mussolini had abandoned him.

On 20 December, the day that Gandolfo dismissed the Militia commanders and also the day of the meeting at Paolucci's house, Mussolini responded. He promised a bill to bring back single-member constituencies, i.e. to hold new elections fairly soon on terms that favoured the Liberals and risked throwing away his huge majority. But it was too late. On 26 December the opposition journal *Il Mondo* published a memorandum written the previous June by Cesare Rossi. It produced no evidence linking Mussolini directly to the murder of Matteotti, but insisted he *was* personally responsible for many other previous attacks. Given the press uproar, this made it likely that the judiciary would feel obliged to investigate Rossi's allegations, and in those innocent days it was inconceivable that a Prime Minister might remain in office while under judicial investigation. Salandra resigned as president of the budget committee, so clearly the two Liberal ministers, Casati and Sarrocchi, were about to resign as well. Indeed, on 30 December in Cabinet these two urged the whole government to resign, although they themselves held on to their own posts temporarily. Some of the other ministers agreed with them. The government appeared to be collapsing. Early on 3 January Salandra even went so far as to meet Giolitti, whom he detested, to discuss the situation, and they boldly agreed to 'seek every means of making our viewpoint known indirectly to His Majesty'.[45] For the *Duce*, all looked lost. He had managed to antagonise both the *squadristi* and the Freemasons, a disastrous combination.

However, he still had some advantages. The opposition parties were still absent from the Chamber. They had most of the press, but they overestimated their support in the country. They also overstressed the 'moral issue', on which the Fascists were united and the people indifferent, and they foolishly relied on the king to do their work for them. They took no initiatives at all except to publish the Rossi memorandum, and they even managed to do that on the day after Christmas when it would have minimum impact. Another advantage for Mussolini was that D'Annunzio kept quiet. Mussolini had carefully sent him money and flattering letters throughout the crisis, and it paid off. The British, too, came to the *Duce*'s aid. In December the new Foreign Secretary, Sir Austen Chamberlain, visited Rome at a delicate moment, and helped to reinforce Mussolini's position (see p. 178). But Mussolini's real trump card was the threat of civil war. For that reason the king still backed him, and for that reason the Ministers of War and Navy did not resign in Cabinet on 30 December. So Mussolini survived, with the help of the king and the military. He could now hold new elections, which would tame his fractious supporters and punish the absentee opposition. The elections would not, of course, introduce a new regime. Indeed, single-member constituencies would probably mean a return to the old 'transformist' practices in parliament.

That prospect had little appeal to Mussolini's followers. In Florence on 31 December 10,000 armed Fascists held a mass rally that soon turned into a riot, wrecking the offices of the Liberal paper *Il Nuovo Giornale* and also the Masonic lodge. The same day 33 furious Militia leaders turned up unexpectedly in Mussolini's office, demanding action at last. Mussolini, they exclaimed, was betraying the revolution. There must be no more pseudo-Liberal talk of 'normalisation' or single-member con-stituencies. The hundreds of Fascists in prison should be released forth-with. It was time for the 'second wave', for 'normalisation Fascist-style'. Mussolini had better set up a real Fascist regime quickly, or the *ras* would do it for him. Here was a real threat to Mussolini's leadership, particularly if Balbo were behind it; and the *ras* were not bluffing. They could certainly cause mayhem throughout the country, and already were. Indeed, what mattered was not the threats of angry provincial thugs in Rome, but the riots in Florence. It was the *threat* of squad violence that had been Mussolini's trump card; the real thing was a different matter. He knew that if he could not control the *squadristi*, the king might give up on him and bring in the army to restore order *against* the Fascists.[46] So Mussolini's hand was forced. He could not achieve 'Liberal normalisa-tion' even if he wanted to, especially since on 2 January the king told him he would not agree to dissolve the Chamber until after the trial of Matteotti's murderers. Mussolini could not hang on for months while Italian justice took its leisurely course. He needed to act quickly to fore-stall a Fascist rising. There was only one way out, and the *ras* had made it very clear. He had to act tough, so as to keep control of his men; but not *too* tough.

On 3 January 1925 he made the speech of his life to the Chamber of Deputies. Initially he spoke as a responsible statesman. He had, he claimed, had nothing to do with the murder of Matteotti; the criminals responsible had been arrested and would be tried in the normal way. As for a *cheka*, it had never existed in Italy, although there was certainly one in Russia with over 150,000 victims already. He stressed that the government had always sought 'normalisation' and had always acted legally: it had, since June 1924, brought its budget proposals to parliament, had reformed the Militia and had proposed electoral reform. It was the opposition that had acted unconstitutionally by deserting parliament and by engaging in a libellous press campaign against a freely elected government, while slaughtering Fascists in the country (11 in the previous two months). Now the government's patience was over. Mussolini had had nothing to do with the murder, but he was happy to take responsibility for Fascism. 'I now accept, I alone, full political, moral and historical responsibility for all that has happened . . . if Fascism has been a criminal association, then I am the chief of this criminal association.' The government had curbed the Fascists and would continue to do so – 'if I were to put the hundredth part of the energy I have used to restrain them into unleashing them, then you would see' – but it would crack down on sedition, particularly the seditious press.[47]

This speech did not quite end the Matteotti crisis – the Chamber's approval of the new electoral system on 17 January did that. But Mussolini had now seized the initiative. He had shown resolution and patience; as he later said himself, 'the blow was struck at the right time, and it was mortal'.[48] He had clearly had to improvise: his speech was not part of a long-term plot to set up a dictatorship, but simply the best way out of a very tricky situation not of his making. On 3 January he did not set up a 'totalitarian' state; he reasserted his authority over the squads, the true fount of his power. The 'intransigents' were temporarily satisfied, thinking they would soon enjoy a truly 'Fascist' regime. But it was not the *squadristi* but the government, via the police and the Prefects, who would repress the Fascists' opponents, and in due course not only their opponents. This was just what the more conservative Establishment wanted to hear. With the king's backing, Mussolini could now crack down hard on the opposition and close their tiresome newspapers without worrying about the remaining Liberals in parliament. As for the Militia, by concentrating on the bogus threat from the opposition Mussolini had diverted attention away from the real threat from the 'consuls'. Gandolfo remained in overall command, but the *consoli* retained their provincial power and were allowed, for a few months, to help repress the 'subversives'. So everybody who mattered was happy, for a time. But of course there was a price: press freedom. And Mussolini paid a price too. He could no longer woo the reformist Socialists. The *squadristi* had pushed him to the right, and changed the nature of his power. He could no longer hope to be the great national reconciler. Like it or not, he would have to become the charismatic Fascist *Duce*.

Notes

1 ACS, RSI, SPD, c. ris., b. 7, f. 33; ACS Fondo Susmel, b. 8; R. De Felice, *Mussolini il Fascista* (Turin, 1966), i, pp. 380–8; C. Silvestri, *Matteotti e Mussolini nel Dramma Italiano* (Rome, 1947), pp. 32–3.

2 Mussolini to De Vecchi, 18 December 1922, in ACS, SPD, c. ris., b. 4; *OO* xxxviii, pp. 173–4, 309–10.

3 Salvemini quoted in A. Aquarone, *Alla Ricerca dell' Italia Liberale* (Naples, 1972), p. 334; Amendola in S. Colarizi, *I Democratici all' Opposizione* (Bologna, 1973), p. 12.

4 Speech to Chamber of Deputies, 16 November 1922; *OO* xix, pp. 15–24, at p. 17.

5 A. Lyttelton, *The Seizure of Power* (London, 1973), pp. 246–7; A. Aquarone, *L' Organizzazione dello Stato Totalitario* (Turin, 1965), pp. 17–22.

6 De Felice, *Mussolini il Fascista* cit., i, p. 407.

7 Y. De Begnac, *Taccuini Mussoliniani* (Bologna, 1990), p. 245.

8 Ibid., p. 230; A. de Grand, *The Italian Nationalist Association and the Rise of Fascism in Italy* (Lincoln, Nebraska, 1978); F. Perfetti, *Il Nazionalismo Italiano* (Bologna, 1977); R. Cunsolo, *Modern Italian Nationalism* (New York, 1990).

9 Speech at the 'Sciesa' in Milan, 4 October 1922; *OO* xviii, pp. 433–40.

10 Mussolini to Prefect of Naples, 27 October 1923; ACS, SPD, c. ris., b. 61.

11 Lyttelton, *The Seizure of Power* cit., pp. 173–5.

12 Mussolini to Prefect of Cremona, 18 September 1923; *OO* xxxviii, pp. 488–9.

13 O. Dinale, *Quarant'Anni di Colloqui con Lui* (Milan, 1953), p. 94.

14 Speech to Chamber of Deputies, 15 July 1923; *OO* xix, p. 316; to Senate, speech of 8 June 1923; *OO* xix, p. 254.

15 Or almost fully. Cf. De Felice, *Mussolini il Fascista* cit., i, pp. 452–3.

16 ACS, *Autografi del Duce*, cassetta di zinco, scat. 1; cf. *OO* xxxix, p. 62.

17 *OO* xxxviii, p. 415.

18 Letter of 22 March 1923; *OO* xix, pp. 361–2.

19 ACS, Carte Finzi, b. 1, f. 2–3; Mussolini to C. Rossi, 28 May 1923, in *OO* xxxviii, p. 346.

20 Speech to Senate, 8 June 1923, in *OO* xix, pp. 258–9; to foreign journalists, 1 November 1923, in *OO* xx, p. 80.

21 ACS, Carte Finzi, b. 1, f. 8; R. De Felice, *D'Annunzio Politico* (Bari, 1978), p. 200.

22 Mussolini to De Nicola, 2 April 1924, in ACS, SPD, c. ris., b. 61; also *OO* xxxix, p. 134.

23 Mussolini to southern Prefects, 20 March 1924; *OO* xxxix, p. 117.

24 See his circulars to Prefects, 20 and 25 March 1924; *OO* xxxix, pp. 117, 122–3; G. Pini and D. Susmel, *Mussolini: l'Uomo e l'Opera* (Florence 1953–4), ii, p. 358; De Felice, *Mussolini il Fascista* cit., i, p. 581.

25 'Forza e consenso', in *Gerarchia*, March 1923; *OO* xix, p. 196.

26 Mussolini to Prefect of Turin, 1 June 1924; *OO* xx, pp. 321, 384.

27 Report by Dumini, September 1923, in ACS, Carte Finzi, b. 1, f. 5; M. Canali, *Il Delitto Matteotti* (Bologna, 1997), pp. 353–9.

28 Sir Ronald Graham's report to Foreign Office, 20 June 1924, in PRO, FO, C9915/490/22.

29 Lyttelton, *The Seizure of Power* cit., pp. 238–9.

30 A. Tamaro, *Vent'Anni di Storia* (Rome, 1971–5), i, pp. 462–3; Silvestri, *Matteotti e Mussolini* cit., p. xx.

31 C. Rossi, *Il Delitto Matteotti* (Milan, 1965), p. 224.

32 *Popolo d'Italia*, 1 June 1924; *OO* xx, p. 303.

33 Speech of 7 June 1924; *OO* xx, pp. 307–25.

34 Silvestri, *Matteotti e Mussolini* cit., p. 104.

35 De Felice, *Mussolini il Fascista* cit., i, pp. 621–4; G. Rossini, *Il Delitto Matteotti* (Bologna, 1966).

36 A. Lyttelton, 'Fascism in Italy: the second wave', *Journal of Contemporary History*, i (1966), pp. 75–100, at p. 79.

37 ACS, *Autografi del Duce*, cassetta di zinco, scat. 2; also *OO* xxxvii, p. 18.

38 Speech to Chamber of Deputies, 13 June 1924; *OO* xx, p. 328.

39 Speech to national council of PNF, 2 August 1924; *OO* xxi, pp. 45–52, at p. 47.

40 Y. De Begnac, *Palazzo Venezia* (Rome, 1950), p. 246.

41 Canali, *Il Delitto Matteotti* cit., pp. 412–38; De Felice, *Mussolini il Fascista* cit., i, pp. 621–4.

42 ACS, *Autografi del Duce*, cassetta di zinco, scat.1, sottof. 2.

43 Lyttelton, 'Fascism in Italy' cit., p. 83.

44 Ibid., p. 91; Lyttelton, *The Seizure of Power* cit., p. 262; De Felice, *Mussolini il Fascista* cit., i, pp. 691–2.

45 A. Salandra, *Il Diario di Salandra* (ed. G.B. Gifuni, Milan, 1969), p. 322.

46 De Felice, *Mussolini il Fascista* cit., i, pp. 714–20; R. Montagna, *Mussolini e il Processo di Verona* (Milan, n.d.), pp. 23–9; A. Turati, *Fuori dell' Ombra della Mia Vita* (Brescia, 1971), pp. 63–6.

47 Speech of 3 January 1925, in *OO* xxi, pp. 235–41.

48 'Note incompiute sugli avvenimenti successivi al delitto Matteotti', in ACS, *Autografi del Duce*, cassetta di zinco, scat. 2; also *OO* xxxvii, p. 22. Harold Nicolson, in the Foreign Office, more or less agreed: 'a fine bit of bluster' (PRO, FO, C365/1/22).

Chapter 4

Making the Fascist State 1925–9

The Uses of Assassination

Mussolini's speech of 3 January 1925 pleased the Fascist zealots for a time, but he still had to retain the support of king, army and bureaucracy; and that meant essentially a tougher version of the 'revisionist' policy of 1922–4. He intended to rule through the state machinery, not the party, but he thought the state was weak and he intended to reinforce the authority of those institutions he thought useful – armed forces, police, courts, Prefects, civil service, etc. The others, e.g. parliament or opposition parties, would be abolished, or at least by-passed. Some specifically 'Fascist' institutions might also need to be founded for specifically 'Fascist' tasks, as the Militia and the Grand Council had already been, but it was not clear what the relationship between these and the older state hierarchies would be. The overriding impetus behind Mussolini's thinking was his memory of the First World War, when a defeatist parliament and a weak executive had allowed the 'shirkers' to flourish and had failed to mobilise the country effectively, with results that were nearly catastrophic. The new regime, whatever it was, would impose the rule of war. Mussolini had turned Clausewitz on his head: politics was war by other means.

But this was all rather vague. Mussolini had no idea *which* new institutions might be needed to achieve these goals, nor what a 'Fascist regime' might mean. He was a political improviser of genius, not a constitutional lawyer or a political theorist. He believed strongly in patriotism and 'national unity' but these were hardly original ideas, and he still saw himself, at least some of the time, as a national reconciler rather than a 'Fascist' leader. In January 1925 he set up an 18-man Commission on Constitutional Reform (the so-called 'Solons'), which turned out to be divided but did recommend a more 'corporate' state structure: half the deputies were to be elected by provincial corporations, but parliament would lose many of its powers to the executive.[1] Mussolini did not like these conclusions and ignored them, although he did adopt the suggestion of making the Prime Minister's Office (Presidency of the Council) into a real ministry. A host of other 'constitutional experts' also produced reports and recommendations in 1925–6, and their efforts were put to a bored and baffled Grand Council. Mussolini simply selected those few items he wanted, including the rather surprising proposal to give votes to women at local elections on the grounds that local government was mainly concerned with schools and welfare 'in which women may display their particular aptitudes', and that other countries had already given votes to women 'which does not seem to have produced greater inconvenience than votes to men'.[2] However, he soon decided to abolish local elections altogether, so neither men nor women had the vote. In fact, Mussolini had little interest in institutions at all, except insofar as they were necessary to contain trouble. However, he had to satisfy his extremists, and that meant cracking down on his opponents.

His first move was to curb the opposition parties, but the problem was to find them. They had already banished themselves from the Chamber and so from public view, and their strident press campaign of November–December 1924 had suddenly fallen silent. They were not, of course, allowed back into the Chamber – some Popular party deputies tried to return in November 1925, unsuccessfully – and so were absent from all the constitutional and legal debates of 1925–6. They were quite harmless and could safely be left to their own impotent devices. True, the police raided a few of their offices and arrested a few Communists, but it was a token gesture. There were only a few thousand Communists by this time, inactive and heavily infiltrated. Until November 1926 the opposition parties were not suppressed, just left to wither away. The one group that *was* suppressed was a recently formed radical Republican organisation, *Italia Libera*, suspected of terrorist plots.[3] The ex-servicemen's association, which had proved surprisingly disloyal during the Matteotti crisis, was also purged and its executive replaced by Fascist commissioners.

As for the opposition newspapers, again there was relatively little direct confrontation immediately, even though the press was the opposition's only weapon. The censorship was tightened and particular issues were seized if they were too critical of government policy, but the opposition press continued to appear. Mussolini, a press baron himself, acted more subtly and put pressure on the owners. It was the proprietors, not the government, who in 1925 dismissed dissenting editors, even greatly respected ones like Luigi Albertini at Italy's most prestigious paper, the *Corriere della Sera*. His successor dismissed all journalists who were not members of the Fascist syndicate. In December 1925, however, the government did bring in restrictive legislation. A new press law laid down that only registered journalists might write for the papers, and after 1928 the party controlled the register. These measures made government 'spin-doctoring' – slanting the day's news in a favourable direction – less necessary. The journalists did it by themselves, although Mussolini's Press Office made sure that they did.[4] This was not true of the *party* newspapers like the Socialist *Avanti!* or the Communist *L'Unità*, which still circulated in the cities until November 1926, although anyone seen reading a copy was liable to be beaten up. In general, however, the opposition newspapers, like the opposition parties, surrendered without a fight. The British ambassador was unsympathetic:

There were constant allegations and innuendoes connecting Signor Mussolini and his principal lieutenants with the Matteotti crime. Trivial incidents were magnified under such headings as 'Fascist murders his grandmother' or 'Fascist robs the post' . . . in England, in similar circumstances, most if not all of the opposition editors and writers would have either been imprisoned or mulcted in heavy fines for contempt of court or libel.[5]

Mussolini's position was still not altogether secure. After 3 January Salandra resigned again, this time from his post as delegate to the League of Nations, and the two Liberal ministers Casati and Sarrocchi went with him. Mussolini also dismissed the Minister of Justice Oviglio and brought in the far more innovative Alfredo Rocco. To placate the 'intransigents', he took a daring gamble and appointed Farinacci to be party secretary (see below). But then, in mid-February, he fell ill with a suspected duodenal ulcer – his first serious illness, apart from war injuries. He had internal bleeding and even some temporary facial paralysis. For a month he could make no public appearances or even give interviews. Mussolini was, of course, a classic ulcer victim: an irritable man who ate far too quickly and had undergone a great deal of stress in the previous few months. But how was he to be treated? Nobody wanted him to have an operation, as it would be far too risky. Every health faddist in Italy, and many abroad, wrote in suggesting improbable remedies or diets.[6] By 28 March he had recovered enough for a bedside Cabinet to meet in his flat, and by early April he was back at work, but his ulcer recurred later and he never fully recovered from it until treated by Hitler's doctor in 1943–4. Still fairly slim and highly active, he had to remain on a strict diet – mostly milk and fruit – for nearly 20 years, and drank virtually no alcohol (although he claimed to have given it up 10 years earlier). Official receptions became an embarrassment. All this contributed to his growing social isolation. He still saw little of his family – his wife Rachele apparently did not visit Rome at all until Christmas 1926, not even while he was ill.[7] But it also boosted his standing. Government had virtually ceased during his illness. He was indispensable, and everybody feared what might happen if he died. He himself joked to a French journalist that the opposition had prayed for his recovery, so as to avoid being left at the mercy of Farinacci and his kind.[8]

But one real threat remained: assassination. Between November 1925 and November 1926 there were four serious attempts on Mussolini's life. On 4 November 1925 the oft-decorated war hero, expert marksman and reformist Socialist deputy Tito Zaniboni, exasperated by opposition inertia, took a hotel room opposite the Prime Minister's office at palazzo Chigi in Rome and planned to shoot the *Duce* as he spoke to the Armistice Day crowds from the balcony. The police had been tipped off, and rushed into the room just in time. Zaniboni was an influential man in his party, particularly so after Matteotti's death. He had had two audiences with the king the previous year, and his fellow-conspirator was General Capello, former commander of the 2nd Army.[9] Furthermore, he was closely associated with the 'Grand Orient' Freemasons, and an intercepted telephone conversation on 29 October between Zaniboni and the Grand Master, Domizio Torrigiani, indicated that the plot was financed by the Masons.[10] At any rate, Torrigiani was arrested along with the other conspirators, and later sent to enforced domicile. The 'Zaniboni plot' was genuine and serious; it might easily have succeeded. But it was also an ideal propaganda gift to Mussolini (and to the police). Zaniboni's trial became a huge media event. It was a trial not merely of a few individuals, but of the opposition parties, of the Freemasons, of *Italia Libera*, and of the anti-Fascists in France. Traitors at the heart of the state, Masonic conspiracies, social-democratic assassins besmirching patriotic ceremonies commemorating the glorious dead – here was a marvellous opportunity to rush through emergency laws, purge the Masons and clamp down further on the murderous opposition and its seditious press. The Zaniboni plot made even moderate 'flankers' willing to accept a more authoritarian regime. It enabled the new press law to pass quickly through the Senate, and by late November parliament had also outlawed secret associations, i.e. freemasonry. The many Masonic army officers, civil servants and judges had been warned. Henceforth they would have to be loyal to Fascism and above all to the Italian state, not to some shadowy international organisation with 'democratic-liberal' views and close connections with France. Furthermore, there would now be nowhere for them to meet, except in the Fascist party framework. The anti-Masonic campaign was an old theme of Mussolini (see p. 20), but the new laws were pushed through in 1925 by the ex-Nationalist ministers Federzoni at Interior and Rocco at Justice: it was the conservative, monarchist Nationalists who detested the Masons, not the raucous lower-middle-class Fascist *arrivistes*, many of whom were Masons themselves.[11]

The next assassination attempt was in April 1926, when a mentally disturbed Anglo-Irish aristocrat, Violet Gibson, fired at Mussolini as he was leaving an international surgeons' congress, which he had just inaugurated on the Capitol. Once again, Mussolini was lucky. He turned his head at the last second and so the bullet grazed his nose but otherwise did no harm. If one has to undergo an assassination attempt, this one was ideal: a very minor injury, and 400 of the world's top surgeons on hand to treat it. Later in 1926 it was the turn of the anarchists. In September Gino Lucetti injured eight people, but not Mussolini, by hurling a bomb at Mussolini's car as the *Duce* was being driven to work in Rome. At the end of October a 16-year-old anarchist, Anteo Zamboni, came closest of all. He shot at Mussolini from a crowd in Bologna. The bullet passed through the *Duce*'s jacket and the ceremonial sash he was wearing, although again it left him unharmed if shaken. Zamboni was promptly lynched by the angry bystanders. The episode remains rather murky: anti-Fascists claimed the shooting was organised by the police, the police thought it was done by local extremist Fascists. At any rate Zamboni's attempt, like that of Zaniboni a year earlier, was used to justify a further clampdown, including the final banning of all non-Fascist political parties and journals. Until November 1926 Italy was arguably still a liberal democracy of sorts: it had opposition newspapers, albeit censored, and opposition parties, albeit under close surveillance. The attempted assassinations in autumn 1926 ended all that. But they, like the previous ones, did not usher in a 'Fascist state'. They simply meant banning opposition, reducing civil liberties and giving the police more powers.

The police, indeed, were the major beneficiaries of Mussolini's innovations. The chief of police from September 1926 until his death in 1940 was Arturo Bocchini, a cheerful and extremely astute official reminiscent of Louis Renault, police chief in *Casablanca*. Bocchini saw Mussolini every day and became arguably his closest confidant, making sure that the *Duce* received plenty of juicy information about Fascists and anti-Fascists alike. Early on, Bocchini had to tolerate a party appointee, Ernesto Guli, at the head of the political police division, but he soon saw him off. He also had to tolerate the Militia setting up 'Political Investigation Offices' (UPI) to report on myriad individuals, but these offices provided low-grade security checks rather than anything more exciting. The real policing work was done by 'Public Security' professionals, not by 'Fascists'; a few 'political' police chiefs (*questori*) were appointed in the provinces, but they were all ex-army officers, not rank-and-file Fascists or *squadristi*. In 1925 a 15,000-strong corps of 'Public Security' agents was founded, to police the cities; in 1927 'Special Inspectorates' were founded, to target anti-Fascist activity; and in 1930 it was announced that a new secret police, the sinister-sounding OVRA, had been set up. The OVRA – no one knew what the initials stood for – turned out to be a fairly small body (only 375 officers and agents in 1940) relying on a host of paid or threatened informers. It is true that police action became very extensive. According to Renzo De Felice, by 1930 the police were carrying out 20,000 searches, arrests, seizures of literature etc., per week, and had over 100,000 regular informants as well as a vast number of files on potential subversives, including every parish priest.[12] Nonetheless, this work was done by career officials, not party zealots. Mussolini did not revive the *cheka*, although he did occasionally use the army's intelligence service for 'special tasks'. There was no serious 'political' police in Italy, unlike Germany or Russia, and this made a huge difference to the nature of the regime.

The police were aided by two major innovations, both introduced in November 1926 after the Zamboni shooting. First, a 'Special Tribunal for the Defence of the State', distinct from the ordinary courts and applying martial law, was set up to try serious political cases. It could apply the death penalty for treason or for attempted assassination of the king, his consort, his heir and the *Duce*. Restoring the death penalty was a dramatic gesture, although in fact only nine people were executed up to June 1940, including five Slav terrorists in north-east Italy.[13] This was a striking contrast to the fate of dissidents elsewhere, and one should remember too that at this time ordinary, non-political criminals were routinely executed in Britain and France (in public in the latter case), and still are in much of the United States of America. Indeed, in 1927 Mussolini himself tried to secure a reprieve for Sacco and Vanzetti, arguing that the Fascists had proved it was possible to defeat Bolshevism without the death penalty.[14] The tribunal handed down almost 4,600 prison sentences (around 4,000 of them to Communists) over the years, of about five years on average. The Communist leader Antonio Gramsci was sentenced to 20 years, but was granted provisional liberty on health grounds after eight. Mussolini's greatest political enemy, Cesare Rossi, the man who had accused him of numerous crimes in December 1924, was seized by the Italian police in Switzerland in 1929, brought back to Italy and given 30 years' imprisonment; but even he was sent off to the islands in 1940.

Indeed, the second major penal innovation of November 1926 was to extend internal exile (*confino*), used since the 1890s for ordinary criminals, to political prisoners. It was clearly preferable to prison, since the 'confined' could live relatively freely as long as they stayed on their compulsory island. They were not forced to work, could summon their families to live with them, and were even paid 10 lire a day to cover expenses. 'Confinement' was also preferable, from the regime's viewpoint, to exiling people abroad, where they might simply plot more effectively. So the government withdrew all passports, and imposed severe penalties for clandestine emigration. About 14,000 people were sentenced to the new internal exile between 1926 and 1943. Sometimes the Special Tribunal would issue the exile decree itself; more usually a special commission in each province would decide, often on grounds of mere suspicion and always without trial. For ordinary Italians, and also for many zealous Fascists as well as known anti-Fascists, the outcome of these laws was extremely unpleasant. The arbitrary new police powers meant constant insecurity and an atmosphere of distrust and suspicion for all. A mild joke about the *Duce* might lead to years on a remote island. It all added to the pressure to conform, very marked after the mid-1920s. Mussolini always claimed he allowed the 'right to grumble' (*jus mormorandi*), but grumbling was a dangerous activity in Fascist Italy. Exile, or rather the threat of exile, soon became the dominant method of political control.

Even so, it was characteristic of Mussolini that he liked to win but was always willing to compromise if his opponent made a serious offer. In the case of *confino* he enjoyed the combination of being able to humiliate his opponents and of being merciful, and he quite often released people early provided they asked for pardon and agreed to accept the Fascist regime. Indeed, he was quite a soft touch, especially to the families of the detained. The notorious ex-Communist Nicola Bombacci was given 20,000 lire and a pseudo-job in 1931; he received another 5,000 lire in 1937, when his daughter married.[15] On occasions Mussolini might even be blackmailed, as he clearly was by Amerigo Dumini, leader of the gang that had murdered Matteotti. Dumini claimed to have lodged documents with his lawyer in Texas, proving Mussolini's complicity in the murder. In 1934 the government bought him a farm in Libya and gave him 1,000 lire a month as well; he and his American mother seem to have received over 2.3 million lire (about £26,000) in the 10 years after 1928, a vast sum in those days.[16] Throughout the 1930s government funds subsidised both Matteotti's family and his murderer.

The four assassination attempts of 1925–6 certainly triggered real political changes and numerous arrests. They enabled the press to be controlled, opposition parties to be dissolved and military courts to apply martial law on civilians. They forced many anti-Fascists into voluntary exile abroad or into officially imposed exile at home. However, there was still little sign of a specifically 'Fascist' regime, nor was there any vast purge or persecution in their wake. The islands of Ustica and Lipari were not Siberia, and Mussolini was not Stalin. Indeed, he was remarkably relaxed about assassination, believing he had been born under a lucky star and would always escape danger unharmed. The surviving would-be assassins themselves were treated with astonishing leniency. Zaniboni was imprisoned and later sent to the island of Ponza, where Mussolini himself turned up as a prisoner in July 1943. He survived the Fascist regime and wrote his memoirs after the Second World War. General Capello was also imprisoned, but released on health grounds in 1936. Violet Gibson was simply sent back to Britain, and the British were very impressed by Mussolini's magnanimity. Lucetti, like Zaniboni, was imprisoned and later 'confined' on Ponza. He was released by the Allies in 1943, only to be killed shortly afterwards by an Allied bomb. From Mussolini's viewpoint, *failed* assassinations were ideal. They justified greater repression, and they also gave him a welcome aura of invincibility and an opportunity to demonstrate fearless calm.

The police were less sanguine. Federzoni put the point very forcibly to Mussolini after the Gibson shooting: 'If a deplorable act were to remove you even temporarily from the leadership of the state, it would be chaos. This constitutes the tragic greatness and at the same time the only weakness of our situation.'[17] But Mussolini was not the man to hide away from adoring crowds, whatever the danger. He was an orator as well as a journalist, and his whole style of leadership, ultimately his whole power, rested on communicating with the public at mass meetings. He insisted on being visible, although to be visible was to be vulnerable. Furthermore, he liked flying and driving fast cars, both of them hazardous activities from which even Farinacci tried in vain to restrain him.[18] The police could not stop him flying either, but they could protect him otherwise. They did so by organising a 'presidential squad' (maliciously known as the 'applause squad') of 500-odd plain-clothes policemen to act as bodyguards wherever Mussolini went. They soon became remarkably familiar figures not only to the *Duce*, but to newsreel viewers in cinemas throughout the country. These were the other horsemen he saw on his morning rides in the villa Borghese, these were the peasants with whom he threshed grain in the Campagna, these were his fellow-swimmers in the sea at Riccione, these were the factory workers toiling at the assembly lines when he visited the Fiat works in Turin. Mussolini lived his life surrounded by ill-humoured policemen. Even they, of course, were not numerous enough to fill the *piazza* for the big mass meetings: on such occasions party members were forced to attend, on pain of losing their party card and so their jobs. The war wounded went along too, for a few lire and some cigarettes, and to make sure their pensions continued to be paid.

In spring 1925 it was not the police that were a problem, but the army. The Minister of War, Di Giorgio, was planning drastic cuts in its size, and had become very unpopular as a result in senior army circles. In March a Senate committee rejected the plan, and Marshals Diaz, Cadorna and Giardino were known to be hostile. Mussolini had to step in quickly to reassure the military Establishment and the king. On 2 April, fresh from his sickbed, Mussolini made one of the key decisions of his life. He caved in to the military. In a full session of the Senate, he humiliated Di Giorgio by withdrawing the proposal. Di Giorgio resigned, and Mussolini took over the Ministry of War himself, with General Cavallero as under-secretary and Marshal Badoglio as chief of staff, not only of the army but also as 'chief of general staff' of all three armed services.[19] This latter was a new post, designed to help coordinate military planning, and it was to be held always by an army officer. The generals were now happy, but the admirals were most definitely not. The new post, in their eyes, was tanta-mount to putting the generals in charge of the navy. Admiral Thaon di Revel resigned forthwith in protest, and Mussolini had to take over the Ministry of Navy as well, adding Aviation in August. The situation was made worse by one of Mussolini's rare gaffes. On 18 May he told the Senate that the new 'chief of general staff' had to be a general, because 'tomorrow's war must be understood as a predominantly land war' like the last, and he went on to 'confess that there was also a moral reason to give this kind of privilege to the army; and this reason has played a part in my decision. It is the enormous sacrifice of blood and lives . . .' At this point a furious Thaon di Revel leaped up and shouted 'And the navy? Everyone did their duty.'[20] Eventually the admirals were reassured and placated, but they never trusted Mussolini thereafter. The navy was an aristocratic service, rather reserved and Anglophile in its values and with limited political interests or influence. It had little time for soldiers or Fascists, and Mussolini – proud of his own service in the *bersaglieri* – did not sympathise with it nor understand its importance. This proved ex-tremely significant in later years. Mussolini had given in to his generals and, as a pilot himself, he favoured the air force – the most modern and 'Fascist' service; but he always distrusted his admirals. He allowed the air force to prevent the building of aircraft carriers, since this would have meant a fleet air arm under navy control. Even worse, the row over

Badoglio's appointment meant that neither he nor anyone else acted as a real chief of general staff, nor managed to coordinate the three services. In 1927 a new decree made it an honorific title, which Badoglio kept even when he became Governor of Libya in 1928. In reality, each service went its own way, run by its under-secretary who was always a senior officer, and remained free of political interference or regulation. Mussolini was nominally the minister and he used his position to prevent any more embarrassing disputes, or indeed any change. There was no attempt at 'Fascistisation', but also little innovation and even less strategic planning.

Mussolini may not have had a blueprint for new Fascist institutions but he knew how to run a government. He ran it as if it were a newspaper, and he the editor. He wrote the 'editorials', made sure the front page had a strong message, and selected and dismissed his specialist 'reporters', the ministers.[21] He was a very competent 'editor', and he chose surprisingly competent 'journalists', most of them not 'Fascist' in origin. Men like De' Stefani or Volpi at Finance, Rocco at Justice, Federzoni at Interior and Costanzo Ciano at Communications were strong-minded, confident people with successful careers behind them. They all pushed through real changes in their respective ministries, and some of them acquired permanent influence over him. Mussolini called them in regularly to report, but they could and did talk to him as equals and they usually got their way even on sensitive issues – although the more astute ones pretended to let him take the final decision. As Minister of the Interior in April 1926 Federzoni, for example, suggested that the Chief of Police should be dismissed and replaced by Arturo Bocchini; a few months later Mussolini did just that.[22] Even when he became Minister of Colonies Federzoni could still suggest (successfully) a suitable candidate to become Governor of Rome. The same was true, but to a lesser degree, of the prominent technical experts whom Mussolini put in charge of the railways, agricultural improvement schemes and the like. It was noticeable that even in 1925–6 few 'Fascists' were given ministerial jobs. They tended to be the under-secretaries and their tenure of office was short, for Mussolini believed that one non-expert was as good as another and that constant reshuffles ('changing of the guard') would keep people alert. He could be extremely curt to these men. In October 1925, for example, he dismissed the under-secretary at Public Works, Petrillo, for casting doubt on the revolutionary nature of the March on Rome: 'You should know that I despise the ridiculous, tranquil bourgeois who, when they are certain, quite certain, of being out of the firing line pose as truculent and bloodthirsty, and this is true in your case.'[23] Only two of the *ras*,

Dino Grandi and Giuseppe Bottai, made the transition to recognised national leader (*gerarca*). Grandi learned English, developed foreign policy interests and made himself a useful counterweight to the professional diplomats; Bottai became the intellectual spokesman for Fascism in general and for corporatism in particular. One or two others, like Arpinati who was interesting and likeable, held a top government job for a time but did not last long. Farinacci and Rossoni had top jobs *outside* government, in the party and the Confederation of Syndicates respectively, but again were soon replaced. Most of the warlords were too quarrelsome, too corrupt, too unreliable and too independent-minded for Mussolini's purposes. They were not officer material, and they were not happy about Mussolini's strong, centralised state.

In general, therefore, the *Duce* preferred to choose bright experts and let them get on with it, as long as they let him know what they were doing. But they had to stick to their last. He did not let them discuss general policy. Indeed, Mussolini never really believed in collective decision-making. As he told his biographer De Begnac years later, 'I would not dream of asking Count Volpi his opinion on Gentile's educational reform, just as I would not dream of asking Gentile what he thought about revaluing the lira.'[24] Only the *Duce* could take a general view; lesser men had to restrict themselves to their narrow, specific tasks. Inasmuch as there was any general debate, it took place occasionally in the Grand Council, not in the Cabinet. The latter met about once a month and only then to hear reports from ministers (often Mussolini himself), and to approve bills and decrees that had already been decided. In fact, Mussolini rarely met his ministers or under-secretaries at all, unless they were at the Interior or Foreign ministries and had to report every morning. None were friends except perhaps Costanzo Ciano, the only one to be invited to his house. The *Duce* had no cronies except his brother Arnaldo, and Arnaldo was in Milan. His ministers rarely met *each other* either, and were suspected of plotting together if they did. It is striking that the Fascist government and party elite hardly ever gathered socially, and met only on formal occasions like Cabinet or anniversary parades. Unlike Stalin, Mussolini held no late-night banquets or drinking sessions with his colleagues; nor, unlike Hitler, did he bore them all with meandering monologues. He just ignored them. Ministers knew that Mussolini did not wish to know their opinions on anything except their departmental remit, and only then when he called them in for a formal report. They developed an ingenious solution to this problem. Since their telephones were tapped, ministers could pass on views and information to some trusted colleague or friend, knowing that the transcript would be on

Mussolini's desk the next day. This was one way to run a country, but it was not collegial debate. On the contrary, it was literally presidential government, for Mussolini's official title until December 1925 was 'President of the Council of Ministers', and his colleagues addressed him as '*Presidente*' – as, apparently, did his wife.

However, in December 1925 Mussolini acquired a new official title, 'Head of Government', and new formal powers over his ministers who became responsible to him rather than to parliament. This meant, in practice, that he had an even better excuse to interfere in a host of matters. In any case, he often *was* the minister – by 1929 he held eight ministries – and as such was responsible to himself; the routine work in such ministries was done by the under-secretaries, but these men had little political influence and no responsibility. The result was predictable. Mussolini could not do everything, so the civil servants took over. Senior bureaucrats had direct access to Mussolini and often reported to him directly, by-passing the under-secretary. They had to be reliable, of course. Another law in December 1925 had laid down that officials 'who do not give a full guarantee of faithful implementation of their duties', or who 'put themselves in conditions of incompatibility with the general directives of the government' might be dismissed.[25] In other words, no anti-Fascism and no freemasonry. This was quite a serious threat while Farinacci was party secretary in 1925–6, and the civil service also had to fight off the 'corporatist' enthusiasts in 1926–8, but they could rely on royal and ex-Nationalist support and as usual they triumphed in the end. Very few civil servants lost their jobs, and the absence of parliamentary control or press criticism of their activities made life considerably easier for them thereafter. Proposals for 'civil service reform' on productivist or 'managerial' lines were soon abandoned. The 'competence groups', outsiders brought in to ginger up key ministries, soon disappeared. There was to be no competence in Fascist government.[26] Indeed, in 1923 Mussolini had given extra powers to the Ministry of Finance and the Public Accounts Office, to the dismay of the spending ministries. So the accountants ruled as usual, although naturally the other civil servants found ways round the new controls. Furthermore, civil service recruitment was frozen from 1926 to 1932, so tiresome young Fascist enthusiasts could not come in and cause trouble. From his early days in office Mussolini declared himself to be the friend of the bureaucrat: 'I am the emperor of the clerks.'[27] A few years later he told the Senate, 'The Italian civil service is much better than its reputation, and I dare to affirm that it has greater competence, initiative and honesty than many other civil services in many other countries.'[28] Leaving matters to the senior civil servants ('senior' in every sense, as they retired only at 70) meant that Mussolini could mediate in a world of inter-ministry conflict. He regarded them, particularly the accountants and the councillors of state, as well educated, loyal and irreplaceable. Perhaps he was right, but his choice inevitably meant there would be no 'Fascist revolution'.

In short, Mussolini ruled through his established civil servants. He trusted them, and he did not trust his Fascists. This meant, of course, that Mussolini ruled through *legal* procedures. Italian civil servants had a highly legalistic training, and would do nothing without official authorisation in writing. They implemented only what had been approved by the Council of Ministers, and if necessary by parliament. 'It is the *Duce*'s wish' was not enough. Indeed, the Council of State, which acted as legal tribunal on administrative matters, became much more significant under Fascism as the powers of parliament declined. It was routinely consulted when legislation or administrative decrees were being drafted, and its president Santi Romano was even asked his views on appointments to government.[29] Fascist government may have been personal and presidential, but it was not arbitrary.

The 1925 law that made Mussolini 'Head of Government' provided him with no institutional machinery for his new tasks. He relied on the existing 'Presidency of the Council of Ministers', with its own undersecretary who soon became his closest daily collaborator in the technical, legal aspects of government.[30] The 'Presidency' controlled some key administrative units, e.g. the Statistical Office founded in 1926, and supervised some others, including the Council of State. It prepared detailed legislation but it was essentially an administrative body and did not provide policy coordination. Nor did the 'Private Secretariat of the *Duce*', run by Alessandro Chiavolini, a former journalist on the *Popolo d'Italia*. The 'Private Secretariat' simply stored all Mussolini's correspondence and 'private' documents, including detailed files on both colleagues and opponents, so that he had access to them at all times without having to request information from the police or the Interior Ministry. They are now the *Duce*'s great gift to historians. Mussolini did merge some ministries and in 1924 set up a Ministry of Communications, covering transport, post and telecommunications, merchant navy, etc., under Costanzo Ciano. The Ministry of Corporations (see below) founded in 1926 was certainly an innovation, and the agencies set up by the Ministry of Public Works to develop the south, while not new, were rather more effective than their predecessors. But there were no other serious reforms, although of course it was significant that the former public-sector trade unions were no more.

There seem to have been three main reasons for this distinct absence of innovation. One was that 'managerial' reforms, although widely discussed and backed by academic experts, would have benefited the spending ministries and cost money at a time when the government was seeking to balance the budget. The second reason was that it was much less trouble to 'hive off' managerial activities either to the private sector (e.g. life insurance) or to specialised functional agencies like the Autonomous Roads Agency set up in 1928, run by technocrats responsible only to Mussolini himself. The Fascists may not have reformed the civil service itself, but they did set up an expanding 'new public sector', i.e. a host of administrative or regulatory agencies run by a 'parallel bureaucracy', a managerial class derived from wartime experience and from Nitti's fitful post-war experiments in radicalism. They set up other parallel bureaucracies too, in the party, the Militia, the corporations and the welfare agencies, although these were largely job-creation schemes.[31] But the third reason was the most telling. A modern 'managerial' elite in the civil service would inevitably have come from northern or central Italy. Mussolini could not afford to alienate the southern middle classes, who held most of the top civil service jobs and needed them. When De' Stefani presented him with a scheme for streamlining the civil service, Mussolini was horrified and even ordered it to be burned: 'We have to adopt a policy of the maximum number of jobs in the state bureaucracy, if we don't want an insurrection on our hands – an insurrection caused by the hunger, I repeat hunger, of intellectuals.'[32] So he placated the civil servants, as he had placated the military. In both cases he praised them in public, and he did not bother about their efficiency.

The most powerful civil servants in Italy were the Prefects, at the head of administration in each province. These were political bureaucrats, who supervised local government, repressed the subversives and organised the police. They had to be politically flexible, and sympathetic to the government of the day as well as to the local elites. Between 1922 and 1929 86 of them retired or were replaced; but 57 of the new Prefects came from the Interior Ministry career service. Only 29 were 'political' appointments, i.e. Fascists, and even they held the smaller and less significant provinces.[33] In other words, Mussolini relied heavily on traditional 'career' officials, even at provincial and local level. Some of them, including Arturo Bocchini as Chief of Police and Cesare Mori as Commissioner in Sicily, became very prominent officials in Fascist Italy. All of them had greater powers than previously, for elected local councils were abolished in 1926 and so the Prefect chose local mayors (*podestà*) throughout his province. He tended to choose respectable landowners or ex-army officers, rather than a local Fascist. Mayors had to be men of independent means, for most of them received no pay.[34] But the problem, from Mussolini's viewpoint, was that the Prefect's authority in central Italy was weak. In many zones the *ras* still controlled local government and the local party branches, told the Prefect what to do, and had him removed if he failed to comply.[35] Mussolini issued instructions stressing that the Prefect, not the provincial party secretary or anyone else, was the man in charge of the province.[36] The *ras* took little notice, so Mussolini said it again and again. On 5 January 1927, for example, he proclaimed that 'the Prefect, I reaffirm solemnly, is the highest state authority in the province. He is the direct representative of central executive power . . . the highest political representative of the Fascist regime.'[37] Nonetheless, a few months later he admitted that there were still around 10 provinces, out of the 91, where there was some ambiguity and power-sharing.[38] By 1930 he thought the problem was solved: 'the federal [party] secretaries are, as they ought to be, at the orders of the Head of the Province'.[39] In fact, disputes between Prefects and party bosses remained endemic throughout the regime. Prefects felt obliged to intervene in local party disputes; provincial party leaders tried to 'Fascistise' local society, with or without prefectoral approval. It was, after all, their job.

Taming the Fascists

Mussolini's strategic choices in 1925–6 were not, of course, what the angry provincial *ras* had envisaged. Before his illness, Mussolini had pleased them by appointing their spokesman, Roberto Farinacci, as party secretary, and also by encouraging the syndicates to become more militant and organise a few strikes. Farinacci was a surprisingly good choice. He was an extremist all right, more Fascist than the *Duce*; but he had the great advantage of hating Balbo, and he was always loyal to Mussolini in his fashion. He enjoyed imposing discipline and he spent a happy few months threatening everybody, especially civil servants and lukewarm Fascists. Naturally he purged the party of dissidents and all those who had wavered during the Matteotti crisis, but he also expelled the two main organisers of the 'consuls' agitation in December 1924, as well as 19 Fascist deputies. Farinacci wanted a small, disciplined party of true believers ('few but good', '*pochi ma buoni*') capable of tackling the decadent ruling class and its 'Liberal' institutions; and for a few months in 1925, while Mussolini was ill, such an outcome looked distinctly possible. Farinacci also had no objection to *squadrismo*, at least if the *squadristi* were his own supporters; and so in 1925 the squads of Blackshirts roamed once more around Emilia-Romagna and Tuscany, while Fascist syndicates led serious industrial strikes throughout northern Italy (see below). Most government ministers, above all Federzoni at the Interior Ministry, were shocked by these developments. The Prefects in central Italy would not obey his orders. They knew where local power lay, and central power too – Farinacci had managed to instal the 'intransigent' Attilio Teruzzi as under-secretary in the ministry, to keep an eye on the minister.[40]

Once again, as in 1921–2, a degree of squad violence was useful to Mussolini, showing the 'flankers' what might befall them without his moderating influence. So he let Farinacci have his head for a time. But, once again, squad violence threatened to discredit Fascism if it became excessive. In October 1925 it did so. Serious riots in Florence killed eight prominent Liberals and Masons. Mussolini had to act very firmly. On 5 October, in furious mood, he addressed the Grand Council: 'A murderer, we admit, may be killed. But the rest? It is not Fascist, not Italian, not timely, chivalrous or surgical violence . . . and all this under the eyes of ten thousand English and Americans . . . the most anarchic party in Italy is the Fascist.'[41] He ordered all the squads to be dissolved, and this time he more or less succeeded (some, as in Genoa, survived by masquerading as 'Fascist sports clubs').[42] Squad members were again made to join the Militia. The Florentine Fascist party branch and Militia were purged and totally restructured, as were those in Parma. Indeed the government's strong response to the Florence riots enabled Mussolini to be, once again, the man who could tame the squads, and helped him to push his repressive legislation through the Senate. Farinacci's day was over, although Mussolini kept him on as party secretary until the trial of Matteotti's murderers ended in the spring of 1926. He was then dismissed and sent back to languish in his home town of Cremona. Mussolini did not need him any more. By then Mussolini fully controlled the state machinery, the squads had been dissolved and the party had been effectively disciplined.

In short, in 1925–6 Mussolini tamed his hard men at last. He succeeded in the most difficult task facing any revolutionary leader – controlling his own supporters – without even needing to shoot anybody. He showed exceptional political skills in doing so: daring to appoint Farinacci, using him to purge the party, biding his time and then acting firmly when needed. He also exploited the rivalry between the two most prominent squad leaders, Farinacci and Balbo. Mussolini clearly suspected that Balbo had been involved in the 'revolt of the consuls' in December 1924, so he put Farinacci in charge of the party a few weeks later. But when

Mussolini wanted to end squad violence in October 1925, it was Balbo he sent to purge the Florence *Fascio*. Mussolini was lucky to be able to play off these two powerful men against each other. Since the extremists had no one generally accepted leader, his own position was far more secure. If only for that reason, he could not throw away the Farinacci card; it might well come in useful again one day. In any case, Farinacci remained very popular in Fascist circles. On his return to Cremona he was greeted by enthusiastic crowds of *squadristi*, who promptly beat up the local Mussolinians.[43] Moreover, Farinacci did not stay in Cremona long. He was a remarkably successful advocate – somehow he always won his cases – and rich enough to keep a suite of rooms in Rome's Grand Hotel. As an ex-party secretary he had a seat on the Grand Council, and he had a newspaper. He claimed to be the conscience of the revolution, and for many years he wrote regular letters to Mussolini telling him in very familiar terms just where the *Duce* was going wrong.[44] This irritated Mussolini intensely and he often replied angrily, but he knew that Farinacci was basically loyal and he was careful not to antagonise him too much. When, on one occasion, he did lose his temper and wrote too toughly ('discontent in the party is largely caused by your attitude of spiritual indiscipline and your claim to monopolise the party's purity and salvation . . . give up this air of anti-Pope awaiting his moment . . . and above all avoid freemasonry'), he changed his mind at the last minute and sent round to the post office to make sure the letter was not delivered.[45]

Farinacci's successor as party secretary was Augusto Turati, syndicalist, ex-boss of Brescia and friend of Arnaldo. Mussolini still wanted the party tamed, and Turati did his bidding. By June 1926 13 provincial federations and innumerable local ones were being run by centrally appointed commissioners. Moreover, party membership was transformed. Just as people had flocked into the PNF in 1923, after the March on Rome, so they did in 1926, once Mussolini had clearly consolidated his power and had dismissed Farinacci. In a year party membership rose from 637,454 to 937,997.[46] In the south, many Fascist branches were founded for the first time, although they often consisted of the same local notables as the former Liberal 'circles' had done. While new men came in, the old ones were leaving, or being forced out. Turati purged the provincial extremists and even the non-provincial ones: the Rome federation expelled 7,000 members in 1927, out of the previous 31,000.[47] Around 2,000 officials and 30,000 members were thrown out in Turati's first year, and over 50,000 in all by 1929; to these should be added the 100,000 or so who left voluntarily, many of them committed Fascists disgusted by what was happening to their party.[48] Farinacci had disciplined the PNF; Turati transformed it, and subordinated it to the state. A new party constitution laid down that all posts were to be appointed from above, not elected from below. When people complained, Mussolini asserted that 'it would be grotesque to abolish elections in the nation and keep them in the party ... the revolution has a leader who prepared it from 1914 to 1922; who willed it in 1922; who has guided it until today; *everything depends on him*'.[49] Local party journals were closed down. National congresses were no more – none was held after June 1925, itself the first since 1921. Even local or provincial ones became rare. In a one-party state, the structure and activities of the one party matter. Ordinary members could not express their views, elect their officers or influence policy. Few complained overtly, but morale collapsed. No wonder the older members left. A bloated, centralised party of careerists and conformists, of local government officials and bank managers, its leaders parachuted in from above: it was the antithesis of Farinacci's ideal, 'few but good'. A further 120,000 members were expelled in 1930–1 by the next party secretary, Giuriati, and this later purge emasculated the party even more. But the real change had been in 1925–6, when the squads were dissolved. *Squadrismo was* Fascism, its essence both ideological and practical. It embodied ardour, youth, enthusiasm, impatience, adventure, imagination and dynamism. Mussolini liquidated the squads, but in so doing virtually liquidated Fascism as a live movement. No *squadrismo*, no Fascism. But also: unless no *squadrismo*, no Establishment backing. Mussolini had made his choice. The party, the Militia, the syndicates and corporations all signified not dynamism but bureaucratic conformity and jobs for the middle-aged. It was amazing how quickly, in the mid-1920s, Fascism became boring.

Yet Mussolini still needed the party. He did not need it to rule Italy, for he could do that through the civil service and the police. Nor did he even need it as a political base, which was now secure. He needed it as a 'church': to transmit 'Fascist' values through society, to train the young and to organise social activities, welfare and opinion. He knew this was vital. He did not want to stay in office for a few years as an Establishment stooge. He wanted to 'Fascistise Italy', and to rear a new generation of faithful enthusiasts who would, in due course, take over the state institutions and run them on 'Fascist' lines.[50] Here again we see Mussolini's characteristic ambiguity. He compromised with existing institutions but always with mental reservations, and he really wanted a far more radical outcome. Of course, he realised the party was not a suitable instrument for his purposes, but he had no other. On Saturday afternoons he would sit in his office, discussing with Turati the difficulty of rousing a non-revolutionary people to revolutionary acts.[51]

The Militia too was transformed in 1925–6, under a new commander, General Gonzaga, who took over in September 1925 after Gandolfo died. The 'consuls' in December 1924 had been mainly troubled by the question of who was to control the Militia. The answer turned out to be: ex-army officers, nearly ten thousand of them by 1928. Nine thousand Militiamen were expelled in two years, but it was more difficult to purge the Militia than the party. After all, the Militia had been founded to *contain* the thugs; what would happen if they were all thrown out? It had to be done gradually, with liberal recourse to police measures and 'confinement', but even then the *squadristi* noticed – this was one of the main triggers of the violence in Florence in October 1925. The Militia members were therefore given some leeway. They were not allowed to go off on squad expeditions any more, but they carried out low-level public order tasks and were conspicuous for their zero tolerance. At local level beatings-up and castor oil 'purgations' never died out, and became quite common again in the late 1930s. The Militia also organised 'pre-military training' for future army conscripts, and held a remarkable number of parades. Mussolini himself often watched these parades, and passed on appropriate comments to the commanders: 'I noticed a hunchback [was he a mascot?] and several cripples, one of whom had a wooden leg . . . some of the officers looked as if they were merely out for a stroll.'[52] Even so, the Militia was a visible reminder of the regime's success, and it made the ageing *squadristi* feel important – a dads' army in black shirts.

Innovation at Last

The one area of true innovation in 1925–6 was in labour relations. Mussolini's attempted flirtation with the reformist unions had been broken off by the Matteotti crisis, so he needed to find something else, preferably something that sounded innovative and revolutionary and would deliver some working-class support. He toyed with syndicalism again, partly as a way to placate the 'intransigents' who often ran the local labour syndicates. But the new Minister of Justice, Alfredo Rocco, had clearer ideas about what should be done, and outlined them in a speech at Perugia in August 1925. Rocco believed in a strong state on 'Prussian' lines, regulating and controlling everything: the economy, the syndicates, the party, the Church and the citizen. It should have 'productivist', technocratic aims, and should mobilise and regulate everybody. Economic decisions should be taken by the state and implemented by joint, 'corporative' bodies of employers and workers, helping to run a planned economy in a spirit of patriotic harmony.[53] Mussolini, searching for some model of a 'Fascist state', was impressed. Here, at last, was a 'Third Way', a new method of managing the national economy and also an answer to class conflict. He congratulated Rocco:

I have just read your magnificent speech in Perugia and I hasten to send you my word of applause. It was a fundamental speech . . . Every Fascist in Italy must read your speech and will find in it, clearly reaffirmed, the fundamental programme of our party and the reasons why Fascism must fight against all other parties, following the method of the most resolute, rational, systematic intransigence. Only thus will the word become flesh and the idea become fact.[54]

Note that this 'fundamental programme of our party' was set out nearly three years after the Fascists had come to power, and even then by an ex-Nationalist; this was particularly striking because some of the basic ideas had been worked out by Alceste De Ambris and implemented by D'Annunzio at Fiume in 1919–20.

Still, Mussolini took them up enthusiastically in 1925–6. The 'corporate state' became a key propaganda slogan at home, and the main source of Fascism's appeal abroad. He did this partly to frighten the industrialists, who had been conspicuously reluctant to back the government in 1924. For the same reason he encouraged the syndicates, which led several large and successful strikes in 1925, particularly in the engineering industry. They secured wage increases, won back the eight-hour day and recruited many new members. In October, by an agreement signed at palazzo Vidoni, Mussolini forced the industrialists' confederation to recognise the Fascist syndicates' *exclusive* right to negotiate labour contracts – although, in a characteristic *quid pro quo*, the elected shop stewards' committees (*Commissioni Interne*) in the factories were abolished. The result was that opposition trade unions, like opposition parties, simply faded away: no employer would talk to them, however competent and representative they might be compared with their Fascist counterparts. The Fascist syndicates were not pleased either, for being excluded from factories meant that any agreement they signed would be unenforceable in practice. Still, they now had sole recognition, and seemed poised to become a basic institution of the new economy and the new state. As for Mussolini, he had been a revolutionary Socialist until 1914 (or later), a 'productivist' in 1917–18, and a 'Manchesterian' free-enterprise economic liberal in 1920–21. Now he had become a 'corporatist'. Clearly he did not much care how the economy was run, so long as he was running it.

In April 1926 Rocco pushed through a law confirming the Fascist syndicates' monopoly of negotiating collective agreements and imposing compulsory arbitration of serious labour disputes. It set up new 'labour tribunals' for this purpose, although they had little effect: judges could not impose their decisions, and in practice disputes continued to be settled by negotiation, often at local level. The law also banned strikes, go-slows and lock-outs as criminal attacks on the national economy; henceforth strike leaders, even Fascist strike leaders, would go to prison. In the public sector syndicates were banned too, although in practice, again, many Fascist 'associations' (including the National Association of Fascist Railwaymen) continued to flourish, syndicates in all but name. Mussolini proclaimed that class conflict had ended for ever, and that Italy was showing the world an example of a 'harmonically organised national society, where the state, with its impartial sovereign justice, achieves a balance of all interests'.[55] But the syndicates were still just old-fashioned trade unions, not 'corporations'. They might have a monopoly but they had little independence, and very little influence on decisions. Their top officials were government appointees and at local or provincial level there was no one to run them except ex-*squadristi*, whose view of labour relations was robust but inexperienced. Moreover, they had to contend with the government's deflationary policy in 1926 (see pp. 126ff.), which kept wages and available jobs low. The industrialists, after a worrying time in 1925-6, had won after all. They kept their decision-making powers, they were no longer bothered by strikes, and in the absence of shop stewards they could ignore any agreements they wished.

Naturally Mussolini had to disguise this outcome. 'Corporations' did not exist, but in 1926 he set up a 'Ministry of Corporations' to coordinate them, with himself as minister and, after November, Giuseppe Bottai as under-secretary. The ministry had nothing much to do except mediate in labour disputes, as the old Ministry of Labour had done – a task, incidentally, which the new labour tribunals were supposed to be doing. In April 1927 the government also proclaimed a 'Charter of Labour', largely written by Rocco, not Bottai: as such documents do, it proclaimed various pious aspirations, but it had no legal force.[56] Bottai's new ministry soon came into conflict with Edmondo Rossoni's confederation of syndicates. Bottai wanted genuine 'corporations', of employers' and employees' representatives with regulatory and planning powers, to be set up quickly; Rossoni wanted this too, but insisted that (genuine) workers' representatives should really share power, and feared (rightly) that Bottai's schemes would simply bring the syndicates under even greater bureaucratic control. Mussolini then made matters worse by announcing, in his highly publicised Ascension Day speech of May 1927, that the 'corporate state' had already been set up, and to prove it the 'corporations' would elect

half the members of the next Chamber of Deputies. Indeed, a new electoral law in May 1928 laid down similar proposals (see below). In other
words, it looked as if Rossoni might soon be able to choose half the new
parliament. The other Fascist leaders were not having that, and united
against him and his confederation. Mussolini, mindful also of the need
to restrain wages, bowed to the pressure. He dismissed Rossoni and split
the confederation into six separate organisations – Agriculture, Industry,
Commerce, etc. – balanced by six corresponding employers' bodies. But
there was also, at last, a 'corporation', i.e. a 'mixed' body, although it
was for professional men and artists, most of whom in any case were
self-employed. The break up of Rossoni's confederation was a classic
Mussolinian manoeuvre. It got rid of the most prominent Fascist labour
leader, and it brought the Fascist syndicates under greater state control.
Each new workers' confederation, on its own and without Rossoni's
leadership, would be no match for government or industrialists. But
Mussolini could claim that true 'corporatism' had begun. The rhetoric of
the 'Third Way' had weakened the unions, not for the last time.

With very few opposition members since June 1924, the Chamber of
Deputies was already a pointless anachronism. In 1927–8, as its five-year
term neared its end, the Fascists debated what should be done with it. The
party wanted to keep control; the existing deputies wanted to be re-elected;
the syndicalists argued that they alone had the right to represent the
people in the new corporate state. Eventually a new electoral law passed
through the Chamber by 216 to 15, only the aged Giolitti daring to speak
against. It was a compromise between party and syndicalist views. A thousand names were to be submitted to the Grand Council by syndicates,
employers' associations, ex-servicemen and a few other prestigious cultural
or welfare bodies. From these, the Grand Council would choose 400 candidates for the 400 seats. So the voter would have no choice of candidate. He
would simply answer 'yes' or 'no' to the question, 'Do you approve the list
of deputies nominated by the national Grand Council of Fascism?' Mussolini praised the Chamber for passing the new law in true Fascist style,
without discussion, and for listening to Giolitti's speech in 'glacial silence'.[57]
In March 1929 a new Chamber was 'elected' under this system. It was a
plebiscite rather than an election, but the usual techniques of persuasion
secured an almost 90 per cent turnout, and of the voters 98.3 per cent
were in favour – a real triumph for the *Duce*. The employers' associations
ended up with 125 of their nominees in parliament and the workers'
syndicates with only 89; the rest had been proposed by other bodies.[58]

It was the Grand Council which chose the 400 future deputies. Previously a purely party body, a new law in December 1928 had made it into

a kind of official Privy Council, consisting of the great and good in the regime: ministers while in office, some permanent members (the *Quadrumviri* of the march on Rome, ex-party secretaries), and some nominated by Mussolini.[59] It was given advisory and in some cases legislative powers on major 'constitutional' issues like choosing deputies, approving international treaties and relations with the Vatican. The law also required the Grand Council to advise on the succession to the throne. Here was a clear warning to King Victor Emmanuel III and especially to his son Humbert (who was believed to have anti-Fascist sympathies) that they had better support the regime. It was issued because Mussolini was about to reach a 'reconciliation' with the Church, which would involve the king ceding territory in Rome to the Vatican (see below). The king was furious, but helpless. By now it was too late for him to turn elsewhere. Another new task for the Grand Council was to draw up a list of possible successors to the *Duce*, to be submitted to the king in case of vacancy. This also threatened the king's traditional prerogative of choosing the head of government, although in practice Mussolini was of course far too astute to allow any such list, and in 1927 proclaimed he intended to rule for another 10 or 15 years (and did): 'my successor is not yet born'.[60] However, he apparently wrote a letter nominating the elderly, moderate Costanzo Ciano as his successor in the case of his own sudden death.[61] I write 'apparently' because the source of this information is the diary of Ciano's son Galeazzo, not too reliable even if family piety were not involved. If there was such a letter, both Mussolini and Ciano kept quiet about it; there was no deputy *Duce*.

The Grand Council acquired, therefore, extensive 'constitutional' powers that even threatened the Crown's prerogatives. But it remained mostly consultative and it met irregularly, indeed considerably less often as time went on.[62] As earlier, Mussolini used it to win the support of his leading *gerarchi*, but he certainly did not intend it to be a collective body that might threaten his own dominance (although that happened eventually, in 1943). Nonetheless, it *was* a forum for debate, and in 1926, for example, it made real changes to the law on syndicates. It provided an outlet for the discontented, and it kept Mussolini aware of what it would be impolitic to attempt. Mussolini disliked collective decision-making but he was, by all accounts, an excellent chairman: he let people have their say, he could always find an acceptable synthesis of different views, and he did not allow factions to develop. In the 1920s there was still an 'inner core' of party and government 'big hitters', who had to be treated with respect. In the 1930s this became less true, but even then the Grand Council provided a focus for the symbolic rallying of the faithful behind the *Duce*'s banner.

These institutional innovations – the 'corporate state', the new parliament, etc. – were certainly novel but they were hardly revolutionary, especially in practice. The 1928 law on the Grand Council may have been a warning to the king, but Victor Emmanuel III was not likely to cause too much trouble. He had backed Mussolini at key crises – October 1922, June 1924, December 1924–January 1925 – and he admired Mussolini's gifts and energy. He was increasingly sidelined during the regime; it was the *Duce*, not the king, who opened exhibitions and attended most ceremonies. Nevertheless, both men knew that it was the king, not the *Duce*, to whom the army and most public officials were loyal. Only the king could deliver Establishment support for the regime. It was the king who had appointed Mussolini Prime Minister in October 1922; it was the king who might, one day, dismiss him (and did). So Mussolini treated the king with outward deference. He visited the royal palace twice a week, reported in detail on political and military developments, and even accepted royal advice on appointments and honours. He left certain institutions, including the military and the judiciary, more or less alone because they enjoyed the king's protection. So, too, did the Senate, which consisted of 'life peers' drawn from the traditional elites and appointed by the king; to dismiss any of them would have been a direct challenge to royal authority. Mussolini not only left them alone, but flattered them with frequent and respectful speeches. Indeed, he made most of his important speeches to the Senate, where there had been no 'Aventinian' secession, where debates were surprisingly lively and well informed, and where for some years the government had no automatic majority. In 1932 there were 148 Senators who were not members of the Fascist party; even in 1942 there were still 34, including 6 Jews.[63] In April 1925 Senator Benedetto Croce organised an 'anti-Fascist manifesto' of fellow-intellectuals, but he remained a Senator and continued to speak out throughout the Fascist regime. In November 1926 49 Senators voted against the new public order laws; 46 of them opposed the 1928 law on elections to the Chamber. Of course, most Senators were, like the king, a support rather than a threat. The Senate's pro-government vote in June 1924 was crucial in enabling Mussolini to survive the Matteotti crisis. But the Senate, like the king, had to be treated with deference. It was the spokesman for the most powerful groups in the country. It was allowed to modify several important pieces of legislation, including the press laws and the ban on secret associations. It remained throughout the regime a tolerated alternative forum of political debate, if only for the elderly and distinguished. This was of huge importance. The Senators, and the king, prevented too many constitutional innovations; arguably they prevented a really tyrannical regime. There were always surprising, and frustrating, limits to Mussolini's power.

The Great 'Reconciliation'

The greatest limit of all was not the king, nor the army, nor the civil servants. It was the one body in Italy that had more adherents than Fascism, the Catholic Church. Mussolini was an atheist and a renowned anti-clerical in youth; but he had realised early on that if he wanted to hold power in Italy he would have to conciliate the Vatican. He showed his good will by a number of real concessions (see p. 66), and Pius XI showed his by remaining silent on the 'moral issue' after the murder of Matteotti. In 1925 Mussolini went further. He banned freemasonry altogether, to clerical approval; and in December he even had a religious wedding with Rachele, 10 years after the civil ceremony, to her disgust. Mussolini was aiming high. Perhaps he was already after the most glittering political prize of all, a settlement of the 'Roman Question', in dispute since Italian troops had seized the papal states in the mid-nineteenth century. More probably he envisaged a less wide-ranging settlement, based on amending the Law of Guarantees of 1871. But the Vatican, once it was sure that Mussolini was likely to stay in office, wanted more. The Church was not content with a few extra concessions wrung from a reluctant state, liable to be retracted at any time. She wanted a full bilateral settlement in the form of a solemn treaty, valid in international law, *between equal partners*. Mussolini had no objection – on the contrary, a full treaty would be the ultimate endorsement of his regime at home, and would make him a popular hero worldwide.

But, as usual, he had to be careful. He could not give too much away. The king disliked the Church and had no intention of abandoning the glorious Risorgimento traditions of his forefathers by allowing the Pope any say in Italian affairs, let alone by giving up any territory to him. Many of the leading Fascists were also strongly anti-clerical, and after the defeat of the opposition parties in 1925–6 these men saw the Church, and in particular Catholic Action and the Catholic lay organisations, as the last bastions of anti-Fascism. They were not wrong. Most of the Popular party and Catholic trade union leaders had, unlike the other anti-Fascists, remained in Italy at liberty. They continued to be active in Catholic Action or in the Catholic Institute of Social Activities (ICAS); they ran sports clubs, welfare bodies and cooperatives; they even founded 'professional sections' – trade unions by another name. Catholic Action, in short, rescued social activities from Fascist control, and also provided a refuge for the ex-*Popolari*, nearly all firm anti-Fascists. It had strong papal backing and the Vatican, indeed, saw a settlement with the state as an opportunity to give Catholic Action – especially its youth movements, now competing with the Fascist organisations – formal state recognition and protection in the future.[64]

Mussolini resolved these problems rather uncharacteristically, by keeping them quiet. Both sides wished to negotiate a deal, but both had many prominent men who detested the whole idea. So the negotiations, which began in late 1926, were secret. Mussolini himself took no part directly until the last few weeks, although he did regularly instruct and consult his chief negotiator, Domenico Barone. Barone was, of course, no Fascist and not a minister. He was a senior civil servant, a member of the Council of State and steeped in constitutional law. His status was similar to that of Torre on the railways or Serpieri in agriculture: a technocrat, charged with an important job and responsible only to the *Duce*. On the Vatican side, negotiations were conducted not by a member of the Curia but by a highly placed lay lawyer, Francesco Pacelli, brother of the next Pope. Mussolini set one condition: the settlement had to be a *final* one, and the Holy See would have to give up any further claims to its former territory.[65] As always, he used both flattery and threats. In 1927, after negotiations had already begun, he insisted that the Catholic Boy Scouts (*esploratori*) be closed down, as too great a rival to the newly formed Fascist youth organisations. The public fuss about this reassured his supporters and served to conceal what was going on; it also helped Mussolini to find out how much the Vatican was willing to concede to reach a settlement. After suitable protests the Vatican agreed to abandon the Boy Scouts, just as it had abandoned the Popular party and the Catholic trade unions; but it insisted on keeping its other lay organisations, including Catholic Action's youth bodies which contained 200,000 young people, far more than in the Boy Scouts. Early in January 1929 Barone died, so thereafter Mussolini negotiated directly with Pacelli, who had to come round unobtrusively at night to Mussolini's flat; but by then most issues had been resolved. The secret was well kept, helped no doubt by the regime's tight control of the press. Apart from the two negotiators, only the Pope, the papal Secretary of State Cardinal Gasparri, the *Duce* and the king knew what was going on, although the Minister of Justice Rocco had been active in promoting the deal early on, and was brought in for advice at the end. On 7 February 1929 Gasparri announced the news of a 'reconciliation' to an astonished group of diplomats, and the news flashed round the world – although even then not round Italy.

Four days later he and Mussolini signed the 'Lateran Pacts'. An international treaty set up a new sovereign state, Vatican City, with the Pope as ruler of around forty-four hectares (about a hundred acres) on the west bank of the Tiber, and 'extraterritorial status' for a few other ecclesiastical buildings, including St John Lateran and Castelgandolfo. All these areas were in papal hands already under the 1871 law, and were tiny – even San Marino has 59 square kilometres. The Italian state also handed over 750 million lire, plus 1,000 million in government bonds, as compensation for the loss of the Pope's previous lands. So the Church was, literally, bought off. Most important of all, a concordat gave the Church a range of privileges in Italy, including religious education in secondary as well as primary schools, a guaranteed status for Catholic Action, and legal recognition of marriages celebrated in church. This last provision meant not only that the Church retained control of the 'rites of passage', but of most family-related issues – for example, only the Church could now annul marriages. Mussolini admitted to the king that this was a real concession on an issue close to his heart:

I do not conceal from Your Majesty that the most serious obstacle to overcome in the concordat is the clause concerning marriage. Here the state withdraws a long way and is almost made extraneous to a fundamental issue like the formation and activities of the family. On the other hand, it seems that the Holy See regards the issue as essential, and on it depends all the rest.[66]

The pacts were, without question, the greatest political achievement of Mussolini's life. He had succeeded where all his predecessors, even Cavour and Crispi, had failed. No longer would the 'Roman Question' bedevil Church–state relations and often dominate domestic Italian politics. A chorus of praise, national and international, enveloped the *Duce*. Even Victor Emmanuel was pleased: Rome had been made safe for the House of Savoy. Indeed, the king offered Mussolini a title, although Mussolini had more sense than to accept. Pope Pius XI called him 'the man sent by Providence',[67] a wonderful phrase repeated for years by all with varying shades of irony. But Providence moves in mysterious ways. The atheist Mussolini, brought up on Machiavelli and still as anti-clerical as ever, made an unlikely defender of the faith. The pacts, for him, were just another necessary compromise. He had wanted them badly, and he knew their importance; but once he had secured them he was none too proud of them, and for once he did not trumpet his achievement to the world. After all, he knew what his Fascists were thinking. Had they marched on Rome only to restore the city to the Pope? Had they defeated the Bolsheviks only to surrender to the clericals? How could a patriotic leader, sworn to defend the national frontiers with his blood, give away territory inside the very capital city? How could a Fascist regime allow an independent Church to run much of welfare, education and the health services and to instruct the young in her own beliefs, totally opposed to those of true Fascists? Worse, might not the Church train a new clerical generation? Had the *Duce* gone soft, and been outmanoeuvred by a Pope? The Grand Council, 'supreme organ of Fascism', had not been consulted, and its members deliberately grumbled to each other by telephone to communicate their displeasure.[68] Reactions on the other side of the Tiber were rather similar, since the Curia had not been consulted either. In the Catholic north they were much stronger. Three hundred priests in Milan wrote to their new Archbishop, Cardinal Schuster, to stress that 'Fascism, which is inspired by state-worship and racist imperialism, will never disguise the fact that it is the antithesis of Christian teaching.'[69]

Mussolini could not, therefore, bask in his triumph. On the contrary, he had to spoil his own feast. Church–state relations grew markedly *worse* just after the Lateran Pacts. The government went into battle against Catholic Action, accused of being run by ex-*Popolari* and of trying to form clandestine trade unions. In May 1929, three months after the 'reconciliation', Mussolini told the Chamber that Christianity would have remained an obscure Jewish sect had it not managed to be diffused by the Roman Empire; it was Caesar, not God, who had ensured its success. The Pope published an acerbic reply, and made clear that it was only Mussolini that Providence had sent, not Fascism.[70] By 1931 there was open conflict. The Pope organised special celebrations to commemorate the fortieth anniversary of Leo XIII's famous encyclical on social issues, *Rerum Novarum*, and issued his own encyclical *Quadragesimo Anno*, relating it to the contemporary scene; this was particularly galling to those Fascists who claimed to have invented corporatism. So the *squadristi* were encouraged to resume their vocation. The real conflict was over the Catholic Action youth clubs, with over 700,000 members in 1930. The Church saw 'reconciliation' as a green light to expand them and to Christianise society, using Fascism as a secular arm. Mussolini, of course, was determined to resist any Catholic *reconquista* of Italian society, and he had his own intentions for Italian youth. In May 1931 the Catholic youth clubs were closed down, to show who was boss. All sides then overreacted. Pius XI publicly denounced the Fascist regime's 'pagan stateworship' and its youth movement, which trained the young only to hate and to be violent. He also recommended that Catholics who had to take an oath of loyalty to the regime should do so with 'mental reservations', so that it did not count. Meanwhile, in Milan, Cardinal Schuster refused to turn up and bless the monumental new railway station, so poor Arnaldo had to find a mere auxiliary bishop to do it instead.[71] Moreover, Mussolini started favouring various Protestant sects, which received far better treatment in Fascist Italy than they were to do later under the Christian Democrats.

Eventually, in September 1931, the Pope backed down and an uneasy peace was restored, largely on Mussolini's terms. The Catholic youth clubs reopened, but were now confined to religious and educational or recreational activities; i.e. no sport. The adult sections of Catholic Action came under direct episcopal control; i.e. no ex-*Popolari* (although in practice most of them stayed in office). The oath of loyalty was tacitly accepted; i.e. no 'reservations'. Mussolini's honour was satisfied. He had taken on the Pope in public conflict and won a victory, or at least a reasonable compromise. He had undermined the ex-*Popolari*, he had warded off a serious challenge to the Fascist youth movements, and he had silenced his Fascist critics. On 11 February 1932, the third anniversary of the pacts, he met Pius XI formally at last – and discussed the Protestant sects.[72]

The 'reconciliation' and its aftermath were excellent illustrations of Mussolini's political skills and approach. He had his own very decided opinions on all subjects, but he never let them stand in the way of a good compromise. A good compromise might be with anyone, even hated opponents; and he could always sense what mattered most to the other side. However, it was always a good idea to browbeat opponents a bit first, if possible; or if not, to make a few trivial unsolicited concessions. Either approach would put them in a more receptive state of mind. This done, Mussolini would settle, provided there was something tangible in it for himself. If the benefit proved to be not tangible enough, he would not go back on his word, but he would reopen the dispute on some partial issue and force a new settlement that could be presented as being more satisfactory. These are, of course, normal political and bargaining skills; for Mussolini by this time they had become instinctive. Note, too, that he neither persecuted the Church, nor wooed her. He kept his distance and negotiated with her via a lawyer, although he did like to stress their common enemies – Bolshevism, freemasonry and inadequate procreation. He won a huge propaganda victory in 1929, and then satisfied his doubtful followers in 1931. The irony is that at the end of it all Catholic Action and its youth clubs remained in being and continued to educate the young in non-Fascist values, thus vitiating Mussolini's long-term hopes for the Italian people. But they were no longer so *obviously* non-Fascist, or anti-Fascist, and that is what mattered most to a politician.

Conclusion

By the time of his triumph in the 1929 plebiscite Mussolini had set up a 'strong state', which clearly enjoyed mass support. He had done it slowly, piecemeal and in response to circumstances and attempted assassinations, without any coherent long-term programme or blueprint. The new state was an 'authoritarian compromise', based more on Nationalist ideas than specifically 'Fascist' ones, and it rested on the traditional state institutions. Indeed, the real Fascists, the provincial extremists, had been defeated in 1925–6 and thrown out of their own party; neither they nor the syndicalists had imposed their will. It was not surprising that Mussolini was greatly admired in Rome's official circles. He seemed energetic, highly competent, and unthreatening. He put on a good show, and he respected the limits set by Italy's exceptionally strong legal, cultural and ecclesiastical traditions. Before 1925–6 the essence of Fascism had been *squadrismo*; by 1929 it had become the cult of Mussolini, the man who had improved public services and balanced the budget, the man who ran eight ministries and took no pay for any of them.

But the traditional state institutions had values and practices of their own. Their members had given up their freedom to be Masons but they still held a great deal of power. Mussolini could not even rely fully on the army. He was surrounded by cautious bureaucrats, money-grubbing bankers and sycophantic courtiers, and he despised them all. Even the police, competent as they were, were still just policemen – the cynical servants of any regime. The 'Fascist state' was too tame, too risk-averse, too essentially 'un-Fascist' for Mussolini's emotional needs. It gave him power of a kind, but not the dynamic, 'Jacobin' power he craved. He was still '*Duce* only in a manner of speaking', dissatisfied and frustrated by his own necessary compromises with Church and state. That was why he was so sensitive to any suggestion that the 'March on Rome' had not been a true revolution, as Petrillo found to his cost. In the late 1930s the *Duce* told De Begnac bitterly that Cardinal Gasparri had apparently replied, when asked who would succeed Mussolini even in a thousand years' time, 'Giolitti'.[73] On another occasion he was rather more defensive:

The *Serenissimo Doge* [Mussolini's epithet for Volpi] is afraid that I have become the prisoner of the system that I created. I did not create the system, I tried to modify the one in which the insurrection of October 1922 enmeshed me. I demolished useless barriers between public administration and the working masses. I removed all authority from disorder, and imposed order on entire regions of the country. I gave authority to the real executive, taking power away from political cliques that had illegitimately seized it. I could do no more. Let no one fool himself that he can carry out a revolution starting from a vacuum, from a state reduced to a heap of ruins. The system continues to live: it is essential to give it some vitality and prevent it from vegetating, which trying to abolish its every function immediately would ensure. This, I told Volpi, does not mean becoming prisoner of the system.[74]

But it did, and he knew it. Mussolini had thought his 'ball of lead' was agrarian *squadrismo*, crude and violent; but actually it was the sedentary, comfort-loving Roman bureaucracy. So he kept the Militia in reserve, and tolerated Farinacci's outbursts. He might yet need them, or the threat of them.

Mussolini's 'strong state' was founded on memories of the World War and the 'mutilated victory'. It was designed essentially to remedy the defects that the war and the post-war instability had made apparent, including the vote and the strike. It sought to mobilise and control 'society'; soon it would seek to transform it. Mussolini's favourite slogan now was 'Everything within the state, nothing outside the state, nothing against the state'.[75] So far that was just a slogan, but not for long. Mussolini might have compromised with the state, but he was not going to compromise with society. Like Machiavelli, he wanted to correct the faults in the Italian national character. It was time to 'Fascistise the nation'.

Notes

1 H.W. Schneider, *Making the Fascist State* (New York, 1928), pp. 321–7; A. Aquarone, *L'Organizzazione dello Stato Totalitario* (Turin, 1965), pp. 55–9.

2 Grand Council document, 5 October 1925; ACS, SPD, c. ris., b. 27.

3 Aquarone, *L'Organizzazione* cit., pp. 48–9; R. De Felice, *Mussolini il Fascista* (Turin, 1966–8), i, pp. 566, 726.

4 V. Castronovo, *La Stampa Italiana dall' Unità al Fascismo* (Bari, 1970), pp. 361–431; E. Decleva, 'Il Corriere della Sera', in B. Vigezzi (ed.), *Dopoguerra e Fascismo* (Bari, 1965), pp. 155–257.

5 Sir Ronald Graham to Foreign Office, 23 January 1925; PRO, FO C1179/1/22.

6 ACS, SPD, c. ris., b. 104, sottof. 6.

7 *Corriere della Sera*, 1 September 2001.

8 *Le Temps*, 23 May 1925; *OO* xxi, p. 324.

9 De Felice, *Mussolini il Fascista* cit., ii, pp. 139–47; *OO* xxi, pp. 539–43.

10 U. Guspini, *L'Orecchio del Regime* (Milan, 1973), pp. 59–60.

11 The Grand Master of the 'Scottish rite' Freemasons wrote a number of whining letters to Mussolini and was eventually given a job in the Ministry of Communications. In 1929 he supported the 'reconciliation' with the Church. ACS, SPD, c. ris., b. 58 'Palermi, Raul'.

12 R. De Felice, *Mussolini il Duce* (Turin, 1974–81), i, p. 83. Cf. also G. Leto, *OVRA* (Bologna, 1951), pp. 31–4, 132–4; M. Franzinelli, *I Tentacoli dell' OVRA* (Turin, 1999); P. Carucci, 'L'Organizzazione dei servizi di polizia', in *Rassegna degli Archivi di Stato* xxxvi (1976), no. 1, pp. 82–114, esp. p. 109.

13 Aquarone, *L'Organizzazione* cit., pp. 103–4.

14 Mussolini to Italian consul in Boston, 23 July, and to US ambassador in Rome, 24 July 1927; *OO* xl, pp. 413–14, 416–17.

15 On Bombacci, see ACS, SPD, c. ris., b. 74; on '*confino*', De Felice, *Mussolini il Duce* cit., i, p. 304; G. Leto, *OVRA* cit., p. 59; L. Musci, 'Il confino di polizia', in A. Dal Pont and S. Carolini, *L'Italia al Confino* (Milan, 1983).

16 ACS, SPD, c. ris., b. 84 'Dumini'. In 1939 he offered his services to Mussolini again.

17 Federzoni to Mussolini, 16 April 1926 (similar letter 26 May); ACS, SPD, c. ris., b. 5.

18 Farinacci to Mussolini, 20 January 1932; ACS, SPD, c. ris., b. 37.

19 Mussolini's speech in *OO* xxi, pp. 270–9; letter to Di Giorgio, 2 April 1925, in *OO* xxxix, p. 390; De Felice, *Mussolini il Fascista* cit., ii, pp. 52–5, 76–9.

20 Speech of 18 May 1925; *OO* xxi, pp. 311–14, at p. 313.

21 G. Bastianini, *Uomini, Cose, Fatti* (Milan, 1959), p. 23.

22 ACS, SPD, c. ris., b. 5, sottof. 2.

23 Mussolini to Federzoni, 29 October 1925; *OO* xxxix, pp. 536–7.

24 Y. De Begnac, *Taccuini Mussoliniani* (Bologna, 1990), p. 527.

25 Law of 24 December 1925 no. 2300; Aquarone, *L'Organizzazione* cit., pp. 71–4; De Felice, *Mussolini il Fascista* cit., ii, pp. 344–6.

26 M. Salvati, *Il Regime e gli Impiegati* (Bari, 1992), pp. 70ff; G. Melis, *Due Modelli di Amministrazione tra Liberalismo e Fascismo* (Rome, 1988).

27 Interview in *Giornale d'Italia*, 5 December 1923; *OO* xx, p. 124.

28 Speech to Senate, 19 June 1929; *OO* xxiv, p. 119.

29 G. Melis, *Storia dell' Amministrazione Italiana* (Bologna, 1996), pp. 343–4.

30 Melis, *Storia* cit., pp. 335–6; E. Rotelli, *La Presidenza del Consiglio dei Ministri* (Milan, 1972), pp. 301ff.

31 Salvati, *Impiegati* cit., pp. 42–54, 218–19; Melis, *Due Modelli* cit., pp. 223, 341.

32 A. De' Stefani, *Una Riforma al Rogo* (Rome, 1963), p. 12.

33 P. Morgan, 'The prefects and party-state relations in Fascist Italy', in *Journal of Modern Italian Studies* iii (1998), pp. 241–72, at pp. 251–2; Aquarone, *L'Organizzazione* cit, pp. 74–5; De Felice, *Mussolini il Fascista* cit., ii, p. 344.

34 See, for example, report of Prefect of Terra di Lavoro (Caserta) to Ministry of the Interior 14 August 1926 on his choices as *podestà*; ACS, Min. Int., Dir. Gen. P.S., AA. GG. e RR., 1926, b. 97.

35 Morgan, 'The prefects' cit.; A. Lyttelton, *The Seizure of Power* (London, 1973), pp.160–75; R. Fried, *The Italian Prefects* (New Haven, 1963).

36 Mussolini to Prefects, 13 June 1923; *OO* xxxviii, p. 355.

37 Mussolini, Circular to Prefects, 5 January 1927; *OO* xxii, pp. 467–70; Aquarone, *L'Organizzazione* cit., pp. 485–8.

38 Ascension Day speech, 26 May 1927; *OO* xxii, p. 381.

39 Circular to Prefects, 15 February 1930; ACS, SPD, c. ris., b. 28, f. 8.

40 Morgan, 'The prefects' cit., p. 246; Lyttelton, *The Seizure of Power* cit., p. 278; L. Federzoni, *Italia di Ieri per la Storia di Domani* (Milan, 1967), p. 100.

41 Lyttelton, *The Seizure of Power* cit., p. 283.

42 Prefect of Genoa to Min. Int., 28 May 1926; ACS, Min. Int., Dir. Gen. P.S., AA. GG. e RR., 1926, b. 95.

43 Prefect of Cremona to Min. Int., 28 June 1926; ibid., 1926, b. 97.

44 ACS, SPD, c. ris., b. 37, 40.

45 Mussolini to Farinacci, 10 July 1926; ACS, SPD, c. ris., b. 37 and b. 40; *OO* xl, pp. 86–7.

46 A. Lyttelton, 'La Dittatura Fascista', in G. Sabbatucci and V. Vidotto (eds), *Storia d'Italia* iv (Bari, 1997), p. 181.

47 P. Morgan, 'Augusto Turati', in F. Cordova (ed.), *Uomini e Volti del Fascismo* (Rome, 1980), pp. 473–520, at pp. 498–9.

48 E. Gentile, *La Via Italiana al Totalitarismo* (Rome, 1995), pp. 171–2; De Felice, *Mussolini il Fascista* cit., ii, pp. 186ff.

49 Mussolini to Turati, February 1927; ACS, *Autografi del Duce*, cassetta di zinco, scat. 3, f. 5; *OO* xxxvii, pp. 53–4.

50 Speech 7 April 1926 at palazzo Vidoni; *OO* xxii, pp. 107–10.

51 De Begnac, *Taccuini mussoliniani* cit., p. 474.

52 Mussolini to consul general Carini, 1 November 1925; *OO* xxxix, pp. 538–9.

53 A. Rocco, speech at Perugia, 30 August 1925; cf. P. Ungari, *Alfredo Rocco e l'Ideologia Giuridica del Fascismo* (Brescia, 1963); E. Gentile, 'Alfredo Rocco', in F. Cordova (ed.), *Uomini e Volti* cit., pp. 305–36; D. Roberts, *The Syndicalist Tradition and Italian Fascism* (Chapel Hill, N.C., 1979), esp. pp. 139–52.

54 Mussolini to Rocco, 31 August 1925, in *OO* xxxix, p. 507.

55 PNF *Foglio d'Ordine*, 20 July 1927; *OO* xxxvii, pp. 320–1.

56 Aquarone, *L'Organizzazione* cit., pp. 142–3; Lyttelton, *The Seizure of Power* cit., pp. 330–1; text in W. Welk, *Fascist Economic Policy* (Cambridge, Mass., 1938), pp. 287–92.

57 PNF *Foglio d'Ordine*, 17 March 1928; *OO* xxxvii, p. 329.

58 De Felice, *Mussolini il Fascista* cit., ii, p. 496; A. Lyttelton, in Sabbatucci and Vidotto (eds), *Storia d'Italia* cit., iv, p. 176.

59 Aquarone, *L'Organizzazione* cit., pp. 169ff.

60 Speech of Ascension Day, 26 May 1927; *OO* xxii, p. 385.

61 G. Ciano, *Diario 1937–43* (Milan, 1990 edn), 3 July 1939; De Felice, *Mussolini il Fascista* cit., ii, p. 349; Aquarone, *L'Organizzazione* cit., pp. 161–2.

62 Aquarone, *L'Organizzazione* cit., pp. 162, 169–72, 184; De Felice, *Mussolini il Fascista* cit., ii, p. 313.

63 De Felice, *Mussolini il Duce* cit., i, p. 281.

64 J. Pollard, *The Vatican and Italian Fascism* (Cambridge, 1985), p. 34.

65 P. Kent, *The Pope and the Duce* (London, 1981); I. Garzia, *Il Negoziato Diplomatico per i Patti Lateranensi* (Milan, 1974); D. Binchy, *Church and State in Fascist Italy* (London, 1941); A. Martini, *Studi sulla Questione Romana e sulla Conciliazione* (Rome, 1963).

66 Mussolini to Victor Emmanuel III, 20 January 1929; *OO* xxiii, pp. 315–17.

67 Pius XI to visitors from Sacro Cuore University, Milan, 13 February 1929 ('e forse ci voleva anche un uomo come quello che la Provvidenza Ci ha fatto incontrare').

68 Pollard, *The Vatican and Italian Fascism* cit., pp. 62–3; Guspini, *L'Orecchio del Regime* cit., pp. 95–6.

69 ACS, SPD, RSI, c. ris., b. 49 'Schuster'.

70 Mussolini's speech to Chamber of Deputies, 13 May 1929; *OO* xxiv, p. 45; Pius' reply in *L'Osservatore Romano*, 6 June 1929.

71 ACS, SPD, RSI, c. ris., b. 49 'Schuster'.

72 *OO* xxxvii, pp. 128–31. They also discussed the Italian Jews, the Pope praising them and in particular his former Hebrew teacher in Milan, rabbi da Fano.

73 De Begnac, *Taccuini Mussoliniani* cit., pp. 522–3.

74 Ibid., pp. 541–2.

75 From his speech, 28 October 1925; *OO* xxi, p. 425.

Chapter 5

Targets and 'Battles' 1925–35

Mussolini's ambitions in 1925–6 were boundless. He was setting up, or claimed to be setting up, a new political system, and he needed to provide real benefits that the previous Liberal regime would not have been able to achieve. He wanted visible, dramatic successes, not mundane administration; and he wanted a leading role for himself. He had already ended strikes and made the trains run on time. Now he launched a series of spectacular 'campaigns', or 'battles' – the military terminology was revealing – on other key economic and social issues. The Fascist regime would save the lira, crush the Mafia, make the country self-sufficient in wheat, drain and resettle the Pontine marshes near Rome, rebuild Rome itself on imperial lines, and even boost the birth rate. These issues were carefully chosen. They were certainly dramatic gesture policies, demanding tough action and determined management; but they were not *too* frightening or disruptive, and they were likely to prove popular. Few people, after all, wanted the currency to collapse or the Mafia to dominate Sicily, and even fewer were against motherhood or pizza pie. Furthermore, Mussolini's 'battles' were part of a comprehensive strategy of social transformation. Mussolini expected to rule Italy for some time and, unlike most politicians, was serious about long-term social change. He did not make grandiloquent promises, soon forgotten. His 'battles' lasted for years – some until the Second World War – and provided the essential justification for Fascist 'mobilisation' of society. Moreover, they were not merely a response to pressing social needs. They were selected by the *Duce* himself, and outlined in his famous Ascension Day speech in May 1927.[1] They reveal what his values really were, or at least what he thought feasible to pursue in the mid-1920s at a time when people wanted peace and quiet rather than more radical change. Call him old-fashioned, but what he wanted, it seemed, was a *rural* Italy, free of crime or dissent, self-sufficient in basic foods, and populated by disciplined, fecund peasants: a land of large, dutiful families and social stability, regulated benevolently from above. He believed in good order, tidiness, hygiene, education, a reliable currency and clearing the slums.

'The Battle for the Lira'

Mussolini's greatest 'battle' in the late 1920s was in monetary policy. Like many entrepreneurs, he knew nothing about money and was notoriously improvident with his own, but running the *Popolo d'Italia* had taught him one lesson: if people thought you were important enough, or might become important enough, they would give you some. So money did not matter, but politics did. Sometimes politics dictated intervention. One of his government's first acts in 1922–3 had been to rescue the (Catholic) *Banco di Roma* and the Ansaldo steel complex. Usually Mussolini left economic and financial policy to his Finance Minister De' Stefani, who cut public spending, balanced the budget and presided over the biggest manufacturing boom until the late 1950s. Industrial output rose by over 50 per cent in three years, and exports doubled.[2] But by 1925 the boom was becoming inflationary, the balance of payments deficit reached 8 billion lire, and the lira fell from 105 to the pound sterling in January down to 120 by late summer. Mussolini began to worry about foreign and domestic confidence. He needed to reassure savers, particularly after the German hyperinflation of 1923–4. He also needed to teach the industrialists a lesson, as they had been conspicuously unsupportive during the Matteotti crisis in 1924. He dismissed De' Stefani and brought in an acerbic banker, Giuseppe Volpi, with a very different remit – to save the lira. For the next two years government pursued a deflationary policy directed initially to prevent the lira falling below 120 to the pound, later on to revalue it at a higher rate. The government cut public spending further, reduced money wages, rents and prices, imposed a credit squeeze, reduced the money supply and consolidated (i.e. lowered the interest payable on) the national debt. The main losers were industrial workers and exporters, but Volpi had little sympathy for them: he thought far too many useless objects were produced, and in any case successful exporting just meant underpaying workers at home.[3]

Mussolini was lucky, as usual. By late 1925 the post-war boom was slowing anyway. Moreover, in 1925–6 Volpi managed to have Italy's war debts to Britain and the United States of America reduced, with the remainder to be paid off gradually with money received from the Germans and Austrians. He was then able to borrow US $100 million from the J.P. Morgan Bank on the basis of these agreements. The lira remained steady at around 120 to the pound. But it declined again in the spring and summer of 1926 to around 150. Mussolini decided to act. On 12 July he told the Prefects to arrange for long bureaucratic delays before passports were issued, so that people could not go abroad and spend lire on holiday.[4] On 8 August he wrote to Volpi, instructing him not just to stabilise but to revalue the lira:

the notes that follow are the result not so much of reflection and study of the problem that has been agonising us all for some time, but of intuition which as far as I am concerned is nearly always infallible . . . the fate of the regime is linked to the fate of the lira . . . it is necessary therefore to consider the battle of the lira as being absolutely decisive.[5]

Ten days later he made an apparently impromptu but actually carefully planned speech at Pesaro on the same lines. He would, he proclaimed, 'defend the lira to the last breath, to the last drop of blood'.[6] The argument was essentially political. Mussolini could not allow the lira to fall below the French franc, or Fascism would appear inferior to democracy. Since the German debacle two years earlier people were not at all confident about the leading currencies, and holding lire was certainly a big risk: everyone realised that both Fascism and the lira would collapse overnight if Mussolini were assassinated, and there were four assassination attempts in 1925-6. Furthermore, most of Italy's public debt was owed to foreigners and payable in foreign currency, so the exchange rate mattered. In short, deflation was the right policy politically and a good case could be made for it economically, whatever its short-term consequences.

Soon the lira began to climb, reaching about 90 lire to the pound sterling ('quota novanta') by May 1927. Mussolini did not need the lira to go any higher, so later in the year he joined the gold standard and fixed the new rate at 92.46 lire to the pound, or 19 lire to the US dollar. Even then, Mussolini knew there were plenty of 'inflation defeatists' selling lire to push the rate down; he told Volpi that if they did not stop he would announce a new rate of 75 to the pound sterling.[7] This was not just bluster. He was determined not only to impose a new exchange rate, but also to tackle the economic Establishment and show them who was in control. The press was censored, of course, but there was still much grumbling, particularly when the interest on Treasury bonds was lowered. Ettore Conti, of the electrical industry, spoke in the Senate in favour of a lower rate, 120 to the pound; Fiat, unable to export its cars at the new high exchange rate, threatened to lay off workers. Mussolini reminded the Prefect of Turin that Fiat was 'not a state institution on a par with the dynasty, the Church or the regime . . . Fiat must be regarded as a private firm, similar to thousands of others'.[8] In fact, the government did make some concessions to industry. It lowered interest rates, granted tax reliefs and permitted further cuts (10 per cent) in money wages on top of those already announced. But this, in turn, only infuriated the Fascist syndicates and led to many clashes, which grand gestures like the 1927 Charter of Labour (see p. 111) were designed to obscure, and which in 1928 contributed to the dismissal of Rossoni and the break-up of his confederation of syndicates. The employers thus won out over labour but they lost to the government, and 'quota ninety' remained. Meanwhile the government had also ordered lower rents, and any landlord who failed to reduce them was dispatched to the islands on Mussolini's specific order.

So the *Duce* managed to alienate employers, workers and landlords, all by a single policy. But he did not care. He disliked the 'bourgeois' industrialists, who were very lukewarm towards Fascism and the 'corporate state', and he had no reason to worry about the workers. He disliked 'parasitic' landlords even more. He needed to reassure foreign investors, and he needed a prestigious policy and a highly valued currency. He was not going to let tiresome money-grubbing businessmen stand in his way. He chose the actual rate, 'quota ninety', not for any economic reason but because it had been the rate in October 1922, when Fascism came to power. It was his choice and he imposed it on a reluctant Volpi (who wanted a rate of 120 lire to the pound) and on Stringher, Governor of the Bank of Italy.[9] He had to manoeuvre, conciliate, and threaten all the most powerful groups in the country, going to their meetings and addressing them personally. He took a big risk, but he knew other countries were adopting similar policies, and he had certain advantages. In 1925 Churchill had put Britain back on the gold standard at the pre-war rate, and the result was a general strike the following year. In Italy there was no general strike, indeed few strikes at all; money wages were cut, and the syndical confederation broken up. This enabled the government to *lower* interest rates even while deflating the economy. In any case, 'there was no alternative'. Germany had shown what happened if foreign confidence collapsed. So the *Duce* gambled, and triumphed.

'The Battle Against the Mafia'

Another of Mussolini's 'battles' was against the Sicilian 'Mafia'. It started partly as a result of reports coming in from ex-Inspector Gasti, famous for his report on Mussolini in 1919 (see p. 43) and now Prefect of Palermo,[10] but mainly because of Mussolini's own visit to Sicily in May 1924. He had not been impressed. The island's Fascists seemed less than zealous, and local government seemed to operate in remarkably traditional ways. At Piana dei Greci the mayor apparently asked the *Duce* why he had brought along his police bodyguards: 'Your Excellency is my guest. You have nothing to fear!' No doubt this was so, but the crime level was alarming. There were 278 murders in Palermo province alone in 1924, and Trapani was proportionately even worse. Here was Italy's 'Northern Ireland', and Mussolini's response was swift. The Fascist regime could not tolerate the apparent existence of rival centres of power. In 1925 the *Duce* decided to impose law and order, once again via the official state machinery. He sent in Cesare Mori, a tough ex-policeman who had even dared to crack down on the local Fascists when he was Prefect of Bologna in 1921-2. Mori behaved true to form, expelling 400 Fascists in Trapani, closing down the Fascist party organisation in Palermo and arresting its secretary, Alfredo Cucco. Eleven thousand suspects were rounded up all over the island (and that was the official figure); a whole town, Gangi, was besieged by policemen who took women and children as hostages.[11] A series of show trials – 15 in all, with a great deal of publicity – ensured that the whole world knew of Mussolini's achievement. All this naturally led to a great deal of protest from influential Sicilians, but Mussolini gave Mori his full backing. He had realised that here was a golden opportunity to demonstrate the acceptable face of Fascism. With parties virtually dissolved and local elections abolished, Mussolini was in a far stronger position than his Liberal predecessors. He had no elections to win and so had no reason to woo the local bosses and their dubious gangs. He could, and did, impose direct rule, and give Mori – a man hated by many Fascists – and the police a free hand. In 1928 murders in Palermo province were claimed to be a mere 25; if true, an astonishing achievement.

However, as usual in these circumstances, Mori had clearly gone much too far. He had arrested more or less anyone denounced to him, but the accusations often came from personal enemies or feuding families. In any case, proof of Mafia connections was notoriously difficult to establish: *mafioso* was simply a term of abuse applied to opponents in the hope of rousing the authorities against them. Moreover, Mori was in charge of the police but not of the judiciary. Most of the accused were soon released without trial or, like Cucco himself, acquitted on all counts. Moreover, the show trials turned out to be not much of a show: Italian court procedure is largely written and therefore undramatic. By March 1928 Mussolini was growing restless, and alarmed at the way Sicilian public opinion was turning hostile to the constant accusations. He told Mori to hurry up the trials, and cut down on any more retrospective enquiries; the whole business should be finished off quickly.[12] In the summer of 1929 the campaign ended, and Mori was sent off into retirement.

Mussolini had won his 'battle', but not the war. He was certainly more effective against the 'Mafia' than any other government in Italy before or since, at least until the 1990s. Many violent thugs were imprisoned and many others were driven abroad, mostly to the United States of America where they found a more welcoming environment. Crime did diminish, and the regime appeared firmly established. But he had not convinced Sicilians of the merits of Fascist rule. He continued to distrust them, and they him. It was noticeable that in later years Sicily was distinctly neglected by the regime, even though it was potentially a very useful grain producer. Socially, the result was paradoxical. The anti-Mafia drive was essentially against 'new money', against the nouveaux riches who had acquired land from impoverished landowners during the war or the post-war inflation, and who were now labelled as *mafiosi* by their many enemies. Mori's activities meant that the old landowners were restored to their lands and their influence, not quite the outcome Mussolini had envisaged. Perhaps the best way of regarding his 'battle' against the Mafia is simply that it was one of a long series of high-minded northern campaigns to transform southern, and particularly Sicilian, values and society, and to convince southerners of the merits of the rule of law and of an effective state (ruled by northerners). In that sense, Mussolini's campaign, like all the others, was an abject failure.

'The Battle for Wheat'

Mussolini favoured rural life, but some kinds of rural life were more favoured than others. The Fascist regime always approved of small peasant landowners, and indeed created hundreds of thousands more by 'persuading' landowners to sell land to deserving ex-servicemen in the early 1920s, and by improvement schemes later. But there was no extra land for shepherds, nor for dairy farmers, nor for fruit and vegetable growers. Such people tended to export their produce, whereas Mussolini was after self-sufficiency in Italy's basic cereal, wheat. Wheat was the vital commodity that could feed an army, and Italy did not grow enough of it; in the early 1920s about 2.5 million tonnes a year, nearly one-third of the requirement, had to be imported, at a cost of almost 3 billion lire.[13] This was about one-fifth by value of all imports. Italy already had to import coal and oil; and could not import basic foodstuff as well. Pre-Fascist governments had run wheat propaganda campaigns, and in 1923 the Fascists, too, launched a wheat-growing competition to raise productivity, but the winner only managed 4.13 tonnes per hectare. Something more was needed.

On 20 June 1925, with much fanfare, Mussolini proclaimed the 'battle for wheat'. Henceforth Italy would grow enough wheat for her own needs, indeed for the needs of a rising population and to provide a reserve in case of war. He already knew, of course, that the 1925 harvest would be good (it turned out to be 6.55 million tonnes, a record) and his technical experts had assured him self-sufficiency was feasible, but even so it was a daring commitment. He promised to 'liberate the Italian people from the servitude of foreign bread',[14] a phrase that became the slogan of the whole campaign. But even Mussolini could not control the weather, and in fact both the next two harvests were poor. The 'battle' was truly military, with the *Duce* as supreme commander. A special 'general staff' – the Permanent Wheat Committee, chaired by Mario Ferraguti – was set up to wage the campaign, with the support of provincial agricultural councils and the Agricultural Confederation. The committee's task was to ensure that selected seeds, grown at the agricultural research station at Rieti, were widely used, and that fertilisers, expert advice etc., became more available. Government grants also poured into arable farming, helping farmers to buy tractors and storage facilities on the cheap, and the tax on agricultural income was halved. In 1931 millers were obliged to use 90 per cent home-grown wheat in making flour. The government imposed high tariffs – 75 lire a tonne initially, 750 lire by 1931 – on imported cereals, thus raising the wheat price, discouraging consumption and protecting farmers. However, despite these last measures the domestic wheat price actually *fell* quite sharply in the next few years, because of 'quota ninety' and later because of the world depression, although it fell less than prices elsewhere. Undeterred, the *Duce* spent huge sums on agricultural improvement schemes (see below) and irrigation, thus bringing more land under the plough; and of course many farmers switched to wheat from other crops, particularly maize. The government became the farmer's friend, pouring funds into arable zones on a scale unmatched even by the European Union's Common Agricultural Policy 50 years later. The Prefects were instructed to reduce local taxes and favour agriculture: 'it should be the object of particular care, taking precedence over all other forms of economic activity . . . the regime is predominantly rural and intends to remain so'.[15]

Above all, there was propaganda. The 'battle for wheat' provided endless photo-opportunities and made a huge contribution to the myth of the *Duce*. In his travels round the country Mussolini could rarely see a group of farm workers without leaping out of his car and joining in. Photographs of the *Duce*, stripped to the waist and threshing corn, were shown in cinema newsreels throughout the land.[16] In any case, he still owned a couple of plots near Forlì, and could always be shown labouring there. The sight of the First Peasant at work aroused much derision in the cities, but wonder and approval in the countryside. Mussolini was, after all, the first Italian ruler since Cincinnatus to go back to the land and dig for victory. Even the Russians' 'rural Stakhanovism' did not involve Stalin personally. Mussolini also held a special ceremony every year in December to reward the most productive grain-growers with large money prizes and a rousing speech, and there was a national 'Bread Day' in April marked by further messages from the *Duce* ('honour bread, the glory of the fields, the fragrancy of the earth, the feast of life'[17]). Rural clergy were expected to encourage their parishioners to grow more wheat, and there was a special competition for the priests themselves. The government also promoted international conferences in Rome on grain productivity, and Mussolini spoke at the opening ceremonies. International approval and worldwide publicity were all part of the 'battle', and brought considerable political rewards.

In a crude way, it worked. The 1929 wheat harvest was an excellent 7.1 million tonnes; the 1929–34 mean was 6.9 million, well up on the pre-war level of around 4.9 million and on the 1921–5 mean of 5.4 million. The yield per hectare rose from 0.92 tonnes in 1922–4 to 1.34 tonnes in 1938–40, still only just over half the British yield but a great deal more than had ever been achieved in Italy. The country really did become virtually self-sufficient in wheat, at least in a good year, although she had to import phosphates instead. Giddy with success, Mussolini in 1933 proclaimed a huge victory in the countryside. Of course, this was not the whole story. The 'battle for wheat' illustrates, yet again, that determined governments are like overzealous doctors: they can usually achieve a limited objective if they throw enough resources at it, provided they ignore costs, side-effects and long-term consequences. In this case, consumers had to pay needlessly high bread prices at a time when wheat worldwide was cheap. So they ate less wheat than they had done earlier,[18] and/or had less money available to spend on other foods. Worse, the 'battle' caused soil erosion and exhaustion as trees were cut down and unsuitable land ploughed up. This had not been intended: Mussolini had told his committee at the outset that the *area* of land under wheat should not increase, but the various incentives ensured that it did.[19] More wheat, particularly in the south, meant fewer cattle or sheep and hence less manure. Mussolini's agricultural policy, like Stalin's, led to a wholesale slaughter of livestock.[20] It also meant a sharp decline in the production of olive oil, wine and silk, together with the loss of export markets and centuries-old orchards. No matter. Mussolini had won his 'battle'. He had also cut Italy's import bill and thus protected the balance of payments and the lira; and he had kept the farmers happy, if farmers are ever happy. Arguably his policy was no more ludicrous than the equally protective policies that were imposed elsewhere in Europe, and still are.

One aspect of this 'battle' deserves particular mention, as it was more innovative and provided a more justifiable propaganda triumph. In December 1928 the famous 'Mussolini law' was passed, setting aside 4.3 billion lire of public money to be spent on highly publicised land reclamation and irrigation schemes, in public–private partnerships with landowners who also had to contribute on pain of expropriation. The best-known example was the Pontine marshes, a notoriously malarial zone which was drained and settled by ex-servicemen from Venetia, and which was conveniently near Rome so foreign visitors could easily be shown around. Land reclamation meant more than just draining the swamps, or improving public health. It meant 'comprehensive improvement' (*bonifica integrale*), promoting real 'sustainable development', with aqueducts, reafforestation, roads, schools and townships all planned and coordinated. In Latium five new agrotowns – 'wheat cities' – were built, with great publicity and ceremony. Similar schemes were pursued in other malarial areas, particularly in the Tuscan *Maremma* and in western Sardinia. Perhaps 250,000 hectares were 'improved' in all by these schemes, although it is difficult to estimate as some works would have been done by landowners anyway, and others were left incomplete.[21] Mussolini often visited these projects and was personally committed to their success. It was a novel experiment and had wider aims: to produce more wheat of course, but also to boost the birth rate, to settle a conservative food-producing class of small landowners and to create jobs during the Depression. By the early 1930s nearly one-third of all public works jobs were linked to land reclamation schemes. But land reclamation was not just a make-work project. Roads and clean water *were* desperately needed in many areas, and malaria was a traditional curse of the countryside that had to be tackled before any rural prosperity was possible. Mussolini's schemes were a rare example of intelligent comprehensive planning, pushed through as usual by a very competent technocrat, Arrigo Serpieri, who in September 1929 became under-secretary at the Ministry of Agriculture. They were the exact opposite of the Soviet collectivisation of agriculture being implemented at the same time (also designed to produce more bread) and they were far more successful. The main criticism of them is that they literally did not go far enough. Mussolini's schemes stopped on the plains. The hill and mountain areas needed water and transport too, but apart from some successful reafforestation the regime neglected them. They did not grow much grain, they were too remote for easy publicity, and they were inhabited by the small peasant cultivators' traditional enemies, shepherds.

'The Battle for Births'

Despite these successes, Mussolini's most important 'battle' failed. From 1926 onwards Mussolini made speeches and wrote surprisingly frequent articles in his newspaper urging the Italians to have more children. He even instructed the Prefects to make sure that sufficient children were born in their provinces, and criticised them strongly if they failed, literally, to deliver.[22] Indeed, Mussolini soon became rather a bore on this theme, and a distinct touch of querulous crankiness was all too apparent. On this issue he did not set up a technocratic agency to achieve his goals, apart from the National Agency for the Protection of Motherhood and Infancy (ONPMI) which produced much useful social legislation and healthcare provision. Instead he preached, and practised what he preached. His third legitimate son, Romano, was born in September 1927, and his second daughter, Anna Maria, exactly two years later. His performance was particularly commendable since he still saw his wife only occasionally; both infants must have been conceived during the Christmas–New Year breaks, just as two of their elder siblings had been. Unfortunately, not all his senior colleagues followed his example. One or two, including the Chief of Police Bocchini, were bachelors, and several of the married ones had no children; none of them had as many as the *Duce*.

Even Mussolini realised he could not make marriage and procreation compulsory, but he could and did provide both incentives and deterrents. In 1926 he had a brilliant idea and introduced a remarkably high 'stealth tax' on bachelors, i.e. on unmarried men aged 25 or over; priests and servicemen were exempt, as were women, since being unmarried was not their fault. Four hundred mayors were dismissed in 1934 because they were bachelors. Top posts in the civil service and education, even in universities, were reserved for married men with children. Women were dismissed from state jobs unless they were war widows. Birth control information was banned, although condoms had to remain available in order to prevent venereal diseases. The proceeds of the bachelor tax went to pay for tax concessions to the fertile – if you had 10 children you paid no income tax at all – and also for marriage grants, birth grants, cheap housing and far better maternity services. Mussolini himself personally handed out quite large prizes (5,000 lire, plus free life insurance) to the nation's hundred most prolific couples, although usually only about ninety-five of them turned up, the others being in labour, or too exhausted.[23] After 1930 the government also provided free seaside holidays for poor children. Unlike most north Italians, Mussolini strongly approved of the southerners' higher birth rate. In his Ascension Day speech he praised Basilicata, a region 'not yet infected by the pernicious currents of contemporary civilisation'.[24] Some years later, on a visit to the appropriate town of Potenza, all the mothers joyfully held up their young children for the *Duce* to admire, to his great delight. Southern Italians, he proclaimed, were doing their patriotic duty, closing their eyes and thinking of Italy, and would receive their reward in the Empire.[25]

Nonetheless in bed, if nowhere else, the Italian people defied their *Duce*. Despite the bachelor tax, people married later: the median age was 28.3 for men and 24.9 for women in 1936–40, almost a year older than in 1921–5. They also had fewer children, down about 10 per cent from 1930–2 to 1935–7. Government policy may have prevented the birth rate falling even lower, but it did not raise it. It was a 'battle' Mussolini could not win. Italy in the 1920s and 1930s was a rapidly *urbanising* society, where millions of people moved each decade from the fecund countryside to the sterile cities. The population of Rome doubled between 1921 and 1940, the fastest increase ever in its long history, and Milan and Turin were not far behind. The *Duce* realised he could not stem the tide, but 'even if the laws prove to be useless we have to try, just as we try all the medicines even when, or especially when, the case is hopeless'.[26] So the 'battle for births' was accompanied by a 'battle for ruralisation', a futile campaign to 'empty the cities' which came a little oddly from a man who himself had moved from a village in Romagna to the provincial capital Forlì, then to Milan and finally to Rome, each time in order to take a better job. Permits became necessary before people were allowed to move from one province to another, and Prefects were encouraged to send newly arrived immigrants back home. They had more sense than to try, for the numbers involved were very high: if the policy had been applied, it would have created a huge class of serfs tied to the land.[27] The only aspect of this 'ruralisation' policy that succeeded was the 'land improvement' schemes, which did mean some new rural settlements, although usually of existing peasants, not townsmen. It is also true that emigration abroad declined very sharply under Fascism, from about 600,000 p.a. pre-war to about 50,000 p.a. in the late 1930s. This was certainly a real boost to the rural population, but it was the result not so much of Mussolini's policies as of the United States of America's new immigration restrictions, and because the Depression made it pointless to look for work elsewhere.[28] So Mussolini may not have produced more people, but like most dictators he did manage to keep most of the existing ones in.

It is easy to mock Mussolini's efforts to boost births, but it is also easy to defend them. Anyone writing 80 years later is mindful that in the early twenty-first century the Italian birth rate is about 1.3 children per woman, 40 per cent below replacement level. A consistently low birth rate means not only fewer soldiers but also, in the long run, demographic and social disaster: fewer workers of all kinds, fewer consumers, economic stagnation and an ageing population – the antithesis of Fascist ideals but also of any successful or sustainable society. Moreover, Mussolini's ideas were a great deal more sensible than those of the 'degenerationist' social scientists (Niceforo et al) of his youth, who regarded southerners as innate criminals; and they were certainly more humane than the 'eugenic' programmes of compulsory sterilisation practised in the 1930s in Scandinavia and in the more progressive states of the United States of America as well as in Germany. If the extra children he hoped to produce turned out to be mainly southern peasants, that was fine by him; when they grew up they would make admirable soldiers, as they had in 1915–18. Nevertheless he failed, on an issue he regarded as vitally important. In 1937 he admitted defeat and blamed it on the Italians' moral defects, on their selfish desire for bourgeois comfort rather than children or Empire.[29] He had a point, and with five legitimate children he was entitled to make it.

Marching in Rome

Mussolini's efforts at improvement schemes were unfortunately not confined to the countryside near Rome, but extended into the city itself. Like many dictators, he wanted a monument, a capital city worthy of his regime. In 1925 he told the new governor of the city to clear the areas round the Teatro Marcello, the Capitol and the Pantheon: 'everything that has grown around there during the centuries of decadence must disappear. Within five years the Pantheon should be visible from piazza Colonna, across open space . . . a third Rome will arise on the hills and on the banks of the sacred river.'[30] His plans had two aspects, both of them designed to emphasise 'Romanness' (*romanità*). First, it meant a free hand for archaeologists, charged with revealing the buildings and streets of the ancient city, e.g. in the Forum area or in piazza Argentina. Even Rome's main concert hall was destroyed in order to leave a space around Augustus's tomb. Secondly, and more importantly to the *Duce*, it meant pulling down existing medieval or Renaissance quarters and constructing imposing new buildings and 'Roman roads', along which Mussolini's new legions might march. A very picturesque zone, from piazza Montanara and the Teatro di Marcello to St Maria Cosmedin at the foot of the Aventine, was laid waste simply to help traffic flow to and from the southern suburbs. The new road, like via dell' Impero, led straight into piazza Venezia which thus became Italy's biggest bottleneck, with main roads flowing into it from all directions. This was terrible planning, but no matter: Mussolini's office in palazzo Venezia was on one side of the square, and he wanted to be at the hub of the city's activity. Sometimes the two aspects of *romanità*, the archaeological and the roadworks, were combined. Via dell' Impero (now via dei Fori Imperiali), between Colosseum and Capitol, was built *over* much of the carefully excavated Forum and opened in 1932 by Mussolini himself, on horseback. It had, and still has, four marble plaques with maps showing the expansion of the Roman Empire at various dates; a fifth plaque, now 'lost', was added after 1936 depicting Mussolini's new empire as well.

The fundamental problem in Rome was that Mussolini had boundless ambition, virtually complete power to decide, and no taste. His mistress Margherita Sarfatti kept him right on paintings but had little interest in architecture, let alone town planning. He had lived in Milan for 10 years and thereafter in Rome, but he had no grasp of what makes a city – its complex diversity, its living traditions, its unexpectedness, its capacity for variety and surprise. Dictators always fear the old quarters of their capital cities, since they are usually overcrowded and it is difficult to know what is happening within them. Mussolini disliked them particularly strongly, as they reminded everyone of the centuries of papal rule. He wanted a planned, orderly, disciplined Rome, to be the fit capital of a planned, orderly, disciplined Italy; and he wanted it quickly. So he pulled down much of the city centre, displaced thousands of the inhabitants, revealed the ancient classical buildings and built a few more of his own as a backcloth to his processions and ceremonies. Rome may not have been built in a day, but much of it was destroyed in a decade. It was a new Sack of Rome, worthy not so much of Charles V's troops as of the Vandals. Of course, he might have done even more damage, for example, by building a genuine political-administrative complex in the centre. In fact, government buildings remained scattered round the city as usual, to no discernible plan, and new ones were often sited on the periphery. Further out, indeed, he actually did some good. The 'University City' proved quite useful and was even admired, and both the new Foreign Ministry building and the sports complex at Foro Italico had at least the great merit of being a long way away. So was the 'Rome Universal Exhibition' (EUR) planned for the regime's twentieth anniversary celebrations in 1942 on a site halfway to Ostia. EUR, with its pseudo-classical buildings in 'Fascist style' and its ultra-wide streets, embodied the Fascist version of 'Romanness'.[31]

What was good for Rome was also good for Mussolini's birthplace. In 1925, after a landslide on the hill at Predappio, he told the Minister of Public Works to move the whole village and all its inhabitants down to Dovia, where decent houses and a school could be built: 'I do not hide from you that many *Predappiesi* will be grief-stricken at having to move their tents to Dovia, but no one, I think, wants to die in an unexpected landslide and the state cannot throw millions away just to meet a few people's parish-pump wishes.'[32] Mussolini was clearly settling some old scores here. He himself came from Dovia and had been bullied as a young child when sent from his mother's schoolroom there to another primary school in Predappio. Settling more scores, he sent both Balbo and Farinacci to the ceremony of laying the first stone at Predappio Nuova, 'New Predappio', but he did not go himself.

Summary

Mussolini's 'battles' were surprisingly successful, apart from the 'battle for births'. It is striking that his policies, unlike most political solutions to socio-economic problems, did not actually make matters worse, except in Rome and some fruit-growing zones. As with the railways, policing and the 'reconciliation' with the Church, Mussolini knew how to get results. He made speeches, wrote articles and allocated resources, but the real key was to find the right man, give him clear instructions, keep an eye on him, back him up for a time and then dismiss him whenever he became too popular or unpopular. To wage his 'battles' Mussolini usually (but not always) used special institutions and handpicked technical experts, by-passing the normal civil service. These men brooked no debate and underwent no normal processes of consultation and scrutiny. They operated on clear lines of command and responsibility, reporting directly to the *Duce*. As in war, any opposition was seen as treachery. Mussolini was normally quite prepared to safeguard established interests but when he seriously wanted something done, that was how he did it. He was a pioneer of 'militarism', the application of military techniques to civilian life, and he chose his men well. They were tough-minded technocrats, for the most part neither 'Fascists' nor from the traditional Liberal elite, and they usually achieved the goals Mussolini had set them. But, of course, they were not really fighting 'battles' at all, except perhaps in Sicily. Unlike many dictators, Mussolini did not use force. He did not need to, since the issues were not too controversial. In any case, he controlled the media and he could use propaganda. He knew, too, that bureaucratic agencies are good at achieving limited specific short-term goals, if given enough resources and political backing. Moreover, he knew that he would take the credit.

But his real 'battle' was more ambitious. He wanted to transform Italian values, behaviour and society: to implement a 'comprehensive improvement scheme' for the whole country. The individual 'battles' were part of an overriding strategy, to found a new Italy, inhabited by responsible, disciplined, healthy and youthful Italians – brave, active risk-takers with a social conscience. As he told the Fascist party congress in 1925, 'We want to Fascistise the nation, to the extent that in future "Italian" and "Fascist", rather like "Italian" and "Catholic", are pretty much the same thing.'[33] But even this was not the whole story. In fact, what Mussolini wanted was a real battle, or rather a real war. In December 1925 he told the Chamber, 'I consider the nation as being in a permanent state of war. I have said, and I repeat, that the next five or ten years will be decisive for the destiny of our people . . . we, who have arrived a little late on the world scene, are not permitted to disperse our energies.'[34] The 'battles' were not ends in themselves but means to an end; an end of greater national power and imperial expansion. A rural Italy would produce more children and therefore more soldiers, as well as more food to feed them. The *Duce* was quite explicit about this. In his Ascension Day speech, he compared the existing 40 million Italians with the 90 million Germans and the 200 million Slavs, to say nothing of the extra millions that the British and French could mobilise from their colonies. He set a target of 60 million Italians by 1950: 'If we become fewer, gentlemen, we will not build an empire, we will become a colony!'[35] Note, incidentally, that he assumed that success in war depended on manpower, on having more recruits than the other side. So his 'battles' were not so conservative after all. They were the first stage of a social transformation, and of an imperial dream.

Notes

1 Speech of Ascension Day, 26 May 1927, in *OO* xxii, pp. 360–90.

2 P. Ciocca and G. Toniolo, *L'Economia Italiana durante il Fascismo* (Bologna, 1976), p. 31; V. Zamagni, *The Economic History of Italy 1860–1990* (Oxford, 1993), pp. 243ff.

3 Y. De Begnac, *Taccuini Mussoliniani* (Bologna, 1990), p. 518.

4 Mussolini to Prefects, 12 July 1926; *OO* xl, p. 90.

5 ACS, *Autografi del Duce*, cassetta di zinco, scat. 3, f. 4; *OO* xl, pp. 110–18. Much the same rhetoric was used by Romano Prodi 70 years later, in his 'battle' to *abolish* the lira; it too led to years of easily avoidable stagnation.

6 Speech of 18 August 1926 at Pesaro; *OO* xxii, pp. 196–8.

7 Autograph note of December 1927, in ACS, *Autografi* cit., cassetta di zinco, scat. 6.

8 Mussolini to Prefect of Turin, 5 July 1927; *OO* xl, p. 393.

9 Mussolini to Volpi and Stringher, 26 April 1927, in ACS, *Autografi* cit., cassetta di zinco, scat. 5; *OO* xxxvii, pp. 73–6; F. Guarneri, *Battaglie Economiche* i (Milan 1953), p. 159; J.S. Cohen, 'The 1927 revaluation of the lira', in *Economic History Review* xxv (1972), pp. 642–54.

10 Mussolini to Gasti, 28 May 1923; *OO* xxxviii, pp. 345–6.

11 C. Duggan, *Fascism and the Mafia* (New Haven, 1989), pp. 136, 245.

12 *OO* xli, p. 67; Duggan, *Fascism and the Mafia* cit., p. 248.

13 C.T. Schmidt, *The Plough and the Sword* (New York, 1938), p. 46; J.S. Cohen, 'Fascism and agriculture in Italy: policies and consequences', in *Economic History Review* xxxii (1979), pp. 70–87; essays by Cohen and Tattara in G. Toniolo (ed.), *Lo Sviluppo Economico Italiano* (Bari, 1973); G. Barone, *Mezzogiorno e Modernizzazione* (Turin, 1986).

14 Speech to agricultural syndicate representatives, 30 July 1925; R. Festa Campanile and R. Fittipaldi, *Mussolini e la Battaglia del Grano* (Rome, 1931), p. 54; *OO* xxii, p. 377.

15 Circular to Prefects, 15 February 1930; ACS, SPD, c. ris., b. 28, f. 8.

16 Example in *OO* xxvii, pp. 100–2.

17 Proclamation, 24 March 1928, for 'Bread Day' 1928; *OO* xxiii, p. 343.

18 Istat, *Sommario di Statistiche Storiche dell' Italia 1861–1965* (Rome, 1968), p. 134. Consumption of wheat fell from 7.24 million tonnes p.a. in 1926–30 to 6.76 million in 1931–5.

19 On 4 July 1925; *OO* xxi, pp. 372–3. But see S. Alberti ('Aspetti statistici dei risultati della battaglia del grano', in *Atti della VII Riunione Scientifica della Società Italiana di Statistica* (Rome, 1943), pp. 531–2), who estimated that the area under wheat increased by 460,000 hectares between 1922–4 and 1938–40; Schmidt, *The Plough and the Sword* cit., pp. 53–4, thought there were 300,000 hectares more in 1936 than in 1921–5.

20 The livestock census of 1930 found fewer cattle than in 1908, with over 11 per cent lost between 1926 and 1930; Schmidt, *The Plough and the Sword* cit., p. 62.

21 M. Bandini, *Agricoltura e Crisi* (Florence, 1937), p. 137.

22 Mussolini to Prefects, 30 March 1928, in *OO* xli, pp. 68–9; Mussolini to Prefect of Novara, 23 January 1929, in *OO* xli, p. 241; also to *podestà* of Asti, 4 March 1928, in ACS, *Autografi del Duce*, cassetta di zinco, scat. 2.

23 Speech at palazzo Venezia, 19 December 1936, in *OO* xxviii, pp. 95–6.

24 Ascension Day speech, 26 May 1927; *OO* xxii, p. 364.

25 Speech at Potenza, 27 August 1936; *OO* xxviii, pp. 30–1.

26 *Gerarchia*, September 1928; *OO* xxiii, p. 215.

27 'Sfollare le città', in *Popolo d'Italia*, 22 November 1928; *OO* xxiii, pp. 256–8.

28 D.V. Glass, *The Struggle for Population* (Oxford, 1936); D.V. Glass, *Population Policies and Movements* (Oxford, 1940), pp. 219–68; C. Ipsen, *Dictating Demography* (Cambridge, 1996).

29 'Cifre in declino', in *Popolo d'Italia*, 30 January 1937; *OO* xxviii, pp. 110–11.

30 Speech at installation of first Governor of Rome, 31 December 1925; *OO* xxii, p. 48.

31 G. Zucconi, *La Città Contesa* (Milan, 1989); A. Cederna, *Mussolini Urbanista* (Bari, 1979).

32 Mussolini to Minister of Public Works Giuriati, 18 March 1925; *OO* xxxix, pp. 337–8.

33 Speech to PNF Congress 1925; *OO* xxi, p. 362.

34 Speech to Chamber of Deputies, 11 December 1925; *OO* xxii, p. 37.

35 Ascension Day speech, 26 May 1927; *OO* xxii, pp. 360–90, at p. 367.

Chapter 6

At the Height of his Power?
The Regime and the *Duce* 1929–35

Family and Personality

By 1929 Mussolini's regime was firmly established, endorsed by Church and king. He had already won some of his 'battles', for example against the Mafia and against the currency speculators, and he was admired both at home and abroad. In September he at last brought his wife and family – which now included two very young children, one just born – to Rome, and settled down with them all (and with his cat Pippo, who came with him from via Rasella) in the villa Torlonia, off via Nomentana. Villa Torlonia was a gloomy building, and Mussolini found little relaxation or enjoyment there. His wife Rachele had no political interests and was far too sharp-tongued. Benito might have been dictator of Italy, but Rachele was dictator at home. She was resolutely determined to remain a peasant woman from the Romagna, and reared hens, rabbits and pigs in the middle of Rome. She despised her husband's job and knew it would all end in tears. Living in villa Torlonia with his family was tantamount to self-imposed 'internal exile' (*confino*) for Mussolini. No longer did he take his morning rides in the villa Borghese; instead, he rode in the grounds of villa Torlonia and he rode alone, or alone apart from his riding instructor Ridolfi. He had been in prison 11 times, and would be again in 1943; but arguably his longest sentence was served in villa Torlonia.

The eldest daughter, Edda, was now in her late teens and causing Mussolini some anxiety. He had, in effect, to veto a couple of suitors, one of them because the young man made the disastrous mistake of asking Mussolini how much the dowry would be. The other applicant was the son of a colonel but Jewish, and both families opposed the union – Mussolini particularly so, as he thought mixed marriages were bound to be unhappy and in any case he had just signed the Lateran Pacts with the Church.[1] Eventually, after some family manoeuvres, Edda married a rising young diplomat Galeazzo Ciano, the son of Mussolini's favourite minister Costanzo. Galeazzo was a good match. He was handsome, clever and rich; he was also likeable and amusing, and Mussolini was delighted. In April 1930 the Mussolinis held a vast wedding reception at villa Torlonia for 500 guests. The king, notoriously tight-fisted, sent Edda a brooch, which she used in 1943 to bribe her children's way into Switzerland. This reception was one of the very rare occasions when other people were invited to Mussolini's house or when anybody ever saw his wife. Rachele disliked her daughter, disliked the wedding ceremonies, disliked the guests and strongly disliked Galeazzo, far too effete and aristocratic for her taste. But Edda was happy, for a time, and by December 1931 Benito, still only 48 years old, was a grandfather; less than five years later Galeazzo was Foreign Minister.

In September 1929 Mussolini not only moved his residence, he also moved his workplace from palazzo Chigi to the far more imposing palazzo Venezia, using the huge *Sala del Mappamondo* as his office. Visitors had to cross it diagonally to reach his desk in the far corner, an intimidating ordeal particularly for ministers, who had to run across the room and were not offered a chair when they finally arrived. They noted that he kept his desk remarkably tidy, demonstrating his love of order; inside the drawer was a loaded revolver. He could see all the busy traffic of Rome from his office window; and he could, on occasion, step out on to the balcony and address the massed crowd below in piazza Venezia. He also had plenty of people to talk to: he saw his top officials in the morning, and a host of visitors in the late afternoon. He preferred to meet people, even journalists, individually and group meetings were rare – mostly the Council of Ministers once a month, and the occasional Grand Council. At around 2.00 p.m. he went back to villa Torlonia for lunch, which rarely took more than 10 minutes and usually consisted of a little pasta and vegetables, followed by a lot of fruit. He drank milk, avoiding wine and even tea or coffee, although he liked camomile tea. Then he might relax with his family, perhaps playing tennis for a time or reading the newspapers. He was very fond of his children, sent them to state schools on principle and spent time with them in the afternoon; his own father had been stern, but he himself was very indulgent. At around 5.00 p.m. he would return to his office. He still liked women and although he at last ditched the ageing Margherita Sarfatti in the early 1930s, he had several other long-standing mistresses as well as brief one-evening stands in palazzo Venezia with admiring 'visitors': as with food, 10 minutes was quite long enough. By 9.00 p.m. he was back in villa Torlonia for some more fast food, a phone call to Arnaldo about the next day's *Popolo d'Italia*, and a film shown in one of the villa's reception rooms. Laurel and Hardy's films were his favourites, not surprisingly for a man with a genius for getting himself into another fine mess. As for his famous violin, Mussolini apparently stopped playing it around 1930, perhaps because of the jokes comparing him to Nero.[2] By 11.00 p.m. he was in bed and, contrary to myth, slept soundly for seven or eight hours. Twice a week he visited the king. Somehow he managed to fit in journalism, writing regular articles for his newspaper and also for American press agencies, which paid well and promptly – he needed the money, for he had five children and he still took no salary for his government posts. This routine was of course disrupted in the summer, when Mussolini took the family to Riccione or to Rocca delle Caminate, a medieval castle which was restored and donated to him in 1930 by the people of Forlì. He also toured the country on occasions, particularly in the autumn, and liked to celebrate anniversaries and attend commemorative parades in the provinces.

In short, Mussolini in the early 1930s led a stable, ordered existence, all work and family, for the first time in his life. He was busy but he organised his time well. He himself, in ironic mood, wrote an article in 1933 entitled 'The Marvellous Activity of the Head of Government', describing a typical day at the office:

After having received early in the morning his customary daily visits from the Commander of the *Carabinieri*, the Under-secretary at the Presidency of the Council of Ministers, the Chief of Police, the Private Secretary, the Head of the Press Office, the Under-secretary at the Foreign Ministry, the Under-secretary at the Ministry of the Interior and the Secretary of the Party, the Head of Government received, the same morning, the British ambassador who engaged him in discussion of current political issues, and Senator Dall'Olio for the monthly report of the Supreme Commission of Defence. After 2.00 p.m. he received continuous visits from the hon. Polverelli and from ministers De Bono, Acerbo, Crollalanza and Jung who reported on matters concerning their departments; the Under-secretaries Baistrocchi at the Ministry of War and Ricci at the Ministry of National Education; the Governor of Rome, who reported on issues concerning the capital; the Director General of the Savings Banks; the hon. De Cicco, Italian consul at Beirut; the German ambassador von Hassell who introduced the three new military attachés; the hon. Barenghi, who reported on the situation at Ansaldo [steelworks]; col. Gambelli of the Supreme Commission of Defence; the hon. Parisio of the Royal Italian Automobile Club and Commendatore Anelli of Cremona who raised some questions concerning pianoforte manufacture.[3]

In 1930–1 Mussolini suffered a huge personal and political loss. Back in October 1922 he had put his brother Arnaldo in charge of the *Popolo d'Italia* in Milan, and this arrangement worked very well. Benito still used the paper as his mouthpiece and told Arnaldo which issues to stress; Arnaldo kept Benito in touch with northern opinion, and did not abuse his position. However, in autumn 1929 Arnaldo's teenage son, Alessandro, contracted leukaemia and died in the following summer. Arnaldo never recovered. Benito invited him down to Rome on lengthy visits and persuaded him to visit Libya in the spring of 1931, but it was no use. He had no wish to live, and in December 1931 he too died, of heart failure. He had been Mussolini's sole brother, friend and confidant, the one person on earth whom the *Duce* fully trusted. Arnaldo had been a generous and religious man, stable and quick to forgive; quite different from Benito, but Benito could appreciate these qualities in others and knew that Arnaldo's advice would be judicious and humane. He had needed Arnaldo, and he knew it. He immediately wrote a quite sensitive, detailed account of his brother's life, published the following year.[4] For the rest of his life Mussolini had no one to turn to for advice or even for reliable information. He had no friends or cronies; he had no religious beliefs; he did not even have a Fool to mock his pretensions. He did have a highly intelligent sister, Edvige, who moved to Rome after Arnaldo's death and lived nearby, but she had her own husband and family to care for and was much involved in charity work. Inasmuch as she had any influence, it was to secure people's release from *confino*, but she could not secure it for the *Duce*.

Government and Colleagues

Mussolini's problem now was boredom. After all, by the summer of 1933 he was 50, had been Prime Minister for over 10 years, and had been a prominent national journalist and politician for 10 years before that. As his article on his own 'Marvellous Activity' implied, he was beginning to wonder if it was all worthwhile. Despite all the bluster and the adaptation to circumstances, he had become stuck in a surprisingly conventional lifestyle that did not provide the stimuli he needed. He was a man who needed challenges. Italian politics no longer provided them, mainly because of his own efforts. Since he now had nothing much to do, he developed a close personal interest in trivialities. He bombarded the party secretary with tales of inactive branches, and reproved ministers for the failings of their departments: the kilometre signs at Fano were too close to each other; the newly planted trees on the road from Lodi to Piacenza needed to be properly staked, or they would fall down in a storm; there was excessive luxury in the new Fascist youth building at Viterbo.[5] He banned Christmas trees, in his view an absurd German custom that impoverished still further Italy's forest resources. At 5.35 p.m. on 31 December 1928, rather late in the day, he sent telegrams to all the Prefects telling them that 'on the last night of last year there was disorder in some towns after excessive drinking. Ensure that scandals of this kind do not occur tonight.'[6] Mussolini had become a 'grumpy old man', forever complaining; or, to put it more politely, a Don Quixote anxious to right all conceivable wrongs. Indeed, he praised Don Quixote precisely for his commitment to his own values and for his resolute lack of common sense: 'Quixote is the best aspect of ourselves.'[7]

All this had its comic side, but Mussolini was serious. He aimed to transform Italian values at home and the image of Italy abroad. Not content with having invented Fascism, he invented health Fascism too. He told the doctors' syndicate in 1931 that 'I am profoundly convinced that our way of eating, dressing, working and sleeping, all aspects of our daily habits, must be reformed.'[8] He himself did not smoke, ate sparingly, drank very little, and took plenty of exercise. He boasted that he had 'made my body into a constantly surveyed and supervised engine, that runs with absolute regularity'.[9] As for Italy's image, here too his constant care was evident. He instructed his diplomats abroad not to promote Italian musical events: 'except for symphony orchestras, whose playing gives an idea of collective discipline. Everything else should be ignored. It is high time that the world, i.e. hundreds of millions of people, begin to know a different type of Italian from the usual tenor or mandolin player performing for the entertainment of others. Caruso and similar people were or are the old Italy.'[10] So to play the mandolin was to be automatically suspected of anti-Fascism. Clearly Mussolini was no longer the acute, streetwise mediator of his early days in office. Despite his claims about his health, in appearance he was ageing fast, going bald and putting on weight, and this was a serious matter in a regime whose very anthem was 'Youth' (*Giovinezza*). He had lost both his best advisers, Arnaldo and Margherita Sarfatti. He was isolated, mistrustful and increasingly frustrated, and he no longer needed to bother much about what was politically feasible. This was not a recipe for good government. Mussolini was already in decline, although it was not evident as yet to the general public.

His ministers, however, did begin to notice. In autumn 1929 Mussolini reshuffled his government again, giving up the three service ministries (Aviation went to Balbo), the Foreign Ministry (to Dino Grandi), the Ministry of Public Works (to Michele Bianchi) and the Ministry of

Corporations (to Giuseppe Bottai). He kept the Interior Ministry, but the government seemed now broader and more 'Fascist', containing not only these four ex-*squadristi* but also others, e.g. Leandro Arpinati, under-secretary at the Interior, Francesco Giunta, under-secretary at the Presidency of the Council of Ministers, as well as the party secretary Augusto Turati. However, this experiment in 'Fascist government' was not a success. The new men were too independent-minded and not respectful enough. Mussolini did not trust them, and could no longer be bothered to argue with them. In August 1931 he instructed the state news agency not to publish any speech by a minister or under-secretary without his author-isation.[11] Soon he began to purge them, not from paranoia (although he did fear Balbo) but from impatience and a sense of superiority over lesser mortals. Turati, at the head of the party, went in October 1930; his successor Giuriati in December 1931. In July 1932 Mussolini took back the Foreign Ministry and the Ministry of Corporations himself, and also replaced Rocco at Justice and Giunta at the Presidency by others. The following year he took back the three service ministries and dismissed the outspoken Arpinati. Even the long-serving Costanzo Ciano left the government in 1934. In January 1935 Guido Jung was dismissed from the Ministry of Finance. When Mussolini sacked people he often did it abruptly, without warning or explanation, and he conspicuously failed to reward success. Several of his top men were not only dismissed, but banished: Balbo was sent off to govern Libya, Grandi to be ambassador in London, Arpinati and Turati to the islands. Meanwhile the *Duce* ran six ministries and in 1935 made himself Colonial Minister as well. As Giuriati put it, he wanted people to believe he was not only the conductor of the orchestra, but that he played all the principal instruments himself.[12]

Once again, the result was that most decisions were taken in practice by under-secretaries or by senior civil servants, who may have been competent administrators but lacked the political standing to innovate or the political motive to check whether decisions were actually proving effective. Alternatively, of course, they were taken in the technocratic specialist agencies, which became ever more significant and took over more functions as 'normal' government declined (see p. 104). The 'Fascist state' was not monolithic. It was a network of politicised institutions, regulating their own spheres and protecting their own interests. Even so, it mattered that the quality of Mussolini's ministers and under-secretaries undoubtedly fell sharply in the early 1930s. In the 1920s he had consistently chosen well: men like Rocco, Federzoni, De' Stefani, Volpi, Gentile, and Costanzo Ciano were all intelligent, able ministers, and Mussolini had allowed them a fairly free hand. Even in 1929-32 the government was reasonably lively and energetic. But the reshuffles of 1932 onwards resulted in a government of pliable men, none more so than Arpinati's replacement as under-secretary at the Interior, Guido Buffarini Guidi, 'the Tuscan secretary, more cunning than any other Tuscan, past, present or future'.[13] Cesare Maria De Vecchi, regarded as a complete buffoon by everybody including the *Duce*, became Minister of Education in 1935. It is clear that Mussolini by this time did not want competent colleagues. As he began to contemplate controversial military adventures abroad and more 'totalitarian' efforts at home, and perhaps half aware that he was easily influenced by strong-minded men who might deflect him from his purpose, he wanted people who would not ask questions or raise objections. So he appointed a Ministry of All the Mediocrities, and furthermore mediocrities who were not subject to press or parliamentary criticism, whose activities were not coordinated, and who knew that their time in office would be limited. Each minister answered individually to the *Duce*, competing to catch his ear and avoid his eye. The best strategy for such men was to do what they were told, flatter Mussolini whenever possible, keep on the right side of Buffarini Guidi and the new party secretary Starace, and cash in while the going was good.

This was evident to his colleagues, but of course they could not speak out. Their wives had more latitude. In January 1935 Serpieri's wife complained bitterly on the telephone to a friend about the latest government reshuffle, which had included her husband's dismissal from his post as under-secretary at Agriculture:

the choice is horrible, people who cannot put any intelligence into their work because they don't know anything . . . for example, that new Finance minister, at such a dangerous time as this! My personal impression is that he [Mussolini] must have had a brain storm! . . . he treats men too much like pawns . . . the newspapers say nothing, nobody dares to criticise what he does, nobody tells him what people are saying . . . don't you see he's becoming more and more despotic? Alas, that nowadays we live in this kind of regime.[14]

The telephone was of course tapped, and Serpieri had to grovel to Mussolini on his wife's behalf ('she is all instinct, spontaneity and nerves'), but the incident shows how disaffected and helpless even the 'technocratic' government insiders felt by this time, and what they thought of Mussolini's decision-making.

It is interesting to look at the fate of Mussolini's two closest collaborators in 1929–30, the party secretary, Turati, and the under-secretary at the Interior, Arpinati. After Turati had been dismissed in October 1930 he became editor of *La Stampa* in Turin, and his many enemies felt free to destroy him. Farinacci spread rumours in his newspaper about sex scandals, and Starace joined in. Mussolini did not believe the stories or care whether they were true or not. He knew Arnaldo was backing Turati and he himself (unusually for Mussolini) rather admired Turati as a man and a politician, but he packed him off to exile for a few years on Rhodes, and later to East Africa. He had two reasons, both revealing. As editor of *La Stampa*, Turati had been distinctly tiresome. He had kept sending in reports about party branches as if he were still party secretary, had stressed how much government policy had annoyed the Catholics in 1931, and had campaigned against high electricity prices even though the electricity companies had just made large financial contributions to the Italian Academy.[15] Mussolini was not interested in these issues. What he wanted now was loyalty, and it had to be profuse and unconditional. The other reason, of course, was that Turati was dispensable. He was no longer party secretary, whereas Starace was; and Farinacci was still very influential. Mussolini did not believe in taking unnecessary risks, and even in 1931–2 he knew the limits to his power. 'Do you really think,' he asked De Begnac years later, 'that Mussolini is enough to quell and cancel the torrent of calumnies that has brought a man down? . . . [the episode was] part of the climate of permanent crisis in the country, which he [Turati] made a vigorous contribution to containing.'[16] The phrase was significant. Even in the early 1930s Mussolini was not sure that the 'permanent crisis' was over, nor that the regime was secure.

Mussolini's other close collaborator in this period, Leandro Arpinati, suffered an even worse fate. Arpinati was an outspoken, independent man, an honest ex-anarchist who was very popular in his native Romagna. As under-secretary at the Interior, he was tough on dissenters and believed very firmly in applying the law, but he wanted a limited state and disliked anything that smacked of religion, monarchy, protectionism or Socialism, e.g. the Lateran Pacts, the syndicates, and the corporations. Clearly he did not approve of the all-embracing, 'totalitarian' regime that was developing in the 1930s, and he had a serious row with Starace that almost ended in a duel. However, his real offence was to have insisted that no favours be granted to Mussolini's wife Rachele when she applied for the concession of the mineral waters at the Terme di Castrocaro. He told the Prefect of Forlì that 'Italy is not a fief of the Mussolini family', and the Prefect reported these words to the *Duce*. This was a direct challenge to the family honour, and no Italian could ignore it. Mussolini told him to resign and Arpinati did, but without the usual sycophancy: 'To His Excellency Benito Mussolini, Head of Government. Following from and in compliance with the invitation sent me in today's letter, I resign from the post of Under-secretary at the Interior. With unchanged devotion, Arpinati.'[17] He was also thrown out of parliament and the party. Soon he was 'confined' on the Lipari islands, and later placed under house arrest at home near Bologna. His fall had a big impact. At Bologna, the Fascist party was hastily purged and the Prefect replaced. Elsewhere, some of the *gerarchi* breathed sighs of relief. Arpinati had been tough on corruption and contemptuous of most Fascists; his successor Buffarini Guidi was far more prudent. On the other hand, Arpinati had been de facto minister of the Interior. If he could be packed off to the islands without having committed any legal offence, indeed merely for being honest, who was safe? Did it mean that the party secretary would always triumph over state officials, quite contrary to Mussolini's repeated declarations? And if Mussolini could not take honest advice from an old friend, what was the regime becoming?[18]

Still, it could have been worse. Despite the occasional disgrace and banishment, Mussolini's colleagues did not really fear him. None of them was shot, at least until 1944, and he tolerated their corruption with resigned good humour: there was 'nothing to be done about the rats in the grain store', for if he dismissed them he would have to appoint new men who would have empty pockets.[19] He was not much of a threat to them, nor they to him. The only one who might have been, Balbo, built an empire at the Aviation Ministry between 1929 and 1933 and became extremely popular worldwide after a daring transatlantic flight with 24 seaplanes to Chicago. Balbo then suggested that the armed forces needed to be better coordinated, and that he himself should become chief of general staff instead of Badoglio. This move would obviously have infuriated the army, and might have given Balbo power over all three services.[20] Mussolini therefore sent him off, at the height of his popularity, to govern Libya – a nice ironic touch, since Badoglio was the existing governor. Balbo grumbled on the telephone so that Mussolini would know, and replied to the *Duce*: 'My Great Leader! Always at your Orders! I have received your letter and while I thank you for your kind words I place my post as Minister of Aviation at your disposal';[21] but he went. The other ex-*squadristi* ministers dismissed in 1932–3 also caused no trouble. They still had status as leading *gerarchi* of the regime and they remained on the Grand Council, although admittedly the Grand Council met less often, and when it did only the top men dared to speak. Farinacci still wrote his letters of complaint and posed as custodian of the Holy Grail, but Mussolini was prepared to tolerate him as a harmless outlet for squad disaffection, and he also enjoyed Farinacci's robust black humour. Throughout the regime Farinacci, with a suspect Masonic past, acted as leader of the rightist opposition, ran his own newspaper and was often openly critical of government policy; yet he was never touched nor exiled, except very notionally to Cremona.

There was, nonetheless, even less debate or sense of collective responsibility in Mussolini's government and entourage than there had been earlier. Indeed, there was quite a strong sense of mutual suspicion, and certainly a reluctance to take initiatives or bear unwelcome news. The frustrated *gerarchi* were a quarrelsome bunch, much given to personal disputes over money, honour or women. Sometimes they fought duels. Several of them took to their diaries, and wrote wonderfully sharp and malevolent accounts of Mussolini's doings. Others denounced their colleagues to the *Duce*, who would pass on these comments to the alleged offender together with the name of the source, thus boosting the atmosphere of intrigue and suspicion. A few, including Grandi and Bottai, flattered Mussolini outrageously; he saw through it, of course, but enjoyed it just the same.[22] Neither of them, however, was in the same league as Buffarini Guidi, a true master of the art of sycophancy. After one of Mussolini's speeches, Buffarini Guidi congratulated him: 'Permit me, *Duce*, to tell you personally that your speech, wonderful in content, attained a form so lofty and perfect that places it among the masterpieces of great classical oratory of all time.'[23] The *gerarchi* had to behave like this because they could not rely on each other for support, and because they depended entirely on Mussolini. In essence they were always divided between the educated 'liberal Fascists' or ex-Nationalists on the one hand, and the rude provincials, frustrated and betrayed, on the other; the split became clear cut in 1943, but had long existed. Mussolini had few illusions about either group. In 1939 he told Galeazzo Ciano that De Bono was 'an old cretin. Not because of his years, which can respect the intellect if it ever existed, but because he always was a cretin and now he has grown old as well.'[24]

Party Matters

Turati, when party secretary, had carried out large-scale purges (see p. 107) and his successor Giuriati was even more zealous, bringing the total membership down to around 800,000 by September 1931. He did, however, found the 'Young Fascists', aged 18–21, as a counterweight to the Catholic youth clubs; their motto, proposed by the *Duce* himself, was 'Believe, Obey, Fight' ('*Credere, Obbedire, Combattere*'). The slogan was significant, and not only for the 'Young Fascists'. The whole party was now to be obedient, socially active and militarist. To achieve this end, in December 1931 Mussolini appointed a new party secretary, Achille Starace, who remained in the post until late 1939. In October 1932, to celebrate the tenth anniversary of the 'March on Rome', Starace opened the party's doors to new members again, and numbers rose 40 per cent in a year; by October 1934 there were 1.8 million members, and by 1936 over two million. Membership was now required for all public-sector jobs, including local government and the agencies. However, it remained true throughout the regime that some were more Fascist than others: to have been in the party before October 1922 gave you higher credentials, to have been a *squadrista* even more, best of all to have been in piazza San Sepolcro at the founding meeting in 1919. At any rate Starace, 'the honest corporal', was just the man to discipline the party. His job, essentially, was to mobilise popular support for the regime. This was an important task, and particularly so during the Depression since unrest was probable. Starace was unquestionably loyal and in his way efficient, but wonderfully limited in imagination or sense. His idea of how to mobilise support was to hold endless parades and to think up ceremonies of increasing complexity. His first act was to introduce a ludicrous ritual known as the 'Salute to the *Duce*'. After that it was downhill all the way. By 1933 the word *Duce* had to be written in capital letters, *DUCE*. In October 1935 he told the party's federal secretaries to be ever vigilant: they should 'sleep for not more than seven hours, with only one eye shut'. Two years later this wimpishness was no more: now they should 'reduce the time of sleeping by 50 per cent and double the number of eyes open'.[25] Even Mussolini sometimes mocked Starace's directives. When Starace decreed that all party communications should henceforth end with the words '*Viva il DUCE*', Mussolini objected that often he had to dismiss people: 'You are sacked. *Viva il DUCE*' did not sound quite right.[26] Still, he kept this absurd man in his key job for eight years. Starace had obvious faults and was a figure of fun, but he had one great virtue: he would carry out Mussolini's wishes. Mussolini wished, as he later put it, 'to satisfy the Italian sense of the picturesque'.[27] He also wished to control every aspect of Italian society and to transform the Italians into disciplined, obedient serfs, and the party was the instrument with which to do it.[28]

The party did not, until 1937, control the Fascist youth movement, the *Opera Nazionale Balilla*, which had been founded in 1926 as an umbrella organisation for 6–18-year-olds. In practice these youth clubs were usually run by teachers, with the local Militia providing some 'pre-military training' for the older boys. Unlike their Catholic rivals, they were allowed to take part in sport; they were, literally, the only game in town.

They also organised the summer camps by the seaside. So there were real incentives to join and indeed while still at primary school it was imprudent not to do so, since the teachers were often zealous Fascists who felt responsible for bringing up the children in the Fascist faith. But sport, physical training and playing at soldiers did not appeal to everyone, and the Catholic clubs grew rapidly in the 1930s. The odd thing about all this is that Mussolini, committed to bringing up a transformed Fascist generation and rearing a new Fascist elite, seems to have taken little practical interest in it. He proclaimed his intentions often enough, and in 1929–31 he fought the Church on precisely this issue, but he did not bother about what the *Balilla* groups actually did. In the schools, teachers had to take oaths of loyalty and textbooks were vetted to ensure they were politically correct, but there was little central control of the *Balilla*. Partly for this reason Starace and the PNF resented the *Balilla's* independence, and in 1937 managed to take it over and rename it the *Gioventù Italiana del Littorio* (GIL).[29]

Finally, I should mention the Fascist student movement, *Gioventù Universitaria Fascista (GUF)*, which also provided sport, recreation and welfare, and ran the very popular annual *Littoriali* athletic and debating contests, where virtually free speech was tolerated. Students, as usual, enjoyed a latitude not permitted to others. By the 1930s they became rather an embarrassing problem, demanding what Fascism had always promised: dynamism, vitality, radical reforms, genuine corporations. It was not that they were anti-Fascist, but that they were *too* Fascist; they took the rhetoric seriously. Mussolini's son Vittorio was friendly with some of the student leaders and used to invite them back to villa Torlonia to meet the *Duce*. They were not impressed.[30]

Coping with Depression

Mussolini, of course, always felt insecure. Even in the early 1930s the Fascist hardliners were unhappy, the Church was worried about her youth movements, and the international scene looked menacing. Above all, the worldwide economic depression might have unforeseeable consequences. True, Italy was relatively sheltered. She had already cut her imports and consumption, and the 'battle for wheat' had made her self-sufficient in basic foods. Even so, Italian exports collapsed, and farm incomes with them. The 'new class' of peasant proprietors, one of the prime beneficiaries of the Fascist regime, was threatened with ruin. Industrial production went down by 23 per cent between 1929 and 1933, while official unemployment rose from about 300,000 to 1.2 million.[31] For two or three years Mussolini had good reason to be worried. The syndicates were still smarting from their defeat in 1928, and their leaders became ever more disgruntled as money wages of state employees were lowered by another 12 per cent. Monetary policy was even tighter than it had been in the late 1920s. Mussolini in 1931 would not follow Britain's example in giving up the gold standard and devaluing, so until he did so in 1936 the exchange rate was around 60 lire to the pound sterling, not 90.

The government's response was unorthodox but surprisingly perceptive. Mussolini realised that the basic problem was that consumers would not spend, partly because there were too few young people. Lowering people's wages was not likely to encourage them, and made it all the more essential for the state to step in. About 200,000 state jobs (and a further 40,000 in local government) were created, mostly in road-building (where spending doubled in four years), marsh drainage, and bureaucratic regulation.[32] Spending on welfare benefits shot up. The party and the syndicates became large-scale distributors of food, clothing, and money. The Fascists set up a welfare state, rather by accident, and it was quite a generous one. Price-fixing and cartels were not only tolerated but encouraged, in some cases even made compulsory, the aim being to *lower* prices as well as to stifle new competitors. This mixture was effective in the short term: real wages in industry held up remarkably well until 1934, although they fell in agriculture, and private consumption fell by only 2.5 per cent in the early 1930s. But it also ensured that Italy acquired a 'regulated economy', with a host of producer-dominated agencies (e.g. for cotton, wool, rice or fashion) fixing prices and production levels, and distributing raw materials among themselves.

The government also had to rescue the banks, as usual in Italy during a recession. Most big firms had borrowed heavily from the banks on the strength of their own shares, and when demand collapsed many could not repay the loans. So the banks found themselves holding worthless shares and became insolvent in their turn. When the Bank of Italy pumped money into them, it too became overcommitted. The regime faced financial disaster. Mussolini had to act decisively. In 1931 he founded the state-financed *Istituto Mobiliare Italiano* (IMI) to replace the banks in providing long-term (even, after 1936, medium-term) industrial credit. In 1933 another agency, the *Istituto per la Ricostruzione Industriale* (IRI), was created to rescue individual firms in trouble. These two agencies, themselves financed mostly by bonds, rescued the banks by paying real money for valueless industrial shares, and took over the banks' traditional long-term investment role. IRI soon held over 20 per cent of all share capital in the country. It was run by one of Mussolini's more inspired appointments, Alberto Beneduce, who had been a follower of Nitti in pre-Fascist days and had served as Minister of Labour in the Bonomi government of 1921–2. Beneduce turned IRI into an effective business school. It held shares in firms, but aimed to restore those firms to health in order to be able to recoup its money. So it taught new business techniques and management skills, suggested opportunities and imposed technical innovations. Mussolini had not envisaged this, but IRI proved one of his more lasting legacies.

It all seemed to show Mussolini's admirable flexibility and *spregiudicatezza*. In the early 1920s he had preached, and even allowed De' Stefani to practise, free trade. In the early 1930s trade collapsed, so he preached, and allowed his technical experts to practise, self-sufficiency ('autarchy') and state control instead. It was more popular, and it was more in character. Yet it is not at all clear how responsible he was for these measures, apart from the decision not to devalue, which was clearly his. Initially, when the Depression first struck, he was out of his depth like all other politicians. He knew he had to rescue the banks, but the initiative for IMI came partly from his Finance Minister Jung, partly from bankers like Raffaele Matteoli of the *Banca Commerciale*, and partly from the former Finance Minister Volpi, who was now at the head of the Industrialists' Confederation and was still a very close adviser to Mussolini on economic issues.[33] In other words, it came from within the banking and industrial Establishment; Mussolini simply provided the political impetus. Some of the other policies were also suggested by others. Leading syndicalists like Capoferri, emboldened by the cool reception Mussolini received in May 1930 when he went to talk to industrial workers in Milan, pressed for job-creation schemes and for speeding up the work of the labour tribunals.[34] Why should Mussolini resist? These were 'Fascist' measures, they helped his 'battles' for land reclamation and urban renewal, and they made the syndicates and the party much more popular. They did, of course, cost money and the budget deficit rose alarmingly, but high unemployment was an even bigger threat, as he well knew. So landless labourers from Emilia were given improved land in the Roman Campagna and the south, and the Turin–Trieste *autostrada* was built in the north. In 1930–1 Mussolini spent much time touring northern and central Italy, explaining government policy and cheering people up. Fortunately, Italy was less exposed to international trade than were other advanced countries. In the short run, she managed to weather the Depression by Keynesian means – government spending and job-creation; and she avoided the customary inflationary consequences of such policies by keeping the currency overvalued, by strict exchange controls, and by lowering money wages. Mussolini was remarkably lucky, as usual.

However, in the longer term the consequences were less benign. IRI's 'public-private partnerships' often suited the private owners and managers so well that they were reluctant to lose the state's protective umbrella. The private firms ceased to be private, in any meaningful sense. The new agencies provided them with state guarantees, cheap finance and technical help. But they also directed long-term finance to whichever industries or cartels they chose, and could deprive other sectors of any chance of expanding. They were run by experts but subject to political direction, and they soon controlled much of the economy, particularly shipbuilding, steel, electricity, armaments and heavy engineering. The state takeover was justified by the immediate crisis of 1931, but it continued for the rest of the Fascist regime (and long afterwards). Mussolini had inadvertently invented a real 'Third Way' after all, quite different from the official 'Third Way' he proclaimed. The new system owed nothing to 'corporatism' and had not been suggested by the Ministry of Corporations. It was undoubtedly innovative, and it gave the state effective leverage over the country's industrial base. But it stifled initiative, and made the leading industrial sectors totally dependent on state support.

However, 'corporatist' ideas were not forgotten. Mussolini may have been cautious about setting corporations up or giving them any powers, but they were, at the very least, excellent propaganda, much needed during the Depression when capitalism seemed to have collapsed and when Mussolini needed to show that he had the workers' interests at heart. In 1930 he set up a National Council of Corporations, with syndical and industrialist members, but it only met five times and turned out to be a mere talking shop. In 1934 he went much further. He founded 22 true corporations, i.e. 'mixed' bodies of workers' syndicates and employers' associations, together with a few party members, each regulating an economic sector. They were still mostly consultative, but had some direct powers: they could fix wage rates and prices, boost productivity and settle industrial disputes. In practice, the existing syndicates and employers' organisations continued to negotiate with each other on such matters outside the corporate framework, bringing the agreement inside for ratification at the end. The corporations were far too centralised and absurdly unrepresentative. The peasants' and workers' 'representatives', advocates and journalists to a man, were of course not elected but appointed from above, usually by party bosses; indeed, they often *were* former party officials. This may have been a 'Third Way', but it was not exactly stakeholder democracy. Furthermore, since the corporations had no real tasks they became simply a tiresome bureaucracy. They did not promote efficiency; on the contrary, by fixing prices and wages centrally, and by controlling import and export licences, they destroyed any chance of it. Like later pseudo-corporatist bodies elsewhere, they regulated, and monitored, and interfered, and obstructed, so much so that people gave up trying to innovate and just obeyed orders from above.[35] But Mussolini proclaimed them as an article of Fascist faith: the corporations were national and inter-class, the only institutions that could overcome class conflict, resolve the basic fault in Liberal, capitalist society, and ensure the national interest would prevail. Perhaps he believed it; more probably, he needed cover on his left. At any rate, the 'corporate state' now existed, allegedly the incarnation of the whole Fascist ideal.

However, the significant institutions were still the syndicates and the agencies. The syndicates did manage to protect industrial workers from the worst of the Depression, and they learned to deal effectively with grievances. There were plenty of *successful* wage claims and agitations, and the syndicates eventually saw off the Bedaux time and motion system at Fiat. In 1934 the 40-hour week was brought in, as a work-sharing device to reduce unemployment, and so were family allowances for industrial workers. Some of the old Socialist union leaders, including the former Socialist mayor of Milan, were very impressed and 'came over' to the Fascist cause. Other measures followed: Christmas bonuses, holiday pay, redundancy money, sickness insurance – all popular, all benefits for which the syndicates could claim the credit, and all sometimes even distributed by the syndicates themselves. In short, faced by the Depression Mussolini made sure the industrial workers were bought off. He gave them what they wanted – jobs, protection, bread, and even something very like a welfare state. He even started denouncing 'bourgeois egotism', a sign of things to come. It seemed to work. Northern workers continued to dislike Fascism because it had defeated them and destroyed their unions, but they realised the regime was providing some real benefits. By the mid-1930s 'anti-Fascism' had become mainly a middle-class, intellectual phenomenon.

Workers' Playtime

Like any other Roman Emperor, Mussolini knew he had to provide not just bread but circuses. He had to entertain the crowd, and he was still very good at it. He became famous for his speeches from the balcony of palazzo Venezia to the 'oceanic assemblies' below. He even entertained

them in the Colosseum, using it as the venue for speeches to huge delega-
tions of northern workers, or peasants, or wounded ex-servicemen – a
much more imposing version of the British 'beer and sandwiches' in
Downing Street. He appeared on cinema newsreels virtually every week,
usually in ceremonial mode but sometimes caught in engaging leisure
moments. A born actor, he had found his true medium, and a captive
audience – going to the cinema was the Italians' favourite leisure activity
in the 1930s, and all films were preceded by compulsory newsreels. Cinema suited Mussolini. Unlike television, it is a dramatic medium, well
suited to heroic poses and patriotic propaganda, and he made full use of
it. The *Duce*'s eldest son, Vittorio, helped to make several well-known
films. The regime trained young directors, and took over *Cinecittà*, Italy's
Hollywood, in 1938. The *Duce* was less effective on the radio – fireside
chats were definitely not his line – and he avoided it, although by the late
1930s many of his public speeches were transmitted by radio to *piazze*
throughout the land.

The Fascists always claimed to be a youthful movement, devoted to
physical fitness and sport. Mussolini himself was regularly seen on newsreels riding, swimming, cycling and playing tennis, and for once this was
quite genuine, for he was an active man who needed plenty of exercise.
In 1924 he and (allegedly) 15,000 followers jogged six miles uphill to
visit the house of his intellectual precursor, Alfredo Oriani. Perhaps significantly, the *Duce* did not play any team games, not even the most
popular sport in Italy, football. But Arpinati was a real fan, and was
president of the Italian Football Association; huge new stadiums were
built in the cities, and in 1934 Italy staged the World Cup. What is more,
the Italians won it, and Mussolini himself handed out the medals to his
victorious team. At the next World Cup, in 1938, Italy won it again.
Moreover, it was not just football. Primo Carnera was world heavyweight
champion from 1933 to 1935, and 'Mussolini's boys' won 12 gold medals at
the Los Angeles Olympics in 1932. The regime was not, of course, directly
responsible for these triumphs, but it certainly encouraged sport and
physical fitness, and so must have improved the nation's health. Mussolini certainly claimed the credit and enjoyed the boost to his popularity.
He knew that it is sport, not religion, that is the opium of the people.

Most important of all were the Fascist local, or sometimes workplace,
leisure centres. These, too, were rather an inadvertent development.
Originally Socialist or Catholic social clubs, the Fascist syndicalists took
them over in the early 1920s and realised they were a good way of
winning popular support. They began to found their own, and in 1925
organised them into a national network, the *Opera Nazionale Dopolavoro*

(OND). In 1927 the party took them over and greatly expanded their activities. They became by far the most successful aspect of the party's work. By the mid-1930s *Dopolavoro* centres were to be found throughout Italy. Public employees had their own, and many private firms also set them up for their workers once the party had 'suggested' the idea. Eventually four million adults were members. The *Dopolavoro* provided billiards, dancing, sport, athletics, music, organised holidays and trips to the seaside. It sent thousands of children off for summer holidays by the sea, or in the hills, all paid for by the proceeds of the bachelor tax. It showed films, brought travelling theatres and put on amateur dramatics, as well as wonderfully bogus folk festivals. This was quite new for many Italians. It was genuinely popular, and participatory too. There was little overt propaganda about it, just enjoyable leisure activities – virtually free entertainment for the masses. It was a brilliant invention. It convinced Italians that Fascism was not all stern duty and patriotism, let alone violence; it was fun as well.[36] Fascist 'consensus' stemmed largely from the *Dopolavoro*, and from the social opportunities it provided. Mussolini, too, enjoyed seaside holidays at Riccione every summer, and would often drop in to visit a 'colony' of urban children on the Adriatic coast, for the benefit of cinema newsreels. Mussolini was happy to pour resources into welfare, and into sport and leisure. He may have despised 'democracy' in principle and destroyed it in practice, but 'social democracy' – benevolent elites providing the 'people' with what was good for them – flourished as never before in Fascist Italy.

The other great 'circus' that the Fascists put on was in the air. This was the heroic age of aviation, comparable to the Space Age 40 years later, and Italy was in the forefront. In 1926 Nobile flew over the North Pole with Amundsen. The new Fascist government in 1923 set up a separate Aviation Ministry, held sometimes by the *Duce* himself, and regarded air travel as quintessentially 'Fascist': it was fast, dangerous, required considerable technical skills and could be put to military use. In 1927 Mussolini congratulated the Fascist deputy Roberto Forni, who had just received his pilot's licence: 'all young Fascist deputies of spirit should follow your example. It is by this means, not by constant squabbles, that we may prepare men and machines for Italy and for Fascism.'[37] It was unfortunate that Forni was killed in an air crash five weeks later, but that did not deter others. Mussolini himself was a competent pilot and flew around the country regularly, although he did not bother to get a full pre-military pilot's licence until 1937. His second son, Bruno, grew up to be a professional pilot, took part in the Ethiopian and Spanish wars and in 1938 even flew across the Atlantic to Brazil. Balbo, as Aviation Minister from

1929 to 1933, devoted himself to organising spectacular formation flights – to Odessa in 1929, across the South Atlantic to Rio de Janeiro in 1930, and to Chicago in 1933. This last, in particular, was a superb act of daring that made him a hero in the United States of America as well as in Italy, and made a suspicious Mussolini banish him to Libya. Still, it was a magnificent show. Even the Roman Emperors had never staged spectacles like that.

The Ideological Front: Myths and Image

Mussolini had wide cultural interests and was a surprisingly intellectual man, perhaps the most intellectual Italian politician since D'Azeglio. He was, after all, the son of a teacher and was a qualified *professore* himself; he had learned to play the violin, and was well read albeit in limited spheres. Every day he tried to see at least one well-known intellectual or artistic figure, and he prided himself on being a non-conformist intellectual still. He wrote articles and reviews on cultural themes, and he even collaborated (with Gioacchino Forzano) on several successful plays, including *Napoleon: the Hundred Days*, which in 1932 was staged at the New Theatre in London and was later produced in Vienna. He was a friend of leading artists, including Marinetti and Mario Sironi, who appointed himself official artist of the regime, but despite obvious Futurist influence there was no 'Fascist art': many artists, including the greatest of them all, Giorgio Morandi, could hardly have been less 'Fascist' in approach. Mussolini's attitude to writers and artists was usually one of benign if often sarcastic interest, tempered by caution. The fact that he was a playwright himself did not stop him censoring other people's plays, and not just those of his contemporaries. Aristophanes' works were banned altogether, being political satire. Shakespeare's *Julius Caesar* presented a particular problem. The hero Brutus is an obvious anti-Fascist of the Zaniboni type, and he succeeds in killing the Roman tyrant. Even so, Mussolini could hardly ban Shakespeare and retain any cultural credentials, so he banned George Bernard Shaw's *Caesar and Cleopatra* instead, for showing Caesar as undignified – and this despite Shaw's well-publicised praise for the Fascist regime.[38] So the Fascists censored publications and even banned books occasionally, but they did not burn them; they drove few artists or writers into exile (and those few for political agitation, not for their cultural activities), and they did not campaign against 'degenerate art'. Mussolini disliked the works of writers like Moravia, but he did not persecute their authors. The major exception was Elio Vittorini, whose *Conversation in Sicily* earned him a prison sentence, although not until 1943. Ignazio Silone, too, would probably have been persecuted for his novels, if he had not prudently stayed abroad. But Italy's best-known intellectual, Benedetto Croce, who had organised an anti-Fascist 'Manifesto' in 1925, remained in Naples and published his very influential *La Critica* throughout the regime, without even being beaten up. Obviously non-Fascist or anti-Fascist publishers, like Giuseppe Laterza in Bari or Giulio Einaudi in Turin, were extremely active and came to dominate the literary scene.

Indeed, most of the intellectuals not only enjoyed remarkable freedom but also patronage and flattery. Some of them, especially the classicists, archaeologists, and town planners, thought Fascism was wonderful. Croce's 'Manifesto' had itself been a response to a pro-Fascist (or anti-Liberal) manifesto issued a few weeks earlier by a cultural congress convened by the philosopher Giovanni Gentile, a manifesto which had been signed by several very distinguished writers including Luigi Pirandello as well as by historians, painters, economists and scientists. The meeting had showed that there was a 'pro-Fascist culture' in Italy, and Gentile soon demonstrated the point more effectively than by a mere manifesto. He persuaded Mussolini to found a 'Royal Academy' on the French model, with perks for the favoured few: a generous 3,000 lire a month, free first-class rail travel, and the right to be addressed as 'Excellency'. More seriously, members could tap into government funds for their research projects and find jobs for their *protégés*. Mussolini himself chose the president and the 60 members, and he selected for intellectual and cultural standing rather than for political conformity. For some years Guglielmo Marconi was president, Italy's leading historian Gioacchino Volpe was secretary, and the physicist Enrico Fermi was admitted to membership at the age of 28. Even so, to have signed the wrong manifesto in 1925 made it unlikely you would be chosen. The whole point of the academy was to demonstrate that Italian culture was not synonymous with Croce, nor with Liberalism. In that sense the 1925 'battle of the Manifestos' went on for years, and the regime won. Men like Marconi, Marinetti, D'Annunzio, Pirandello and Fermi were certainly prestigious. Croce himself was kept out of the Academy by the device of excluding all Senators, even though (or possibly because) this also applied to Gentile.[39] But the academy had two great defects. One was that Italian intellectuals, like those elsewhere, usually loathed each other, so Mussolini could not appoint worthy new members without mortally offending some existing ones and risking embarrassing scenes in public. The other problem with the academy was that it was academic. Mussolini had hoped that it would help him create a new avant-garde that would transform intellectual life and stimulate enthusiastic consensus for a new social order. 'Fascist culture' was supposedly dynamic, innovative and anti-conformist. But the dead hand of Academe stultified any such aspirations. The academics, like Mussolini himself, were ageing and increasingly uncreative. He enjoyed meeting his old friends and mentors, but even he recognised that these men were not likely to found a new Roman civilisation, particularly since they tiresomely objected to his pulling down much of the old one.[40]

Gentile's other great scheme was an Italian encyclopaedia, again directed against Croce and his school. Here was the sum of human knowledge, published under Fascist auspices but objective rather than partisan, and with far-reaching educational aims. It contained some articles written by people who had signed Croce's Manifesto, and many written by foreigners. Once again, Volpe was deeply involved, choosing the authors of the historical sections. The encyclopaedia contained a famous article on 'The Doctrine of Fascism', drafted by Gentile but revised and signed by Mussolini himself in his role as philosopher king. The *Duce* also added some material, particularly in the second part. 'War alone,' he characteristically proclaimed, 'brings up to their highest tension all human energies, and puts the stamp of nobility upon the peoples who have the courage to meet it.'[41] Nevertheless, the stress elsewhere in the article, particularly on the 'ethical state', was recognisably Gentilian. The article was soon approved, *faute de mieux*, as the canonical version of Fascist ideas, and was much used in schools and colleges. It is worth noting that on intellectual matters, as on others, Mussolini adopted his typical method of government. He chose a highly competent expert, Gentile, and let him do the rest, under supervision. The result was an academy and an encyclopaedia, an official creed, and very little trouble from the intellectuals. Men like Marconi, Gentile and Volpe were a match for Croce and Salvemini. They gave the regime much of its legitimacy, and prevented the fatal growth of a dissident intelligentsia.

The academy and the encyclopaedia were not alone. The government also, in effect, took over the Dante Alighieri Society, which promoted Italian culture abroad, and founded a National Fascist Institute of Culture (INFCI) to do the same task at home. INFCI became quite an important meeting place for the educated, with over 100,000 members by the mid-1930s, although it, too, was distinctly traditional in its activities, and it attracted the jealousy of the party's propagandists. Mussolini also founded the National Council for Scientific Research in 1925, with Marconi as president, and was quite lavish with prizes and grants to artists and writers. He knew that it paid to keep the chattering classes happy and that he could do it relatively cheaply, and in any case he often had a genuine interest in their activities. As he put it semi-ironically to Ada Negri in 1925, 'my tyranny is concealing its chains by placing laurel wreaths on poets' brows'.[42] Mussolini even saw *himself* as an artist, working in the most intractable medium of all, human nature. But he always watched out for signs of dissent, and of course he did not win everybody over. His most conspicuous failures were the historian Gaetano Salvemini (who, in a splendid gesture, sent the *Duce* a copy of his very critical book on Fascist foreign policy, *Mussolini Diplomatico*, inscribed 'to the leading actor, the first copy', '*al primo attore, la prima copia*'[43]) and the conductor Arturo Toscanini, who went into voluntary exile in 1931 after refusing to play the Fascist anthem at the beginning of concerts. Moreover, when university professors throughout Italy were forced to take an oath of loyalty to the regime, 12 of them actually refused.

Mussolini still owned the *Popolo d'Italia*, derived most of his income from it, and remained a journalist at heart. He knew the press was the key to public opinion, and public opinion was the key to power. As earlier, it was not difficult to control the press. The party controlled the register of official journalists, the only people permitted to write; his close colleague Mario Morgagni ran the official news agency, Stefani. Most papers simply took their 'news' from the agency communiqués, then as now. Mussolini played fair in a way, and did not ensure that his own paper had all the scoops. After Arnaldo's death he made Arnaldo's son Vito the editor of the *Popolo d'Italia*, but the real work was done by Sandro Giuliani, deputy editor since 1914. Mussolini still read the papers carefully, particularly after one of his own speeches to see how it had been reported; and he wrote regular book reviews and articles on demography and foreign policy. The newspapers, censored and monotonous, carried little news since any unwelcome topic like crime or financial scandal was strictly curtailed – not more than 30 lines, it being one of the Prefects' key duties to count them and fine offending editors. However, the press did manage to debate serious political or economic issues on occasions. There was, for example, much discussion about the desirable exchange rate in 1926, before Mussolini laid it down in public; and the reconciliation with the Church in 1929 was by no means universally welcomed. Even in the 1930s there were some newspapers, e.g. Farinacci's *Il Regime Fascista*, which took an independent line and could also be used to spread rumours and calumnies that the government wished to diffuse. The liveliest papers, indeed, were the 'extremist' ones like Settimelli's *L' Impero* or Interlandi's *Il Tevere*, defending the original ideas of the Fascist revolution against the complacent conformists.

Mussolini himself usually preferred to read the foreign press, since it was more interesting and it enabled him to keep up his languages.

In 1934 press control became more centralised and 'positive'. No longer were editors merely told what *not* to print, but what their papers should contain, even down to the detailed clichés ('the unsleeping *Duce*, his masculine profile forged in bronze, marched at the head of his invincible legions') and the photographic poses. Mussolini was usually shown smiling, or (if examining a project) frowning with concentration, or (if marching) sternly martial. The *gerarchi* were always depicted looking admiringly at the *Duce*.[44] Mussolini's Press Office became a proper under-secretariat of Press and Propaganda, with his son-in-law Galeazzo Ciano in charge; the following year it became a full ministry, the nucleus of the future Ministry of Popular Culture that from 1937 controlled not only the press and radio but also cinema and theatre as well. Here was a real 'mediacracy', government by a handful of journalists who vetted all ministers' speeches and had a big influence on policy. They took a stern, Reithian view of the journalists' calling. The Fascist ideal was to keep the message simple and repeat it often, and this could be done even more effectively via radio and cinema newsreels. However, like most press manipulation it failed in the long run. Italy was a gregarious country and by no means isolated. Foreign newspapers were freely on sale, foreign radio broadcasts could easily be heard, and there were always thousands of tourists. News and opinion spread rapidly by word of mouth, as the secret police kept discovering.

Mussolini knew that his regime rested ultimately on the acceptability of its ideas. But what were its ideas? They were certainly incoherent, for Fascism was a broad Church and harboured people of wildly different views – syndicalists and bankers, revolutionaries and monarchists, anti-clericals and Catholics. True, they were all patriotic and looked back to the First World War and to the comradely virtues of military activism. Nevertheless, Mussolini always had to compromise among the factions and leave his options open, even on ideological issues. He stressed that Fascism was a practical viewpoint, activist and impatient. It had led Italy to victory, had rescued her from Bolshevism and corrupt Liberalism alike, and had redeemed her from centuries of stagnation. It rejected the 'immortal principles of 1789', which provided benefits only for bourgeois lawyers, just as it rejected the collectivist principles of 1917. But it favoured nothing very specific, except good order and nationalism. It certainly had its own 'ethos', essentially *squadrista*, but this was virtually abandoned in the mid-1920s. After that, Fascism meant nothing more than *Mussolinismo*, the cult of the *Duce* – who was often supported precisely because he seemed to be the *alternative* to the squads, and because he had no evident blueprint for either state or society.

However, he did of course have decided opinions, which had not changed a great deal since 1914-15. He was still a romantic nationalist, anxious to expand Italy's influence and power. The Italians, in his view, were hugely gifted but undisciplined; with the right leadership they would soon become pre-eminent. He regarded Liberalism as pernicious and defeatist, parliamentary government as utterly incompetent and corrupt, and democracy as either illusion or, if genuine, the rule of the stupid and ignorant. As in Venice or Britain at their peak, the honest, patriotic few should rule, natural aristocrats who would ignore vested interests and welcome responsibility and command. A single lion would always put to flight a million sheep. The economy should be planned and run on 'corporate' lines, with all legitimate interests represented. There was no justification for class conflict or strikes, nor for any defeatist chatter. The state should intervene and regulate all social activities including private ones, but it should respect legal procedures and property rights, and it should provide the honest citizens with effective protection and social welfare. The dishonest ones should be treated with 'zero tolerance'. Moreover, the regime should, by education and example, transform the people into dedicated protagonists of community values and of the national cause. This was a coherent view, based on wartime experience and values but also reflecting avant-garde literature and art. But it was also, in peacetime, impractical. It curtailed men's freedoms too much, and eventually they came to resent this. Italian society was not so easy to transform; nor were Italian mentalities. Mussolini could not dictate to the king, nor to the Senate, nor to the Church, nor to the courts, nor to the industrial and commercial elites. 'Zero tolerance' was not an option; Italy's legal and religious traditions were too strong. Mussolini's vision was also too idealistic. Fascism, to Mussolini, meant heroism. The movement itself had been founded in 1919 as the *Fasci di Combattimento*, the '*Fasci* of Combat'. He assumed that the Italians could be made into a nation of heroes, fighting for the collective good. He was simply not interested in providing peace and prosperity. When asked to define 'Fascism' in a single phrase, he replied 'we are against the comfortable life!'[45] He hated capitalism not because it exploited the workers but because it made people mercenary and ignoble. No doubt he was right, but for a single lion there were a million sheep.

In any case, the regime could not really be founded on the principle that 'Mussolini is Always Right' (a slogan coined with ironic intent by the maverick journalist Leo Longanesi, and soon plastered all over Italy by Starace).[46] Mussolini himself recognised that as an Italian intellectual he needed a doctrine. So he wrote his article in the encyclopaedia, and constantly resented any suggestion that Fascism was not 'revolutionary'. In 1929 he told Bottai that Fascism 'is indeed a revolution, not just a way of making the trains run on time. We would have been in real trouble without that shift in thinking. Without it, the Fascist movement would have been pure reaction or mere restoration of an old political and social regime, whereas in fact it has created and will create a new world.'[47] It had not, but to do so remained an aspiration or rather a burning ambition in the *Duce* – not because of any ideology, but because of his personality.

Mussolini, never reluctant to promote himself, had written his autobiography as early as 1911–12 (see p. 16). In the 1920s another alleged autobiography appeared, with a preface by the American ambassador, Washburn Child, although in fact it had been written by Arnaldo. Mussolini was also the subject of a best-selling biography in English entitled *Dux*, written by his mistress Margherita Sarfatti, an influential work that stressed the *Duce*'s cultural sensitivity. In 1932 he had another propaganda triumph when he gave a series of interviews to a rather naive German journalist, Emil Ludwig, a man who was not only Liberal but Jewish and was almost certainly selected by Mussolini in order to annoy Hitler. Ludwig wrote up these interviews as a book, *Talks with Mussolini*, which became a best-seller and was translated into a dozen languages. Although a close reading of Ludwig's book clearly revealed Mussolini's deep insecurity and his tendency to pose, it was nonetheless a real publicity coup worldwide for the *Duce*. However, the Italians themselves were less impressed, particularly by Mussolini's uncomplimentary view of their sheep-like national character, so the *Duce* tried (in vain) to buy up the entire Italian edition on the grounds that the translation was 'horrible'.

Inasmuch as the regime after 1930 had any other unifying idea apart from the cult of the *Duce*, it was *romanità* (Romanness). Rome was not just a city, she was a myth. Mussolini deliberately presented himself as the heir of the Caesars. He, too, had crossed the river Rubicon and ordered his legions to march on Rome. He, too, had restored order and the rule of law. His very title, *Duce*, was from the Latin *Dux*; the *Fasci* had been the Roman lictors' symbol of office; and the Militia, organised into 'legions' and 'cohorts', was led by 'consuls'. Its members greeted each other with the 'Roman salute'. The anniversary of the city's foundation, 21 April, was celebrated as a public holiday, the 'Birthday of Rome'. In April 1933 Mussolini gave the *podestà* of Rimini a statue of Julius Caesar, telling him to put it on top of the column near which Caesar had addressed the XIII Legion immediately after crossing the Rubicon. Fresh flowers were to be put on the statue every year, on the Ides of March.[48] The Italians were not Italians at all but Romans, or might become so again. This Roman rhetoric had much appeal in a country where ancient ruins were difficult to avoid, and where the regime's archaeologists were daily uncovering more. It was also a nice snub to Fascism's true birthplace, Milan – industrious but all too bourgeois. And Rome meant Empire. In 1937 a big exhibition of Roman civilisation was held at the Tomb of Augustus, pointing the obvious comparison between the first Roman Emperor and the current ruler. 'Romanness' had another useful implication. Rome, after all, had been a vast bureaucratic structure, ruled from the centre. To stress 'Romanness' was to abandon the original 'Fascist ethos' of initiative and insubordination, and replace it by discipline, order and Caesarism.

Mussolini was still popular abroad, at least in the more conservative circles. He corresponded with some highly improbable people, including Mahatma Gandhi who came to Rome on Mussolini's request and enjoyed the rare honour of being invited to villa Torlonia, accompanied of course by his goat. In the late 1920s and early 1930s, indeed, there was something of an international 'cult of personality' around the *Duce*. Many intellectual foreigners made the pilgrimage to Rome to visit the great man, who flicked through their works before they arrived, found something interesting to say, and sent them on their way with a glow of satisfied recognition. His most famous visitor was the British Chancellor of the Exchequer Winston Churchill, who came to Rome on a private visit in January 1927, had a very warm meeting with the *Duce* and later told the press:

I could not help being charmed, like so many other people have been, by Signor Mussolini's gentle and simple bearing and by his calm, detached poise in spite of so many burdens and dangers. Secondly, one could see that he thought of nothing but the lasting good, as he understood it, of the Italian people . . . If I had been an Italian I am sure that I should have been wholeheartedly with you from start to finish in your triumphant struggle against the bestial appetites and passions of Leninism.

Mussolini's greatest achievement, in Churchill's eyes, was to have shown the world that Bolshevism could be defeated, and that people could be rallied against it: '[Italy] has provided the necessary antidote to the Russian poison'.[49] This was flattery indeed, and irresistible coming from a man like Churchill. No wonder the *Popolo d'Italia* immediately serialised Churchill's First World War memoirs, paying him generously. It was not only conservatives who admired Mussolini. Lloyd George was enthusiastic too, and the future Labour Chancellor of the Exchequer Hugh Dalton was so overwhelmed when he met Mussolini in 1932 ('charm, intelligence, energy and no play-acting. That is for the gallery. There is no other living man whom it would have thrilled me more to meet') that his wife grew jealous.[50] British admiration for Mussolini cooled abruptly in 1935 because of Ethiopia, but until then the *Duce* was widely regarded in Britain as upright, heroic and, best of all, a sportsman.

Conclusion: Consensus or Repression?

Mussolini's regime rested, as he recognised, on both 'consensus' and 'repression'; or rather, on weaker forms of both: 'acquiescence' and 'implicit threat'. There is little doubt that Mussolini himself was genuinely popular, except perhaps in 1930–2 during the worst of the Depression and the conflict with the Vatican. He co-opted virtually everybody into his system, and provided benefits both material and psychological. The 'myth of the *Duce*', of an ultra-competent man of infallible intuition and huge talents who could be trusted to resolve any problem, was surprisingly widely accepted, although people were critical of the *gerarchi* and of the ludicrous Starace. Mussolini toured the country, distributed handouts to war veterans and prolific mothers, put on a good show and was manifestly a 'man of the people' – a picturesque and energetic one to be sure, but still a blacksmith's son with the same values and tastes as most other Italians. His policies usually turned out to be successful, and he was clearly not a zealot. People trusted him and were grateful to him. The streets were clean, the marshes were drained, the beggars and the *mafiosi* were out of sight, and the trains not only ran on time but made a profit. He was now a successful elder statesman in Europe, and at home seemed a truly enlightened despot, patronising artists and architects and flattering the learned. He provided welfare, entertainment, financial stability and public order, and he even guaranteed religious liberty as well.

On the other hand, police informers were everywhere, the post was intercepted, the telephones were tapped, there was no freedom of speech or association, and there was no press or parliamentary check on government activities. Mussolini, ever insecure, kept the Militia in reserve, just in case: in January 1930 he remarked to the party bosses in Ravenna and Forlì that the Po valley could mobilise over 200,000 men in 48 hours, enough to control the rest of Italy.[51] Moreover, a host of local *mini-Duci* had sprung up, interfering with every aspect of life and demanding conformity. These pests were tiresome at best, and could turn nasty. At any moment the police might send you off to the islands, for no apparent reason. This threat made life unpleasant and you had to be careful, but it was a reign of intimidation and nervous conformity rather than of terror. Only the Communists were arrested en bloc, and this only because they foolishly adopted a policy of 'going back' to Italy in the early 1930s. The anti-Fascist parties were still conspicuously ineffective. However, there were still plenty of agitations over bread shortages or food prices, and over a hundred unofficial (and unreported) strikes in 1933 on economic issues. In the south the traditional land occupations and riots against taxes and oppressive mayors remained endemic, particularly in the early 1930s, although these were not necessarily 'anti-Fascist' and the cry 'down with the mayor, long live Mussolini' was both common and prudent. Other forms of protest, such as jokes, graffiti on toilet walls or the occasional drunk singing the 'Red Flag' at night on the street, were quite common too, and solemnly recorded in police files. Most common of all was *afascismo*, non-Fascism: passive resistance, or rather passive acceptance. You joined the party, you kept your job, and you carried on exactly as before. This was the *normal* response of professional people like teachers and lawyers to the regime, and of course it had to be tolerated. It is clear, therefore, that Fascism was not universally loved. 'Consensus' was never total, and is in any case an unattainable goal. However, it is also clear that dissent was limited, except at local level; it was not an overt challenge to the regime.[52]

In short, the regime imposed tough policing and tougher social discipline but it allowed sufficient legal and property rights to be tolerable, and it was not founded on a mountain of human bones. To most Italians it seemed just another top-down bureaucratic regime with a democratic deficit, very familiar in the contemporary world. Like all such regimes, it was not so much tyrannical as corrupt and increasingly inefficient. The ending of public debate – or even internal government debate – on public issues was the key problem. People lobbied the *Duce* with their various requests, and he then proclaimed his decision; raising objections or asking questions was automatically 'subversive' or 'defeatist'. Mussolini was, after all, always right. Moreover, since he possessed neither a religious nor a historical perspective, he had little to indicate to him the likelihood of being wrong. In any case, he was simply far too insecure to seek advice or allow debate. He had no 'think-tank', no circle of close advisers and no cronies. He met his ministers and officials one at a time, not to debate but to instruct. He often heard informed views but he rarely heard unorthodox ones, and nor did anyone else. However expert the technocrats, and however disinterested the dictator, banning open discussion of alternatives guaranteed bad government in the long run. Mussolini, like any good journalist, had always simplified issues; now he became remote and arbitrary as well, his colleagues ever more disillusioned and resentful. Indeed, Mussolini's rule illustrates yet again the banal truth about dictatorship: it may be effective and even necessary as a temporary measure, but eventually all power corrupts, i.e. grows rotten. In October 1932 the regime held huge festivities to commemorate the tenth anniversary of the 'March on Rome'. It was a splendid celebration, but it was also a reminder to Mussolini and to everyone else that even if he really had saved the country from Bolshevism, he had done it 10 years earlier. The emergency was long over; the dictatorship remained.

Mussolini, too, was in decline. Aged 50 in 1933, and already in power for over 10 years, he was beginning to believe his own myth. Perhaps he really had been sent by Providence? But over the previous couple of years he had lost some essential supports. Without Arnaldo or Sarfatti to keep him in touch, and without Arpinati or anyone else to argue with, he was lonely and became ever more introspective. His journalism was less incisive or persuasive, and his serious speeches fewer. Perhaps he was 'burning out': for years he had faced huge stress on an unbalanced diet and without much emotional support, and now it was beginning to tell. He lost the bloody-minded sharpness, the sarcastic wit and dynamism of his early days, and took to pontification, always a sign of failing powers. He wrote and spoke increasingly about his big issues – the demographic crisis, the yellow peril, the decline of the West, etc. His daily visitors noticed that he no longer held conversations, nor showed much curiosity about others. Instead, he delivered monologues, usually about the past. This tendency is also evident in a series of interviews Mussolini gave to Yvon De Begnac between 1934 and 1943. These interviews are his 'Table Talk', reminiscences and reflections on political and cultural matters.[53] They are extremely well informed and often penetrating; but what they really show is that Mussolini entered his anecdotage early.

He also became dangerously bored and dissatisfied. After all, he was a journalist. An editor's office is far more stimulating than a Prime Minister's, and furthermore editors can have a private life. Dictators, in particular, lead lives of uneasy leisure. They issue the orders and sign the documents; their officials carry out the tasks. So Mussolini read widely, made commemorative speeches and gave his interviews; not much stimulus there. At the end of his life he reflected bitterly: 'the trouble with power is twofold: to have to deal with all kinds of imbeciles, and to be under constant scrutiny even in intimate matters'.[54] He had set up a system based on multiple compromises but he could not abide being bound by it, presiding over a world made safe for the Establishment. Always an emotional, insecure man, he had achieved much but he always needed to win even greater glory and play an even more dramatic role, upon an even wider stage. He despised stability and order, even his own stability and order. Moreover, after 10 years in office he had grown less cautious. He knew that time was running out, and he still had to transform the Italians and found an Empire. As Ludwig perceptively noted in 1932, Mussolini's 'fundamental moral problem must be to hold a revolutionary temperament in check'.[55] For the next few years he struggled with exactly that task, but he struggled in vain. He had grown older, but he had not mellowed with age. He was not one of Nature's elder statesmen. On the contrary, he was a born troublemaker, and he needed to make more trouble.

Notes

1 Edvige Mussolini, *Mio Fratello Benito* (Florence, 1957), pp. 122–5; *OO* xxxv, pp. 242–3.

2 E. Ludwig, *Talks with Mussolini* (London, 1932), p. 210.

3 'La Meravigliosa Attività del Capo del Governo', in *Il Popolo d'Italia*, 8 August 1933; *OO* xxxvii, p. 557.

4 'Vita di Arnaldo'; *OO* xxxiv, pp. 139–92.

5 These examples are in *OO* xli, pp. 379, 394–5; xliii, p. 71.

6 Circular to Prefects, 31 December 1928; *OO* xli, p. 234.

7 N. D'Aroma, *Mussolini Segreto* (Bologna, 1958), p. 143.

8 Y. De Begnac, *Palazzo Venezia* (Rome, 1950), p. 323.

9 *Popolo d'Italia*, 9 March 1937; *OO* xxviii, pp. 136–9.

10 Circular to diplomatic and consular representatives, 12 March 1931; *OO* xli, p. 425.

11 Mussolini to Stefani agency, 10 August 1931; *OO* xli, p. 454.

12 G. Giuriati, *La Parabola di Mussolini nei Ricordi di un Gerarca* (Bari, 1981), p. 50.

13 O. Dinale, *Quarant' Anni di Colloqui con Lui* (Milan, 1953), p. 320.

14 ACS, SPD, c. ris., b. 93 'Serpieri'. Guido Jung had just been replaced as Finance Minister by Paolo Thaon di Revel.

15 ACS, SPD, c. ris., b. 96, f. 1.

16 Y. De Begnac, *Taccuini Mussoliniani* (Bologna, 1990), p. 486.

17 ACS, SPD, c. ris., b. 79, sottof. 1; V. Cattani, *Rappresaglia* (Venice, 1997), p. 83; *OO* xlii, p. 45.

18 A. Iraci, *Arpinati l'Oppositore di Mussolini* (Rome, 1970), pp. 127ff, 181; R. De Felice, *Mussolini il Duce* (Turin, 1974), i, pp. 297–300.

19 Dinale, *Quarant' Anni* cit., p. 140.

20 De Felice, *Mussolini il Duce* cit., i, pp. 283–6.

21 Balbo to Mussolini, 5 November 1933, in ACS, SPD, c. ris., b. 69, sottof. 11. Cf. also U. Guspini, *L'Orecchio del Regime* (Milan, 1973), pp. 117–18; *OO* xlii, p. 70.

22 ACS, SPD, c. ris., b. 14 (Grandi, 19 June 1929: 'In your presence, *Presidente*, the good become better, the patriotic filter and purify their patriotism, the intelligent sharpen their wits and become both harmonious and aristocratic') and b. 69 (Bottai, on being dismissed, 19 July 1932: 'the only regret I will have is nostalgia for the Leader, for your presence and for your orders. I will seek to overcome it with the thought that even in private life Mussolini will be acting as an unceasing power of improvement').

23 ACS, SPD, RSI, c. ris., b. 7.

24 G. Ciano, *Diario 1937–43* (Milan, 1990 edn), 26 March 1939.

25 S. Setta, 'Starace', in F. Cordova (ed.), *Uomini e Volti del Fascismo* (Rome, 1980), pp. 443–72, at p. 453.

26 De Felice, *Mussolini il Duce* cit., i, p. 226.

27 Mussolini, 'Soliloquy on Trimellone island', 20 March 1945; *OO* xxxii, pp. 170–1.

28 D. Germino, *The Italian Fascist Party in Power* (Minneapolis, 1959), pp. 174–5; E. Gentile, *La Via Italiana al Totalitarismo* (Rome, 1995), pp.180ff.

29 Germino, *Italian Fascist Party* cit., p. 98; Gentile, *La Via Italiana* cit., p. 192; T.H. Koon, *Believe, Obey, Fight* (Chapel Hill, N.C., 1985), pp. 60–89.

30 R. Zangrandi, *Il Lungo Viaggio Attraverso il Fascismo* (Milan, 1962), pp. 198–200.

31 P. Ciocca and G. Toniolo, *L'Economia Italiana durante il Fascismo* (Bologna, 1976), p. 36; G. Tagliacarne, 'The evolution of Italian exports during 115 years of national unity', in Banco di Roma, *Review of Economic Conditions in Italy* xxx (1976), pp. 171–92, Table One. Exports fell from 11.3 per cent of Gross National Product in 1928 to 6.7 per cent in 1933.

32 S. La Francesca, *La Politica Economica del Fascismo* (Bari, 1972), p. 29; G. Toniolo, *L'Economia dell' Italia Fascista* (Bari, 1980), pp. 197–268; V. Zamagni, *The Economic History of Italy 1860–1990* (Oxford, 1993), pp. 243–71.

33 Mussolini to Jung, 9 January 1933, in ACS, *Autografi del Duce*, cassetta di zinco, scat. 9, f. 11.

34 P. Capoferri, *Vent'Anni col Fascismo e con i Sindacati* (Milan, 1957), pp. 62–3; F. Grossi, *Battaglie Sindacali* (Rome, 1988).

35 A. Aquarone, *L'Organizzazione dello Stato Totalitario* (Turin, 1965), pp. 189ff.; E. Conti, *Dal Taccuino di un Borghese* (Milan, 1946), pp. 508–9; G. Pini and D. Susmel, *Mussolini: l'Uomo e l'Opera* (Florence, 1953–4) iii, p. 309.

36 V. de Grazia, *The Culture of Consent* (Cambridge, 1981).

37 Mussolini to Forni, 3 September 1927; *OO* xxiii, p. 322.

38 L. Zurlo, *Memorie Inutili* (Rome, 1952), p. 29.

39 De Begnac, *Taccuini Mussoliniani* cit., pp. 308–9.

40 Ibid., p. 350. When D'Annunzio died in 1938, Volpe suggested that Fermi be made President of the Academy. Mussolini said he was too young. 'But *Presidente*, he will rejuvenate us all.' 'Not Fascist in spirit' (pp. 351–2). That was what really mattered.

41 'La dottrina del Fascismo'; *OO* xxxiv, pp. 115–38; in English, 'The doctrine of Fascism', in A. Lyttelton (ed.), *Italian Fascisms* (London, 1973), pp. 37–57.

42 Letter of 9 June 1925 to Ada Negri; *OO* xxxix, p. 443.

43 ACS, SPD, c. ris., b. 48. The book was banned, but Salvemini was given his citizenship back.

44 F. Flora, *La Stampa dell' Era Fascista* (Rome, 1945), pp. 90–1; Celso Luciano, *Rapporto al Duce* (Rome, 1948), p. 12.

45 Ludwig, *Talks with Mussolini* cit., p. 191 (the translation of this passage as 'life must not be taken easily' is inadequate); also Mussolini's speech to 2nd quinquennial assembly of PNF, 18 March 1934, *OO* xxvi, pp. 185–93.

46 But with Mussolini's approval; De Begnac, *Palazzo Venezia* cit., p. 652. The phrase became the 'tenth commandment' in the *Decalogo del Legionario* (Rome, 1938), written by Mussolini himself; *OO* xxxvii, pp. 219–20.

47 Mussolini to Bottai, 4 June 1929; *OO* xxiv, p. 348.

48 Mussolini to *podestà* of Rimini,15 April 1933; *OO* xxv, p. 287; G. Gattei, 'Bagni e guerre 1914–44', in G. Gattei and A. Gardini (eds), *Storia di Rimini* (Rimini, 1977), vol. ii.

49 *The Times*, 21 January 1927.

50 B. Pimlott (ed.), *The Political Diary of Hugh Dalton* (London, 1986), pp. 173–4; also H. Dalton, *The Fateful Years* (London, 1957), pp. 33–9.

51 ACS, *Mostra della Rivoluzione Fascista*, b. 53.

52 See, especially, M. Chiodo (ed.), *Geografia e Forme di Dissenso Sociale in Italia durante il Fascismo* (Cosenza, 1990); P. Bevilacqua, *Le Campagne del Mezzogiorno tra Fascismo e Dopoguerra* (Turin, 1980), pp. 122–44; De Felice, *Mussolini il Duce* cit., i, pp. 77–82.

53 De Begnac, *Taccuini Mussoliniani* cit.

54 Mussolini, 'Soliloquy on Trimellone island', 20 March 1945; *OO* xxxii, pp. 168–82, at p. 169.

55 Ludwig, *Talks with Mussolini* cit., p. 37.

Chapter 7

The *Duce* Abroad: Propaganda, Peacemaking and War 1922–36

From Lausanne to Locarno 1922–5

Mussolini had come to national power partly by stressing Italy's 'mutilated victory', the idea that at Versailles Britain and France had cheated her of her just reward for a victorious war. The reward, in his view, should consist of former German territory in Africa, former Turkish territory in the Middle East, and dominance of the Mediterranean and Adriatic. The Liberal governments' failure to stand up for Italy's rightful claims was intolerable, and a Fascist regime would swiftly put matters right. From 1919 to 1921 he wrote many articles and made a number of fiery speeches on these lines. The British and French, acquisitive and greedy, had carved out these areas for themselves. If need be, Italy should rouse up the native peoples against their colonial oppressors: 'we are in touch with the British colonial empire. From Egypt to India the whole world is in ferment. If we are betrayed we must without hesitation prepare our revenge!'[1] At Trieste, in March 1921, he proclaimed that 'it is destiny that the Mediterranean should become ours again. It is destiny that Rome should become once more the city that leads civilisation in the whole of Western Europe.'[2]

On the other hand, he was always more cautious on more northerly issues, where Italy had done remarkably well at Versailles: she had acquired easily defensible frontiers together with Trent, the South Tyrol, Trieste, and Istria. Mussolini favoured a cautious rapprochement with wartime enemies, sympathised with Germany's protests about the burden of 'reparations' and even claimed to be 'revisionist', i.e. in favour of altering the Treaty of Versailles; but he knew that any serious revision would threaten Italy's newly acquired northern and north-eastern provinces and might lead to the dreaded *Anschluss*, a German takeover of Austria. The one real problem was on the Adriatic. Versailles had set up a strongish Yugoslavia, usually backed by France; even so, the new state was too unstable to be a real threat, and Mussolini realised it was wise not to become involved too openly in Balkan conflicts. So he welcomed the Rapallo settlement in autumn 1920 and he abandoned D'Annunzio at Fiume, at some risk to his own position (see p. 46). In 1922, realising he might soon have to deliver on European issues, he became more circumspect still. In January he went to the inter-Allied conference at Cannes to spy out the land, and in the spring he visited Berlin. He went as a journalist, but like all good journalists he managed to secure interviews with some of the leading statesmen, for example the French Prime Minister Briand, and assess their personalities – whereas they, for the most part, had little idea who he was. He listened respectfully to what they said, and reported it straight. After all, he was there to gain credibility. He intended to play the responsible European statesman, and he knew he had little option.

But in Africa and the Mediterranean he could try his luck. He had made his position clear in 1919–21 and at Naples, four days before the 'March on Rome', he again proclaimed 'the Mediterranean for the Mediterraneans'.[3] He never forgave Britain and France for ignoring Italy's claims and he never gave up his ambition to make Italy a truly Great Power, dominating the East Mediterranean and with an African empire. He was not alone. Many influential Italians, including Liberals and anti-Fascists, agreed with him. The problem was not so much that the World War and the Versailles settlement had failed to give Italy any colonies, but that they had also thrust an apparent Great Power status upon her. The Austro-Hungarian and Turkish empires had vanished; Russia had become a pariah; the United States of America was in self-imposed isolation; Germany was prostrate and her economy ruined; Japan was too remote. Only the three western European allies remained as significant powers. The Italians thus acquired ideas considerably above their station. Might it not be sensible to help themselves while the going was good?

After the 'March on Rome' Mussolini took the Foreign Ministry himself and held the post until 1929. His most radical early act was to move the ministry itself from palazzo della Consulta to palazzo Chigi, ostensibly so that possible demonstrations would be further away from the king's palace. The ministry's work continued to be run by the secretary-general, a tough-minded Sicilian named Salvatore Contarini, and the ambassadors remained the same type as before: aristocrats with wide connections. Sforza resigned as ambassador in Paris but otherwise there were few changes either of policy or personnel. War debts and German reparations still dominated the European agenda. Mussolini's first appearance on the diplomatic stage was at a conference on ex-Turkish territories, held in Lausanne where 20 years earlier he had slept under a bridge; the Swiss had hastily revoked his expulsion order so that he could attend. It was a successful trip, resulting in agreement that the Italians could continue to hold the Dodecanese islands in the Aegean, which they had taken from the Turks in 1912 and which were also claimed by Greece. Mussolini made one dramatic gesture (dramatic by diplomatic standards). As the British Foreign Minister Lord Curzon had already met his French counterpart Poincaré in Paris en route, Mussolini insisted that they should both have a preliminary conversation with him too, and this was held at the station hotel at Territet, one stop before Lausanne. Mussolini felt he had safeguarded Italian honour, and the other two were prepared to humour him.

In December 1922 Mussolini made another foray abroad, this time to London for one of the interminable conferences on German reparations. Here he behaved more diplomatically and produced quite a sensible scheme to resolve the issue, although as usual the French rejected it and indeed shortly afterwards occupied the Ruhr.[4] Mussolini did not like London. It was too big and too damp. Hardly anybody knew who he was, and those who did were either too patronising like Lord Curzon, or too disrespectful like the journalists. He drew the obvious lesson. After two trips abroad in his first two months, he stayed put and expected others to come to him. The only exceptions, apart from his visits to Hitler before and during the Second World War, were when he turned up at the Swiss town of Locarno to sign the treaty in 1925 (see below), and when he took centre stage at the Munich conference in 1938. This self-imposed isolation may have saved him from assassination but otherwise it was a bad mistake, especially for a Foreign Minister. Since 1909 he had hardly travelled abroad, and so he had very little up-to-date first-hand information about other countries or about the changes that the World War had brought.

Foreign policy remained as yet fairly traditional, based as usual on alliance with the most powerful European country, Britain. In 1923 the British ambassador reported, with some surprise, that 'we are not only respected but liked here, both individually and as a nation. My impression is that Italy is the only important Continental country where such a statement can truthfully be applied.'[5] Britain was, in fact, Italy's protector: both countries feared French obstinacy and German revival. So Fascist Italy supported Bonar Law's project on reparations, and played her part at the League of Nations in Geneva. Mussolini still nursed his Mediterranean ambitions, but they were directed against France, not Britain. He suggested to Marshal Diaz (who took no notice) that a Corsican 'foreign legion' be formed in the Italian army, for future use in seizing the island;

and, as 'Latinus', he wrote a preface to a book by Margherita Sarfatti about the 100,000 oppressed Italian settlers in French-held Tunisia.[6]

The only exceptional adventure in these early years was the 'Corfu incident' in 1923. In August the Italian General Tellini and four other members of the international Boundary Commission defining the Greek-Albanian border were killed inside Greece (although possibly by Albanians). Italo-Greek relations were already very poor, and Mussolini seized his chance. He demanded an official apology from the Greek army, an international investigation, capital punishment of the guilty, 50 million lire as indemnity, and full military honours for the deceased with the entire Greek government attending the funerals.[7] The Greeks demurred and suggested referring the dispute to the League of Nations, so Mussolini ordered the Italian navy to take the island of Corfu as a pledge. On 31 August it did so, bombing the old fort and killing 16 people, mostly refugees. Within 48 hours an entire Italian division had landed. This all aroused a great deal of international indignation, but Mussolini held firm. The League, he claimed, had no role since there was no threat of war. In any case, occupying territory temporarily as a pledge to ensure good behaviour was recognised international practice and had just been done in the Ruhr by the French. This was a valid argument, and certainly France had no wish to see the League deciding the issue and setting a precedent. So Mussolini got his way. The 'Conference of Ambassadors', i.e. the old wartime Allied War Council, took over the negotiations. The Greek government, now isolated, agreed to most of the conditions, and in late September the Italians evacuated the island. Mussolini naturally claimed a huge Fascist success, unthinkable under the despised Liberals. A robust, independent approach had paid off, and taught the foreigners not to mess with Italy.

Corfu was, perhaps, a harbinger of things to come, but it was so far an isolated incident. The traditional business of foreign policy continued undisturbed. The Yugoslavs had been rather frightened by Mussolini's gunboat diplomacy at Corfu, and agreed to settle the Fiume issue at last. In January 1924 Fiume became part of Italy and Mussolini could proclaim another triumph. First the Dodecanese, then Corfu, now Fiume; it was a good record, and a grateful king gave Mussolini Italy's highest honour, the Collar of the Annunziata. Relations with Yugoslavia improved for a time, but soon worsened as Italy manoeuvred for advantage in Albania's complicated internal disputes. In February Mussolini set up full diplomatic relations with the USSR, partly to show realism and freedom from ideological constraints. In the summer of 1924 Britain handed over Jubaland, on the Somali–Kenyan border, as a cheap concession to Italy's imperial ambitions. Jubaland was not worth having – it was the first of what Mussolini later called his 'collection of deserts' – but it was, undeniably, colonial territory in Africa. It had been won not by conquest nor, needless to say, out of any regard to its inhabitants' wishes, but by old-fashioned diplomatic haggling. Eighteen months later, in February 1926, Mussolini acquired another desert, Jarabub on the Egyptian–Libyan border.

In late 1924, when the Conservatives came back to power in Britain, Mussolini and the new Foreign Secretary, Sir Austen Chamberlain, came together to oppose one of Ramsay MacDonald's legacies, the League of Nations' proposed 'Protocol for the Peaceful Regulation of International Disputes'. This provided for compulsory arbitration of disputes by the International Court at the Hague, and also imposed an obligation to go to the aid of a country under attack. Mussolini, mindful of Corfu, did not like the sound of that; and nor did Chamberlain, anxious to avoid any British commitments in Europe except for the obligatory one on the Rhine. In December 1924, at the height of the Matteotti crisis, Chamberlain visited Rome for the League Council and made some very flattering remarks about the *Duce*. Mussolini was grateful and used his visit to maximum political effect. A real friendship began between the two men, which lasted until Chamberlain lost office in 1929 (and later). Britain and Italy became close partners, and in May 1925 the English-speaking, Anglophile Dino Grandi was made under-secretary at the Foreign Ministry.

The 'Protocol' soon collapsed but this made a general European settlement, to contain Germany and reassure France, all the more necessary. Stresemann suggested a four-power treaty guaranteeing existing frontiers, which would give Germany the Ruhr back. Mussolini initially welcomed the idea since it would presumably also guarantee the Austrian frontier and indeed the whole independence of Austria; and the one event Italy did not want to see was a German annexation of Austria. In May 1925 Mussolini made it clear to his ambassador in Germany that 'I would consider the war lost and the victory totally cancelled on the day that Germany managed to carry out her annexationist programme.'[8] An *Anschluss* would mean German troops stationed on Italy's least easily defended frontier, the Brenner. Italy could not, by herself, prevent Germany taking over Austria, but international guarantees might prevent it or deter it, particularly if Germany were herself committed to them. But as negotiations went on it became clear that the treaty would be essentially a Franco-German non-aggression pact, guaranteeing the Rhine frontier and Belgium but nowhere else. It would ensure the demilitarisation of the German Rhineland, which France therefore evacuated, and the admission of Germany to the League of Nations, but it would not guarantee

Austria or other central or south-eastern European countries and there was nothing in it for Italy. So Mussolini did not take much part in the negotiations and did not intend to go to the final conference, held in October 1925 at Locarno at the Swiss end of Lake Maggiore.

But Chamberlain knew his man, and made him an offer he could not refuse. Italy was to be, with Britain, a 'co-guarantor' of the treaty, i.e. of European peace and security. Here was Great Power status at last. Overcoming his reluctance, Mussolini took a speedboat from Stresa and turned up at Locarno, unexpectedly and at the last minute. He braved the anti-Fascist demonstrators (and the anti-Fascist delegates, especially from Belgium), signed up to European peace, posed for the cameras and sped off again across the waters. He came, he signed, he postured. Italy had done very little to secure the treaty but ended up the arbiter of European peace, on the same plane as the British Empire. It was all very satisfying, and was meant to be. Mussolini told Chamberlain he had not raised the Brenner issue, because he did not want the possibility of an *Anschluss* discussed at an international conference.[9] In any case, there was no need. Locarno applied to the Rhine, but it would obviously inhibit aggression elsewhere. In fact, the astute Chamberlain had quite deliberately flattered the volatile and potentially very troublesome Mussolini into taking the role of responsible European statesman, on a par with – i.e. under the control of – Britain. It was a brilliant piece of diplomacy, helped by Chamberlain's genuine liking for the *Duce*: 'I thought Mussolini a strong man of singular charm and I suspected not a little tenderness and loneliness of heart.'[10]

A year later, after another enjoyable meeting with Mussolini on a Mediterranean yacht, Chamberlain reflected again on his relations with the *Duce*:

What Italy may want ten or twenty years hence is a problem that often recurs to my mind; but what she wants before all things *now* is to be treated as *a Great Power on a footing of equality* with France, Germany and ourselves. For perhaps the first time since the Crimea what she asks is more a moral satisfaction than material concessions. Let us keep this constantly in mind. Mussolini said to Sir William Tyrrell: 'you treat me like a gentleman and the others don't', or something to that effect. Let us rather seek opportunities for consultation, for confidences and the like. Fine manners (if not fine words) will butter more parsnips in Italy than anywhere else; and *it is essential* that we should keep Italy, a growing power, in sympathy with our policy and in co-operation with us. This may be vital in the future either to maintain peace in Europe or to restrain or guide Italy outside Europe.[11]

In other words, British policy to Mussolini should be flattery, known more politely as 'parity of esteem'. Britain should make him think he was the great peacemaker. It worked, for some years. But Mussolini was astute too, and he knew he was being fobbed off. Only a month after Locarno he told his ambassadors in Paris and London that Italy, not Germany, still had first call on any colonial mandates that were available, and that, if the British and French did not recognise this, 'Italy is determined to re-examine the whole situation including the Locarno policies, and in any case to refuse to accept decisions which do not recognise her rights and interests.'[12] He was willing to cooperate in Europe, but the Empire came first. And, as Chamberlain forecast with great prescience, he could not be fobbed off for ever. Within 10 years Italy would want some real rewards, and Britain might not be willing to deliver. Harold Nicolson, with equal prescience but greater wit, had also noted the difficulty of satisfying the Italians: 'It would be easy enough to ask them to dinner; but the bother of it is that when they arrive they are apt to order their own wine; and when it comes to pay the bill it is discovered that they have selected the most expensive.'[13]

From Locarno to Rome 1926–35

The Locarno treaty settled the vital European conflict for some years. The other major issue, war debt, was also partly resolved in 1925–6, and Italy secured a distinctly favourable treatment. There was nothing much left in Europe to interest Mussolini, except Italy's traditional pastime of meddling in the Balkans. In those areas he was far from being a responsible statesman. In November 1926 he signed a pact with Albania, which made her virtually a client-state and gave Italy an apparent stranglehold on the Adriatic. Mussolini also financed Croat and Macedonian terrorists in the hope of breaking Yugoslavia up, and signed a treaty with Hungary, one of the big losers of Versailles and therefore a strong 'revisionist'. All this guaranteed Serb hostility and contributed to the formal Franco-Yugoslav alliance of December 1927. Mussolini resented French efforts to dominate south-east Europe and regarded France as an even bigger menace there than Germany. He also objected to France's efforts to exclude Italy from any say in the international administration of Tangiers. The two biggest issues bedevilling Franco-Italian relations were the Italians in Tunis (not treated, in Italian eyes, in ways laid down by the 1896 agreement) and the Italians in Paris. Mussolini complained that the French (unlike the Swiss) were far too tolerant of the anti-Fascist exiles, who were plotting to kill him and nearly succeeded in September 1926; he demanded effective policing and a curb on the anti-Fascist press, but in vain.[14] It was true that the French were sympathetic to the exiles and even subsidised some of them, as Mussolini well knew, but he could hardly complain too much; he had received French subsidies himself in the past. In spring 1929 an international 'anti-Fascist conference' was held in Paris, which further worsened relations, and in October an exile based in Paris tried to shoot the Italian Crown Prince who was on a visit to Brussels. These constant quarrels with France and Yugoslavia were not a fruitful policy and in spring 1926 they led Contarini to resign. Mussolini also tried to 'Italianise' the German-speaking inhabitants of the South Tyrol, which led to protests from both Austria and Germany; and he even quarrelled occasionally with the British, over oil concessions in Albania and Iran. But these minor quarrels were just that: minor quarrels, not serious disputes, and nothing that the diplomats could not handle. Meanwhile, of course, Mussolini was preparing his greatest diplomatic triumph of all, in Rome itself (see pp. 115ff.), and doing it unknown to the diplomats.

It has often been claimed that it was Contarini who had kept Musso-lini under control during the early years, and that his resignation in 1926 marked the beginning of Mussolini's assertive, expansionist policies.[15] The diplomatic documents do not seem to me to support this argument. From very early on Mussolini was manifestly the man in charge. He had always been passionately interested in foreign issues, he quickly mastered the techniques of diplomacy and he soon learned who was trustworthy and who was not (few were). His summary of Italian policy on the Locarno negotiations, sent to his ambassadors in Paris and London, was a model of clarity and precision.[16] In some ways he was the ideal boss. He was decisive but he listened to advice, he laid down clear directives, and he was not overbearing although he could be demanding and very sharp when occasion arose. He let other people take initiatives and supported them even when he himself disapproved of what they had done, as happened at the settlement of the Corfu dispute which was negotiated by his am-bassador in Paris. He was a dynamic, imaginative minister, respected and liked by his officials and by many of his counterparts abroad. In any case, Mussolini's desire for colonies and Mediterranean expansion was shared by his officials, including Contarini. The alleged endemic contrast between moderate, sensible diplomats and a hysterical, ultra-nationalist *Duce* was a myth put about after Mussolini's fall by officials anxious not to share the blame. It is true that Italian foreign policy was less coherent after 1926, but this was because after Locarno the focus shifted to the

Balkans and the Danube basin, where political reality was highly volatile and where the officials were divided too.

However, Mussolini as Foreign Minister also had serious faults. He was easily flattered, as Austen Chamberlain had discovered and as Hitler was to exploit. He was too obsessed by Italian prestige, he despised most foreigners and he would not travel or go to conferences. He was impulsive, as Corfu had shown; he had acted there without considering the impact on Britain or France. He was not, to put it mildly, a natural diplomat. Not for him the patient pursuit of concealed objectives; he preferred novelty and public acclaim, like any actor or journalist. He had little time for discussion and compromise, which is after all the whole point of diplomacy; and he detested the pious platitudes of the League of Nations, far too tedious and parliamentary for his taste. Nor was he keen on what became, by the late 1920s, the most prominent international issue, disarmament. After late 1926 Mussolini left much of the routine work to his under-secretary Grandi and made only one major speech on foreign policy in the next three years. In September 1929 he promoted Grandi to be Foreign Minister. But Mussolini still spoke occasionally on foreign affairs, and since he was no longer Foreign Minister he felt he could say what he liked. When Grandi complained in 1930 about one of Mussolini's inflammatory speeches, the *Duce* retorted that this was the reason why he had been given his job: 'What does it matter what I say to my crowds? Why do you think I made you Foreign Minister, except to be able to talk here exactly as I please!'[17]

Grandi soon became a respected Foreign Minister, i.e. he went to the League of Nations, favoured disarmament and spoke English. Hoping as always to win Mediterranean or African concessions, he wooed France, which as always was unresponsive. Italy managed to secure an agreement with France on shipbuilding, but it meant that France kept virtually all her existing naval superiority and the Fascists back home were unimpressed. However, Grandi did stumble on one possible basis of Italo-French understanding. In July 1931 he met the French Foreign Minister Pierre Laval and was pressing the usual line on Italy's need for colonies in Africa as some small recompense that might allay her legitimate bitter disillusionment, when Laval interrupted: 'Ethiopia, for example?'[18] The Italians initially took this, probably rightly, as an attempt to divert them away from the Adriatic and ensure they became bogged down in Africa. But it was tempting, and it could clearly be done without French opposition. Meanwhile the various disarmament conferences – first naval, then from 1932 general – achieved nothing significant except to increase mutual suspicion. Furthermore, Italy had become dangerously isolated. Sir Austen

Chamberlain was no longer British Foreign Secretary, and in Germany Hitler was about to seize power. Despite Locarno and the disarmament conferences, Europe was dividing into two poles again, amidst all the tensions of the Depression. Mussolini grew discontented with Grandi; he had obviously spent too long among the diplomats, and gone native.

In July 1932 Mussolini sent his Foreign Minister a characteristic note: 'Dear Grandi, I have decided to take back the reins of foreign policy into my own hands. Come to palazzo Venezia tomorrow morning at 8.00 a.m. to hand over the documents.'[19] Grandi was sent to London as ambassador, and the *Duce* took over the Foreign Ministry again, with Fulvio Suvich as under-secretary. Suvich was from Trieste, a former Austrian citizen guaranteed to be anti-Serb and anti-*Anschluss*. But policy did not change. Mussolini continued to play his Locarno role, wary of the French but even more wary of the Germans. The French might be blocking Italian moves in the Balkans and Mediterranean, but at least they were not threatening the Brenner. When the Germans floated the idea of a 'customs union' between Austria and themselves, Italy protested very strongly. A customs union might be the first step towards full merger, or *Anschluss*. Italy was anxious to expand somewhere – perhaps in the Balkans, perhaps in the Mediterranean, certainly in Africa – but could not risk paying too high a price.

Mussolini's first task was to win some allies. He knew Hitler would soon take over Germany, and had few illusions about the likely results. Hitler, Austrian by birth, would certainly want to take over Austria as well, and would probably also seek to restore Austria's pre-war central European empire as soon as he was strong enough. So Mussolini cultivated his few friends, Hungary and Austria, and in October proposed a 'new Locarno' – originally a German idea designed to make the Franco-British alliance less significant, but welcomed elsewhere as a device for containing Germany. At the end of January 1933 Hitler did become Chancellor in Germany. One of his first acts, on the day he took office, was to send a message to Mussolini expressing his 'strong admiration and homage' for the *Duce*, and stressing that he would never have succeeded without Mussolini's example.[20] This was not just flattery. Hitler, in fact, genuinely admired Mussolini and had been trying to make contact for years. Mussolini did not reciprocate Hitler's esteem. He regarded Hitler as a sexually degenerate fanatic with lunatic ideas, and always referred to him as 'that madman' ('*quel pazzo*'). He also disliked the Nazis in general, for upstaging his own Fascist movement. However, it was obvious that Germany was now diplomatically isolated too and that Italy was Germany's only possible friend, so Mussolini began to think he might be the man to contain the madman in Berlin. He was astonished by Hitler's anti-Semitism and advised him paternally to give it up ('a racial struggle always has a bit of the flavour of the Middle Ages'), and he was worried by Hitler's obvious contempt for disarmament talks.[21] So in March Mussolini produced a draft treaty of a 'Four-Power Pact' to guarantee consultations on all disputed issues, and hence European stability. The British were happy to go along with it, the French less so – it might turn out to be an excuse for 'revision' of the Versailles settlement, and therefore disruptive – but the British persuaded them, for a time. The Germans welcomed it as recognition at last of their equal status in Europe, free of the restraints of Locarno and of the Italo-British *gendarmerie*. In June the pact was signed in Rome. The European powers had, it seemed, once again avoided a split into two blocs. Once again, and this time more genuinely, Mussolini had been the improbable angel of European peace. In early September Mussolini rounded off his achievement by signing a 'Pact of Friendship, Neutrality and Non-Aggression' with the USSR, obviously another move to contain Germany and preserve stability, this time in Eastern Europe.

But on 14 October 1933, without warning, Germany walked out of the League of Nations. This unexpected blow killed the Four-Power Pact and threatened the remaining prospects for disarmament. Worse, it indicated that Hitler was about to seize Austria. Mussolini was furious. He threw Italian support behind the Austrian Chancellor Dollfuss, a conservative Catholic who proceeded to crush the Social-Democrat/Communist opposition in February 1934. Mussolini had suggested this, in order to prevent the German-backed 'Austronazis' posing as saviours of the country from Bolshevism.[22] However, Dollfuss was still faced by constant riots and terrorism from the 'Austronazis', so Mussolini also financed Starhemberg's *Heimwehr* movement, a nationalist but anti-Nazi version of the Italian squads. In March he signed the 'Rome Protocols' with Austria and Hungary, emphasising Italian support for both, and in the summer he stepped up his public denunciations of anti-Semitism: 'a policy of this kind, a policy that cannot help but be obscurantist, exclusivist, chauvinist and imperialist, can not be a policy for the twentieth century'.[23] But it was clear that Britain and France were not interested in Austrian independence, and Mussolini soon became pessimistic about the prospects. In June he agreed to meet Hitler at last at Stra, near Venice. It was a personal visit, not official, and it did not go well. They discussed disarmament, anti-Semitism and the position of the Church in Germany. On all these issues Hitler was inflexible, indeed fanatical. Mussolini thought he had told Hitler clearly to keep his hands off Austria, but

Hitler later said he had been told that Italy had no objections to new elections in Austria (which the Nazis would probably win), nor to the inclusion of some Nazis in a new Austrian government (which would mean a de facto German takeover).[24] This claim was not credible. The two men spoke together in German and certainly Mussolini's knowledge of the language was quite inadequate for serious political discussion,[25] but Mussolini was obviously supporting both Dollfuss and Starhemberg. No doubt Hitler, who in any case rarely listened to what anyone else said, deliberately 'misunderstood', as he was to do many times in future.

In July 1934 Dollfuss's wife was staying with the Mussolini family at Riccione, where Dollfuss himself was to join them. But on 25 July he was assassinated in Vienna by Nazis, and a Nazi coup seemed imminent. Mussolini himself had to break the news to Frau Dollfuss. So this was no ordinary diplomatic crisis: Mussolini was personally engaged as a human being. He was convinced that Hitler had ordered Dollfuss's murder, perhaps as a personal insult to himself. The Fascist press raged against the Germans, and Mussolini rushed four divisions to the Brenner frontier. He threatened to send them over the Austrian border if need be, to help the new Austrian government suppress any Nazi coup. Hitler realised he meant it, and told his men to back down. The *Anschluss* was postponed for a few years – just as well, for Mussolini was bluffing. His four divisions would not have lasted long against an Austrian uprising backed by Germany. The whole episode wrecked any chance of Mussolini establishing good relations with Germany. Hitler became a legitimate figure of abuse and mockery in Fascist Italy. At carnival time in Bologna in 1935, one of the floats depicted Hitler as a clown; when the German embassy staff complained about this outrage to their head of state, the police said they had allowed it because they had thought it was meant to be Charlie Chaplin.[26]

Mussolini, by contrast, was the toast of Europe. Honest, forthright and effective, he was the man who had consistently urged a fair settlement of the war debts issue, who had pushed through the Four-Power Pact, who had pressed hard for disarmament, who had safeguarded Austrian independence and who had stood up successfully to Hitler – ironically, the only European statesman to do this before 1940 was Mussolini. He really was the elder European statesman, a reliable defender of the peace. The British and French – who, needless to say, had themselves done nothing whatsoever to save Austria, or Locarno – beamed their approval. He deserved the adulation for he had genuinely tried to build bridges, although some of the credit should go to the unsung hero Suvich. At his best, Mussolini had a thoughtful, pan-European perspective. He grasped that Europe was still in a desperate political and economic crisis that might well lead to war and/or to internal chaos and revolution in several more countries, and he proposed some realistic remedies. In July 1932, when Grandi had been dismissed, people had expected Italian foreign policy to become more aggressive and irresponsible. Instead, Mussolini had pursued exactly the opposite line, with great success. He had organised the Four-Power Pact, he had kept Hitler out of Austria, and he had even played his part at the League of Nations. The whole Austrian crisis had stimulated him and on foreign issues, at least, he was far livelier and alert in 1933–4 than he had been a couple of years earlier. Indeed, he appeared to be the only sane, decisive statesman in Europe (the British, under Ramsay MacDonald and Simon, were sane but indecisive, Hitler was decisive but insane, and the French, apart from Laval, were both indecisive and insane, or at least insanely obstinate).

At any rate, the first *Anschluss* crisis of 1934 was his finest hour. Italy was isolated no longer. In October 1934 Britain's top Foreign Office official, Vansittart, went to Rome and assured the *Duce* that all British opinion was anti-Nazi. That was nice to know, but Mussolini naturally expected a more tangible reward. In January 1935 he received it, although it turned out to be not tangible enough. The new French Foreign Minister Laval went to Rome and signed a firm agreement (the 'Rome Accords') with Italy on arms, the Balkans and Africa, to strong British and Russian approval. The French handed over 110,000 sq km of desert on the Libyan border and 20,000 sq km near Eritrea, to add to Mussolini's collection. In return, Italy gave up the special status of Italians in Tunisia. This was, on the face of it, a terrible deal for Mussolini. He abandoned a long-held demand in Tunisia and gained only 'half a dozen palm trees in one place, and a strip of desert which never contained a sheep on another'.[27] But the French also handed over 2,500 shares (out of 34,000) in the railway from Djibouti to Addis Ababa, and above all Laval pledged the famous *désistement*, i.e. the French would turn a blind eye to Italian activities in Ethiopia, except inasmuch as they affected French economic interests associated with the railway. This is what Mussolini really wanted – a free hand in Ethiopia, as well as an alliance in Europe. The Italians in Tunisia and the Ethiopians were to pay the price of the Franco-Italian alliance. But so, as it turned out, were Mussolini and Laval. *Désistement* was a verbal agreement, which could hardly be made explicit in the published accords. The agreement was too personal, and too dependent on Laval – virtually the only Frenchman willing to compromise – continuing in office. Even a year later Mussolini and Laval were corresponding with each other about its exact meaning, and Mussolini had to concede that

Laval had not necessarily agreed to an Italian war in Ethiopia, merely to increased Italian influence there.[28] Even so, at the time it was an astonishing transformation. Italy and France had, it seemed, made up their long-standing quarrels at last, and had realised they must stand together against Hitler. Soon the two countries' chiefs of staff were consulting together and planning direct military cooperation.

From Rome to Addis Ababa, via Stresa 1935–6

By this time Italy was already committed to conquering territory in Ethiopia. This was a long-held dream, pre-dating Fascism. The Italians had invaded Ethiopia in the 1890s and had suffered a shameful defeat at Adowa in 1896. It was the first occasion an African country had successfully resisted European colonisation, and it had made a strong impression on the moody, 12-year-old Mussolini. But now Italy was a Great Power, and wished to prove it. Mussolini's great ambition was to found an African empire and the obvious place was Ethiopia, virtually the only part of Africa left uncolonised. Italy had spent much of the 1920s 'pacifying' Libya with considerable brutality. Her other existing colonies, in Eritrea and Somalia, were on either side of Ethiopia; the frontier lines were unclear and border incidents were frequent. The British and French would not be too offended provided their interests were safeguarded, since they too suffered from Ethiopian border raids and would welcome greater security for their own neighbouring colonies. The Italians could invade from both directions, win military glory, expunge the shame of Adowa and revenge their ill-treatment by the Allies at Versailles. Mussolini had domestic reasons too. He needed to maintain morale at home, especially among the young. He could hardly keep proclaiming his martial values and the need for Empire for over a decade, without actually fighting anybody. Why have a *Duce* or a Fascist regime at all, if Italy were simply to remain a peaceful European backwater? Mussolini, like that other great newspaper proprietor Lord Copper, needed a war: a quick, easy war against carefully chosen, weak opponents. It should provide opportunities for some noble and well-publicised acts of heroism, and should end in a colourful march through the enemy capital.

So he set his sights on Ethiopia. As early as 1925 he ordered military and diplomatic preparations in case Ethiopia collapsed: 'while waiting, work in silence, as far as possible in collaboration with the British, and try to allay the suspicions of Abyssinian officials'.[29] In 1928 Italy signed a

'Pact of Arbitration and Friendship' with Ethiopia, agreeing to refer disputes to arbitration and proposing a road into Ethiopia from Eritrea (it
was not built). But border incidents and tribal conflicts continued. The
Ethiopian government was weak and had little control over the outlying
parts of the country. In the summer of 1932 De Bono, the Italian Colonial
Minister, visited Somalia and Eritrea and reconnoitred the prospects for
an attack on Ethiopia. On his return to Rome he drew up a plan and
sent it round the various general staffs and service ministries, which
were unenthusiastic.[30] But Mussolini approved. In October De Bono
triumphantly told another general that the campaign would take place
in 1934–5, and that he himself would be in command: '[Mussolini] wants
to give the East African operation a characteristically Fascist imprint.
Nobody except myself is qualified to do that, don't you think?'[31]

The military, as always, demanded far more men and resources than
De Bono had envisaged, and Mussolini was not in a mood to stint. Somalia and particularly Eritrea saw a flurry of improvements: the port of
Massawa was widened, roads were built and makeshift barracks constructed. In 1934 the king visited both colonies, for the first time. In
Somalia he was presented with a golden bunch of bananas, a symbol of
Somali 'efforts to emancipate the Motherland from a product of which it
was a tributary to the foreigner'.[32] In Italy herself, foreign military attachés
noted greater military preparations.[33] In the summer and autumn of 1933
Mussolini took over the three service ministries himself, and appointed
new under-secretaries. He also brought Badoglio, chief of the general
staff, back from Libya so that he could assist in the planning. In February
1934 the diplomats were brought into the plan and the Grand Council
was told – although not, of course, asked for its opinion. Many of its
members were dubious, as was Badoglio. Even Mussolini himself wondered in the summer of 1934, during the Austrian crisis, if this were
quite the time to send thousands of troops off to East Africa.[34]

Other powers were aware of these developments, and they had interests in Ethiopia too. Early in 1934 Britain secretly offered the Red Sea
port of Zeila in British Somaliland to the Ethiopian Emperor Haile Selassie,
in return for grazing rights for local tribesmen in Ogaden – including
Walwal, which was claimed by Italy as part of Italian Somalia, and where
there was an Italian garrison already. In late November 1934 a British/
Ethiopian Boundary Commission, tracing the Ethiopian/British Somaliland
boundary with the aid of an 'escort' of 600 Ethiopian soldiers, came to
Walwal, and fighting soon broke out. The 'Italian' garrison troops (all
Somali in fact) drove out the Ethiopians, but 150 people were killed. Mus-
solini was not pleased, either with Ethiopia or Britain. On 30 December

he finally issued orders for the total conquest of Ethiopia: 'there is no other way to found the Empire'.[35]

Mussolini's memorandum of 30 December 1934 was none too popular with the army high command. It was about to begin staff talks with the French, and did not want to risk alienating its new partners; nor did it want to see all the available resources being swallowed up by a futile colonial campaign.[36] Badoglio, as chief of staff, had spent most of 1934 arguing against the Ethiopian campaign; but if there had to be a war at all, it should be run by the army, not the Colonial Ministry.[37] In his view De Bono, now High Commissioner for East Africa, was too old (aged 68) and too incompetent to be given the command, and De Bono's original plan had been hopelessly optimistic about the number of men – 20,000 Italians, plus 60,000 local troops – that would be required. Mussolini, as usual, mediated. He left De Bono in charge but prudently poured extra men and equipment into Eritrea and Somalia, in case Badoglio turned out to be right. His December memorandum spoke of 60,000 Italians and 60,000 natives, 'even better if 100,000 Italians'; by February he told De Bono he would provide 100,000 Italians and 100,000 natives; by March it had gone up to 200,000 Italians; by October, when the war actually began, there were 135,000 Italian soldiers and about 85,000 local troops in the colonies, plus around 50,000 civilian Italian workers in Eritrea alone, building roads and barracks.[38] This was not serious military planning; it was, literally, doubling the number he first thought of. It was also far more than any of his military commanders had requested or recommended, but Mussolini was taking no chances. The Ethiopian campaign was to be no colonial skirmish but a real national war, personally supervised by the *Duce* and with all the regime's prestige, indeed its whole future, at stake. The cost was irrelevant; there could not be another Adowa. De Bono soon had 30,000 vehicles and nearly 250 planes available as well as huge numbers of troops, sitting out the rainy season without accommodation. However, although De Bono was left in nominal charge of the overall operations and held the command on the Eritrean front, he had little or no influence over Graziani, commander of the troops in Somalia, let alone over naval or air operations. Each commander made his own plans, ignoring the others, and neither Mussolini nor his chief of staff, Badoglio, seriously attempted to coordinate war preparations.[39]

Mussolini had squared the French with the 'Rome Accords'; but Italy's most important ally was Britain, and it was vital to win *her* tacit consent to Italy's ambitions in Ethiopia as well. Hitler did his best to help, by reintroducing conscription in Germany and repudiating the arms restrictions laid down in various treaties. So in April 1935 Mussolini invited the

British and French Prime and Foreign Ministers to Stresa, just further down Lake Maggiore from Locarno, essentially to discuss the German threat but also to sound out British reactions to what were already manifest Italian intentions. It was to be the last formal meeting of the wartime allies, and Mussolini seems to have been a decisive, practical chairman. The three powers reached a broad agreement that European stability was a good thing. Each would oppose any attempt to change the existing frontiers, and would consult together if Austria were threatened. Sir John Simon, British Foreign Secretary, was happy to see the French and Italians on such good terms, but Britain did not commit herself to fighting over Austria or anywhere else. The British did not yet distrust Hitler that much, nor fear his rearmament. With their customary well-meaning naivety, many of them thought that Germany needed to be reassured rather than restrained, let alone encircled. Certainly Britain did not expect to pay a price for Italian support in Europe.

The Stresa agreement applied only to Europe. Ethiopia was politely avoided in the main discussions, although each country's African experts debated the issue among themselves. Everyone knew by this time of Italy's war plans. Troopships were to be seen sailing through the Suez Canal, and in any case Mussolini had informed the British in January 1935 of the Italo-French 'understanding'.[40] True, the British ambassador warned Mussolini in February that British public opinion might prove hostile to an Italian attack on Ethiopia, which had been a member of the League of Nations since 1923; and Vansittart repeated this warning to Grandi on 27 February and 7 March.[41] Mussolini therefore knew of British concerns, but assumed that some sort of compromise could be patched up, especially because of Hitler. He promised to safeguard British interests in the region and was anxious to know what those interests were, so as to avoid future misunderstandings. The British set up a commission under Sir John Maffey to find out, but it could not discover any apart from Lake Tana and the Nile waters. Naturally neither Mussolini nor the British government took British public opinion too seriously. So Mussolini at Stresa assumed that silence meant consent. Here, he thought, was another tacit understanding that Italy could go ahead; another *désistement*. He was not wrong. There really was very little ambiguity at Stresa, even if matters were not spelled out there any more than they had been four months earlier in Rome.

But the tacit African agenda at Stresa turned out to be a diplomatic catastrophe. As war grew closer, British public opinion underwent one of its periodic fits of morality. To its horror, the British government found itself faced by a sudden, unexpected outburst of enthusiasm for the League of Nations, whose covenant forbade any attack on a member state on pain of collective reprisals. The Liberal press leaped to the defence of Ethiopia. In June the famous 'Peace Ballot' against war, any war, collected 10 million signatures. No government could ignore these popular protests, particularly as it was likely to be election year. Within the government Anthony Eden, Minister for the League of Nations, became spokesman for 'collective security'. Confirmed Italophiles like Churchill or Sir Austen Chamberlain (the one out of office, the other semi-retired) were silenced. Chamberlain and the senior Foreign Office officials were desperate to keep Italy as an ally against Hitler and were therefore quite willing to let Mussolini have Ethiopia if he wanted it; but their views seemed far too cynical in the inflamed atmosphere of 1935. They were reduced to warning the Italians that the war might weaken Italy's military strength and allow Germany to move south-eastwards.[42] The argument was perfectly valid but unconvincing, since Britain had shown very little concern about the fate of Austria the previous year. An alternative approach was to let Mussolini know indirectly what Ethiopia was like: 'if it was worth anything we would have taken it already'.[43] The real problem was that the Italians had been given a nod and a wink at Stresa – time-honoured diplomatic devices, of course, but not bankable. The British had said nothing explicit and had put nothing in writing. They could deny everything and, with an election to win, they did.

Mussolini, always given to resentment, was furious at this volte-face and felt betrayed. He urged Grandi to tell Britain to give normal support to her ally, and not to treat Italy on the same footing as backward Ethiopia: 'by doing so [Britain] would act exclusively to the future advantage of forces that are undermining European peace and security'.[44] Hitler, delighted by these developments, made a speech in the *Reichstag* promising not to interfere in Austrian affairs. This was an obvious approach to Mussolini, indeed a guarantee that nothing would happen behind his back while he was busy in Africa, and the British began to be alarmed. On 21 May the British ambassador put a more promising suggestion to the *Duce*: Italy should be given a 'protectorate' in Ethiopia, like Britain in Egypt or France in Morocco. Ethiopia would remain formally independent, but Italy would decide all the key issues.[45] Mussolini was quite interested in this possibility but it would not satisfy the League, which could hardly impose a mandate on one of its own members. In June Anglo-Italian relations became even worse when the British signed an unexpected naval agreement with Hitler. It limited the German navy to 35 per cent of the British (apart from submarines, where parity was allowed), but that meant that it might become as large as the French and larger than the Italian. This naval agreement, coming when it did, was crucial. It showed the British could not be trusted to contain Germany or to oppose German rearmament, and it undermined the Stresa agreement after only two months.

Later in June 1935 Eden went to Rome to placate the *Duce*. He took another compromise plan, essentially the same scheme Britain had offered Haile Selassie the previous year. Britain would hand over the port of Zeila and part of British Somaliland to Ethiopia; in return Ethiopia would give Italy most of the Ogaden, including Walwal, and Italy would enjoy economic dominance. Mussolini turned this down flat: another desert. It was far less than the British ambassador had thought feasible a month earlier. He did not want to give Ethiopia a port, and he did not want to see Britain becoming de facto protector of Ethiopia. He stressed that a peaceful outcome was possible, but Ethiopia would have to concede all the outlying (non-Amharic) provinces to Italy and also give Italy control, presumably via a mandate, over the central nucleus. These were clearly impossible demands, and the meeting broke up. Mussolini disliked the fastidious Eden ('I have never seen a cretin so well dressed'), and Eden more than reciprocated the *Duce*'s feelings. British attitudes began to change. Until late June Britain had sought a compromise, without commitment to either side; thereafter, spurred on by opinion at home, she became a more active advocate of the League and of collective security. Just as France began serious staff talks on military collaboration with Italy, Britain moved the Home Fleet to the Mediterranean. The two parties to the dispute were no longer Italy and Ethiopia; they had become Italy and Britain. The Ethiopian issue had triggered an Anglo-Italian 'Cold War'. It continued for the next five years, before eventually turning hot.[46]

This 'Mediterranean crisis' in late summer 1935 was a nasty shock to Mussolini and to most Italians. He had not foreseen the force of British enthusiasm for the League; but then, nor had the British. On 9 August he told Badoglio to prepare plans for a war against Britain. Badoglio consulted the three service chiefs of staff and under-secretaries, and reported back – without a plan – that such a war would be an unequivocal disaster, to be avoided at all costs:

Your Excellency has brought enormous benefits to our country. You have given it a place of honour in the world. Your Excellency cannot now break off this magnificent action, nor, even less, expose the country to a disaster that would plunge us down to a Balkan level. Your Excellency, with your inexhaustible resources of which you have given such evident proof, will surely be able to find an honourable solution to the current dreadful situation, and avoid a war with Britain.[47]

In other words, the army did not think a war against Britain could be won; nor did the navy, nor the diplomats. Even the police were seriously worried, for fear of popular unrest. But Mussolini ignored them all. His secret services, raiding the British ambassador's safe, had told him that the British Home Fleet had very little ammunition, especially against aircraft; the British were bluffing. Mussolini also realised that the British Admiralty would not risk a Mediterranean war: Britain would win, but at the cost of losing a few ships at a time when Britain was already short of vessels to protect her Far Eastern possessions against Japan. Moreover, the British would have no support from France, nor from the Dominions.[48] Above all, even a British Cabinet would surely not be so stupid as to wage war for peace, i.e. to make war on Italy so that Italy might not make war on Ethiopia. Mussolini simply could not understand why Britain was siding with a barbarous, slave-owning feudal state like Ethiopia against her First World War ally, and he took it as an affront to Italy. He was willing to respect Britain's colonial interests but he was not going to listen to hypocritical anti-colonial sermons from people who controlled half of Africa themselves and who had certainly not acquired it peacefully.

Mussolini had guessed right. The British Cabinet had no intention of going to war with Italy. Many of its members desperately wanted to keep Italy as an ally against Hitler, and cared not at all about Ethiopia. They knew that European peace depended on a 'Stresa' alliance, not on the League of Nations. But they had to do something, and they had to appear devoted to the League. On 22 August they agreed that the League should impose moderate economic sanctions on Italy if she attacked Ethiopia. Such sanctions were not likely to be effective, but stronger ones (e.g. on oil) or tougher measures like closing the Suez Canal might well have forced Mussolini to retaliate. In fact, Mussolini was shocked by the threat of sanctions. This was something he had *not* foreseen.

Meanwhile, negotiations continued. In August representatives of the three Stresa powers met in Paris, to no avail. Mussolini told his negotiator simply to play for time: 'I don't want an agreement unless they concede me everything, including the head of the Emperor.'[49] In September a 'Committee of Five' (Britain, France, Spain, Poland and Turkey) at the League produced a plan whereby Italy would have economic control of Ethiopian development, while the League itself exercised a political mandate. The Italian diplomats recommended that this should be accepted, but the *Duce* refused, and kept his nerve. It is worth noting that at this stage it was always the British, not Mussolini, who tried to find a compromise. Mussolini simply carried on with his war preparations. Usually so obsessed with his image abroad, he even ignored the foreign press. Nor, apart from one memorandum to the League council in September, did he soften up the League with talk of a civilising mission or 'humanitarian war', although he had quite a good case: Ethiopian government was mostly extortion, the outlying non-Amharic peoples were cruelly exploited and slavery was widespread – the Italians later claimed to have freed two million slaves. The result was that Italy lost the propaganda war before a shot had been fired. The great journalist, the man who had virtually invented government control of information, could not be bothered to argue his cause. Perhaps doing so would have made little difference, but it was worth a try. If the British favoured the Ethiopians it was largely because they knew nothing about them. To virtually everybody outside Italy the Ethiopian war seemed a brutal conquest and an attack on the very principles of the League of Nations rather than an emancipatory crusade, and Mussolini did very little to alter this perception.

On 23 September the British ambassador saw Mussolini, who stressed the menace of Hitler but otherwise appeared

calm, affable and unperturbed. If mad, he is a very singular madman . . . he seems astonishingly untroubled by the remorse of conscience. The explanation lies probably in his philosophy and creed. He believes in war as the means by which a country can be kept vigorous, young, powerful and progressive. He believes also that Italy is the heritor of the ancient traditions of the Roman Empire. He finds his country lacking space, raw materials and the place in the sun which he holds to be its due. These reasons combined have rendered him oblivious of other considerations such as economic or financial facts.[50]

Or, he might have added, diplomatic and military ones. Mussolini should have been preoccupied with Germany, not Ethiopia; with the crisis in Europe, not Africa. And even the Ethiopian campaign itself presented a huge risk. As Churchill said at the Carlton Club the same week,

to cast an army of nearly a quarter of a million men, embodying the flower of Italian manhood, upon a barren shore two thousand miles from home, against the good will of the whole world and without command of the sea, and then in this position to embark upon what may well be a series of campaigns against a people and in regions which no conqueror in four thousand years even thought it worth while to subdue, is to give hostages to fortune unparalleled in all history.[51]

However, Fortune still smiled on Mussolini. On 3 October 1935 the war in Ethiopia finally began. De Bono pushed into Ethiopia and within three days took the symbolic town of Adowa. Then he stopped, to Mussolini's chagrin, although in early November he did take Makale after much agitated prompting from Rome. But diplomacy did not stop. At Geneva a flurry of activity led by Eden resulted in economic sanctions, excluding oil, being imposed on Italy from mid-November. League members promised not to import Italian goods, to stop some exports to Italy and to end financial credits. However, several major countries, including Germany, Japan and the United States of America, were not League members. The United States of America, which continued to send arms as well as oil, was a more useful friend to Italy than was Germany, for Hitler imposed an arms embargo on both sides and did not seek to break sanctions.[52] Other countries, e.g. Austria, Hungary and Argentina, were in the League but had no intention of imposing the new measures; nor did Switzerland, apart from an arms embargo. Even Britain continued to send coal. The new measures were economically and militarily ineffective, as predicted. Eden tried early in 1936 to have oil included, but the French would not support him. The Italians tightened their belts, and the balance of payments deficit on trade was lower during the sanctions period than it had been earlier.[53]

But sanctions had very significant political and diplomatic consequences. The Italians – not just Mussolini, but nearly all Italians – were furious. They regarded themselves as a civilised nation fighting against barbarians, and they expected sympathy and support from their friends. There had been no League sanctions on Japan over Manchuria, nor on Germany for reintroducing conscription. Why had Italy been singled out for denunciation? Mussolini caught the national mood of defiance and resentment. Italy could stand alone, against her false friends and the hypocritical League. Italian public opinion, hitherto extremely sceptical about the whole enterprise, swung round rapidly. Sanctions made the war hugely popular in Italy, to everyone's surprise including Mussolini's. When the government asked citizens to donate gold for the cause, there was an enthusiastic response. Even Benedetto Croce gave his Senator's gold medal and, in a stupendous propaganda coup, Queen Elena handed over her wedding ring, an example followed by millions of others. Mussolini was in luck. He might easily have found himself fighting an unpopular colonial war with little support at home and none abroad. Instead, the British kindly ensured that the sacrifices of war could be blamed on them.

Throughout the autumn of 1935 Britain and France sought to find a compromise, especially once the British election of 14 November was safely over. Mussolini, too, characteristically left the door open for compromise, in case the war went badly. Despite sanctions, his representatives stayed at Geneva throughout the war, put the Italian case and won some tacit support from the neutrals, who were just as anxious as he was to keep the other Great Powers out of the conflict. Soon a new compromise was worked out by the senior French and British officials in Paris and London, and approved by both Foreign Ministers. This scheme, the famous 'Hoare–Laval pact', proposed that Italy should receive eastern Tigray outright; there would be frontier changes in the Ogaden and on the Eritrea/Danakil border; the central Amharic areas would remain under the *Negus*, the Emperor Haile Selassie; and most of southern Ethiopia, south of the 8° parallel and east of the 35° meridian, would remain under Haile Selassie's sovereignty but be administered for 99 years by a chartered company chaired by a delegate from the League. The company would give Italy exclusive economic rights and a 'preponderant but not exclusive' role in development and welfare administration. This, it was hoped, would block any further overt political expansion by Italy but would allow her strong economic influence, and furthermore would link her into the League system. Ethiopia would also be given an outlet to the sea, either by Italy handing over Assab and a band of territory to reach it, or by a corridor through French and British territory to Zeila.[54] Formally, this proposal was for an exchange of territory, as it had to be if British public opinion were to accept it. In practice, it was very similar to what Mussolini himself had requested via the French and via his unofficial envoy to London, Ezio Garibaldi. It is worth stressing that Mussolini did not, in late autumn 1935, necessarily envisage conquering the whole of Ethiopia. Ethiopian resistance showed no sign of collapsing; De Bono showed no sign of advancing; oil sanctions were still very possible, especially if the war dragged on. Mussolini wanted quick gains, presumably in the peripheral regions, a link between his existing colonies of Eritrea and Somalia, and economic concessions.[55] The 'Hoare–Laval pact' gave him most of what he wanted, including a virtual mandate in southern Ethiopia. He was minded to accept, naturally extracting a few further concessions if possible.

So he summoned the Grand Council to discuss the plan, and drafted a motion accepting it. But then, before the meeting, a French official leaked the scheme to the press. There was a public outcry both in France and Britain. After all, the British government had just been re-elected on a platform of 'collective security', so why was Britain forcing the Ethiopians to surrender? As the Grand Council began its debate in Rome, the House of Commons debated the scheme in London. Soon Grandi telegraphed the news: the Commons, with a Conservative majority, had turned it down. So the scheme collapsed, and Mussolini managed to avoid having to take a tricky decision. A week later he told Laval that if the Grand Council meeting had run its normal course 'the reply would not have been un-favourable'.[56] Hoare had to resign forthwith. He was replaced as Foreign Secretary by the symbol of sanctions, Anthony Eden, since Sir Austen Chamberlain was passed over as being too old. Laval fell too, a few weeks later. Mussolini was quite shocked by the failure of the 'Hoare–Laval pact', and by these consequences. It was not his fault; he would probably have accepted the scheme. It was French officials who had leaked it, and the British parliament that had rejected it. It had been the last real chance of a negotiated settlement. Now it was war or nothing, and most people expected Italy to lose – or, at least, to have to accept eventually a less than satisfactory outcome. And Italy's arch-enemy had now become Brit-ish Foreign Secretary, and would certainly try to secure oil sanctions.

Meanwhile the war continued, Mussolini's war in every sense. He was Minister of the Interior, Foreign Affairs, War, Navy, Aviation and Col-onies. He had always been an empire-builder, even in his early days at *Avanti!*; now he was building a real empire. He sent out his younger colleagues to fight and to enhance their Fascist credentials, and his two elder sons both flew as pilots in the war. He tried, not very successfully, to be a hands-on military strategist. After Makale, he urged De Bono to push on to Ambi Alagi; when De Bono refused on strategic grounds, Mussolini replaced him by Badoglio. This was a mistake, from Musso-lini's viewpoint. Badoglio was a more experienced and prestigious com-mander than De Bono, and he had the king behind him. The *Duce* showered him with detailed instructions to press forward, but Badoglio took even less notice than De Bono had. The *Duce* was in a hurry – he had to win quickly, before Eden managed to impose oil sanctions or the existing sanctions started to bite – but his military commanders would not move until they were sure of winning, and they were not sure yet. In mid-December the Ethiopians won some territory back. But their efforts were not coordinated. Each *ras*, or local warlord, fought on his own with his own men; worse, they insisted on fighting set-piece battles against more numerous and much better-equipped troops. This was a losing strategy, especially as the Italians had over 250 aircraft. Mussolini also demanded that his generals should not be squeamish about bombing civilians, nor about using mustard gas against troops. Both Badoglio and Graziani, commander of the southern front, made their own decisions about this, with Mussolini issuing 'authorisations' or 'prohibitions' as the needs of diplomacy or propaganda dictated.[57] It seems that around 1,150 bombs of mustard gas were dropped during the war, i.e. nearly 250 tonnes, although over half failed to explode, and many of the rest fell in the wrong place.[58] The gas was disabling but not usually lethal and it probably had little impact on the war, certainly less than aerial machine-gunning to which the Ethiopians had no defence.

By 20 January Badoglio was ready, and the real Italian offensive began. He had the largest army ever used in a colonial war, between 350,000 and 400,000 men including about 100,000 Eritreans and Somalis; he also had 250 planes and 30,000 vehicles. By early March his troops held all Tigray; at the end of the month they defeated the Emperor himself near Lake Ashangi, and took Gondar the next day. Badoglio then advanced on the capital, Addis Ababa, and took the city on 5 May – just in time, before the rainy season really began. Three days earlier the *Negus* had fled, or rather had calmly caught the train down to Djibouti – greatly to Italian relief, as they had no idea what to do with him if he were captured. Even in mid-April Mussolini had been contemplating giving him nominal authority over part of Ethiopia, under Italian control.[59] Meanwhile Graziani, coming up from the south, took Harare on 8 May, and organised resistance collapsed. Guerrilla warfare, of course, replaced it and continued for the five years that the Italian occupation lasted, but Mussolini could claim a famous victory, well prepared and well executed. Fewer than 3,000 Italians and about 1,600 colonial troops had been killed.

The Triumph of the *Duce*?

On 5 May 1936 Mussolini proclaimed victory to a huge crowd in piazza Venezia. Four days later, once he was sure that the *Negus* had left Ethiopia, he also proclaimed Victor Emmanuel III as the new Emperor of Ethiopia: 'salute the reappearance, after fifteen centuries, of the Empire upon the sacred hills of Rome'.[60] It was a great personal triumph. In seven short months he had defeated Africa's oldest state and 52 'sanctionist' countries as well, and done so without provoking a wider war. He had overcome hostility abroad and military scepticism at home. He had avenged Adowa, and had even proved Churchill wrong. It was Mussolini, and he alone, who had wanted the Ethiopian war, and who had imposed it on a reluctant army; it was he who had insisted on sending huge numbers of troops, and who had supervised the logistics; it was he who had laid down the broad lines of strategy, and who had urged on his cautious generals; it was he who had redeemed Italy's military reputation. He had shown courage, foresight and even patience.

His political achievements were no less impressive. He had won over the French in January 1935, kept his nerve when sanctions were imposed the following autumn, and roused overwhelming patriotic sentiment in December. He had remained in the League despite sanctions and a great deal of sanctimonious abuse, and he had made sure there was someone else (Eden) to blame if things went wrong. He had defeated not only the Ethiopians but also the might – or rather, the peevish petulance – of the British Empire. He had won 'the greatest colonial war in history'. It was, in the historian Gioacchino Volpe's sarcastic phrase anticipating Andy Warhol, 'Mussolini's quarter of an hour'[61] – or rather his few weeks, while he and many Italians lived on a high peak of exaltation. Henceforth Mussolini was addressed officially as 'The Founder of the Empire'. The king even offered him the title of 'Prince'. Italy, despised and neglected by her allies at Versailles in 1919 and subjected to sanctions by them in 1935–6, had at last become a truly Great Power.

However, Great Powers have great burdens, and great expenses. Ethiopia proved a troublesome colony – Eden called her 'the greatest sanction of all'.[62] Most of the western zones had not been conquered and guerrilla war continued there for years. In July Mussolini authorised the new viceroy, Graziani, to adopt a terror policy of reprisals against rebels, and Graziani needed little encouragement. He was not the most tactful of rulers. In February 1937 he told an assembly of chiefs that 'your main fault is your habit of lying. Falsehood is the basis of your every thought.'[63] The basis of Graziani's own thought seemed to be to provide jobs for his numerous poor relatives. Soon there was an attempt to assassinate him, which resulted in massive reprisals (at least 5,000 Ethiopians killed). The Italians controlled the towns and were relatively welcome in the peripheral Muslim areas. They gave money to Islamic schools and paid for some influential people to go to Mecca. They even built a mosque in Addis Ababa, while shooting two bishops of the Coptic Church and expelling all foreign missionaries including the French Catholic bishop Monsignor Jarosseau, who had been there for 50 years. In true Roman fashion they built over 3,000 km of roads, including the highway from Adowa to Addis Ababa; and they built hospitals, schools and aqueducts. They intended to stay, and to 'develop' the country. Thousands of 'experts' and colonists poured in. A tour of duty in Ethiopia became very popular among young Italians. They were attracted by adventure, by good jobs, by extra pay, by a marvellous climate, and above all by beautiful, bare-breasted and available girls. But the cost was huge. Ethiopia provided no loot, indeed swallowed up Italian resources. By 1937–8 about 12.5 per cent of the total state budget was being spent in East Africa alone, and the total national debt rose by almost 70 per cent in five years.[64] Ethiopia bled Italy dry, just when all the other powers were rearming.

It is easy to say this with hindsight, and admittedly both Britain and France had greatly *extended* their empires as recently as 1919, but the fact remained that Mussolini was 40 years too late. He had founded an African empire just when colonialism was going out of fashion, and when existing empires were struggling to hold on to what they already had. The *Negus*'s propaganda victories at the League of Nations, indeed the very existence of the League, showed that Great Powers henceforth could not throw their weight about too obviously, at least against other League members. Mussolini did not care. He had won his war and avenged Adowa. Now it was time to move on. After 1936 he paid little attention to Ethiopia and never went there. Ethiopia became the viceroy's problem, or the Colonial Minister's, and these two were usually at loggerheads.

The other consequences were diplomatic and psychological, and even more serious. When the Hoare–Laval scheme collapsed in December 1935, the 'Stresa front' against Germany collapsed with it. Mussolini was still unsure of military victory and unsure of the effects of sanctions. He faced a possible oil embargo and now had little chance of a satisfactory compromise. He drew the obvious conclusion. France and Britain had proved faithless friends, so it was time to consider changing sides. On 28 December he wrote to Laval telling him the 'Rome Accords' were over. Germany had not backed Mussolini either – on the contrary, Hitler had sold arms to the *Negus* before November 1935, and had even offered arms and planes to Britain – but at least the Germans had not imposed sanctions nor delivered high-minded lectures about colonialism. Mussolini realised, of course, that Hitler was a dangerous psychopath, but that simply made it easier to play the 'German card'. As early as May 1935 the German ambassador in Rome, von Hassell, had reported signs of a better relationship with Italy, and the British ambassador in Berlin had also noticed that Hitler was 'posing as Mussolini's best friend with the possible risk of an Italo-German understanding concluded behind our backs'.[65] But there was an obvious obstacle to this understanding: the corpse of Dollfuss. Just as he had ditched the Italians in Tunisia the previous year in order to win French support, so Mussolini now prepared, with characteristic *spregiudicatezza*, to ditch the Austrians in order to win over the Germans. On 6 January 1936 he told the astonished von Hassell that he would no longer oppose German designs on Austria. Austria might become a German satellite, provided she remained formally independent.[66] Both Hitler and the German Foreign Office were initially sceptical, but the *Duce* meant it. Suvich, the under-secretary at the Italian Foreign

Ministry, was horrified. He had been kept out of the meeting on 6 January, and since it was his job to take notes, there was and is no Italian record of the conversation. When he found out what had happened, he tried to persuade Mussolini to preserve Austria as a buffer state at all costs, stressing Germany's constant aim to expand to the south and east: Germans in Vienna today would mean Germans in Budapest and Prague tomorrow.[67] Suvich came from Trieste and was a known *austriacante*. In the new climate his days at the Foreign Ministry were clearly numbered, and the following June the failure of the Hoare–Laval pact claimed yet another victim.

The Italo-German rapprochement was hesitant and did not run smoothly. For some time Mussolini simply used it as a threat, particularly against France. On 22 February 1936 he saw von Hassell again, and gave him even more startling news: Italy would not cooperate with Britain and France, under the Locarno treaty, if Germany reacted strongly to the new Franco-Russian agreement.[68] This was a coded way of saying that Germany could move her troops into the 'demilitarised zone' of the Rhineland (i.e. the left bank of the Rhine, and a 50-km-wide strip on the right bank). On 7 March Hitler took a huge gamble, and did just that. It was quite contrary to the Treaty of Versailles and also to Locarno, but the Western powers did not react. France, immersed in a serious domestic crisis at the fall of the Laval government, would not act alone; Britain and Italy, the guarantor powers under Locarno, were not willing to act at all. Mussolini was not going to cooperate with Britain to impose sanctions on the one major European country that had not imposed them on him. Britain, still obsessed by Ethiopia, thought Hitler had simply moved his troops from one part of his country to another. This was foolish, for the whole point of the demilitarised zone was to make it easier for France to attack Germany if Germany attacked any other country. Now France could not do so, and hence central Europe was exposed. Furthermore, Locarno was dead too, like Stresa. Mussolini told his Austrian *protégé* Starhemberg to adapt to the new situation. In late March he summoned the leaders of Austria and Hungary to Rome, and made it clear that the days of a virtual Italian protectorate were over. He also told the Austrian Chancellor, Schuschnigg, to come to terms with Germany, and he did not object when Schuschnigg reshuffled his government and excluded Starhemberg. Neither the Italians nor the French were now willing to protect the small states of central Europe. The whole post-war security system had collapsed.

On 5 June Suvich sent Mussolini a memorandum asking the *Duce* to work towards a new system of security, with guarantees for the small states.[69] He was promptly dismissed. This was a highly significant move. Suvich was an intelligent, professional man willing on occasion to stand up to the *Duce*. He was replaced by Edda's husband, Galeazzo Ciano, who became not under-secretary but Foreign Minister outright, in a rare example of Mussolinian nepotism. Ciano was 33 years old, and as the *Duce*'s son-in-law was highly unlikely to argue for any independent views. His job was not so much to be Foreign Minister – Mussolini continued to decide policy, as previously – but to be the *Duce*'s crony, a cheerful young companion with whom Mussolini could let off steam. Hitherto Mussolini had been counselled by men like Contarini, Grandi and Suvich, all willing to give unwelcome advice. Now there was no one to put an alternative view, to help Mussolini to control his emotions or even to keep him informed.

On 11 July 1936, after weeks of negotiation, Germany and Austria reached an agreement, a *modus vivendi* whereby Austria remained form-ally independent but allowed some of her Nazis into government. This was an *Anschluss* in all but name: 'one people, two states'. Mussolini permitted this without protest, indeed he encouraged it, although he did insist that Hitler had to stop at the Brenner: the South Tyrol, acquired in 1919, might have mainly German-speaking inhabitants but it was now sacrosanct Italian soil. Hitler was happy to promise this, and for once he meant it. But everyone knew Austria herself was doomed. With his usual cheerful cynicism, Ciano later told the new Italian ambassador to Vienna to act like 'a doctor who has to give oxygen to the dying patient, without the heirs noticing. If in doubt, we are more interested in the heirs than in the patient.'[70] Two years after his firm pro-Austrian stand, Mussolini had abandoned her. In return, he had secured support and gratitude from Europe's new strongman, the real winner of the Ethiopian war.

Meanwhile the Ethiopian war was over, but sanctions continued for another two months. To call them off would have been to admit failure. Only on 18 June did Eden ask the League to lift them, and only then because the Chancellor of the Exchequer, Neville Chamberlain, inter-vened by publicly calling the policy of sanctions 'midsummer madness'.[71] They were eventually lifted on 6 July, but Britain still refused to recog-nise the Italian Empire. In British eyes Mussolini was the arch-villain of Europe, far worse than Hitler. He had made a fool of them, and they never forgave him. The whole Ethiopian episode was arguably Britain's most humiliating defeat since the loss of the American colonies. Nor was Mussolini likely to forget the threats and condescension of the previous seven months.[72] His country had been deliberately impoverished by sanctions and made a pariah, and he himself had been denounced by foppish politicians like Eden for doing what the British had been doing for centuries. Moreover, Italy's relations with France were even worse than with Britain. In January 1935 France had, after all, signed the 'Rome Accords', a close agreement including military cooperation; she had then promptly gone off with Britain, betraying her partner before the honeymoon was over. Now Laval had been overthrown and a Popular Front government of the left had come to power, led by men who had been denouncing Mussolini and Fascism for years and who were often in close touch with the anti-Fascist exiles. With Léon Blum in Paris and Anthony Eden in London, there was very little chance of Mussolini making it up with the Western powers.

However, Mussolini always liked to hedge his bets and he still had some influential friends in the west. Lord Rothermere's *Daily Mail* was virtually Mussolini's house journal in London, and would print anything suggested to it by the Italian ambassador, Grandi. At the end of April 1936 Mussolini told Grandi to spread the word in friendly British circles that Anglo-Italian conflict could 'only have one result: the continental hegemony of Berlin'.[73] Grandi showed this telegram to Churchill, who agreed completely. Churchill, like Neville Chamberlain, spoke out firmly to end sanctions but he also advised the *Duce*, via Alberto Pirelli, that he should 'sugar the pill that Britain was having to gulp down'.[74] Similar advice came from Vansittart, who saw Grandi on 21 May: Britain would need time to recover, and Mussolini should make some face-saving concession to help her.[75] Mussolini's old friend Austen Chamberlain also made encouraging remarks and said he was sure that Mussolini had no personal rancour against Eden – a diplomatic way of saying that of course he had, but he should try and overcome it.[76] But Mussolini, in the exalted euphoria of May 1936, was not in the mood to overcome rancour or to sugar pills. He had never understood why sanctions had been imposed, and he wanted them ended immediately. He replied to Austen Chamberlain that there was no alliance as yet between Italy and Germany, only an improved atmosphere; but 'there might be something more in the future if the madmen of Geneva and London continue their policies hostile to Italy and to the regime'.[77] This was a familiar Mussolini ploy. He was using the threat of Hitler as he had once used the threat of *squadrismo*, to frighten others and to win greater influence for himself. He wanted a closer relationship with Germany, especially since it was the Austrians who had to pay for it; but not too close.

Like any insecure man who has reached the top, what Mussolini really sought was recognition – recognition that Italy was a Great Power, on a par with Britain or France. Austen Chamberlain had wisely granted him this at Locarno in 1925; now, in the midst of conflict, Mussolini floated the idea of a 'Mediterranean agreement' with Britain, to secure the same end. Mussolini also, of course, wanted personal recognition for his own achievements and high European status, and for the Fascist regime as modern and progressive. It always paid to flatter Mussolini. The British had grasped this back in 1925 (see above, p. 179) and Churchill knew it too, but he was not in office and the man who was, Eden, was just as unforgiving as the *Duce*. Recognition was the last thing on his mind. Commenting on Vansittart's talk on 21 May with Grandi, Eden characteristically noted 'there is a touch of blackmail about this and we are not in a mood to be blackmailed by Italy . . . if Mussolini thinks he has only to beckon and we will open our arms, he is vastly mistaken'.[78] Hitler was far more generous.

Finally, the Ethiopian war had wider consequences still. The war, the rapid military victory, the Empire, the adulation at home, above all sanctions and his successful defiance of the Western powers – they all gave a huge boost to Mussolini's already excessive self-esteem, just as the British and French 'betrayal' greatly boosted his already strong sense of grievance. 'Mussolini is Always Right' proclaimed the posters; and so it seemed. In reality, he was already showing signs of decline (see pp. 146ff.), yet just at this point he had the greatest triumph of his life. It confirmed his loathing of 'bourgeois' society, of Leagues and parliaments, and of the whole mercantile mentality. It convinced him that the Italian people really had become disciplined and warlike, and that he himself was a gifted military leader. Self-confidence soon began to shade into megalomania. As in domestic politics, he lost one of his greatest assets, prudence. It was not Italian foreign policy alone that changed; so did the *Duce*, and so did the regime. Fascism had always been a nationalist movement, preaching duty and valour. Now it became overbearingly arrogant, all jack boots and militarist posturing. The British ambassador noted in June 1936 how unpleasant life in Rome had become: 'the arrogance, the exhibitionism, the unrestrained nationalism and the frightening egoism and vanity have been such as to revolt the weaker Anglo-Saxon stomachs'.[79] Mussolini became convinced of his own infallibility, and that of his magnificent soldiers. This was the real legacy of the Ethiopian war. He had gambled, and won; but now he could not leave the table. His 'quarter of an hour' of triumph was leading him to years of disaster.

Notes

1 'La Rivincita di Domani', in *Popolo d'Italia*, 23 April 1919; *OO* xiii, pp. 75–6.

2 Speech of 6 March 1921; *OO* xvi, pp. 150–60.

3 Speech of 24 October 1922; *OO* xviii, pp. 453–61.

4 *OO* xix, pp. 68–71; E. Di Nolfo, *Mussolini e la Politica Estera Italiana 1919–33* (Padua, 1960), pp. 65–7.

5 Sir Ronald Graham to Lord Curzon, 7 June 1923; *DBFP*, s. 1, xxiv, no. 412.

6 Mussolini to Diaz, 12 April 1923; *OO* xxxv, p. 314. 'Latinus', *OO* xxxv, pp. 76–84.

7 The ultimatum is in *OO* xxxv, pp. 75–6; see also p. 338 and xx, p. 392. Cf. Di Nolfo, *Mussolini e la Politica* cit., pp. 80–3, 92–5; A. Cassels, *Mussolini's Early Diplomacy* (Princeton, 1976), pp. 99–101; R.J.B. Bosworth, *Italy and the Wider World* (London, 1995), pp. 36–54.

8 P. Pastorelli, *Dalla Prima alla Seconda Guerra Mondiale* (Milan, 1995), p. 214; cf. also *OO* xxi, pp. 315–21.

9 Archivio De Felice; *OO* xxxvii, p. 15. Cf. D. Grandi, *Il Mio Paese* (Bologna, 1985), pp. 217–23.

10 C. Petrie, *Life and Letters of Sir Austen Chamberlain* (London, 1939–40), ii, pp. 295–6.

11 Minute by Sir Austen Chamberlain, 7 October 1926; *DBFP*, s. 1a, ii, no. 243.

12 Mussolini to Italian ambassadors in Paris and London, 25 November 1925; *OO*, xxxix, p. 555.

13 H. Nicolson, memo on Sir Ronald Graham's 'Review of Italian Political Situation', 23 July 1925; PRO, FO, 1925, C 9899/1/22.

14 Mussolini to ambassador in Paris, 16 September 1926, 14 April 1927, 26 November 1927 and 9 October 1928; *OO* xl, pp. 142–3, 318–21, 515–19 and xli, p. 201.

15 Cf. Di Nolfo, *Mussolini e la Politica* cit., pp. 139ff; Cassels, *Mussolini's Early Diplomacy* cit., pp. 286–7.

16 Dispatch of 28 March 1925; *OO* xxxix, pp. 384–5.

17 Graham to Henderson, 28 May 1930; *DBFP*, s. 2, i, no. 210. Cf. Di Nolfo, *Mussolini e la Politica Estera* cit., pp. 282–3; H. Stuart Hughes, 'The early diplomacy of Italian Fascism', in G. Craig and F. Gilbert (eds), *The Diplomats* (Princeton, 1953), pp. 210–33, at p. 228.

18 Grandi to Mussolini, 25 July 1931; *DDI*, s. 7, x, no. 413. Cf. F. Perfetti, 'Alle origini degli accordi Laval–Mussolini', in *Storia Contemporanea* viii (December, 1977), pp. 683–748, at pp. 688–9.

19 D. Grandi, *Il Mio Paese* cit., p. 354.

20 Report of Major Renzetti, Berlin, 31 January 1931; ACS, SPD, c. ris., b. 71. Cf. R. De Felice, *Mussolini e Hitler. I Rapporti Segreti* (Florence, 1983), pp. 212ff.

21 R. De Felice, *Mussolini il Duce* (Turin, 1974), i, p. 452.

22 Mussolini to Dollfuss, 1 July 1933; *OO* xxvi, pp. 405–7.

23 'Teutonica', in *Popolo d'Italia*, 26 May 1934, in *OO* xxvi, pp. 232–3; also 'Fallacia ariana' on 14 August, p. 298; and 'Alla Fonte' on 29 August, pp. 309–10.

24 De Felice, *Mussolini il Duce* cit., i, pp. 493–6.

25 For examples of Mussolini's execrable German, see his letters to Leni Riefenstahl, 11 July 1936 and to Alvine Dollfuss, 30 July 1937 ('bitte meine herzliche Gruesse zu annehmen'); *OO* xlii, p. 167 and p. 191.

26 Prefect of Bologna to Minister of Interior, 11 March 1935; ACS, SPD, c. ris., b. 71. Note that this is some years before Chaplin's film *The Great Dictator*.

27 Mussolini–Eden conversations, record sent by Drummond to Hoare, 24 June 1935; *DBFP*, s. 2, xiv, no. 320. Cf. De Felice, *Mussolini il Duce* cit., i, pp. 525–30.

28 Mussolini to Laval, 25 December 1935 and 19 February 1936, in *OO* xxvii, pp. 279ff.; *DDI*, s. 7, xvi, nos 399, 403; s. 8, ii, nos 904, 915; and s. 8, iii, nos 106, 252.

29 Mussolini to Minister of Colonies Lanza di Scalea, 10 July 1925; *OO* xxxix, p. 465. Similar instructions to ambassador in Addis Ababa, 1 March 1926; *OO* xl, p. 27.

30 G. Rochat, *Militari e Politici nella Preparazione della Campagna d'Etiopia* (Milan, 1971), pp. 26–31.

31 De Bono telephone conversation with another general, 18 October 1932, in U. Guspini, *L'Orecchio del Regime* (Milan, 1973), p. 112.

32 ACS, Fondo Primo Aiutante di S.M. il Re, sez. spec., f. 135.

33 Report of British military attaché to Foreign Office, 19 September 1930; PRO, FO, 371/14419, C7163/951/22.

34 Mussolini to Badoglio, to under-secretaries of War, Navy and Aviation, and to Minister of Colonies, 10 August 1934; *OO* xlii, pp. 84–5.

35 Mussolini to Badoglio and others, 30 December 1934; *DDI*, s. 7, xvi, no. 358 and *OO* xxxvii, pp. 141–3. Cf. Rochat, *Militari e Politici* cit., pp. 376–9.

36 De Felice, *Mussolini il Duce* cit., i, pp. 633ff; Rochat, *Militari e Politici* cit., passim.

37 Badoglio to Mussolini, 26 April and 29 May 1934; Rochat, *Militari e Politici* cit., pp. 323–4, 349–51.

38 *OO* xxvii, pp. 275–6; *OO* xlii, pp. 96–9. Cf. De Felice, *Mussolini il Duce* cit., i, p. 637; Rochat, *Militari e Politici* cit., pp. 146–7, 407.

39 Rochat, *Militari e Politici* cit., pp. 128–9.

40 Mussolini's instructions to Grandi, 25 January 1935; *DDI*, s. 7, xvi, no. 492.

41 Sir John Simon to Drummond, 29 January 1935, in *DBFP*, s. 2, xiv, no. 143; *DDI*, s. 7, xvi, no. 670.

42 Buti to Suvich, 23 April 1935; *DDI*, s. 8, i, no. 70. Chamberlain wrote to Grandi on 10 May warning that an Italian invasion of Ethiopia would enable the Germans to take Austria; ASAE, Grandi papers, b. 43, f. 105.

43 Message via Alberto Pirelli, October 1934; Y. De Begnac, *Taccuini Mussoliniani* (Bologna, 1990), p. 121.

44 Mussolini to Grandi, 20 April 1935; *DDI*, s. 8, i, no. 60.

45 Mussolini–Drummond conversation, 21 May 1935; *DDI*, s. 8, i, no. 253.

46 On Mussolini–Eden meeting, see *DBFP*, s. 2, xiv, nos 301, 308, 318–20, 323, 325; *DDI*, s. 8, i, nos 430–3; P. Aloisi, *Journal* (Paris, n.d.), pp. 281ff.; A. Eden, *Memoirs, vol. 2: Facing the Dictators* (London, 1962), pp. 220–9.

47 Rochat, *Militari e Politici* cit., p. 229.

48 Cf. Chatfield to Vansittart, 8 August 1935; *DBFP*, s. 2, xiv, no. 431. Cf. also R. Mallett, *The Italian Navy and Fascist Expansionism 1935–40* (London, 1998), pp. 33–7; A. Marder, 'The Royal Navy and the Ethiopia Crisis of 1935', in *American Historical Review* lxxv (1970), pp. 1327–56; R. Quartararo, 'Imperial defence in the Mediterranean on the eve of the Ethiopian crisis', *Historical Journal* xx (1977), pp. 185–220.

49 Aloisi, *Journal* cit., 9 August 1935, p. 293.

50 Drummond to Hoare, 23 September 1935; *DBFP*, s. 2, xiv, no. 630.

51 W. Churchill, *The Gathering Storm* (London, 1948), p. 151.

52 M. Funke, *Sanktionen und Kannonen* (Düsseldorf, 1970), pp. 72–83.

53 Ibid., p. 59; De Felice, *Mussolini il Duce* cit., i, pp. 702–6.

54 Text of 'Hoare–Laval Pact' is in *DBFP*, s. 2, xv, no. 336. Cf. D. Waley, *British Public Opinion and the Abyssinian War* (London, 1975), ch. 2.

55 Mussolini to De Bono, 20 October 1935, in *OO* xxvii, pp. 298ff; Aloisi, *Journal* cit., p. 310 and pp. 318–19 (1 and 31 October); De Felice, *Mussolini il Duce* cit., i, pp. 687–8, 719–20.

56 Mussolini to Laval, 25 December 1935; *OO* xxvii, p. 280. Cf. also Grandi, *Il Mio Paese* cit., pp. 397–400; Aloisi, *Journal* cit., pp. 328–31. According to Alberto Pirelli (*Taccuini* (Bologna, 1984 ed.), p. 147), both Volpi and Costanzo Ciano favoured acceptance.

57 Example of authorisation, Mussolini to Badoglio, 29 March 1936 in *OO* xxvii, p. 316; of prohibition, Mussolini to Graziani, 10 April 1936, in *OO* xxvii, p. 317. See also A. Del Boca, *I Gas di Mussolini* (Rome, 1996), pp. 145–62.

58 Del Boca, *I Gas di Mussolini* cit., esp. pp. 96–7, 139–41, 178; A. Mockler, *Haile Selassie's War* (Oxford, 1984), p. 409.

59 Aloisi, *Journal* cit., 14 April 1936, pp. 373–4; Pirelli, *Taccuini* cit., p. 177.

60 *OO* xxvii, pp. 268–9.

61 ACS, SPD, c. ris., b. 93; *OO* xxxvii, p. xlvi.

62 L.A. Pratt, *East of Malta, West of Suez* (Cambridge, 1975), p. 29.

63 ACS, SPD, c. ris., b. 26, f. 1.

64 G. Maione, *L'Imperialismo Straccione* (Bologna, 1979); S.B. Clough, *The Economic History of Modern Italy* (New York, 1964), p. 259; C. Segre, *Fourth Shore* (Chicago, 1974), p. 83; F. Repaci, *La Finanza Pubblica nel Secolo 1861–1960* (Bologna, 1961), pp. 168–70, calculated the combined cost of Ethiopia and Spain as 12 billion lire in 1935–6 and 18 billion in 1936–7; total state spending, around 25 billion lire p.a. in 1930–4, rose to over 40 billion p.a. in 1935–9.

65 Phipps to Sir John Simon, 20 May 1935; *DBFP*, s. 2, xiv, no. 276. Von Hassell's report of 30 May 1935 is in *DGFP*, s. C, iv, no. 120.

66 Von Hassell to Auswärtiges Amt, 7 January 1936; *DGFP*, s. C, iv, no. 485.

67 Suvich to Mussolini, 28 January and esp. 7 February 1936; *DDI*, s. 8, iii, nos 131, 194.

68 *DGFP*, s. C, iv, no. 579.

69 Suvich memo to Mussolini, 5 June 1936; *DDI*, s. 8, iv, no. 193.

70 G. Ciano, *Diario 1937–43* (Milan, 1990 edn), 24 November 1937.

71 *DBFP*, s. 2, xvi, no. 360. A delighted Mussolini told Grandi on 11 June to congratulate Chamberlain; *DDI*, s. 8, iv, no. 236.

72 Matters had not been improved in May 1936 when the press officer at the British embassy in Rome, Sir William McClure, a man perhaps not best suited to a diplomatic career, reportedly told journalists that 'for us Englishmen the Italo-Abyssinian conflict was nothing more than a war between one brown-coloured people and another even browner one'; ACS, Min. Int., Dir. Gen. P.S., Div. Polizia Politica, b. 171, f. 2.

73 Mussolini to Grandi, 25 April 1936; *DDI*, s. 8, iii, no. 758; for Churchill's agreement, see Grandi's dispatch to Mussolini, 1 May, no. 808. On 2 May Mussolini replied asking Grandi to tell Churchill that 'the future of Anglo-Italian relations, which for my part I wish to be stronger and more fruitful, depends on his attitude and speeches'; no. 815, also in *OO* xlii, pp. 157–8.

74 Pirelli, *Taccuini* cit., p. 180.

75 Vansittart–Grandi conversation, 21 May 1936; *DDI*, s. 8, iv, no. 91.

76 Grandi to Mussolini, 29 May 1936; *DDI*, s. 8, iv, no. 134.

77 Mussolini to Sir Austen Chamberlain, 3 June 1936; *DDI*, s. 8, iv, no. 172. The message was repeated via Grandi to Churchill (Grandi to Mussolini, 11 June, ibid., no. 251).

78 *DBFP*, s. 2, xvi, no. 347 note.

79 Drummond to Eden, 6 June 1936; ASAE, Grandi papers, b. 43, f. 107.

Chapter 8

Electing a New People 1936–40

The *Duce*'s Cultural Revolution

In his hour of triumph Mussolini faced personal tragedy. In June 1936 his youngest daughter Anna Maria, not yet seven, contracted polio. For some weeks her life was in serious danger, and Mussolini was distraught. He was a devoted father, and he spent long hours at her bedside. Eventually she recovered (she died in 1969, aged 40) and Mussolini's normal life resumed. But it had been a real shock, coming on top of all the stress he had undergone during the war. He had already lost a nephew and a brother; now he had nearly lost a daughter. He himself was 53, and looked older. He had aged very markedly, both physically and mentally, in the previous five years. He was bald, heavily built, with a swollen neck, a red face and protruding eyes. He was still reasonably fit, but less active than earlier. Time was running out. His wife Rachele told him to retire at the top, covered in glory after 14 years in office. But Mussolini was far too restless and could never retire. He still had vast ambitions, and knew he had better act quickly if he were to achieve them.

He soon acquired one great consolation. In September 1933 he had met by chance a young admirer named Claretta Petacci, engaged to an air force officer. By autumn 1936, aged 24, she had married, separated and become the *Duce*'s favourite mistress, while her husband had been packed off to be air attaché in Tokyo. Claretta gave Mussolini just what he needed – cheerful, unconditional devotion. She visited him regularly at palazzo Venezia in the late afternoon, had her own apartment at the back, and waited there for the *Duce*'s busy day to end. She was not, of course, his only mistress but she was sensitive to his needs and he became very fond of her. Their phone calls, monitored by the police, show Mussolini as remarkably sentimental, even adolescent ('I live only for you . . . I love you, I'm afraid and am jealous . . . I long only for your kisses').[1] Claretta was attractive, intelligent and uncritical: she did not try to boss Mussolini around, unlike his wife Rachele and his former mistress Margherita Sarfatti. On the other hand, she did not offer the intellectual stimulus or useful criticism that Mussolini now needed more than ever. She also had a family – a brother, an actress sister, various cousins and uncles, all expecting favours and subsidies which Mussolini grudgingly handed out. The 'Petacci clan' soon became notorious in Rome. So poor Claretta was good for Mussolini, but bad for his reputation and for his regime.

Despite Claretta, Mussolini was now dangerously isolated. Most of his children had grown up, he had no friends or companions except Galeazzo Ciano, and the flow of admiring foreign visitors had dried up after Ethiopia. He had no court, and no court jester. His wife and his sceptical children had far more sense than to listen to his reflections. Never had Arnaldo been so missed. Moreover, Mussolini now saw himself as a hugely successful statesman, who had challenged the entire world and prevailed. He turned in on himself and became the great leader, far-seeing in his Olympian detachment and incomprehensible to ordinary mortals. He was obsessed by foreign affairs, a wider stage where alone glory might be found; and he identified his own interests with those of his country. He thought that the world in 2000 would be dominated by Russia, Germany, Japan and Italy. His rhetoric became relentlessly militarist. In the past he had, as a magnificent ham actor, played many roles: peasant, pilot, sportsman, etc. Now he played only one, the imperious commander of invincible armies, always scowling. When he took Italy out of the League of Nations in December 1937, for example, he proclaimed to a huge crowd that 'we have the weapons on land, sea and air, plentiful and tempered by two victorious wars, but above all we have the heroic spirit of our revolution, which no human force on earth can ever resist'.[2] Furthermore, he half-believed it.

Even so, he knew that he needed to transform the whole of Italian mentality and society, to ensure Italy stayed in the race and took over from the decadent bourgeois democracies. The domestic history of Italy from 1936 to the Second World War is essentially that of Mussolini's efforts to complete his revolution, to 'elect a new people' and found a warrior race. He had little time now for astute political compromises, nor for ordinary domestic administration. He might easily have played the grand old man of European politics, but he had a new young mistress and wanted to reassert his virility, the revolutionary vitality of his youth. Indeed, Mussolini strongly stressed the cult of youth, a big mistake given his appearance and that of his *gerarchi*. He was clearly dissatisfied and bored by his own regime, still based on earlier compromises with Church and king; soon he quarrelled with both. He was ever more contemptuous of the 'comfortable life' and of the bourgeois mentality, reluctant to fight or even to breed. Mussolini no longer bothered to conciliate important interests and was no longer content to fight specific 'battles' on limited issues. He revived the austere rhetoric (although not the practice) of *squadrismo*, the stern comradely vigilantism of the 'harsh vigil'. By 1940 preference was given in public appointments to those who had been *squadristi* before 1922. Above all, he preached 'totalitarianism', state control of all aspects of social life, and tried to implement it. No independent institutions were to be allowed in case they challenged the regime's values and authority.

In 1939, after some years of debate, Mussolini took a further step towards 'totalitarianism' by in effect abolishing the Chamber of Deputies and replacing it by a new 'Chamber of *Fasci* and Corporations'. The new body was not elected, even in the 'plebiscitary' manner of 1929 or 1934. It consisted of members of the National Council of Corporations – i.e. the usual advocates and ex-deputies – and of the National Council of the Fascist party, i.e. the 'federal secretaries' at the head of the party in each province. So if anyone lost his corporation or party post he automatically ceased to be a deputy, or rather ceased to be a 'national councillor' as the members were now called; about a hundred of them changed each year. The councillors' task was not to legislate, but to collaborate with government to introduce new laws. Ministers no longer presented their bills to parliament; the *Duce* did it instead.[3] The change marked yet another breach with parliamentarianism and the former constitution. It was partly aimed at the king and his constitutional scruples; partly it was a snub to the Grand Council, which would no longer choose the approved candidates; but mostly it was directed against the 'bourgeoisie' and against old-fashioned ideas like representation and voting. The Senate, however, remained untouched, perhaps because it had never been elected. Mussolini's regime was now curiously ill-defined. Government legitimacy had rested ultimately on parliamentary approval, but the Chamber of Deputies was no more. Was the *Duce* himself an institution, like the king or the Pope, or was '*Duce*' simply a courtesy title like 'Founder of the Empire' or '*squadrista*'?[4] When he died or had to be replaced, would he have a successor, and if so who would decide who it should be? Would his successor, if there were one, have to be approved by the new (unelected) Chamber, or by the Grand Council, or merely by the king? Above all, was the monarchy to survive? These were not so hypothetical questions, at a time when Mussolini was inveighing against the king, war was approaching and popular discontent growing.

The diplomat Bastianini, returning to Rome in 1936 to become Galeazzo Ciano's under-secretary after 10 years abroad, was shocked by the change: the whole atmosphere of government was suspicious and mistrustful. Mussolini treated his ministers disdainfully and expected them to do as they were told without discussion.[5] His expectations were fully justified. His colleagues had no idea what the aims of his policy were, so they did nothing on their own initiative for fear of being repudiated. He left most domestic issues to his Interior under-secretary Buffarini Guidi and to the Chief of Police, Bocchini – and Bocchini became by 1939 so worried about Mussolini's moods that he wanted him treated intensively for venereal disease.[6] About the only independent-minded minister left was Guarneri at Foreign Trade, and he was mostly ignored. Balbo thought, and said openly, that Mussolini now deliberately picked mediocrities because he was afraid of competent men of value who might question his policies.[7] The *Duce* knew of these remarks and made sure Balbo stayed in Libya; in March 1938 he told Galeazzo Ciano that he would make Balbo suffer the same fate as Arpinati.[8] The Grand Council met infrequently and was expected to listen, not discuss; if it voted at all, it voted unanimously. Moreover, it was not only the institutions of government itself that were affected. Many familiar bodies underwent a similar Rake's Progress, the inevitable result of politicisation. In the 1920s the firemen, for example, had been 'Fascistised', i.e. castor-oil for the dissidents, Socialists dismissed, strikes and unions banned. In the 1930s they were 'Staracised': they wore splendid uniforms, had gleaming engines and paraded every Sunday, but received little training and were not much good at fighting fires. In the 1940s reality caught up with them: suddenly bombs were falling, there were plenty of fires and the firemen's skills really mattered. In the long run posturing was not enough.

Mussolini had grown frightened or intolerant of any challenge or even of any advice, let alone discussion. He rarely listened to anybody and became increasingly ignorant of political developments, indeed seriously out of touch, and he confessed to D'Aroma that he now found taking decisions much more difficult than previously.[9] In the Vatican, the under-secretary of state Monsignor Tardini went so far as to confide to a British diplomat that 'he had of late thought that Signor Mussolini was a little losing his sense of balance and restraint', and the officials in London agreed: 'His rages are becoming more violent and more frequent. I do not believe that he is going mad, as is sometimes alleged, but I do think he has lost the calm judgement which used to be one of his outstanding characteristics.'[10] In fact, Mussolini had now reached that dangerous but all too familiar mental state in which solitary, insecure leaders under strain deliberately avoid unwelcome information and punish those who bring it. They need to think that everything is wonderful and that they are infallible, and the only way to do this is denial.[11] In Mussolini's case this was particularly evident about the state of the armed forces, of which he was the minister and about which he made quite sure he knew little. In short, Mussolini was psychologically no longer up to his job. That was clear to his inner circle and even to outside observers, but he had tenure.

In 1938 Mussolini launched his greatest peacetime 'battle', this time an all-pervasive one against the 'bourgeoisie', understood sometimes in the sense of a social group but more often as a 'mentality'. His target was those prudent Italians, of all classes, who preferred a comfortable, pros-perous peace to the heroic sacrifice of war. The 'bourgeois' was a cautious egoist who calculated the cost, disliked the Nazis, and preferred man-dolins to trumpets. He opposed 'autarchy' because it stopped the import of luxuries, and he was 'a great enemy of sport, of anything that might disturb his perennial state of quiet. He is naturally pacifist, sentimental, full of compassion, always humanitarian, infertile.'[12] In historical per-spective, there was nothing very new about all this. Machiavelli had complained that the Italians of his day lacked the martial qualities of ancient Rome, and Mazzini had also deplored their lack of revolutionary fervour. And it must be said that Mussolini did try to live up to his own ideals. He himself was part peasant, part natural aristocrat, but never a calculating, conformist 'bourgeois' – although the Fascist extremists had privately thought him such in the early 1930s. If there was one thing he enjoyed, it was fighting privileged, defeatist elites. He had done it bril-liantly in 1914–15 and in 1917–18, and in 1938–9 he tried it again.

So Mussolini opened up the home front against the sceptics and the closet peacemongers, and founded institutions to promote the message of heroism. In 1937 the Ministry of Press and Propaganda became the 'Ministry of Popular Culture', or Minculpop, with an ambitious programme to control all cultural activity from Rome. The Fascist youth movement was brought under party control, to ensure propaganda was always uni-form, and in 1939 membership became compulsory. The party itself, still run by Starace, was given a new set of regulations, much concerned with details of how to give the 'Salute to the *Duce*'. In 1939 it organised an 'Anti-Bourgeois Exhibition' in Rome, illustrating the contemptible life of the bourgeoisie through paintings like Pullini's mournful the *Only Child*.[13] The battle of the bourgeoisie took extraordinary forms. Starace extended his party exhortations to the whole people, and forbade every-body to shake hands (which most Italians did frequently, when they met someone for the first time *that day*). They had to give the 'Roman salute' instead, and might be beaten up by party zealots if they forgot. This 'reform of customs' did not go down well. Even some of the *gerarchi* turned out to be 'devoted to the handshake' and had to be disciplined. The regime became a laughing stock overnight. Italians were also instructed not to use the normal polite form of address, 'Lei', as it was deemed too 'bourgeois'; they should use the more comradely 'voi' instead. This was even more difficult to enforce than the 'Roman salute', since the party could not monitor every private conversation in the land. It also gave anti-Fascists, or sceptics, an easy way of making their views known: they just used 'Lei'. In the Naples region, where 'voi' was normal in any case, Benedetto Croce switched to 'Lei' for this reason.

The 'anti-bourgeois' campaign was not just a matter of imposing politically correct language, nor even of mobilising the toughs against the toffs. It was also an internal dispute within Fascism itself. It widened the perennial divide between the crude party men and the more sophisticated ministers and officials, a divide that had already become very evident over foreign policy. Many of the Fascist leaders themselves, particularly Balbo, detested Mussolini's policies. But Balbo was in Libya, and in Italy herself the party machine became ever more influential, to the dismay of ministers.[14] In 1937 the party secretary became a minister, and within two years *all* the provincial party secretaries were members of the Chamber. They had no autonomy there, of course, but they did have a key role in implementing Mussolini's 'totalitarian' zeal for control. The party aspired to control, even to micro-manage, every social activity, and to colonise every institution with its own men and its own values. Party officials came to interfere in every aspect of civil society and private behaviour. The aim was to politicise everything, and to break down the old distinction between party and state. Even the civil servants were put in uniform, each rank carefully denoted. This was very expensive (over 300 million lire) and also highly unpopular, as Mussolini realised: 'Another thing that has annoyed many people is uniforms for civil servants. People ask "So everybody in Italy has to be a soldier?" Exactly. Everything in Italy should be military, everything in Italy must be militarised.'[15]

However, the military themselves were treated no better. A few months after visiting Berlin and seeing the German army on parade, Mussolini ordered the Italian army to adopt the 'Roman step' for ceremonial occasions, i.e. the goose step that had so impressed the *Duce* in Germany. The 'Roman step' was even less popular in the army than the 'Roman salute' was among civilians – although for some years officers, too, had been expected to salute each other 'Romanly' when not wearing a hat, and civilians on parades also had to adopt the 'Roman step'.[16] Even the cultural elite of the Royal Academy of Italy had to parade in front of the *Duce* on their anniversary, wearing black shirts and fez, and naturally marching with the 'Roman step'.[17] The king, aged 69 and with creaking joints, simply could not do it, and so royal appearances at military parades had to be carefully stage-managed. Mussolini characteristically told Ciano it was not his fault if the king was physically a 'half-cartridge', a phrase repeated in public the next day in a speech to the Militia, and soon passed on to the king.[18] The *Duce* later made a rather confused speech claiming the 'Roman step' was not Prussian at all and was not even a goose step, although in any case geese were a revered Roman bird and the ones on the Capitol had rescued the city in ancient times.[19] This was all fairly amusing but was also a very imprudent policy for Mussolini. Fascism had little backing among the top army officers, who regarded Mussolini as quite a good corporal but little more. They were loyal to the king, not to a regime which they regarded, rightly, as run by a parvenu bunch of small-town lawyers and stationmasters on the make.

Indeed, the best illustration of Mussolini's increasing megalomania and lack of political caution came in March 1938, when he provoked a completely needless quarrel with the king. The deputies, led by Starace, passed by acclamation a one-clause bill creating a new army rank, 'First Marshal of the Empire', and giving it to both the *Duce* and the king. The Senate naturally approved it too, also by acclamation. But this new law not only created two 'First Marshals', it also literally ranked ex-corporal Mussolini equally with the king, and Victor Emmanuel (who had not been forewarned) was furious. The king took military matters very seriously. He reviewed army manoeuvres every year, visited regiments round the country, and was known flatteringly as 'the Soldier-King', '*Il Re Soldato*'. Moreover, it was not just a matter of protocol, nor of improper parliamentary procedure, nor of Mussolini's pretensions to military expertise. The king was the head of the army. Mussolini, by now impatient with the 'dyarchy' of power at the top, and with a visit by Hitler to Rome imminent, was deliberately challenging not just the king's constitutional position but the army's political neutrality. In the mid-1920s Mussolini had shown far more sense than to attempt to 'Fascistise' the army; now, having founded an empire, he was impatient with any restraint on his military or 'totalitarian' ambitions, and he resented the fact that he still had to share power with a mere king. 'I'm fed up with him,' he told Ciano bitterly, 'I do the work and he signs.'[20] Relations between monarch and *Duce* became very cool in 1938 and never really recovered. Hitler's visit in May 1938 worsened matters, since Mussolini had to play second fiddle while Hitler, as Head of State, drove round with the king and stayed, much to the king's disgust, at the Quirinal palace (see p. 241). Moreover, Mussolini henceforth had to make his visits to the king, even during the war, in civilian clothes; it would have been too embarrassing for the two men to have worn the same First Marshal's uniform. In the long run, i.e. after a victorious war, Mussolini planned to rid himself of the monarchy, and the king knew it.

Just as it was dangerous for Mussolini to attack king and army, so it was absurd to attack the bourgeoisie merely for being bourgeois. These people had kept much of their economic independence and social prestige, and they had sympathisers among the more intelligent Fascist leaders. They had accepted Mussolini in the early 1920s because he had rescued them from strikes and Communism, without asking for real sacrifices. He had genuinely represented important groups and values in post-war society. He had controlled his own zealots and had based his regime upon a satisfactory compromise. But they did not support his efforts after 1936 to create a warrior race, and they certainly did not appreciate finding themselves the target of government hostility in 1938. Now Mussolini himself was the zealot, and his 'battle' was directed against the Establishment. He had undermined the whole basis of his own regime. Mussolini was no longer rescuing the bourgeoisie from anything and he *was* asking them for real sacrifices. So they turned on him; quite right too.

Economic Problems

In November 1936 the lira was devalued at last, by around 40 per cent, and the cost of living rose by 30 per cent over the next three years. At the same time the budget deficit grew alarmingly to nearly 20,000 million lire by 1939–40, and resources were poured into Ethiopia and Spain rather than used productively in Italy. Both ordinary consumers and businessmen suffered from these developments. Moreover, the Ethiopian war and international sanctions had meant a big drive for 'autarchy', i.e. self-sufficiency in vital commodities, and 'autarchy' remained the basis of economic policy thereafter. It was both unpopular and unrealisable: unpopular, because nobody liked the substitutes that soon replaced normal products ('*Lanital*', made from cheese, replaced wool, and rabbit became the basis of fur coats); unrealisable, because Italy had neither coal nor oil, and her supply of iron was very limited. The only major commodity in which Italy achieved self-sufficiency was wheat, and that only in a good year. After 1936 – a bad year – grain producers were no longer allowed to sell their wheat on the market, but only to the state at state-fixed prices, in order to build up stockpiles for use in war. Farmers naturally complained about this and so did consumers, for bread was now made from a mixture of wheat and maize. Indeed, consumers' interests were largely ignored. In 1938, i.e. before the war, the Commission on Autarchy imposed quite severe rationing of luxuries like coffee or petrol, all part of the anti-bourgeois campaign.

In practice, 'autarchy' meant even greater state control – for most of industry the only consumer was the state – but it did not mean effective state planning. Industrial production was now increasingly organised by 'consortia' of the leading firms (there were 300 of them by 1938), who kept prices high and competitors out. A new banking law brought credit under greater government control, and foreign trade could be conducted only by those with licences issued by the Ministry of Trade and Currencies. A quarter of Italian exports went to Germany, and a further quarter to Ethiopia. The largest firms continued to be 'rationalised', i.e. merged, by IRI, which owned some of them and supervised the rest. Indeed, IRI owned over 20 per cent of all the shares in the country, and dominated shipbuilding and steel production. These firms became virtually monopolies in their sectors. As previously, 'corporations' played little part in all these planning and regulatory processes, except as propaganda devices to legitimise them. The consortia, IRI and the other specialist agencies, the various ministries and the corporations all busied themselves regulating, controlling and protecting. Mussolini kept setting up new bodies as well – a Commissariat for War Manufactures in 1935, a Supreme Commission for Autarchy in 1937 – that also had to find a self-important role for themselves. So there was plenty of competition in the Fascist economy: competition to tell other people what to do. But note that this was not a 'Fascist economy', nor even a 'Third Way'. Mussolini relied not on his 'Fascist' institutions but on technocrats (Beneduce, Volpi, Guarneri) and semi-independent agencies, who imposed a variety of controls – taxes, licences, quotas, tariffs, subsidies, control of credit, fixed prices, etc. This bleak picture was mitigated by the black economy, by small family firms and by the tourist trade, but nonetheless Italy had acquired a ludicrously over-regulated, high-tax 'official' economy that was becoming extremely uncompetitive.

Businessmen could no longer influence Mussolini's policy; they merely paid his bills. Tax receipts went up from 16,500 million lire in 1935 to 24,000 million four years later, and there were very unpopular 'forced loans' (e.g. a 5 per cent levy on land and property) as well. Even so, the Minister for Trade kept warning of imminent bankruptcy. By late 1939 there were practically no gold reserves left and the Finance Minister was proposing to sell off Italy's art treasures, to Mussolini's approval but general dismay.[21] Mussolini, like so many others, had started prudent but ended profligate. Affluent people shifted their wealth into gold, or jewellery, or Switzerland. In May 1937 a Militia informer in Milan reported that business leaders were exasperated by the regime's continual demands for money, e.g. for Fascist youth organisations or for the *Popolo d'Italia*: 'any occasion is now thought appropriate to send people round asking for money'.[22] It was reminiscent of the situation in 'Tangentopoli' 50 years later, except that Mussolini needed the money for his empire and his army. In 1938–9 the regime began its 'anti-bourgeois' polemics, and matters grew even worse. The government favoured the syndicates and in 1939 allowed shop stewards inside the factories. Even Volpi apparently remarked that if you scratched Mussolini you would find a revolutionary Socialist. All this was not the welcome stability that Mussolini had once provided. On the contrary, it was a typical 'welfare-warfare' economy, full of hopeless over-subsidised public enterprises and over-regulated private ones, a 'total' system guaranteed to break down under the weight of bureaucracy and serfdom – or war.

Race and Religion

Mussolini still worried about the anti-Fascists, and now with more reason. The Spanish Civil War brought Italian Fascists and anti-Fascists into direct conflict, and the battle of Guadalajara in March 1937 was greeted widely as an anti-Fascist victory (see p. 234). Carlo Rosselli, leader of the 'Justice and Liberty' (GL) group based in Paris, recruited Italian anti-Fascist volunteers for Spain and fought there himself with his (mostly anarchist) troops in autumn 1936. After Guadalajara his slogan, 'Today in Spain, Tomorrow in Italy', began to appear on walls in Italy. Mussolini was not going to tolerate this. It was one thing to put up with anti-Fascist exiles in Paris, even if they occasionally tried to assassinate him; it was quite another to allow them to recruit Italian troops to fight against his Fascist Militia, and all with the support of the French Popular Front government. Ciano, and the head of his cabinet Anfuso, had a word with the heads of military intelligence. In June 1937 Carlo Rosselli was murdered at Bagnoles sur l'Orne in Normandy by French right-wingers, at the request of the Italian intelligence service.[23] His brother Nello was also killed, as an eyewitness. Here, potentially, was another Matteotti affair, although this time the murder was far more official and had been organised by the military. And this time there was no opposition press in Italy to report it, let alone to exploit it. As for Mussolini, as usual he was not *directly* involved. He spoke to De Begnac of the 'Rosselli tragedy': 'not always does a government manage to control the activities of the machinery that represents it'.[24] But it is impossible to believe that he had not known of the plan to kill Carlo (not Nello), or that he had not approved it. He would have had no moral qualms: he knew that GL had been trying to assassinate *him* for years. Moreover, he regarded Italians who fought in Spain for the Republic as traitors, and regularly urged Franco to shoot any Italian prisoners he might take. In fact, the murder of Rosselli turned out to be a successful political move. It remained little known in Italy, and it seriously weakened organised anti-Fascism abroad just when it might have become a real threat.

In 1938 Mussolini's policy turned overtly anti-Semitic. This was not entirely new for him. There had been brief anti-Semitic campaigns in 1933–4,[25] and he had often inveighed against Jewish financiers and businessmen as being too 'cosmopolitan' or Masonic. But that should not be taken too seriously: Mussolini denounced everybody on occasions. He had had Jewish mistresses for years, including the most significant one Margherita Sarfatti, and he had appointed Jewish ministers like Aldo Finzi or Guido Jung to key government posts, Interior and Finance. Even his dentist was Jewish, a sure sign of trust. Jews were welcome as party members and appear to have been Fascist in proportionately greater numbers than other people. Even the hall in piazza San Sepolcro, Milan, where the Fascist movement was founded in 1919, was made available to him by the Jewish president of the Commercial Association.[26] Both the best-known books about Mussolini – Margherita Sarfatti's biography and Emil Ludwig's *Talks with Mussolini* – were by Jewish authors chosen and assisted by him. Once Hitler came to power, Mussolini made it clear that Italian Fascism was not a racist doctrine and that he thought racism was scientific nonsense, and he advised Hitler accordingly.[27] He certainly disliked Zionism and detested the thought that Italian Jews might become loyal to some state other than Italy,[28] but he did not discriminate against them until 1938. Neither he nor the vast majority of Fascists held anti-Semitic views. In any case, Italian-born Jews were few (about 37,000 with two Jewish parents in 1938, plus nearly 10,800 with one[29]), well integrated and long established. They were not seen as a threat to any established interests, and there had been a Jewish community in Rome since ancient times.

The explanation for Mussolini's sudden switch to racism in 1938 is not ideological but political, and the switch was not restricted to Jews alone. It owed something, of course, to the prominence of Jews in anti-Fascist movements, particularly GL, and in the Popular Front government in France. It was also part of the general 'anti-bourgeois' campaign of 1938–9. But two new factors seem to have been particularly significant: the Empire, and the Nazis. As elsewhere, colonial experience encouraged racial distinctions. The Italian troops and officials in Ethiopia had shown an all too enthusiastic *lack* of racial sentiment, and Mussolini had begun to worry about mixed unions and mixed offspring. He wanted an Italian Empire, not a half-breed one. He thought it self-evident that an empire could survive only if the people running it thought themselves superior to lesser breeds. Racial consciousness was needed to make empire viable. He, of all people, urged the viceroy to take a stern line on illicit unions and demand 'racial dignity, or dignity of the Italian people . . . too many Italians have given serious grounds for scandal'.[30] Nobody took any notice. Mussolini sat in Rome and brooded on the racial problem. Perhaps it was a wider issue, not restricted to the colonies? As for the Nazis, although there is no evidence of any German pressure for anti-Semitism, clearly the policy was designed to please Mussolini's new ally Hitler and demonstrate that Italy would prove a faithful friend. Italy could not enter a European war with Jewish officers and officials having to fight and work side by side with the Germans. Such men would never be loyal, and it was best to purge them all first. Furthermore, the purge would have to be publicly proclaimed and practised throughout society, so that no Jew could rise to responsible positions later.

In July 1938 Minculpop issued a 10-point Manifesto on Race, drafted by a 'group of Fascist scholars teaching in Italian universities' and revised by Mussolini himself. It asserted that biological races exist, that the Italians were a pure 'Italian race', Aryan in origin, that Jews were not part of this race, and that 'the purely European physical and psychological characteristics of the Italians should not be altered in any way'.[31] In the autumn a series of laws followed, passed in the Chamber by acclamation but in the Senate by vote; and it is worth recording that several famous non-Fascists, including Benedetto Croce (who *had* turned up to vote against the Lateran Pacts in 1929), De Nicola and Albertini, simply absented themselves from this vote. The laws expelled all foreign Jews (including the queen's private doctor, to her fury) and even those with citizenship if granted after 1919. All native-born Jews were excluded from public office or from attending schools and universities either as students or teachers; textbooks written by Jews were replaced. Jews were also expelled from the Fascist party and forbidden to own over 50 hectares of land, or to have 'Aryan' servants. 'Mixed' marriages would not be permitted in future. Admittedly the definition of 'Jew' was not too rigorous: those with two Jewish parents, or with one but practising the Judaic religion. Hence the children of mixed marriages could become 'Aryan' by being baptised, and there were 4,000–5,000 conversions in autumn 1938 (many of them so that children might be admitted to Catholic schools, having been expelled from state ones). There were also plenty of 'exemptions' allowed for war service or exceptional merit, brought in to placate the king: more than 20 per cent of Jewish families were exempted in this way.[32] Moreover, the laws certainly discriminated but did not actually permit physical persecution, nor interference with Jewish religious practice. And, of course, Italy was not Germany. The laws were not likely to be implemented with zeal; indeed, at local level people were often reluctant to implement them at all. Police informers reported that Jews were greatly respected citizens – doctors, teachers and the like – and that their treatment had aroused a great deal of resentment and shock.[33]

Nonetheless, the laws had a big impact. Jewish businesses closed down; schools lost their teachers; one in twelve university professors were dismissed, including the Rector of Rome University. The laws also wrecked Italian physics for a generation. Enrico Fermi, whose wife was Jewish, went with her to collect his Nobel Prize and promptly moved to the United States of America, there to make a huge contribution to American nuclear research; this was also true of Emilio Segrè. Even Mussolini regretted Fermi's departure, because it left his academy looking old and boring.[34] Above all, the laws were a further blow to Mussolini's image and popularity, both at home and abroad. Most people, indeed most Fascists, opposed them and thought that Mussolini was simply toadying up to Hitler. The Grand Council meeting on 6 October had a very unusual acrimonious debate on the subject, with Balbo and De Bono objecting strongly and several others being manifestly reluctant. The laws were approved but Balbo, in Libya, made sure they were not applied there; Costanzo Ciano, in Livorno, ostentatiously invited Jewish friends to official ceremonies. Mussolini's own children and his sister protected and helped their Jewish friends, as he well knew. Even Farinacci, one of the leading Fascist anti-Semites, turned out to have a Jewish secretary, and was extremely reluctant to dismiss her after 20 years' service. It was widely believed in northern Italy that the laws were simply a 'stealth tax', a way of seizing land and businesses at a time when the state was desperately short of cash.

The anti-Semitic agitation was, as I have argued, part of a more general 'anti-bourgeois' and pro-Empire campaign, designed to make Italians nastier: 'tough on sentimentality, tough on the causes of sentimentality'. The biggest cause of sentimentality was undoubtedly the Church, given to peacemongering and protecting the weak. Early in 1938 the squabbles with Catholic Action began again, as in 1929–31, and continued until autumn. They were exacerbated by Hitler's visit to Rome in May. Pius XI protested about a 'rival Cross', the swastika, being shown on banners throughout Rome, denounced 'exaggerated nationalism' and hastily left for Castelgandolfo in case Hitler wanted to visit the Vatican. Soon Catholic Action members were expelled from the Fascist party, and Farinacci's newspaper was in full cry. When the race 'manifesto' emerged in the summer, relations became really tense. The king accepted the new laws once sufficient 'exemptions' had been allowed, but the Pope did not, if only because the ban on 'mixed' marriages between Catholics and even baptised Jews clearly contravened both canon law and the 1929 Concordat. Eventually the Catholic Action dispute was resolved on the 1931 terms; i.e. Mussolini had to retreat. But the 'wound' to the Concordat remained, as did the more general issue of racism. Relations between government and Vatican remained icy until Pius's death in February 1939. The Church feared war, feared Hitler and feared that the Jews might be merely the first target; after them would come the Catholics, and events in Germany and Mussolini's increasingly violent expostulations seemed to show this was quite likely.

Mussolini had, indeed, realised that the Church was a real obstacle to his plans. He told his Minister of Education, Giuseppe Bottai, that 'the Church has always, I say always, been the ruin of Italy. While other people were dividing up the world she gave Italians a substitute imperialism in the form of a spiritual universalism, which enfeebled us.' The conversation dismayed the sensitive Bottai, who noted perceptively in his diary, 'His antagonist is this [Italian] people, whose history he would like to rewrite and remake in his own way. The Church has softened and emasculated us, deprived us of the taste for rule, has disarmed us. I listen, but I cannot reply. This is a soliloquy, not a dialogue. When I leave I have a sense of bitterness and unease that lasts all evening.'[35] In practice, however, Mussolini might denounce the Church as he did the king, but he could not really crack down on either. As war approached, the churches were full to overflowing and the Vatican newspaper *L'Osservatore Romano* regularly sold out. The king, too, was being greeted everywhere by larger and more enthusiastic crowds than usual, the implied message being 'keep us out'.

The Ciano Cabinet

In September 1939 the Italians *were* kept out, and were greatly relieved not to be taking part in the war (see pp. 247ff.). Many people in the northern regions remembered the Austro-German occupation of 1917–18 and detested the Italian alliance with Germany. The government's anti-French campaign (the 'claims') fell very flat there. The Nazi–Soviet Pact was particularly unpopular. The Church was naturally sympathetic to Catholic Poland and German atrocities there were widely known and deplored, as was the fact that the eastern zones of the country had been handed over to the godless Bolsheviks.[36] In December the king and queen exchanged courtesy visits with the new Pope, Pius XII, and this was widely interpreted as a joint royal–papal effort to keep Italy at peace. People prayed for peace, and stocked up on food.

At the end of October came another 'changing of the guard', this time very significant. Mussolini dismissed Pariani and Valle from their posts as under-secretaries at War and Aviation; they were the scapegoats for military weakness, and were replaced by General Soddu and General Pricolo respectively. He also dismissed the pessimist Guarneri from Trade and at last replaced Starace as secretary of the party, a move generally seen as the end of the 'anti-bourgeois' campaign. The new secretary was Ettore Muti, an ex-*squadrista* and a *Romagnolo* like Mussolini, but one who soon proved incapable of keeping the Fascists disciplined. Pavolini moved to Popular Culture. Grandi, former ambassador in London, had already been made Minister of Justice in July and soon became Speaker of the Chamber as well. Most of these men were now linked to Galeazzo Ciano, and indeed the new government was soon known as the 'Ciano Cabinet' – a government of the more educated and sophisticated Fascists, who had finally defeated the rude provincials and the southerners. But in reality its members owed little loyalty to Ciano, who was extremely un-popular in the party and the country, indeed was a symbol of corruption and nepotism.

He was also, after August 1939, a symbol of 'neutralism'. For that reason the provincial zealots, hostile to Ciano's snobbish cliques, became more pro-German and pro-war; whereas the acting minister of the Royal Household, Pietro Acquarone, met Ciano several times over the winter and assured him of royal favour, if the moment ever arrived when the king needed to intervene. Ciano's diary for 14 March 1940 mentions one such meeting, naturally at the Golf Club:

[Acquarone] speaks openly to me of the situation in preoccupied tones, and assures me that the king is well aware of the discontent disturbing the country.

According to him, His Majesty feels that he might have to intervene at any moment to give a different course to events; he is ready to do so with great energy. Acquarone repeats that the king feels towards me 'more than just benevolence, a real affection and much trust'. Acquarone – I do not know whether on his own initiative or on orders – wanted to push the argument further, but I kept it to generalities.[37]

This was extraordinary. The king, via his minister, was sounding out the *Duce*'s own son-in-law about a possible change of government, and doing so in the crucial few days of March 1940 between Ribbentrop's visit to Rome and Mussolini's trip to meet Hitler at the Brenner (see p. 252). Clearly the king thought that Mussolini was about to decide to join the war, and was trying to find out whether Ciano would support, or perhaps lead, a peace party. The answer was clearly no. Ciano had little backing of his own, and could not risk trying to overthrow his father-in-law. He could not even risk asking him to convene the Grand Council. After December 1939 Mussolini had no intention of doing so, particularly as he knew that the three surviving *Quadrumviri* of the March on Rome – men of huge status in Fascist circles, and in the Council – had met on Rhodes at the end of January 1940 and were all against the war, indeed by now against Mussolini. Balbo, indeed, had referred to 'that madman' ('*quel pazzo*'), meaning not Hitler but the *Duce*.[38]

With a tame parliament and a Grand Council that did not meet, there was no way of deflecting Mussolini from his plans. Even the 'Ciano Cabinet', containing the most prestigious historic leaders of Fascism and backed by king, Church, and businessmen, would not do it openly. Its members grumbled and knew that Mussolini's war policy might prove disastrous, but they still revered the man and would not speak up in public against him, nor form factions against him. In any case, Cabinet meetings were usually little more than monologues by the *Duce*. He was the grand old man, and his status was unquestioned. Until July 1943 Mussolini never had to face a Cabinet revolt, or worry about his colleagues' views. He had amassed plenty of ammunition on each of them, and he received a daily transcript of their telephone calls. Ciano himself had little influence, feared Mussolini's not so oblique threats, and by mid-May realised that the game was up: 'he has decided to act, and act he will'.[39]

A Warrior Race?

To make the Italians into disciplined warriors was not a realistic goal. Whatever Mussolini might proclaim from his balcony, the Italians were not 'a people of heroes, saints and navigators'. They quite enjoyed the rhetoric and they welcomed the prospect of spoils, but they did not share the ambition. Most of them wanted a 'comfortable life', and by the late 1930s they realised that Mussolini had no intention of providing it. He still represented order and stability, and people still feared what might follow him, but they feared the prospect of endless wars even more. The Ethiopian war had been short and popular; the Spanish war (see pp. 230ff.) was neither, and the likelihood of a major European war was even worse. Mussolini was implacable. He told Ciano, 'When Spain is finished I will think of something else; but the character of the Italian people must be moulded by fighting.'[40] This became a constant theme. He also told him that 'Italy will never be Prussianised enough. I will not leave the Italians in peace until there is six feet of earth on top of me', and he boasted to the Fascist national council about the 'kicks in the stomach' he had given the bourgeoisie.[41] To Mussolini, as to Coriolanus, it might truly have been said:

You speak o' th' people
As if you were a god, to punish; not
A man of their infirmity.[42]

However, the Italian people did not wish to be Prussianisèd or to have their characters moulded. Mussolini may have wanted them to be born again; they were quite happy as they were. Starace's constant parades had become a boring embarrassment, and pre-military training was disliked and if possible evaded. People joked that 'we were better off when Mussolini was in charge'.[43] But no ironic jokes could cope with constant bombast and parades, with manifest corruption and obsequious incompetence, with the persecution of Jews and the rush to a hated war. Most intelligent Italians knew perfectly well that Italy's arms, wealth, resources and population were insufficient for a European war, and feared the outcome. Police informers reported a marked shift in opinion between 1936 and 1938: a 'wave of pessimism' swept the country as the regime, after 17 years of repression, promised only further subjugation and conflict.[44]

Mussolini, in earlier years a consummate politician, had now deliberately alienated king, Church, army, bourgeoisie, and indeed most ordinary Italians as well. He should have tried to unite and mobilise the nation together, but he chose the opposite course. The danger to him came not from outside but from within: from his own beliefs, which were absurd but could not be questioned. His regime, after Ethiopia, was imploding from his inability to leave people alone, and from his boundless sense of self-importance. In 1936 it was even proposed to put up a colossal statue in the Foro Mussolini – not explicitly of Mussolini himself, but very similar ('it will be future generations that will recognise the *DUCE* in the quasi-mythological figure of this modern Hercules, the Protector of Rome'[45]). Unfortunately the French anti-Fascist press found out about the project and dubbed it the 'Statue of Tyranny', so it had to be abandoned. But it symbolised what was going wrong. Back in March 1914, at one of his trials in Milan, Mussolini had demanded what an Italy of 36 million inhabitants would be like if everyone thought the same: 'a madhouse, or rather a kingdom of boredom and imbecility'.[46] Now, 25 years later, Mussolini was seeking to achieve just that. It was a sad decline, but not unusual. After an initial honeymoon period, most dictators end up losing touch, mouthing stale platitudes, organising constant parades, persecuting any obvious target group, wrecking the economy and, above all, fighting wars.

By 1938–9 the regime had generated the familiar psychological distortions of over-regulated societies. Constant propaganda and repetition had ensured that even genuine virtues – courage, patriotism, responsibility – could only be mentioned ironically; cynical disaffection had set in. Mussolini recognised this and tried to counter it, but the audience had grown bored with his performance. He had held power too long, and people had forgotten why he had come to power in the first place. By 1939 he was quite often perceived as a ranting old fool, to be humoured rather than admired. His speeches developed a wonderful pantomime quality, with the crowd hissing the villains: 'Some imbeciles on the other side of the Alps [*the whole crowd boos and hisses lengthily*] have imagined that the Italian people has become less devoted to the regime [*the multitude reply with a single cry of 'No!'*] . . . people and regime are completely united (*Yes, yes*).'[47] Oh no they weren't.

Notes

1 U. Guspini, *L'Orecchio del Regime* (Milan, 1973), p. 143.

2 Speech of 11 December 1937; *OO* xxix, pp. 32–4.

3 G. Giuriati, *La Parabola di Mussolini nei Ricordi di un Gerarca* (Bari, 1981), pp. 184–6.

4 E. Gentile, *La Via Italiana al Totalitarismo* (Rome, 1995), p. 213.

5 G. Bastianini, *Uomini, Cose, Fatti* (Milan, 1959), p. 40.

6 G. Ciano, *Diario 1937–43* (Milan, 1990 edn), 27 December 1939.

7 ACS, SPD, c. ris., b. 61, sottof. 2; A. Lessona, *Memorie* (Florence, 1958), pp. 186, 333–6.

8 Ciano, *Diario* cit., 18 March 1938.

9 N. D'Aroma, *Mussolini Segreto* (Bologna, 1958), p. 151.

10 D. Osborne to Foreign Office, 7 July 1938; minute by A. Noble; PRO, FO, R 6217/281/ 22.

11 N. Dixon, *On the Psychology of Military Incompetence* (London, 1976).

12 'Luoghi comuni', in *Popolo d'Italia*, 2 August 1933; *OO* xxvi, pp. 38–9.

13 P. Meldini, *Sposa e Madre Esemplare* (Milan, 1975), pp. 128ff.

14 E. Sulis, *Processo alla Borghesia* (Rome, 1940), esp. pp. 167–9; Gentile, *Via Italiana* cit., pp. 115–16, 184–5, 196–7.

15 Speech to National Council, PNF, 25 October 1938; *OO* xxix, pp. 185–96, at p. 187.

16 ACS, Min. Int., Dir. Gen. P.S., Div. Polizia Politica, b. 191, f. 2.

17 *OO* xxix, p. 73.

18 Ciano, *Diario* cit., 31 January 1938; also speech to Militia, 1 February, in *OO* xxix, pp. 52–3.

19 Speech to National Council, PNF, 25 October 1938; *OO* xxix, at pp. 188–9.

20 Ciano, *Diario* cit., 2 April 1938; also 3 June 1939 and 14 May 1940. On the 'First Marshal' dispute, see L. Federzoni, *Italia di Ieri per la Storia di Domani* (Milan, 1967), pp. 168ff; R. De Felice, *Mussolini il Duce* (Turin, 1974–81), ii, pp. 23ff.

21 Ciano, *Diario* cit., 7 February and 3 March 1940. On Trade Minister Felice Guarneri, see his *Battaglie Economiche* (Milan, 1953), esp. i, p. 317; and F. Zani, *Autarchia e Commercio Estero* (Bologna, 1988).

22 Report of 3 May 1937; ACS, SPD, RSI, c. ris. b. 49 'Schuster'.

23 C. Conti, *Servizio Segreto* (Rome, 1946), pp. 259–60.

24 Y. De Begnac, *Palazzo Venezia* (Rome, 1950), p. 613.

25 M. Michaelis, *Mussolini and the Jews* (Oxford, 1978), pp. 57–80; R. De Felice, *Storia degli Ebrei Italiani sotto il Fascismo* (Turin, 1961), ch. 3.

26 A. Tamaro, *Vent' Anni di Storia* (Rome, 1971–5), iii, p. 356; M. Sarfatti, *Mussolini contro gli Ebrei* (Turin, 1994), p. 105; Michaelis, *Mussolini and the Jews* cit., p. 11.

27 See Chapter Seven, p. 184 and notes 21 and 23. See also *OO* xlii, p. 36; D'Aroma, *Mussolini Segreto* cit., p. 86.

28 'Religione e nazione', in *Popolo d'Italia* 29–30 November and 15–16 December 1928; *OO* xxxvii, pp. 333–7.

29 Sarfatti, *Mussolini contro gli Ebrei* cit., pp. 113–14; Michaelis, *Mussolini and the Jews* cit., pp. 59ff.

30 Mussolini to viceroy, 18 November 1937; *OO* xxxvii, p. 148. Cf. A. del Boca, 'Le leggi razziali nell' impero di Mussolini', in A. del Boca et al., *Il Regime Fascista* (Bari, 1995), pp. 329–51.

31 Sarfatti, *Mussolini contro gli Ebrei* cit., pp. 18–20, 103.

32 Buffarini Guidi to Mussolini, 12 September 1938; ACS, SPD, c. ris., b. 30; Michaelis, *Mussolini and the Jews* cit., pp. 255–6; De Felice, *Storia degli Ebrei* cit., pp. 251–3.

33 ACS, Min. Int., Dir. Gen. P.S., Div. Polizia Politica, b. 219, f. 2, e.g. report on Cuneo, 19 March 1939 (where local priests visited Jewish homes to show solidarity); S. Colarizi, *L'Opinione degli Italiani sotto il Fascismo* (Bari, 1991), p. 309.

34 Y. De Begnac, *Taccuini Mussoliniani* (Bologna, 1990), pp. 317–18, 358–65.

35 G. Bottai, *Diario 1935–44* (Milan, 1982), p. 187 (15 April 1940).

36 S. Colarizi, *L'Italia Antifascista dal 1922 al 1940* (Bari, 1976), ii, p. 474 (report from Milan, 24 January 1940); also Colarizi, in E. Di Nolfo (ed.), *L'Italia e la Politica di Potenza in Europa* (Milan, 1985), pp. 295–6.

37 Ciano, *Diario* cit., 14 March 1940.

38 De Felice, *Mussolini il Duce* cit., ii, p. 721.

39 Ciano, *Diario* cit., 13 May 1940.

40 Ibid., 13 November 1937.

41 Ibid., 18 June 1938.

42 W. Shakespeare, *Coriolanus*, III, i, 80–2.

43 Bottai, *Diario 1935–44* cit., p. 140 (23 January 1939).

44 Colarizi, *L'Italia Antifascista* cit., ii, pp. 428ff; Colarizi, *L'Opinione* cit., pp. 272ff.

45 Ricci's phrase, 22 June 1936, in ACS, Ricci papers, b. 2, f. 4, sottof. 7.

46 M. Sarfatti, *Dux* (Milan, 1926), pp. 143–4; P. Monelli, *Mussolini Piccolo Borghese* (Milan, 1968), p. 68; *OO* vi, pp. 128–31.

47 Speech at Reggio Calabria, 31 March 1939; *OO* xxix, p. 257.

Chapter 9

The Approach of War 1936–40

The Spanish Civil War and the Axis

Mussolini's Ethiopian triumph had given Italy an empire and made her, in his eyes, a Great Power at last. But she was still a militarily weak country, and as Germany recovered Italy became the least of the four major West European nations, to say nothing of the United States of America, USSR or Japan. Despite the bombast and the militarisation at home, Mussolini knew this perfectly well. His only hope of success was to ally, or threaten to ally, with the strongest other power, and rely on another country's efforts winning benefits for Italy. This was, after all, traditional Italian policy, adopted long before Mussolini and long after him.[1] By 1936 the strongest other power was, or soon would be, Germany, which was rearming very quickly. Mussolini could not hope to beat Germany, so he joined her. His strategy was simple: to use the German alliance to threaten France and Britain and so make gains in the Mediterranean and Africa – Tunisia, perhaps, or Corsica or Nice, or even Malta. Meanwhile Germany, having won de facto control of Austria in July 1936, would no doubt wish to expand in central and eastern Europe, and Mussolini would raise no objection. The whole focus of Italian foreign policy had shifted from the Danube and the Balkans southwards.

It was, of course, a risky strategy. Italy became a destabilising power, a troublemaker in the Mediterranean. But Mussolini had always liked a bit of risk, and never more so than in 1936. He was the magnificent *Duce* who had defied the world; he could get away with anything. He calculated that the decadent Western powers would never oppose him seriously, as they had just proved. In any case, they were scared of Germany and needed him; soon they would come begging for his support, and would bring concessions. Italy would exact vengeance for the shameful sanctions that the West had imposed upon her. In Berlin, a respectful Hitler was full of gratitude to the *Duce* for (virtually) letting him have

Austria. It was too good a chance to miss. Furthermore, Mussolini *needed* more triumphs. He had been in power for 14 years and he only had Ethiopia to show for it. The whole point of being a Great Power is to become greater still.

This calculation was superficially rational, but it was extremely short-sighted. The French and British would obviously ignore Italian claims, as they had in 1919. They may have been decadent but they had no intention of yielding their key Mediterranean bases. Italy was not indispensable and her military machine frightened nobody. As for Germany, her ambitions lay to the east. However grateful Hitler might be, it was difficult to see why Germany should be willing to act as the instrument of the Italian Empire in the south. Worse, German ambitions had the potential to trigger a full European conflict. Mussolini certainly did not want that. He wanted colonies and a bigger say in the Mediterranean and Adriatic, and thought he could use Hitler to win them. However, he realised that he could not be sure of controlling the highly unstable Hitler. So he hesitated; in mid-1936 he was by no means committed to a German alliance. But he had strong anti-League of Nations sentiments, or resentments, and he wanted revenge on those who had insulted him. Moreover, events conspired to draw him closer to Hitler's side.

On 18 July 1936 a group of military conspirators in Spain rose against the left-wing government. Mussolini had been in touch with similar plans a year or two earlier, but he had no prior knowledge of this rising, apart from a report by the Italian consul in San Sebastian on 22 June saying a military coup was imminent (the consul's boss, the Italian ambassador in Spain, called it a wild rumour and asked for the consul to be transferred).[2] The coup was not an immediate success. Many army garrisons and most of the navy stayed loyal to the Republican government. Francisco Franco, commanding the 47,000 Spanish or local troops in Morocco, needed to transport his men across the Straits of Gibraltar quickly to join the uprising, but he had only three aircraft and he could not risk crossing by sea against a hostile navy. The Italian military attaché in Tangiers, Major Luccardi, took up his cause and requested that Italian planes be sent. Mussolini initially refused, for supplying Franco might be hazardous. The French had just elected Blum's 'Popular Front' government which would certainly help the Spanish Republicans, and there was an obvious risk of being dragged into a Mediterranean war against France. However, within a few days Italian policy changed. Galeazzo Ciano had just been made Foreign Minister and was anxious to establish his rather tenuous Fascist credentials; Major Luccardi reported that the Germans were sending planes and pointed out that if Franco won he would be grateful to whichever country had backed him. Prompted by Ciano, on 26 or 27 July Mussolini gave in and took the risk. He knew that Britain, at least, would not back the Republic, and that the French armed forces were conservative and favoured Franco. So he sent a ship full of arms and munitions, and 12 unmarked S.81 transport planes – although one crashed in the sea, and two ran out of fuel and had to land in the French-controlled zone of Morocco. A week later he sent 27 fighters and other material, including 5 armoured cars.

His decision was revealing. He had refused several times, but eventually he agreed because of pressure from Ciano, from some of his diplomats and from Franco himself. Yet the danger of a European conflict over Spain was a real one, and Mussolini had no allies. So he took a big gamble, apparently in the belief that a few planes would enable Franco to win quickly. Militarily, this was a real strategic blunder, revealing complete ignorance of the situation on the ground and a willingness to be overruled by others – unhappy omens for the future. But essentially his motives were not military but political. Mussolini sent the planes not out of any desire to win territory in Spain (although he may have hoped for air bases in the Balearics) but to tip the balance against the 'Social-Communists' not only in Spain but also in France, and to ensure that a French–Spanish alliance of the left did not dominate the western Mediterranean. He knew Franco was not a Fascist, but he *was* certainly anti-Communist. Mussolini's fear of Communist contagion, of hostile anti-Fascist governments in Spain and France, was a real one even before the Russians started supplying arms to the Republic; when they did, it became a dominant theme. Moreover, he did not want the Germans to be Franco's only supplier. But he did not intend to become any further involved. He was sending a few planes in an emergency, and a shipload of arms; no more.

However, in the next few weeks a 'Fascist alliance' unexpectedly emerged. It did not make sense for Germany and Italy to send arms to Spain independently, without consulting each other. Göring, at the German Air Ministry, took the initiative. On 6 August the two heads of military intelligence, Canaris and Roatta, met in Bolzano and agreed to communicate daily on Spain. On 23 August Hitler sent the Prince of Hesse to Rome to suggest closer military collaboration in Spain, and Mussolini – in need of an ally – agreed enthusiastically. A few days later Canaris and Roatta met again and agreed to dispatch more supplies, and technicians to maintain them; only the largest items, like warships, should not be sent because they were too obvious. In addition, a senior military officer from each country should go to Spain to liaise between Franco and their respective governments; these men should also advise Franco on military operations, 'making him understand that since he receives so much help from Germany and Italy, he should accept their advice as well'.[3] So only a month after the Spanish civil war had begun, Italy and Germany were being sucked in, both thinking that Franco would win easily if he had just a few more arms. Moreover, they were becoming committed to close, top-level military planning and collaboration (although not, as yet, to sending troops). The Axis was gestating, in Spain.

During the autumn of 1936 this process continued further. In September the former German Justice Minister came to Rome, and saw Mussolini. In late October Ciano went to Germany and showed Hitler a purloined copy of the 'Eden dossier', documents by British diplomats describing the Nazi leaders in less than flattering terms ('dangerous gangsters').[4] The two agreed that the Mediterranean was an 'Italian lake', and that Germany should have both a free hand in east-central Europe and her old colonies restored in Africa. They also agreed to increase still further their help to Franco and to recognise his Nationalist government as the legitimate one in Spain. A month later Italy signed a secret treaty with Nationalist Spain, whereby Franco promised benevolent neutrality in case of war between Italy and another European country (i.e. France).[5] That was the greatest reward Mussolini ever received from Franco. By then Mussolini had made his famous speech of 1 November, in piazza del Duomo in Milan, announcing the birth of the 'Axis' (a term first used by the Hungarian premier Gömbös in October 1935): 'this Rome–Berlin meridian is not a diaphragm, it is rather an axis around which all the European states animated by the will to collaboration and peace can also collaborate'.[6] The die was cast, although not irrevocably. The Axis was not yet a formal treaty nor a formal alliance, merely a 'special relationship' founded to rescue Spain, to threaten France and to destroy Austria.

Franco, secure in Italian and German backing and armaments, was clearly in no hurry to win the war. The Italians and Germans became alarmed and agreed that Franco's troops were so hopeless that both Germany and Italy should send their own men to Spain, and that an Italo-German 'high command' should be set up to coordinate operations with Franco. In practice, Italy soon became more involved than Germany. Both countries sent troops, but Italy sent more – a whole army division and also 'volunteers' from the Militia, chosen for their height and imposing physical bearing.[7] By the end of December there were 10,000 Italian troops in Spain, to Franco's dismay; he had not requested them and did not want them. By February 1937 the number had gone up to over 48,000, over half of them from the Fascist Militia and 'volunteers' only in name.[8] Moreover, Italy became even more involved by sea. Only Italy could cut off Russian supplies moving through the Mediterranean, but could only do so by sinking formally neutral ships. Of the German leaders, only Göring was keen on helping Franco, which is why German support was mostly in the form of aircraft. Most of the other prominent Nazis detested Franco as a reactionary general, far too Catholic and old-fashioned for their taste, and thought the Spaniards should be left alone to fight their own civil war. Mussolini had no love for Franco either and did not really want to be in Spain at all, but he was genuinely worried about the spread of Bolshevism and after November 1936 his prestige was too deeply committed for him to withdraw. For the next two years or more he tried to spur Franco into action, nearly always in vain. He knew the war was extremely unpopular at home and he wanted it over quickly, whereas Hitler was quite happy to let Franco drag it out: the war in Spain distracted world attention from his own designs in central Europe, and it kept Italy firmly committed to the Axis cause.

Mussolini still kept lines open to Britain. Despite sanctions and Eden, his quarrel was more with socialist France than conservative Britain, which tacitly preferred Franco to the Republicans and which certainly sought to restrict the conflict to Spain herself. From Britain Mussolini wanted, essentially, 'recognition' of the conquest of Ethiopia and of the Italian Empire, and partly for this reason he tried to make it clear that Italy was not dependent on Germany. The British were not, as yet, willing to give 'recognition'. They did not take the Italian Empire seriously, to Mussolini's chagrin. However, they ended League sanctions and sent the Home Fleet back to its ports. What the British government wanted was a thaw in Anglo-Italian relations, for fear of Hitler, and also some reassurance that Mussolini was not seeking to threaten France or to take over the western Mediterranean, e.g. by acquiring the Balearics. Eden thought the *Duce* was seeking exactly that and told the Cabinet so,[9] but his ambassador in Rome thought otherwise, and so did Franco. In practice, Mussolini's policy in Spain suited Britain fine, indeed far more than it suited Italy: he helped Franco, he stopped the Germans having too much influence, he kept the Russians away from Gibraltar, and he was too busy there to cause trouble anywhere else. Both Britain and Italy hoped to detach the other party from her main ally, respectively France and Germany; but neither succeeded. Both public and statesmen were acting emotionally. The British left had always loathed Mussolini, and now felt very strongly that Italy had betrayed the League over Ethiopia; in their eyes Mussolini was simply a bully, and was proving it yet again in Spain. The British right also now disliked Mussolini, because of his threat to the Empire. The Italians felt betrayed too, by sanctions. To them, Eden was an arch-hypocrite, and he too was performing true to form. Politicians and public approached the great crises of 1938–9 in the spirit of three or four years earlier. The 'Mediterranean crisis' of 1935 cast a long shadow.

In January 1937 Britain and Italy managed a feeble reconciliation by signing the so-called 'Gentlemen's Agreement' – a term chosen by Mussolini, revealing yet again how he wished to be regarded by others. The gentlemen agreed to respect the status quo in the Mediterranean, but the agreement did not bind either side to do anything. It did not stop Mussolini sending thousands of troops to Spain, it did not include the French, and it did not provide for recognition of the Italian Empire – so the British invited the *Negus* to George VI's coronation the following month, and the Italians boycotted the ceremony in protest. It did not even stop the Italians bombing British merchant ships off Spain a few months later, and it certainly did not stop both sides rearming as quickly as possible. It was, in fact, a remarkably vague document, soon forgotten; a temporary armistice in the clash between two empires. Its main purpose was to signal that the Germans should be kept out of the Mediterranean, and it achieved that for the simple reason that the Germans had no intention of going there.

Throughout 1937 the Spanish war dominated European politics, and European politicians tried to dominate the Spanish war. In February Mussolini sent the diplomat Roberto Cantalupo to 'monitor' Franco and try to prevent Spanish excesses of retribution, but he was not welcomed at Burgos and stayed only about seven weeks. Mussolini also sent Farinacci, of all people, to press Franco to adopt a corporative state and to offer him Victor Emmanuel's cousin, the Duke of Aosta, as potential king of Spain. Farinacci's real purpose was to establish close links with the Spanish 'Fascist' movement, the *Falange*, in case it overthrew Franco – a distinct possibility at that time, and one the Germans were inclined to back. On his return to Italy Cantalupo wrote a memorandum advising Ciano strongly to pull out of Spain, but he did not manage to see Mussolini, nor any senior diplomats or military leaders.[10]

By this time it was, in fact, impossible for Mussolini to withdraw from Spain. In March the motorised troops of the Italian Volunteer Corps were defeated at Guadalajara, north-east of Madrid, partly by other (anti-Fascist) Italians in the Garibaldi brigades. The Corps' battle was unsuccessful because Franco, well aware of the Italians' political manoeuvres, had no intention of allowing foreigners to take over his war. He did not want the Italian General Roatta to triumph and so he did not send in

Spanish reserve troops, nor attack along the nearby Jarama valley.[11] He achieved his purpose. Guadalajara was a massive *political* defeat for Mussolini. The Italians' military reputation, as the victors of Addis Ababa, was in ruins. The British press mocked him mercilessly. Now Mussolini was stuck: for prestige reasons he had to keep his troops in Spain, at least until they had redeemed themselves and won a famous victory. Ludicrously, he expected this to happen within a couple of weeks.[12] But Franco was not going to let them triumph. In fact, the Italian volunteers were very unpopular in Nationalist Spain. Franco did not need them, could not afford politically to rely on them and did not use them for major actions, although they did help take Santander in August and this was portrayed at home as a great Italian victory. Franco – cautious, clerical and reactionary, a man who detested both pagan Germany and revolutionary Italy – remained in charge, and Mussolini had to leave his troops in Spain. They were a real waste of resources and a constant source of friction with France and Britain, and Mussolini could not even control how they were used.

In August 1937 Mussolini agreed to Franco's request that Italian submarines should torpedo Russian and Spanish Republican supply ships near Spanish ports. They went on to attack other neutral merchant ships, including British ones, and even a Royal Navy destroyer, the *Havock*. This was going too far, and might easily have led to general war. It was also a ludicrously inconsistent policy by Mussolini, who was trying to reach an overall 'Mediterranean agreement' with Britain. At Nyon, near Geneva, a hastily convened conference of Mediterranean powers (minus Italy) agreed to set up naval and aerial patrols: all submarines, surface ships or aircraft attacking non-Spanish vessels would be destroyed forthwith. Mussolini had to call off his submarines. But he got away with it. Italy, still protesting her innocence, was invited to join the Nyon scheme and cheerfully did so. As Ciano remarked in his diary, 'It is a fine victory. From suspected pirates to policemen of the Mediterranean – and the Russians, whose ships we were sinking, excluded!'[13] The Nyon agreement settled little – arms continued to flow to both Spanish governments and ships continued to be sunk, although henceforth from the air rather than by submarines – but international interest in the war soon subsided. Stalin realised that Franco was not likely to join the Axis and so he could be allowed to win; the British had already come to the same conclusion. By spring 1938 the focus of European tension had moved to central Europe.

The Spanish war dragged on until Franco was finally victorious in spring 1939, and in June the Italian Volunteer Corps returned in triumph to Naples, after losing nearly 4,000 dead and 11,000–12,000 wounded. The war had been a financial, military and diplomatic disaster for Mussolini. It cost the Italian Treasury 8.5 billion lire in arms and munitions, not counting the costs of the 'volunteers' (the Spaniards paid about 5 per cent back during the war, and the rest later in devalued lire).[14] The Italian troops lost prestige at Guadalajara, and Mussolini himself was out-manoeuvred consistently by Franco. The war also, of course, committed him to the Axis and kept him at loggerheads with Britain and particularly with France. But Mussolini drew a different conclusion. Germany and Italy had passed the test: they had been willing to fight, and had won. Britain and France had shown nothing but pusillanimity, and always would.

1938: The *Anschluss* and Easter

Intervention in Spain had initially been the project of the new Foreign Minister Galeazzo Ciano, the husband of Mussolini's daughter Edda. Ciano had charm, but he was a spoilt upper-class playboy, a *'figlio di papà'*, convinced of his own brilliance and of his right to rule, even to succeed the *Duce*. The leading Fascists loathed him, since he did not share their background or values and owed his position entirely to nepotism. The diplomats disliked him too, since he was convinced he knew far more about international affairs than they did and because he was unwilling to read reports more than a page long or to receive foreign ambassadors, particularly from the smaller countries.[15] Often he could not be bothered to record diplomatic conversations in full, either his own or Mussolini's. He so neglected the Italian ambassadors abroad that his man in Moscow finally lost all patience and in November 1939 wrote privately to Ciano's head of Cabinet: 'in the last two years there have been events of exceptional importance: the Czechoslovak crisis, then the Anglo-French efforts to reach an agreement with Moscow, then the Nazi–Soviet Pact . . . etc. etc. On all these issues I have done my best to provide information, judgements and impressions. However, I have never received a word from Rome to let me know our aims, our points of view or our interests.'[16] Ciano was also amazingly indiscreet, rather a disadvantage in a Foreign Minister, and he spent much of his time gossiping with his friends at the Rome Golf Club or in aristocratic salons. He was, in short, a 'comic opera' minister, much mocked both at home and abroad. However, this cheerful dilettante had hidden depths. He was perceptive, and he had considerable literary skills. From mid-1937 he kept an incomparable diary, recording Mussolini's moods and pronouncements. Clearly the *Duce* liked to unwind and to impress his young admirer, now virtually his only crony. The result was often hilarious, but also revealed the *Duce*'s profound reflections. On the English, for example, Ciano recorded for posterity Mussolini's judgement: 'a people that thinks with its arse'.[17]

For two years Ciano did what Mussolini wanted. He was lively, stimulating and amusing; above all, he admired the *Duce*'s every word. But he saw the *Duce* virtually every day, and no man is a hero to his valet or to his close relatives. Like many other leading Fascists, by 1938 he was beginning to have doubts about the Nazis, about the Axis, and about the *Duce*. His relationship with his father-in-law went sour. By 1939 Ciano thought Mussolini was hopelessly erratic and out of touch. He began to patronise the *Duce*, and mocked him to others. Yet for Ciano, even more than for the others, it was impossible to raise policy options or to express dissent. He could not make foreign policy on his own, and he had no status in Fascist politics except as the *Duce*'s son-in-law. He was totally dependent on Mussolini and when their views began to differ he had little influence on him, less than Grandi or Suvich in their day. Ciano became frustrated and bitter. When his under-secretary Bastianini complained of not having enough work to do, Ciano replied that nobody in government could do anything on his own initiative, nor hope to see any advice or suggestion accepted: 'we all have useless jobs'.[18] As for Mussolini, the coolness between the two men left him more isolated than ever.

After autumn 1936 Mussolini's foreign policy rested essentially on support for, or rather from, Germany. Spain kept the two partners together; so did Mussolini's dreams of a Mediterranean Empire, and German ambitions in Austria. In January 1937 Göring visited Rome and made it quite clear that Germany intended to annex Austria shortly: 'If Italy still wants a buffer state between herself and Germany, then that means that Italy does not have full confidence in Germany. If the two countries were allies in the true sense of the word it would be better if they had direct contact and a common frontier.'[19] In September 1937 Mussolini visited Germany at Hitler's invitation. Apart from a couple of trips to Libya, it was the *Duce*'s first trip abroad since Locarno in 1925; and he was Germany's most important official visitor since 1914. He was given a tremendous welcome, although it turned out marvellously farcical. Mussolini addressed a huge crowd in Berlin, but it poured with rain and the water ruined the notes for his speech, so he had to extemporise in his dreadful German which the half-million people present could not understand.[20] Still, he was greatly impressed by the German army's parades and weaponry, as he was meant to be. He spent little time talking to Hitler – this was to be a feature of their meetings – but that was not the point of the visit. He had gone to the Nazi heartland, demonstrated the Axis alliance in public and been flattered by everyone he met. This was real 'recognition' at last. He returned to Italy convinced that Germany was a dynamic, virile state bent on glory; she would easily defeat her plutocratic, decadent enemies. A few weeks later he told the German Foreign Minister Ribbentrop that he accepted that a full German take-over in Austria was inevitable, and signed up to the 'Anti-Comintern Pact', a German–Japanese alliance ostensibly directed against Russia, in practice largely against Britain. He also, in December 1937, finally left the League of Nations, a pointless gesture at this stage except to signal in-transigence and to please the Germans.

The German alliance had a high price: Austria. Since July 1936 the Germans already dominated much of Austrian life, but Austria re-mained a formally independent state with a Social-Catholic Chancellor, Schuschnigg. In November 1937 Ribbentrop checked up again on Musso-lini's reaction to an annexation. The *Duce* could hardly object, especially as many Austrians seemed to favour it. In the spring of 1938 the Ger-mans adopted tactics that soon became familiar: local Nazis demonstrated against the government, Hitler thundered his support and the govern-ment was forced to appoint Nazis to key posts in the police and army. Schuschnigg, increasingly isolated, called a plebiscite in the hope that the Austrians would reassert their independence. The Nazis prevented any such vote, German troops massed on the border and Schuschnigg was forced to resign. Then the German tanks moved in, followed shortly by Hitler himself visiting the graves of his parents. Mussolini had not been told in advance.

Mussolini would, of course, have preferred Austria to be independent, but he could not prevent the *Anschluss* and was certainly not going to fight against it and thereby wreck the Axis. So he made the best of a bad job, and told the Chamber that 'when an event is inevitable it is better that it happens with your support than despite you, or worse still against you'.[21] He used Austria to win German gratitude and future support. Hitler was indeed grateful. On 13 March he sent the *Duce* a telegram from Linz: 'Mussolini, I will never forget what you have done.'[22] Even so, the *Anschluss* was a dreadful blow to Italy, and to Europe. For the next 18 months, until war broke out, European politics were essentially a footnote to the *Anschluss*. Attention now focused on central and eastern Europe, and in effect Mussolini had given Hitler a free hand there too. The Germans in

Austria meant the Germans dominating the whole Danube basin and probably also the Balkans, where Mussolini had constantly sought to expand Italian influence. The *Anschluss* signalled future German moves to 'safeguard' German minorities in Czechoslovakia, Poland or Rumania, countries which soon became remarkably friendly towards Italy in the hope that the *Duce* might protect them from the *Führer*. Their hopes were in vain. Italy had become a helpless spectator, less relevant to events than at any time since 1915. No longer could Mussolini or anyone else believe that he was the senior partner in the Axis, or that he could control Hitler.

Worse still, the *Anschluss* threatened all Italy's First World War gains. It brought a strong, aggressive Germany right up to Italy's frontier on the Brenner, and threatened to bring her further – the South Tyrol, acquired by Italy only in 1919, was inhabited mostly by German-speakers who also wished to join the *Reich*. Hitler repeated his very explicit promise to respect the Brenner frontier,[23] but the local Nazis there were provoking unrest as they had done in Austria, and Mussolini did not want to suffer the same fate as Schuschnigg. Göring, as so often, came to the *Duce*'s aid. He suggested that the 'German' inhabitants of South Tyrol be given a choice: those who wished, could move north of the Brenner; the rest would renounce their 'Germanness'. This was ethnic cleansing Italian style – by the ballot. Rather surprisingly, Mussolini accepted the plan. After over a decade of battling for births, he now began organising a vote to depopulate his northern region.

Even before the *Anschluss*, Mussolini had become increasingly worried. Hitler was turning out to be more formidable than he had expected. The *Führer* owed him a debt of gratitude, but would he pay up? Might it not be wiser for Italy to hedge her bets? That meant reviving the approach to Britain, which had foundered in 1937 over the naval clashes in Spain and more generally over Mussolini's continuing Mediterranean ambitions. In March 1937 Mussolini had visited Libya and been presented there with the 'sword of Islam', mostly because of the subsidies he had given to the Grand Mufti to help the Arab revolt against British rule in Palestine.[24] Indeed, Anglo-Italian relations in the first half of 1937 had remained very poor. Mussolini was still seen in London as the great threat to the Empire, more so than Hitler, and the propaganda efforts of Radio Bari to stir up the Arab world (particularly Palestine and Iraq) were much resented. But in the summer of 1937 Neville Chamberlain became Prime Minister, and he had other ideas. He rightly saw Hitler as the real menace, and thought it possible to detach Mussolini from him.

On 28 July Chamberlain wrote a personal letter to the *Duce*, and Musso-lini replied in his own hand. The two leaders began to communicate, by-passing Eden by using Chamberlain's 'secret channel', i.e. meetings between the Conservative party treasurer Sir Joseph Ball and the legal adviser at the Italian embassy, Adrian Dingli, who was of course in touch with Ambassador Grandi and hence with Mussolini.[25] Chamberlain was also helped by his sister-in-law, Sir Austen's widow, who stayed in Rome in 1937–8 and passed messages to Ciano and the *Duce*.

By early 1938 Eden's position as Foreign Secretary had become impos-sible. On 18 February he and Chamberlain saw Grandi together, and Grandi later reported to Rome: 'Chamberlain and Eden were not a Prime Minister and a foreign minister discussing with the ambassador of a foreign power a delicate situation of an international character. They were – and revealed themselves as such to me in defiance of all estab-lished convention – two enemies confronting each other, like two cocks in true fighting posture.'[26] Eden resigned forthwith, and serious Anglo-Italian negotiations began. On Good Friday, 16 April – a month after the *Anschluss* – an agreement was signed in Rome. Britain swallowed hard and agreed to recognise the Italian Empire, i.e. the conquest of Ethiopia, although this would not come into force until some Italian 'volunteers' had left Spain (they did so in November). Territorial disputes between Ethiopia and Sudan were resolved, and Italian propaganda in Arab countries was to be toned down (German efforts soon replaced it). The agreement was a great diplomatic success for Grandi, but among the plaudits he also received some abuse.[27] The 'Easter Agreement' showed that Mussolini was still willing to manoeuvre, but it also showed how limited his room for manoeuvre was. Even in the most favourable circumstances – a well-meaning, naive British Prime Minister willing to ignore his own Foreign Secretary, much of his own party and most of public opinion – it proved impossible to reach a real understanding with Britain, let alone to detach her from France. The Spanish war prevented it; so did Mussolini's own rhetoric, not to mention his evident ambitions in the Mediterranean and the Middle East; and so did the Germans. Despite his qualms about the *Anschluss*, Mussolini *had* to play the Ger-man card if he were to achieve his long-term aims. Britain was, inevit-ably, an obstacle to these aims. From Britain's viewpoint, the agreement brought not trust but time – time to strengthen her Mediterranean de-fences and to work on Mussolini. Relations between the two countries were certainly better in 1938–40 than they had been in the previous three years. But it was a lukewarm rapprochement nonetheless. It was no challenge to the Axis, and it was swept away by events in 1940.

From Munich to the Pact of Steel 1938-9

In May 1938 Hitler made his return visit to Rome. It was not a success. Popular enthusiasm was noticeably muted, the Pope had moved hastily out of town, and the king detested his guest. At the royal palace Hitler caused consternation (and some surprise) at 1.00 a.m. by asking for a woman, although it turned out he only wanted the chambermaid to remake his bed.[28] Still, Mussolini took him down to Naples to see a naval review, and the *Führer* enjoyed that; and they also visited Florence, where Hitler, the artist *manqué*, went round both the Uffizi and the Pitti palace meticulously, while a bored Mussolini and entourage tagged along in the rear. The two men's personal relationship was friendly but not close, and in Rome they had only one two-hour talk. They had very different personalities: the one insecure, sarcastic, hard-working, obsessed with his image and status abroad; the other a fanatical dreamer who cared not a fig for world opinion.[29] Hitler admired and flattered Mussolini, but the two men were not on the same wavelength and Mussolini literally did not understand Hitler. The Axis, like the Stresa agreement before it, held up only because the most important things were left unsaid or, if said, were not understood. During the visit the Germans suggested a formal military alliance, but Mussolini refused; it was just after the *Anschluss* and the Easter Agreement with Britain, and he did not want to encourage any further German ventures in central Europe.

By summer 1938 the 'Czech problem' was dominating European diplomacy. Czechoslovakia, created at Versailles, was undoubtedly unstable. Apart from the rivalry between Czechs and Slovaks, the country contained three million 'Germans', mostly in the Sudetenland; they were citizens of Czechoslovakia but anxious to join the powerful new *Reich*. Hitler intended to liberate them from the Czech yoke, but Czechoslovakia had a respectable army of 34 well-equipped divisions and furthermore was allied to France and Russia. Britain, or at least Chamberlain, was as usual guilt-ridden (over Versailles) and naturally thought Hitler was justified in taking up the Sudeten Germans' case; Britain urged the Czech government to grant them 'autonomy'. The Czechs agreed, under pressure, but with German prompting the Sudetens' terms then went up, and in late September the Germans massed their troops on the border and issued an ultimatum. Hitler guessed that neither France, nor Britain, nor Russia wanted to fight Germany over Czechoslovakia if it could be avoided. He ordered his troops to invade on 1 October, and awaited developments.

Mussolini's role in all this was minimal until 28 September. He was still busy with his Mediterranean ambitions and with Spain. He thought

Czechoslovakia was an unstable conglomerate, bound to collapse, and he disliked the Czechs who were far too democratic and Francophile for his tastes. He therefore made a series of bellicose speeches in late September, backing Hitler's views. He proclaimed, both publicly and privately to Ciano, that if France and Britain really did go war with Germany, then Italy would join in on the German side despite having no treaty obligation to do so.[30] Possibly, but she was totally unprepared. Fortunately for him, Britain was not going to war with Germany, at least not over Czechoslovakia. Chamberlain flew to Germany twice in September to fix acceptable terms. When neither trip succeeded, he tried the Italian route, via Grandi and Dingli/Ball.[31] Grandi also persuaded the former British ambassador in Rome, Sir Ronald Graham, to urge the Foreign Office to bring on the *Duce*.[32] These initial soundings succeeded, and so on 28 September Chamberlain made it official. With French backing, he suggested to Mussolini that the *Duce* should persuade Hitler to attend a last-minute international conference of the four major European powers, to be held at Munich the next day to settle the Czech issue. Mussolini forwarded Chamberlain's appeal and Hitler agreed, since the conference was obviously designed to concede all his immediate demands. Göring and two top German diplomats drew up a list of German requirements, i.e. cession of Sudetenland to Germany, in stages; the Italian ambassador in Berlin telephoned them through to Rome; Mussolini then added a few concessions to his friends the Hungarians, and took the document with him on the train to Munich as his own compromise proposal. By the time the conference met on the evening of 29 September Hitler had changed his mind and wanted more, but he could hardly object to a set of proposals that had come from his own colleagues 24 hours earlier, especially if put forward by his one ally. So early in the morning of 30 September he agreed, and the Second World War was averted.[33]

Mussolini had, apparently, stopped Hitler again, as in 1934, and had outmanoeuvred Hitler's last-minute efforts. He thus became yet again the improbable Angel of Peace. On his return to Italy, his train was delayed by cheering crowds at every station. Even the king turned up at Florence to greet the saviour of Europe. The demonstrations dismayed Mussolini, who had hoped the Italians were thirsting for blood. In fact, he had been extremely lucky at Munich. Italy had very nearly found herself dragged into a German war against France and Britain, a war which she was in no position to fight. Mussolini had done nothing to prevent this outcome, and had made speeches welcoming it. He had not even mobilised his troops. Other people, not Mussolini, took the initiative and avoided war: it was Chamberlain and Grandi who had suggested the conference, and it was the Germans who had drawn up the proposals. Mussolini just took the credit.[34]

But the credit for Munich did not last long. No one was really happy with the outcome, except Göring in Germany and Grandi in London. Czechoslovakia, excluded at Munich and then dismembered, was open to further German attack. The French had betrayed their most important continental ally and were ashamed, though also relieved. Britain had also appeased too far. Chamberlain and his Foreign Minister Halifax were heroes for a few weeks but soon became the 'men of Munich', the pusillanimous weaklings who had allowed Hitler to take over yet another country. Hitler was dissatisfied too. True, he had won the Sudetenland without a fight, but by 29 September he had wanted the whole of Czechoslovakia, and had been rebuffed by Mussolini. Moreover, perhaps he had missed his best opportunity for a real war. As for Mussolini, he could boast about Italy's great status and about how Munich had been a defeat for the Russians, but he worried about Hitler's next move and he recognised that Hitler was now the more powerful partner in the Axis. He also realised that he, the great *Duce*, had been used by the decadent plutocracies to persuade Hitler to accept a deal and to *avoid* a war. That was not what Fascism was all about.

So Mussolini reflected on his noble mediation. Blessed are the peacemakers, for they shall play off each side against the other and make a killing.[35] But where were the benefits of Munich for Italy? The real gains could only come from France, a rather tougher proposition than Czechoslovakia. Early in 1938 there had been some French–Italian talks, but negotiations had failed in the summer. The French had British backing, and while they were willing to discuss Djibouti and the Ethiopian trade they saw no reason to make serious concessions to Italy, especially as it was obvious Italy could not make effective war. But that did not stop Mussolini. In autumn 1938 Italian 'foreign policy' became a frenetic search for quick returns. On 30 November Ciano spoke to the Chamber, outlining the 'natural aspirations of the Italian people'. At this point a group of deputies stood up and shouted 'Nice! Corsica! Savoy! Tunisia! Djibouti! Malta!' while the newly appointed French ambassador, the first for two years, looked on from the public gallery. So these were now the publicly proclaimed Italian 'claims', made manifest in an obviously staged demonstration designed to win maximum publicity and to cause maximum offence. It was terrible diplomacy, but Mussolini was probably trying to prevent the 'Franco-German Declaration' of a week later, which Hitler was agreeing in order to have a freer hand in central Europe.[36] At the Grand Council, meeting later on the same day as the scenes in the Chamber,

Mussolini added a few more 'claims'. Albania should become Italian, as a counterweight to the Germans on the Danube. Moreover, 'we have our sights on Switzerland. Switzerland is collapsing. The young Swiss have no affection for Switzerland. We will push our frontier to the Gothard.'[37] Clearly Mussolini had never got over his youthful resentment of the Swiss. His problem was that Italy, unlike Germany, had very few 'co-nationals' elsewhere whom she could 'liberate' – only the inhabitants of Corsica and of canton Ticino in Switzerland, and neither of these seemed at all anxious to be liberated by Fascist Italy. But that did not stop him having 'claims'.

In January 1939 Neville Chamberlain and Halifax came to Rome to further the Anglo-Italian détente. Mussolini was not impressed by his guests: 'These men are not of the same stuff as Francis Drake and the other magnificent adventurers who created the empire. They are the exhausted sons of a long series of rich generations.'[38] Fair comment, but there were other statesmen in Britain, and the more perceptive Italians noted signs of a more resolute attitude even in Chamberlain. The Rome crowds (and even Ciano himself) found Chamberlain, with his old-fashioned clothes and his umbrella, a welcome contrast to the militarist bluster of everyday Rome and of Hitler's visit the previous year. The visit passed amicably enough but achieved little. Anglo-Italian relations remained correct, but no more. The Italian 'volunteers' came back from Spain when Franco finally won in April, and were welcomed back as heroes of the fight against the 'plutodemocracies', not the Bolsheviks.

A week after the Chamberlain visit Mussolini revealed his true think-ing. He spoke fervently to the Grand Council about how Italy was a 'prisoner in the Mediterranean' (and he spoke as a man who knew all about being in prison): 'The bars of this prison are Corsica, Tunisia, Malta, and Cyprus; the guards of this prison are Gibraltar and Suez. Corsica is a pistol pointed at the heart of Italy; Tunisia is one pointed at Sicily, while Malta and Cyprus are a threat to all our positions in the central and western Mediterranean.' Although he left out Savoy and Nice, these aspirations went even further than the 'claims' of autumn 1938, especially as his Mediterranean strategy now envisaged attacking Greece, Turkey and Egypt as well, since they were all allies of Britain and enemies of Italian expansion. The aim of Italian policy must be to 'break the bars of the prison', and then 'march to the ocean', either the Indian or the Atlantic. This would naturally mean conflict with the British and French; hence the historical necessity of the Rome–Berlin Axis.[39] Musso-lini had made up his mind. If the French and British would not concede his 'claims', then he would have to throw in his lot with the Germans.

But on 14 March 1939 Hitler overthrew the Munich agreement and invaded the rest of Czechoslovakia, without informing Mussolini in advance. This was the decisive moment, the point at which the Second World War became virtually inevitable. The French and British did nothing to help the Czechs, but within a month Chamberlain had pledged British support to those countries seen as Hitler's most likely next victims – Poland, Rumania and Greece. Britain also began negotiations with the USSR. Meanwhile there was total disarray in Rome. The seizure of Czechoslovakia was a far bigger shock than the *Anschluss*, and it also destroyed Mussolini's status as peacemaker. Ciano was horrified by the German move. He told the *Duce* that he was now opposed to any alliance with Germany, which would only encourage the Germans to expand elsewhere. He noted that Mussolini was 'very pensive and depressed. It is the first time I have seen him like this.'[40] Mussolini was, in fact, furious with Hitler – 'every time he takes a state he sends me a message' – but he stood firm. He had given his word. 'We cannot change our policy now. After all we are not whores.'[41] He had little choice. Without Hitler, he was isolated and friendless. The French and British did not trust him; where else could he turn? Certainly there was no chance of securing his Mediterranean 'claims' unless the Germans did it for him. On 21 March he spoke to the Grand Council of the 'necessity of adopting a policy of uncompromising loyalty to the Axis', challenging them to disagree. Some did. Balbo angrily replied, 'you are shining Germany's shoes',[42] and others concurred. The deep Fascist hostility to the *Duce*'s foreign policy had surfaced at last. Hardly anybody in Italy cared about Corsica or Djibouti, let alone Ticino; but most of the top *gerarchi* had spent their youth fighting against Germany and Austria. Now Italy was becoming virtually a German protectorate, and they hated the thought even more than they disliked racialism and the anti-bourgeois campaign. Above all, they could see that Mussolini's policy had failed. He had allowed Hitler to move up to the Brenner, without securing any compensation.

The classic answer in these circumstances is to defuse discontent at home by adventures abroad. Ciano's initial reaction on hearing of the invasion of Prague was that now Italy must take Albania, where she already enjoyed a virtual protectorate. Mussolini hesitated: taking Albania might lead to the break up of Yugoslavia and eventually to a German satellite in Croatia, on Italy's border. However, Ciano soon persuaded him, and after bribing the local chiefs and arranging some bogus anti-Italian demonstrations in Tirana the Italians sent in the troops and took over the country. King Zog was generously allowed to flee over the mountains with his Hungarian wife and baby son, born the previous day, and

Victor Emmanuel became king of Albania as well as of Italy. This time it was the Italians who had not told the Germans in advance. Indeed, the invasion was essentially anti-German: to assert Italy's rights in the Balkans against a Germany that had taken Austria and Czechoslovakia. However, Hitler did not object and nor did anyone else, although the British regarded it as a breach of the Easter Agreement and the Greeks worried about having Italians on their frontier. But Italy had controlled Albania for years; invading it was, in the words of one Italian diplomat, 'like raping your own wife'.[43] As triumphs go, Albania was small beer. Militarily, the campaign was singularly unimpressive; politically, it brought little prestige and even less profit. It certainly did not compensate for Hitler taking Vienna and Prague, but at least it showed that the Axis might deliver *some* rewards, however paltry.

Early in May Ribbentrop visited Ciano in Milan, and during their talks Mussolini rang from Rome to say he had finally decided to accept a military alliance. On 22 May Ciano was sent to Berlin to sign it. The 'Pact of Steel' pledged each side to come automatically to the other's aid in the event of hostilities. This would apply even if the other were the aggressor, although there would be 'consultation' between the two countries in advance of any aggressive move – a weak clause, since 'consultation' might mean anything and did not necessarily mean agreement. Mussolini had written Ciano a set of guidelines for the treaty in early May and Ciano had passed these on to Ribbentrop. They included a key provision that there should be no European war for at least three years, so that Italy would have time to 'prepare' and so that Mussolini could hold his Universal Exhibition in Rome in 1942 on the twentieth anniversary of the regime. But it was the Germans who drew up the final text, and it contained no mention of three years. True, Ribbentrop made a verbal promise to that effect, but his assurance was not in the pact and was valueless. It seems that the notoriously idle Ciano did not examine the text closely enough, and that Mussolini – who was touring Piedmont at the time and could only be reached by telephone or telegram – also did not notice, or more probably was not exactly informed. To accept the Germans' text without reading it carefully was staggering ineptitude, showing total lack of competence or prudence by Ciano, possibly by both Ciano and the *Duce*. Ciano should have been instantly dismissed; but he was the son-in-law.[44]

Hitler, of course, had no intention of waiting three years. The day after the pact was signed he ordered his generals to start preparing a war against Poland. The pact had covered his weak southern flank; it would tie down French and British troops in the Mediterranean, and give him a free hand in central Europe. In any case, he did not expect a general war.

He was only going to move on Danzig and the Polish corridor, and the French and British were unlikely to intervene. Mussolini, by contrast, thought he had won three years' peace, and even after three years the bellicose-sounding 'Pact of Steel' would curb German aggression since it stipulated 'consultation', i.e. a period of notice which would give Musso-lini time to mediate another deal. Furthermore, France and Britain would surely now be grateful to Italy for preserving the peace, and/or would be intimidated by Italy's powerful ally. If war did come, Mussolini had covered his northern flank and might concentrate his forces in the south. He had allied with the strongest power in Europe, and that power had given him a free hand in the Mediterranean. Thus each partner inter-preted the pact in quite different ways. But Mussolini was the more deceived. It was astonishingly naive to suppose Italy could restrain Ger-many, especially just after the seizure of Czechoslovakia and at a time when the Germans were already laying claim to Danzig. All Europe was worrying about an imminent German attack on Poland, and Italy had allowed herself to be dragged in.

Keeping Out of War: Summer 1939

Italy's diplomatic activity in the few crucial months after May 1939 was essentially an (eventually successful) attempt to wriggle out of the com-mitment she had just made. Just as Hitler, the day after the Pact of Steel, started to prepare war, so Mussolini began to backtrack. On 30 May he sent Hitler a memorandum, delivered to him by the vice-president of the Italo-German military commission General Cavallero, agreeing that war with the decadent democracies was inevitable eventually but stressing Italy's need for at least three years' delay. She needed to pacify Ethiopia, build six warships, renew all her medium and heavy artillery, become economically self-sufficient, hold her exhibition to bring in foreign cur-rency, and bring back the Italians resident in France. Moreover, it was desirable that the Italian and German *peoples* should have closer rela-tions, which would be helped by less Church-state tension in Germany. He went on to suggest undermining France and Britain meantime by assassinating key individuals and encouraging regionalist and anti-war movements, and gave Hitler some advice about how to win the war when it came, i.e. a land war would be too static, so the Axis should rely on aerial and naval offensives.[45] Hitler was unimpressed, and did not reply. He continued to prepare his Polish campaign, and he opened 'trade talks' with the USSR. Mussolini, on the sidelines, could only watch.

In the summer of 1939 it became obvious to all that Hitler intended to take Danzig. Police informers reported public nervousness on the issue as early as April.[46] Attolico, the Italian ambassador in Berlin, sent in repeated and insistent reports about German war preparations, and suggested an urgent meeting between Hitler and Mussolini at the Brenner. One was fixed for 4 August, and Mussolini even drafted a communiqué calling for an international conference, i.e. another Munich but with Polish and Spanish participation. But Hitler did not want a conference and did not come to the Brenner, and so there was no communiqué and no conference.[47] Instead, Ciano went to Salzburg on 11 August and met Ribbentrop, and later Hitler at Berchtesgaden. The previous day he had been enjoined by the *Duce* not to let the Germans launch a war. But now Ribbentrop told him the awful news: Germany intended to invade Poland – all of it, not just Danzig. Ciano was furious: 'They have deceived us and lied to us. Now they are about to drag us into an adventure which we do not want and which may compromise the regime and the country.'[48] But he cannot have been at all surprised. He had received warnings about the likelihood of war from Attolico in Berlin, from Grandi in London, from the *Duce* and from the Vatican. That was why he had gone to Salzburg at all, and why he had met Ribbentrop – it was a Pact of Steel 'consultation'. Ciano was the man responsible for the fiasco over the text of the pact, and for it omitting any mention of three years' peace. He must have felt guilty, and he needed to pass the blame; he certainly detested the men who had made a fool of him.

Mussolini and Ciano fully realised by this time that a German invasion of Poland meant European war, but Hitler and Ribbentrop did not, or pretended that they did not. The Germans knew how well their negotiations with the USSR were going, and they assumed Britain and France would not dare to defend Poland if Russia were on the German side. This view helped Italy, because if the war against Poland stayed purely local there was no reason for Italy to join, and the whole aim of Italian policy now was to keep out. On the other hand, if Mussolini were right and the war became general the Pact of Steel would apply. On 18 August he again urged Ribbentrop to seek a peaceful settlement, presumably by a conference.[49] Mussolini was seriously worried about his honour, and Italy's, if he reneged on his promise in the pact. Besides, everyone remembered how Italy had abandoned her treaty commitments to Germany and Austria in 1914; she could hardly do so again, and might face Hitler's vengeful wrath if she tried. So he searched for a way of staying out of the war but staying in the Axis. It was not easy. It was his biggest decision since 1914. Honour, fear, betrayal, prestige, booty: all revolved in the *Duce*'s frenetic mind. For some days he drafted letters to Hitler but did not dare to send them. On 20 August Chamberlain asked him to mediate again, by calling an international conference on Danzig.[50] The invitation was not too serious since Chamberlain could not afford another Munich, but it was useful to Mussolini since mediators clearly have to be neutral and that was exactly what he wanted an excuse to be. On 21 August he and Ciano, with Attolico's help, drafted a letter to Hitler urging a conference and making it clear that Italy would stay out, even of a general war. Ciano was to take this to Ribbentrop the next day.[51]

But the letter was never sent. Ribbentrop cancelled the meeting; he was off to Moscow to sign the Nazi–Soviet Pact. This was a real surprise in Rome, although again Attolico in Berlin and Rosso in Moscow had been warning of the possibility for some months.[52] The Nazi–Soviet Pact covered Hitler's eastern flank and made war inevitable, but it was a godsend to Mussolini. It was a wonderful excuse not to join the war. Why was Hitler making an alliance with his, and Mussolini's, arch-enemy? What about the Anti-Comintern Pact? Why had thousands of Italian 'volunteers' died in Spain, fighting Communism? Fascist Italy could never be expected to ally with the USSR. On 25 August Hitler wrote to Mussolini explaining why he had signed the pact with Russia. Mussolini seized his chance. Now he was the injured party, and he could safely tell Hitler about *his* decision.[53] He justified it by stressing Italy's lack of munitions and war materials. Unfortunately, Hitler then asked exactly how much Italy needed, so Ciano and the high command drew up a ludicrously long list including 6 million tonnes of coal and 2 million of steel – in all, 40,000 trainloads! Moreover, Attolico in Berlin cheerfully claimed, on his own initiative, that it was all required immediately. That did the trick. Italy stayed out of the central European war. It was Mussolini's decision, although much influenced by Ciano and Attolico (the idea of a huge list of requirements was probably Attolico's, on 24 August[54]). It is difficult to see how he could have managed it safely without the Nazi–Soviet Pact, or Attolico's private intervention in Berlin. Mussolini's luck had held. Now he could stay out, not as a 'neutral' with its overtones of Liberal defeatism and Giolitti, but as an honourable 'non-belligerent' untainted by the Soviet alliance.

Hitler accepted Mussolini's decision with remarkable magnanimity. He sent Mussolini a telegram confirming that he had not asked for Italian help, and he shook hands with the Italian ambassador very publicly on 3 September before going off to the front. But he was not going to let the *Duce* off the hook. He also sent him a letter the same day, stressing that the fate of the two regimes was interlinked: if the Western powers defeated Germany, Fascist Italy would soon be overthrown.[55] The other German leaders were more overtly resentful, particularly because Mussolini had continued his attempts at mediation. Even on 31 August, when the German tanks were poised to move, he proposed a pan-European conference including the USSR. But by this time it was obviously too late. Hitler was not going to be cheated of his war again, and the Poles were not willing to make concessions; they had seen what had happened to the Czechs. In any case, the issue was no longer Danzig or Poland. It was Hitler, and how to contain German expansion. Even Chamberlain could see that.

Mussolini and Ciano could see it too. Since his experiences at Salzburg Ciano had turned virulently anti-Nazi, and even Mussolini hesitated in autumn 1939. He hoped for a quick end to the Polish war and a compromise peace. The Nazi–Soviet Pact dismayed him, the future of the South Tyrol worried him and the eventual partition of Poland disgusted him. But he could not change sides. He might be 'non-belligerent' but he was still Hitler's ally, and he had to keep Hitler on his side. He knew that Germany was stronger than France and Britain. She alone could help him realise his Mediterranean ambitions; he feared her more; he could not betray her. Certainly he could not allow the USSR to become Germany's chief partner – where would that leave Mussolini's Mediterranean 'claims'? He would join the war eventually, when he could; or, of course, if the war dragged on it might prove possible to negotiate a profitable peace. But essentially Mussolini wanted military glory. His whole career, his whole image, was based on contempt for neutralists, and now he was one. Even on 26 August Ciano had noted that 'the *Duce* is really upset. His military instincts and his sense of honour drew him to fighting. Reason has stopped him, but he is suffering a great deal from it.'[56]

Joining After All: Spring 1940

The Italians were greatly relieved to be spared war, as they had been a year earlier after Munich. But Mussolini, yet again, was not. The next few months were one of the most frustrating times of his life. He became irritable and incoherent. The proud leader of a warrior race could not sit in Rome while others fought for empire. For 15 years he had boasted of transforming the Italians. He had founded an empire, and become First Marshal. His whole regime was founded on war and on the idea that Italy was a Great Power. Yet now Italy was not ready to fight. Why not?

It must be the fault of the generals, or the king, or the people. He knew the Italians were mocking him and he denounced them vehemently. Furthermore, he thought Germany would probably win if anybody did, and he could not keep Hitler waiting for ever. Since Italy could not fight a long war, she should join in later, but not too late; her intervention would have to be seen to make a difference, and deserve some reward at the negotiating table. But perhaps nobody would win, or win quickly; the door to peace negotiations should be kept open. After a time he worked out another possibility, a 'parallel war'. Italy would help herself in the Mediterranean and Balkans, while Germany pressed east. This 'parallel war' was not a popular idea: Italy would have to fight it herself.

Meanwhile Ciano cultivated the British and French ambassadors – in these months Italian relations with the Western powers were considerably better than those with Germany – and was seen conspicuously at the Rome Golf Club, with its British ambience and its whisky. Ciano thought the West would win; in any case, war on the German side 'would be a crime and idiotic'.[57] Until February 1940 Italy continued to sell arms and even aircraft to the French and British. Ciano and Mussolini agreed only in hoping for a compromise peace with Italy as mediator, so there was a tacit division of labour: the *Duce* tried to keep the Germans happy while the Foreign Minister fed information to the British, for example about German massacres in Poland. In mid-December 1939 Ciano spoke to the Chamber, his speech vetted by Mussolini in advance. He explained why Italy had not joined the war: it was because a three-year delay had been agreed in May. He also expressed open hostility to the Nazi–Soviet Pact and admitted it had come as a surprise.[58] The speech went down well. Many Italians, and many others, were more worried about the aggressive re-emergence of Russia in Poland and the Baltic than they were about Germany. Italy, like Britain, sent arms to Finland during the Russo-Finnish 'Winter War' of 1939–40. Russia might also threaten Turkey and the Balkans. The Italians thought that the Nazis had let the Russian bear out of his cage and could not get him back in; they were absolutely right, as events were to prove.

On 3 January 1940 Mussolini took the initiative and wrote to Hitler, his first letter to the *Führer* since 29 August. He told Hitler that he would never defeat the democracies, for the United States of America would not permit it. In any case there was no need to fight the decadent plutocracies, since they were collapsing anyway. He should treat the Poles less appallingly, restore a small Polish state to satisfy the Western powers, make a compromise peace with them and attack the USSR instead: 'the solution to your *Lebensraum* is in Russia and not elsewhere'. In Italy, he emphasised, 'anti-Bolshevik unanimity among the Fascist masses is absolute, rock-solid, unmoveable'.[59] Here was a huge split in the Axis. Mussolini, a non-combatant, was lecturing his junior partner not only on how to fight his war, but on which war to fight. He reaffirmed his support, but he clearly feared an outright German victory in the west because it would bring the United States of America into the war, and he hoped that, with Poland defeated, negotiations might now be possible to end the wider conflict. He was also trying to keep both Hitler and the Russians out of the Balkans. Mussolini's new-found zeal against the USSR is worth a comment, since he had always enjoyed rather good relations with her earlier and in 1938 had gone so far as to call Stalin a 'crypto-Fascist' – high praise, coming from the *Duce*.[60] But now Russia was competing for influence in the Balkans, and for status as Hitler's chief ally. Ironically, Stalin in 1939–41 was acting in much the same way as Mussolini. Both men, faced by Hitler, decided to join him in order to win some booty (e.g. in the Baltic) and a 'free hand' (against Finland). For Russia the policy succeeded, although only in the short run. For Italy it did not work at all.

Mussolini's letter was probably a serious effort at peacemaking or at least at diverting the war elsewhere, but Hitler took no notice and for two months Berlin remained silent. At last, on 10 March, Ribbentrop came to Rome bearing Hitler's reply. Hitler asserted that a negotiated peace was impossible, that the USSR was no threat, that Germany would supply Italy's coal requirements by rail (a serious issue, since Italy required over 1 million tonnes a month and the British had just decided to cut off German supplies sent by sea), that Italy should keep out of the Balkans, and that he intended to launch a *Blitzkrieg* (all-out attack) in the west very shortly. The war would decide the fate of Italy too. Italy should join, or remain a 'European state of modest claims'.[61] The implication was clear: now or never. Mussolini, initially taken back, soon grasped the point, particularly when Ribbentrop assured him the war would soon be over. He told Claretta on the phone that evening that he had decided on war.[62] Ribbentrop had apparently achieved his goal, although his visit to the Vatican was less successful: he ended up arguing with the Pope over religion. Mussolini met Hitler a week later at the Brenner (the *Zweikaporalkonferenz*). He agreed to join the war when he could be of real use, but made no commitment about the timing.[63] He was still playing for time and trying to string Hitler along. Despite Ribbentrop's bluster and despite his own anger at the British naval blockade, Mussolini thought the war would be a long one and that a compromise peace was possible. He told Franco on 8 April that he intended to join but to delay as long as possible, and he was still talking to Chamberlain via Dingli.[64] He offered to transmit to Hitler, as his own, any acceptable proposals Chamberlain might make. But Chamberlain had nothing to offer. In fact, there was no chance of a settlement. Germany (and the USSR) would not give up her gains; Britain and France would not settle unless she did.

At the end of March Mussolini wrote a 'top secret memorandum' to clarify matters for the king and his military chiefs.[65] Italy, he said, would have to enter the war eventually or be reduced to the level of a Switzerland multiplied by 10; but not yet. Indeed, he would seek to delay entry as long as possible 'compatibly with honour and dignity'. Italy should prepare to intervene at a time when her intervention would determine the outcome, and when her war would be short. He did *not* think the Germans would attack in the west, and he argued again for a 'parallel war' in the Mediterranean, repeating his usual phrases about the bars of Italy's prison and the need for a 'window on the ocean'. Mussolini also laid down a strategy for each front: defensive in the western Alps and Libya; mistrustful on the Yugoslav border, unless the country collapsed; offensive towards Djibouti. All this was designed to keep the small pro-war camp happy but also to reassure the majority, who included the king and the military chiefs. At any rate, Badoglio and the service chiefs of staff accepted the plan with only feeble protests. They knew, of course, how poorly equipped the armed forces were, far worse in 1940 than they had been in 1935. Most of the arms and equipment had been worn out or lost in Ethiopia, Spain or Albania. Italy's aircraft were now old and slow, her artillery ancient, her oil supplies inadequate. She was in no position to fight a war, and both military chiefs and *Duce* knew it. After all, they had drawn up an enormous list of vitally needed equipment and sent it to Germany only six months earlier. As for a 'parallel war', that was manifestly strategic nonsense and they should certainly have squashed the suggestion forthwith. Why, then, did the military – apart from the Duke of Aosta, who made it clear that Ethiopia could not be defended if war came – not protest more vigorously? Partly it was because they realised that Mussolini had not really decided on war at all; he had merely issued a statement of intent. War delayed might be war averted. In any case, he was not actually expecting them to attack anybody. But perhaps the main reason is that the military chiefs had warned of multiple disasters before the war in Ethiopia in 1935, and had been proved conspicuously wrong. They were now less self-confident and less willing to stand up to the *Duce*, who might, who knows, turn out to be right again.[66]

In April 1940, therefore, Mussolini anticipated joining the war but not fighting it. He told his new ambassador to Germany on 25 April that Italy would join only when she had 'a quasi-mathematical certainty of winning'.[67] He intended to 'be present', or perhaps to mediate, and he still expected a long war. Years later he admitted that at the time of the memorandum in March he had intended not to join until 1942, as originally envisaged.[68] But when the Germans swept through Holland, Belgium and northern France after 10 May, Mussolini knew he could delay no longer, and so did others. Roosevelt appealed to him on 14 May to stay out, and on 16 May he received this message from Churchill, now installed as British Prime Minister:

Is it too late to stop a river of blood from flowing between the British and Italian peoples? We can no doubt inflict grievous injuries upon one another and maul each other cruelly, and darken the Mediterranean with our strife. If you so decree, it must be so; but I declare that I have never been the enemy of Italian greatness, nor ever at heart the foe of the Italian law-giver ... I beg you to believe that it is in no spirit of weakness or of fear that I make this solemn appeal, which will remain on record. Down the ages above all other calls comes the cry that the joint heirs of Latin and Christian civilisation must not be ranged against one another in mortal strife. Hearken to it, I beseech you in all honour and respect, before the dread signal is given. It will never be given by us.[69]

Even this had no effect, although Mussolini rightly much admired it. He replied that he had committed himself to the German camp and intended to honour his word. But he still did not name the date.

Hitler helped him out. Within a few days the German armies advanced further, and the collapse of France was imminent. That made it essential for Mussolini either to end the war quickly by mediation, or to join it quickly before France had been finally defeated. It was a superb opportunity either for profitable peacemaking or for a 'parallel war' in the south, so as to win his 'claims' in the Mediterranean and Africa. He preferred the latter option, as more satisfying. Fortune comes only once, and must be seized. Mussolini had always resented the French, with their huge empire and their pretensions to superior civilisation; now he could have his revenge. Moreover, Mussolini certainly could not allow a victorious Germany to mass on his vulnerable Brenner frontier, feeling betrayed and bent on vengeance. He had just seen what happened to neutral countries in prime strategic positions. So far he had been able to rely on Hitler's personal admiration and good will, but this was a wasting asset after August 1939, and few other Germans felt it. In that sense

Mussolini's decision to join the war was simply a higher stage of appeasement, although greed was probably a stronger motive than fear.

In any case, greed and fear pointed the same way for once, and not only for Mussolini. Anti-war feeling in Italy, previously strong, melted away overnight and was replaced by impatience and concern. Germany had obviously won the war. Mussolini was clever to have spotted the winner, but had not put his bet on in time. People were saying, as the *Duce* later put it, 'What is Mussolini doing? Has he gone soft? A golden opportunity like this will never come again.'[70] The decision to join was *not* taken by 'one man, and one man alone', despite Churchill saying so[71] and despite the Italians wanting to believe it later. True, the king was still sceptical and thought the war would be neither popular nor short. Balbo and Badoglio, who knew the state of the army, remained strongly opposed. Bocchini, the Chief of Police, reported with considerable exaggeration how hostile public opinion was to war – a manoeuvre attempted in 1914–15 by his predecessor Vigliani, with more truth and equal lack of success. But most people, and most Fascists, assumed that Britain would soon come to terms, or be invaded. So the state of the Italian army was irrelevant. Mussolini himself, who four months earlier had warned Hitler he could never defeat the democracies, now thought he was probably joining too late.[72] Hardly anybody envisaged defeat, let alone the catastrophic 'unconditional surrender' and civil war that were to follow.

Even so, Mussolini agonised over his simple decision. Long after everybody else knew what he was going to do, he was still trying to make 100 per cent sure. He decided finally only on 28 May or possibly even early on 29 May, telling the chiefs of staff on 29 May and Hitler on 30 May. Why then, and not earlier? The answer is probably that until 28 May Mussolini expected that France and Britain would settle quickly with Hitler, that Italy would be the mediator and that she would thereby secure a Mediterranean reward without fighting. On 25 May the new Italian ambassador in London had in fact met the British Foreign Secretary, Lord Halifax, and discussed a possible British approach to Mussolini for a peace settlement. Such an approach was discussed in the British War Cabinet on 26–8 May.[73] However, Churchill prevailed over Halifax and there was no approach to the *Duce*, for fear of destroying home morale. So by 28 May Mussolini had no other option. If he wanted the spoils of war he would have to fight for them and/or receive them from Hitler, not the Western powers. So he decided that Italy would enter the war on 5 June, although at Hitler's request the date was postponed until five days later. On 10 June Mussolini finally came out on to his balcony at palazzo Venezia, and proclaimed war: 'a people of 45 million souls is not truly free if it does not have free access to the oceans'.[74] It was not one of his greatest speeches and it did not convince the crowd ('who is stopping us going to the oceans?'), nor perhaps Mussolini himself.

Conclusion

Mussolini's decision was not, of course, purely rational or diplomatic. He had been frustrated for months, desperate to play his role on the world stage but aware of Italy's military weakness. He wanted his 'claims' and as a politician he wanted to secure them peacefully if possible, but like all Fascists he remembered 1914–15, when Giolitti had been willing to accept 'a considerable amount' ('*parecchio*') from the Austrians in return for staying out of the war. Mussolini had campaigned frenetically then against such ignoble cowardice; how could he now turn round and do the same himself? He was committed to the German alliance and could not betray it. Ultimately it did not matter what the French or British offered, Mussolini would still want to say no, although his head would probably overrule his heart at least temporarily. Ciano noted acerbically, 'It is not that he wants to obtain this or that; he wants war. If he could obtain by peaceful means twice as much as he is asking for, he would refuse.'[75] But that was unjust. Mussolini might have lost the streetwise opportunism of his youth but he was still shrewd enough not to take unnecessary risks. He liked war and he liked to pose as a warrior, but his behaviour in 1939–40 was not that of a bombastic imperialist, let alone of an ideological zealot. On the contrary, he was hesitant and fearful, took a long time to make up his mind and decided on war only when he thought it was safe. He acted largely in response to events and to shifts in Italian public opinion. When the Italians wanted peace, as in September 1938 or August 1939, they got peace; when they wanted war, as in June 1940, that is what Mussolini provided.

After 10 June 1940 both President Roosevelt of the United States of America and Prime Minister Reynaud of France used the same phrase about Mussolini's decision. It was a 'stab in the back' against France, already defeated and prostrate. It also turned out to be a disastrous political mistake. But was it really less honourable than the behaviour of Salandra and Sonnino in 1914–15, negotiating with both sides in the First World War to see who would offer the better terms? Mussolini, in fact, did *not* negotiate with both sides. The issues, for him, were the timing, his state of readiness and the possibility of a compromise peace. Most other Italian politicians, in the circumstances of May 1940, would have made the same choice. Mussolini was not the only one who believed in pushing at an open door; it is how the political mind works. Nor was he the first Italian politician devoted to 'sacred egoism' and to playing a weak hand for more than it was worth. Every reasonably ambitious Italian statesman had wanted colonies and Mediterranean gains; some of them had invaded Ethiopia and Albania; even Giolitti had invaded Libya in 1911 and taken the Dodecanese islands as well. Mussolini could hardly stay on his balcony in Rome, mouthing martial slogans while Hitler helped himself to Nice or Corsica. In any case, he thought he was joining a short war against France, not a long war against Britain. It is fairer to say that no Italian politician except Mussolini might, in those circumstances, have kept his country *out* of the war without provoking a German invasion; but he might have done so, as Franco did (and on 30 April 1940 Franco had warned him that the war would be 'long and difficult'[76]).

However, it is also fair to say that no other Italian politician would have been in those circumstances. It may not have been just 'one man, and one man alone' who joined the war, but it *was* one man who had defied the Western Powers over Ethiopia, who had become deeply involved in the Spanish civil war at ruinous cost, who had connived in the Nazi takeover of Austria, who had committed his country to alliance with Nazi Germany without even reading the treaty, who had constantly and publicly demanded territories long held by more powerful neighbours, who had persecuted Jews and militarised the country, who had ignored public opinion, his ambassadors, his king and even his son-in-law; and who had, at the same time, neglected his armed forces and his munitions industry so that he was totally dependent on an overbearing ally controlled by a manifest lunatic. No one else would have done all that, and ended up in that situation. Mussolini was too restless, too impetuous, too keen on war, too insecure, too full of rancour and mistrust, too contemptuous of others, too jealous of Hitler's success, too ignorant (unlike Franco) of why sea power mattered, and too lacking in knowledge about the rest of the world.

Above all, he was too much the politician, in the sense of being too opportunist and too convinced that a short-term political solution can always be found for any problem. The very qualities and values that had brought him to power in the 1920s were now his downfall. Even joining the war was essentially a piece of short-term opportunism, to ensure his presence at the peace conference and thus a few undeserved gains. Mussolini had ended up behaving exactly as Sir Austen Chamberlain and Harold Nicolson had predicted back in 1925 (see pp. 179–80). It had happened not for any reasons inherent in Fascism, but because of his personality. He needed status, he needed an empire and, like Malvolio, he needed to 'be revenged on the whole pack of you'.

Notes

1 Comparable examples are 1858–9 (Plombières), 1914–15 (Treaty of London), 1948–9 (Nato), 1955–6 (European Economic Community) and 1997–8 (the euro).

2 *DDI*, s. 8, iv, nos 341, 414.

3 *DDI*, s. 8, iv, no. 819.

4 *DDI*, s. 8, v, no. 277 note 1.

5 *DDI*, s. 8, v, no. 504; R. Cantalupo, *Fu la Spagna* (Milan, 1946), pp. 78–80.

6 Speech of 1 November 1936; *OO* xxviii, pp. 67–71.

7 Mussolini to his secretary, 30 December 1936, for head of Militia: 'The Germans are admired for their physical bearing. We should avoid sending men who physically resemble the local population too much'; *OO* xxxvii, p. xlv.

8 ACS, SPD, c. ris., b. 71; J. Coverdale, *Italian Intervention in the Spanish Civil War* (Princeton, 1975), pp. 172–5, 181, 396; A. Rovighi and F. Stefani (eds), *La Partecipazione Italiana alla Guerra Civile Spagnuola* (Rome, 1992), i; V. Giura, *Tra Politica e Economia* (Naples, 1993).

9 On 14 December 1936; *DBFP*, s. 2, xvii, no. 471.

10 *DDI*, s. 8, vi, no. 432; Cantalupo, *Fu la Spagna* cit., pp. 267–72.

11 Coverdale, *Italian Intervention* cit., p. 254; R. Carr, *The Civil War in Spain* (London, 1986 edn), pp. 162–5; M. Tuñón de Lara et al., *La Guerra Civil Española* (Barcelona, 1985), pp. 226ff.

12 Mussolini to Grandi, 25 March 1937, in *OO* xlii, pp. 184–5; *DDI*, s. 8, vi, no. 334.

13 G. Ciano, *Diario 1937–43* (Milan, 1990 edn), 21 September 1937.

14 Giura, *Tra Politica e Economia* cit., pp. 68, 92; *DDI*, s. 9, ii, Appendix V.

15 M. Donosti, *Mussolini e l'Europa* (Rome, 1945), pp. 43–5, 87; Cantalupo, *Fu la Spagna* cit., pp. 50ff; R. Moseley, *Mussolini's Shadow* (New Haven, 1999), esp. ch. 3.

16 Rosso to Anfuso, 13 November 1939; *DDI*, s. 9, ii, no. 208.

17 Ciano, *Diario* cit., 14 September 1937.

18 G. Bastianini, *Uomini, Cose, Fatti* (Milan, 1959), p. 242.

19 Göring's declaration at meeting with Mussolini, 15 January 1937; *DDI*, s. 8, vi, no. 60.

20 His speech is in *OO* xxviii, pp. 248–53.

21 Speech to Chamber of Deputies, 16 March 1938; ACS, *Autografi del Duce*, cassetta di zinco, scat. 11.

22 *DDI*, s. 8, viii, nos 312, 316.

23 *DGFP*, s. D, i, no. 352; Ciano, *Diario* cit., 12 March 1937.

24 *DDI*, s. 8, vii, no. 365. Mussolini gave £5,000 a month in 1937.

25 *DDI*, s. 8, vii, nos 136, 155. On the 'secret channel', see ASAE, Grandi papers, esp.
    b. 66, f. 158; L.A. Pratt, *East of Malta, West of Suez* (Cambridge, 1975), pp. 82–3;
    R. De Felice, *Mussolini il Duce* (Turin, 1974–81), ii, pp. 452–3.

26 Grandi to Ciano, 19 February 1938; *DDI*, s. 8, viii, no. 186; *Ciano's Diplomatic Papers*
    (London, 1948), pp. 164–84, at pp. 182–3.

27 Letter from R.C.K. Watson to Grandi, 7 May 1938: 'Your gallant sailors murder defence-
    less seamen! No wonder the name of Italy stinks in the nostrils of Englishmen.' ACS,
    Grandi papers, f. 10.

28 Ciano, *Diario* cit., 7 May 1938; A. Lepre, *Mussolini l'Italiano* (Milan, 1995), p. 226.

29 Donosti, *Mussolini e l'Europa* cit., pp. 82–3.

30 Ciano, *Diario* cit., 17 and 25 September 1938.

31 De Felice, *Mussolini il Duce* cit., ii, pp. 520ff; P. Pastorelli, *Dalla Prima alla Seconda
    Guerra Mondiale* (Milan, 1997), p. 131; ASAE, Grandi papers, b. 66, f. 158.2; b.151
    f. 199.4.

32 'All I did was to go to the Foreign Office after lunching with you on Monday [26 Sept.]
    and repeat and support what you had said. Whether this had any effect I have not the
    faintest idea – very likely the policy of bringing in your great *Duce* had already been
    decided – anyway it proved the right one, thank goodness': Graham to Grandi,
    30 September 1938, in ACS, Grandi papers, f. 12.

33 Donosti, *Mussolini e l'Europa* cit., pp.118–29.

34 G.L. Weinberg, *Germany, Hitler and World War II* (Cambridge, 1995), pp.112–18;
    F. Anfuso, *Da Palazzo Venezia al Lago di Garda* (Bologna, 1957), pp. 71–8.

35 G. Gafencu, *Gli Ultimi Giorni dell' Europa* (Milan, 1947), p. 137.

36 Pastorelli, *Dalla Prima alla Seconda* cit., pp.130–2; R. Guariglia, *Ricordi 1922–46*
    (Naples, 1949), p. 370.

37 G. Bottai, *Diario 1935–44* (Milan, 1989 edn), p. 139.

38 Ciano, *Diario* cit., 11 January 1939. Cf. *DBFP*, s. 3, iii, no. 500; P. Stafford, 'The
    Chamberlain–Halifax visit to Rome', in *English Historical Review* xcviii (1983), pp. 61–
    100, at p. 71; G. Ansaldo, *Il Giornalista di Ciano* (Bologna, 2000), p. 161.

39 Speech of 4 February 1939; *OO* xxxvii, pp. 151–7; cf. also De Felice, *Mussolini il Duce*
    cit., ii, pp. 321–5; ACS, Fondo Valigia, b. 1, sottof. 5.

40 Ciano, *Diario* cit., 17 March 1939.

41 Ibid., 20 March 1939.

42 Ibid., 21 March 1939.

43 Donosti, *Mussolini e l'Europa* cit., p. 166.

44 *OO* xxix, pp. 524–5; *DGFP*, s. D, vi, pp. 445–9; Pastorelli, *Dalla Prima alla Seconda* cit.,
    pp. 136–53; Donosti, *Mussolini e l'Europa* cit., pp. 179ff.; M. Toscano, *Le Origini
    Diplomatiche del Patto di Acciaio* (Florence, 1948), ch. 4.

45 The 'Cavallero memorandum' of 30 May 1939 is in *OO* xxxv, pp. 135–7; *DDI*, s. 8, xii,
    no. 59; cf. Toscano, *Le Origini Diplomatiche* cit., pp. 186–8.

46 ACS, Min. Int., Dir. Gen. P.S., Div. Pol. Pol., b. 216.

47 *DDI*, s. 8, xii, nos 647, 662; *OO* xxxvii, pp. 157–61.

48 Ciano, *Diario* cit., 13 August 1939.

49 Mussolini's draft note of 14 August, handed to German Foreign Office, 18 August; *DDI*, s. 8, xiii, no. 27.

50 *DBFP*, s. 3, vii, nos 79 and 98; *DDI*, s. 8, xiii, nos 117, 167, 205.

51 *DDI*, s. 8, xiii, no. 123.

52 See dispatches of Attolico in Berlin, 29 May, and of Rosso in Moscow, 17 August 1939; *DDI*, s. 8, xii, no. 53 and xiii, no. 69. Ribbentrop also informed Attolico on 18 August, in Salzburg (xiii, no. 102).

53 *OO* xxix, pp. 415–17.

54 *DDI*, s. 8, xiii, 24–26 August, nos 218, 245, 250, 262, 263, 293; Ciano, *Diario* cit., 26 August 1939; Donosti, *Mussolini e l'Europa* cit., pp. 213–14, claims Mussolini personally doubled the quantities requested.

55 Hitler to Mussolini, 3 September 1939; *DDI*, s. 8, xiii, no. 639.

56 Ciano, *Diario* cit., 26 August 1939.

57 Ibid., 31 December 1939.

58 Ibid., pp. 701–24.

59 Mussolini to Hitler, 5 January 1940; *DDI*, s. 9, iii, no. 33 and *OO* xxix, pp. 423–7.

60 *OO* xxix, p. 63.

61 *DDI*, s. 9, iii, no. 512.

62 U. Guspini, *L'Orecchio del Regime* (Milan, 1973), pp. 167–8.

63 *Ciano's Diplomatic Papers* cit., pp. 361–5; *OO* xxxv, pp. 166–71.

64 Mussolini to Franco, 8 April 1940; *OO* xxxv, pp. 248–9; on Dingli, see ASAE, Grandi papers, b. 66, f. 158.

65 *OO* xxix, pp. 364–7; *DDI*, s. 9, iii, no. 669. Cf. De Felice, *Mussolini il Duce* cit., ii, pp. 772–5.

66 R. Mallett, *Mussolini and the Origins of the Second World War* (London, 2003), pp. 217–18; G. Contini, *La Valigia di Mussolini* (Milan, 1996), pp. 148–54; E. Faldella, *L'Italia nella Seconda Guerra Mondiale* (Bologna, 1959), pp. 85–6; L. Ceva, *Le Forze Armate* (Turin, 1981).

67 Ciano, *Diario* cit., 25 April 1940.

68 ACS, Fondo Susmel, b. 7 (conversation with Silvestri 1944).

69 W. Churchill, *Their Finest Hour* (London, 1949), p. 112.

70 Mussolini's interview with Cabella, 20 April 1945; *OO* xxxii, p. 194. Cf. A. Imbriani, *Gli Italiani e il Duce* (Naples, 1992), pp. 93ff.; S. Colarizi, *L'Opinione degli Italiani sotto il Regime* (Bari, 1991), pp. 336–9; ACS, PNF, Situazione politica per provincia, 1940.

71 W. Churchill, broadcast to Italy, 23 December 1940; *Their Finest Hour* cit., p. 488.

72 Celso Luciano, *Rapporto al Duce* (Rome, 1948), p. 14; De Felice, *Mussolini il Duce* cit., ii, pp. 818–19.

73 Bastianini to Ciano, 26 May 1940; *DDI*, s. 9, iv, no. 589; A. Roberts, *The Holy Fox* (London, 1991), pp. 212–28; J. Lukacs, *Five Days in London* (New Haven, 1999), pp. 92–4, 108–19, 146–9, 180–6.

74 Speech of 10 June 1940; *OO* xxix, pp. 403–5.

75 Ciano, *Diario* cit., 27 May 1940.

76 Franco to Mussolini, 30 April 1940; *DDI*, s. 9, iv, no. 260. Salazar sent a similar message to Ciano on 13 May (no. 404).

Chapter 10

The *Duce* at War 1940–3

Italy's Campaigns

In June 1940 Mussolini claimed to be fighting a 'parallel war' with his own *aims* – Corsica, Tunisia, Djibouti, etc. – but he had no military means to achieve them. He did not really need them. He needed a quick campaign against France on Italy's north-western border, enough to demonstrate Italy's martial valour and help finish off the French. Then he would sit at the peace conference, sharing out the booty with a respectful Hitler. On 18 June he went to Munich and agreed all this – including the rewards – with a very excited *Führer*, but it was clear that France was about to collapse and Italy had better start her campaign quickly or she would have to receive her new territories purely as a gift from German hands. Mussolini was just in time. On 20 June he ordered a reluctant Badoglio to advance at dawn the next day into the French Alps, but on 22 June France signed an armistice with Germany, and two days later with Italy. So Mussolini's Alpine campaign ended too, rather ingloriously. It had been an exceptionally short war, although long enough to reveal inadequate supplies and organisation.

However, Britain did not surrender and so there was no peace conference, and very little booty as yet. Hitler had long-term aims in eastern Europe. He did not want to tie down too many German troops in France and he certainly did not want French North Africa to continue fighting on the British side, so he offered the French reasonable armistice terms. Mussolini, too, did not want the Germans to have to move into North Africa, nor did he want to keep Italian troops stationed in France. In any case, after a mere four-day war he could hardly be more beastly to the French than the Nazis were. So on 22 June he wrote to Hitler saying that he had changed his mind. In order to persuade the French to accept the armistice, Italy would accept a 'demilitarised zone', i.e. a 50-km strip of French territory along the frontier, plus a smaller zone that had already been occupied by Italian troops. Her other 'claims' could wait until the eventual peace settlement, although of course he expected his full pound of flesh then.¹ This was an extraordinary move, coming only four days after the Munich meeting. It was exactly the kind of 'renunciation' Mussolini had denounced very strongly in 1919. It meant that Italy received virtually nothing from her war: not Corsica, nor Djibouti, nor Tunisia. Needless to say, Mussolini had not consulted anybody, least of all his military advisers. Tunisia and the naval bases at Bizerta were vital for any power seeking to control the central Mediterranean, and to have bases there, supplied by a short sea crossing, would have made it far easier for the Italians to fight against Britain from Libya. Possibly Mussolini was misled by poor intelligence reports, showing French forces in Tunisia as larger than they were in reality; no doubt he did not want to risk having to fight in Libya on two fronts; more probably the political motive – of smoothing the French path to an armistice – prevailed, as it usually did with Mussolini. At any rate, within the first two weeks of war he had thrown away, or rather failed to pick up, one of his strongest potential cards. The failure to take Tunisia may have determined the outcome of the whole Mediterranean war.² He had fought the French, but he remained a 'prisoner in the Mediterranean'.

For the rest of the summer in 1940 Italy enjoyed her own 'phoney war'. People went on holiday as usual, and the Italian troops did very little anywhere except to shoot down Balbo's plane on 28 June with 'friendly fire' – an ill omen, and the superstitious Mussolini took it very seriously. On 4 October Mussolini met Hitler again at the Brenner, and told him Italy was about to attack Egypt through the desert from Libya. The Führer offered specialist troops and armoured vehicles, which were seriously lacking in the Italian army, but Mussolini refused: he wanted to win his own 'parallel war'.³ He did not tell Hitler about his other plan, to invade Greece, but it was true that North Africa was, and remained for three years, the main theatre of operations. Mussolini's original intention in March 1940 (see p. 253) had been to stay on the defensive there, but by June he had changed his mind. He realised that Egypt was badly defended and that Italy needed to take the Suez Canal if she were going to supply her troops in East Africa and Ethiopia. On the other hand, he thought Britain would soon collapse; so he let Marshal Graziani, his commander in North Africa, waste much of the summer and then in September, when Britain had not collapsed, urged him into ill-prepared action. Graziani probably had enough men but he certainly did not have enough armoured vehicles, let alone tanks. He moved 70 miles east and took Sidi Barrani – an untenable position, as he knew. In December the

British counter-attacked with 30,000 *mobile* troops and pushed the Italians back beyond Benghazi. The Italians lost all Cyrenaica including Tobruk, and 130,000 of their men were taken prisoner.

This was a massive blow to Mussolini's prestige and that of Italy, and it was not alone (see below). Graziani was dismissed and was lucky not to be shot, even though he had advanced only under protest and on Mussolini's direct and repeated orders. The Germans had to step in, to Mussolini's chagrin. Field Marshal Rommel, with his tanks and his mobile Afrika Korps backed by efficient air power, took over effective command of the desert campaign. Within a few months he won back most of Cyrenaica, although not Tobruk until a year later. But in June 1941 the Germans invaded Russia and had to switch most of their resources to the eastern front. By then the failure to take Suez had produced its inevitable consequences. No supplies of fuel or arms could reach the Duke of Aosta's forces in Ethiopia, or those in Eritrea and Somalia. In the spring of 1941 he had to surrender and Italian Ethiopia, after five years of huge expense, was no more. It had been perhaps the shortest-lived empire in history.

In North Africa, however, the battles raged back and forth for 18 months or more. Each side would advance; each would then find itself a long way from base, running short of water and supplies; each would then retreat. The Italians fought hard and well, surprisingly so given their lack of equipment and transport, although the British could usually tell where they were because they sang at night. Once again, the real Italian problem was supply. Italy had only one large North African port, Tripoli, but it was constantly bombed by the RAF from Malta, and it was so far away from Italy that convoys could easily be spotted and sunk before they arrived. Around 60 per cent of convoys were lost by late 1941; on 7 November the Italians lost seven supply ships in one day. Few arms or vehicles could reach the battle zones. Mussolini and his chief of staff Cavallero recognised that the answer was to use Tunisian ports, but by then the Italians were not in a state to take them, and in any case Hitler would still not allow an attack on Tunisia for fear all of French North Africa would go over to de Gaulle. So the *Duce* was reduced to pleading with the Vichy French to be allowed to use them; in vain. It was a bizarre outcome. Mussolini could not, in mid-war, impose his will on the defeated French, nor secure German support even when faced with the loss of the whole of North Africa.[4] Italy, not yet defeated, lost her African empire; whereas France, which had collapsed a year earlier, still retained hers.

If Tunisia could not be taken, then the British bases at Malta had to be eliminated. The Italians should have attempted this early in the war, and might then have succeeded; as it was, after spring 1941 there was no question of the Italians acting on their own in Malta or anywhere else, and equally there was little chance of persuading the Germans to fight the Italians' battles for them. In 1941–2 Mussolini wrote regularly to Hitler (often at Cavallero's instigation) explaining why taking Malta was vital for the Mediterranean convoys and hence for Axis operations in North Africa, and the German naval chiefs agreed. However, in the summer of 1942 Hitler backed Rommel's all-or-nothing drive into Egypt instead: 'the goddess of fortune in battles passes near warriors only once!'[5] So the Italians' Malta scheme was abandoned, and the convoys continued to be sunk.

In the spring and summer of 1942 Rommel retook Tobruk and managed to push eastwards again as far as Alamein, only 60-odd miles from Alexandria. Mussolini, scenting victory at last, came out to visit in June, hoping to enter Cairo shortly in triumph. But Rommel by this time had almost no air cover and little oil; the British controlled the air and the sea, and he could not make them retreat further. In any case, Rommel refused to meet the *Duce* and Mussolini had to go back to Rome humiliated without even visiting the front line, although he did fly over it. The British and Commonwealth troops, under Montgomery, built up their forces and supplies, and on 24 October 1942 launched their attack. Within two weeks they had won the decisive battle of El Alamein, taking most of the Axis tanks and nearly half their troops, prisoners or killed. Finally, on 8 November American troops landed in Morocco and Algeria, and the local Vichy French troops joined them. At last Hitler agreed that Italians and Germans should occupy the Tunisian ports. But it was too late. The Tunisian ports proved useless, since the RAF and the Royal Navy made sure that Italian ships never reached them. The Italians found themselves now in a hopeless fight on two fronts. They were forced back and compelled to surrender in May 1943. The Italian army had fought well in North Africa, sometimes spectacularly so. It might well have won, i.e. taken Egypt, if Mussolini had been able to occupy the Tunisian ports in 1940, or if he had occupied or destroyed Malta, or if he had not diverted scarce resources from October 1940 onwards towards far less vital campaigns in Greece and Russia.

The other main campaign of Italy's 'parallel war' was even more disastrous than North Africa. On 28 October 1940, anniversary of the March on Rome, Italy invaded neutral Greece from Albania. Once again, it was Ciano who instigated the venture, as he had done in Albania 18 months earlier. His aim was to establish Italy firmly in the southern Balkans and, above all, to keep the Germans out. Indeed, the campaign had been planned in the summer but the Germans had found out and made clear their opposition: it would let Britain into Greece, and Russia into the

Balkans.[6] Mussolini was forced to give the idea up, despite his habitual dislike of Greeks and his wish to show off Italy's martial valour. On 2 October he even ordered over half a million troops to be demobbed and sent home. Only when Hitler, anxious to secure oil, moved his troops into Rumania on 12 October – an act seen in Rome as yet another betrayal – did Mussolini revive his Greek scheme. The campaign was, in short, a direct rebuff to *Germany*, showing that the two Axis powers were at loggerheads over the Balkans. Mussolini even tried to fool Hitler by informing him of the invasion by letter dated 19 October but sent only on the 22nd, when the Italians knew Hitler was travelling to meet Franco and Pétain; he received it only on the 25th.[7] This ruse was infantile and predictably counter-productive: Hitler never trusted Mussolini again. Indeed, the whole Greek scheme was dreadful decision-making by any standards. Mussolini acted very suddenly in a fit of frustration and mistrust. He invaded Greece mainly because there was nowhere else to go. He was not making any progress against the British in North Africa, he thought Malta was too well defended, he knew Yugoslavia was off limits and he was furious with the Germans. As he told Ciano, 'Hitler always presents me with a *fait accompli*. This time I will pay him back in the same coin; he will learn from the newspapers that I have occupied Greece. Thus the equilibrium will be restored.'[8]

On 15 October, three days after the Germans had moved into Rumania, Mussolini summoned his reluctant army commanders – but not those of the navy or air force, nor the intelligence chiefs, an astonishing blunder for a man planning a seaborne invasion. He told them to invade the Epirus region of Greece a fortnight later. This was a ludicrous order if only because of the timescale, and the army high command should have vetoed it forthwith. They already knew the proposed attacking force of 9–11 divisions was far too small, indeed smaller than the Greek defending forces, and General Roatta had told the *Duce* so the previous day. Badoglio was worried, and argued that *all* Greece would need to be conquered and that therefore 20 divisions should be sent; but he did not press his points forcefully. He knew the *Duce* was determined. Mussolini told the military commander in Albania, General Visconti Prasca, not to worry about losses, and was assured that the general had given orders that battalions should attack at all times, even against a division. Visconti Prasca also told the meeting that 'the operation has been prepared down to the slightest detail and is as perfect as humanly possible'.[9] This was an absurd claim. In fact, moving men, arms, clothing and equipment from Italy through the inadequate Albanian ports was a logistical nightmare, as events soon showed. Furthermore, Visconti Prasca relied for intelligence on his Albanian sources. He ignored reports by the Italian military attaché in Athens and therefore completely miscalculated Greek military strength.[10] But nobody queried his sources or spoke out firmly against the venture. It was an extraordinary meeting of incompetents that decided on invasion. Two days later Badoglio told Ciano that all three service chiefs were opposed and that the campaign would exhaust Italy's meagre resources, but he did not dare speak to Mussolini.[11]

Ciano thought that he had ensured the senior Greek officials and commanders were well bribed, and that therefore there would be no resistance. But the Italians, like the ancient Trojans, found that the Greeks were untrustworthy. They could not even be relied on to betray their own country. The Greek gods were untrustworthy too: the autumn rains, or snow in the mountainous zones, poured down on the ill-equipped invaders. Within a fortnight the Greeks, with greater numbers, better weapons, more vehicles and detailed local knowledge, had beaten off the Italians; soon they took over a quarter of Albania. Italy's Albanian troops refused to fight and deserted over the hills; whereas the Greeks made their airfields available to the British, who could therefore now bomb both the ports of southern Italy and the Rumanian oilfields. Even as early as 10 November it was obvious that the invasion had gone disastrously wrong, and Mussolini called in his military again, this time including the other services. This time Badoglio did speak up, telling Mussolini very firmly that the army was not to blame:

neither the general High Command nor the army High Command had anything to do with the organising, which was done in a way completely contrary to our system based on the principle of planning thoroughly beforehand and *then* showing daring . . . when I think of the Greek affair I feel the blood rushing to my face.[12]

This sort of language in public was devastating, particularly as Badoglio repeated it a few days later to General Keitel. Mussolini encouraged Farinacci's paper to stir up opinion against Badoglio and the 'incompetent military caste', and dismissed Badoglio a month later. The meeting of 10 November decided to send thousands of vehicles to Albania, in the hope that they could be unloaded; they were *not* sent, therefore, to North Africa. Furthermore, 100,000 more men were dispatched to Albania, although not from among the ones who had just been demobilised.

Hitler was highly displeased. However, to ensure his Rumanian oil he had to rescue his ally and dislodge the RAF from Greek airports. In the spring of 1941 German troops swept through Yugoslavia and occupied most of Greece, while Mussolini urged his commanders to attack before the Germans arrived ('the military prestige of the Italian nation is at stake'[13]). Eventually the Italians were allowed zones in western Greece, Montenegro and the Croatian coast. The Italians had already lost over 20,000 dead and henceforth they had over 30 divisions tied down uselessly in Albania, Greece and Yugoslavia, fighting against both Communist and nationalist guerrillas with much brutality but little success.[14] The Greek campaign was not just a single, temporary setback. It immobilised virtually half the Italian army for the rest of the war, and the Italians suffered more casualties there than in North Africa. Mussolini was left alone with his anger and his humiliation. He raged against the high command and the collapse of all his hopes, and was bitterly resentful of the Germans. He tried to convince people that the Italians by themselves would have defeated the Greeks eventually, without German intervention.[15] He could also, of course, blame Ciano and the political governor of Albania, Jacomoni, whose fatuous optimism had deceived him. But it was his job not to be deceived. He had managed to turn a pan-European war into a Balkan conflict – 1914 in reverse.

If the Greek campaign was ignominious, the Russian campaign of 1941–3 was, for the troops, far worse. Once again, Mussolini was not consulted in advance when Hitler invaded Russia in June 1941, and was initially dismayed: the Germans were committing the classic error of fighting on two fronts, and would no longer be able to give much help in North Africa. Mussolini had no military reasons to join in and might easily have declared Italian neutrality against Russia, as the Japanese did. He did, however, have his usual political preoccupations: prestige, greed, and a desire to prevent Hitler winning alone. So he sent an expeditionary force of, initially, 60,000 men, and told his Cabinet he was doing so in order to prevent Hitler dominating the Axis![16] Hitler had not requested these troops, indeed had warned that they would disperse Italy's strength, a point also stressed by the new Italian chief of the general staff, Cavallero.[17] Unbelievably, the next year Mussolini poured far more troops into Russia, at a time when they were needed in North Africa for Rommel's big push to Cairo and long after it had become clear that the Russians were not going to be defeated quickly. By the late summer of 1942 there were 227,000 Italian troops in Russia (more than the Germans had in North Africa), often crack troops at that, but mostly without usable transport and utterly ill-equipped for the climate. Moreover, Mussolini personally ordered that Italy's few modern anti-tank guns and her armoured cars be sent to Russia, instead of to Libya where they might have made a big difference in the summer of 1942.[18] His foolishness was not the result of any ideological hatred of Communism, but simply because he did not want to be the junior partner. If the Germans were helping the Italians in

North Africa and Greece, the Italians must help the Germans in Russia. In 1943, as the Germans retreated after the battle of Stalingrad, the Italians were left behind to walk back; they lost 90,000 dead and 60,000 prisoners in remote camps, often for years to come.

The war went badly enough on land, but was even worse at sea. The merchant fleet was given no notice of impending war in 1940, and so over a third of Italy's ships and thousands of trained seamen were caught outside the Mediterranean and unable to sail home. The navy proper adopted a defensive strategy, convinced it could not beat the British in open combat. It turned out to be right. The first clash was at Punta Stilo, off Calabria, in July 1940, when a superior Italian force intercepted Admiral Cunningham's ships moving from Alexandria to Malta. It should have been a decisive Italian victory and might have led to the capture of Malta, but the Italian air force tried to bomb its own ships and the chance was lost. In November the British Fleet Air Arm, using antiquated seaplanes and aerial torpedoes, carried out a very successful surprise attack on the Italian fleet in Taranto harbour: virtually half the Italian fleet, including three battleships and two cruisers, was immobilised for the loss of two ancient planes and four men. In February a British naval convoy from Gibraltar sailed all the way to Genoa and bombed it with impunity. At the battle of Matapan, in March, Cunningham's fleet sank three heavy cruisers and two destroyers, killing 2,500 men. Apart from two planes, the Italian air force arrived on the scene too late, whereas the British had air cover. They also had an aircraft carrier nearby, they had effective radar, and above all they had Ultra's decoding of enemy signals, which told them the Italian Admiralty's detailed instructions and order of battle.[19]

Like most naval encounters, Taranto (allegedly the model for Pearl Harbor) and Matapan had huge results. They made it very difficult for Italy to ship supplies and men across to North Africa; by late 1941 a third of the tanks and a quarter of the artillery sent across the Mediterranean were lost. The navy, lacking oil itself as well as air support, could not protect vital imports of raw materials. Above all, these defeats made it impossible to realise Mussolini's whole strategy. Italy really was a 'prisoner in the Mediterranean' now, with no chance of her ships passing Gibraltar or Suez. Mussolini must take much of the blame. The Italians had no aircraft carriers because he had declared, years earlier, that they were unnecessary: Italy herself was one large aircraft carrier. But Italy was too far away from Gibraltar or Alexandria to be useful for naval aircraft, and indeed Mussolini changed his mind in 1941 and ordered two carriers to be built, although they were not ready by the end of the war.[20] Furthermore, Mussolini made no serious effort to take Malta early in the war, nor even to use the Dodecanese islands, held by Italy since 1912, as key naval bases. Despite his rhetoric about the Mediterranean, he was an ex-soldier who did not understand the significance of sea power and strongly distrusted his navy – too aristocratic, too traditional, too Anglophile and altogether too 'unFascist'. Even when the navy had a spectacular success, e.g. when Italian torpedo boats blew up two destroyers and an oil tanker in Alexandria harbour in December 1941, Mussolini drew no conclusions for tactics or strategy.

Either by land or sea, Italy's war was a story of failure and defeat. This was not surprising. The king and the armed services had let Mussolini have his war in June 1940, provided they were not expected to fight it. Mussolini, too, did not expect to fight. He joined the war for diplomatic reasons, knowing that the troops were badly equipped even for a quick Alpine campaign against France. Without German help Italy would have been out of the war by spring 1941, after losing in Libya, Ethiopia, Somalia and Greece. As it was, she lost her East African empire and was dragged along into a war on distant fronts – North Africa, the Balkans and Russia – none of which she could supply. Furthermore, there were other *potential* fronts, e.g. southern France, Tunisia and Croatia, where troops and arms had to be deployed. In December 1941, after Pearl Harbor and the German declaration of war on the United States of America, Mussolini joined in the war against the Americans too – another front, and even more distant. In each case Mussolini acted for 'prestige', or in order to prevent the Germans winning alone. The problem was that the Italian army and navy could not fight a lengthy war, and if opponents were not defeated quickly they would not be defeated at all. Mussolini's many enemies – the British in 1940, the Greeks in 1940–1, the Russians in 1941 – all surprised the *Duce* by failing to surrender quickly. The result was that morale sank and could not be restored. Every time the troops lost, Mussolini would send them off again on some new ill-considered campaign to restore his military prestige. Then they would lose again. This was not a winning strategy.

The *Duce* as War Leader

Mussolini's whole regime, even in peacetime, had been modelled on the values of the First World War: mobilisation, heroism and national unity. He thought in terms of numbers – '8 million bayonets' – and morale, and he was obsessed by national prestige. He was essentially a 'histrionic' journalist with a simple message: he could command and the Italians could fight. Before the war even started, he had another row with the king over who should be 'supreme commander of the armed forces', a title the king refused on constitutional grounds to give up; Mussolini had to be satisfied with being 'commander of operational troops on all fronts'. Early in the war he constantly urged his generals to attack, essentially for prestige reasons and more or less regardless of circumstances. In January 1941, for example, he told Cavallero to attack in Albania: the action 'must eliminate all reasons for world speculation about Italian military prestige, of which prestige I have been, am and will be a very jealous defender', and it should make German assistance unnecessary.[21] However, he had absolutely no grasp of *long-term* strategy and no knowledge of technical or tactical innovations. Mussolini simply did not think strategically; he could not grasp the big picture, or could not grasp it for long enough. The essence of military success is to know what the enemy is up to, to know when and where to attack or defend, to put enough forces there, and to have a feasible, unpredictable and flexible plan. Mussolini failed all these basic tests. He ignored intelligence and information, he was indecisive, and he spread his men and resources around everywhere: early in 1942 the ninety-odd Italian divisions were deployed in North Africa, Greece, Albania and the Balkans, the Aegean, the USSR, France, the Alps and of course in Sicily and Sardinia. Not surprisingly, none of them was effective. Moreover, he appeared to have no war plan at all, just aspirations. He made an extraordinary series of basic blunders. He accepted the armistice with France, although it gave Italy no immediate gains and failed to strengthen her position in the Mediterranean; he failed to launch a real onslaught on Malta early on; he sent around 170 planes to northern France in 1940 to help invade Britain, although his troops in North Africa urgently needed air cover; he demobilised 600,000 reservists in early October 1940, then decided a week later to invade Greece; and he refused the German offer of armoured cars and tank units in Libya, although his army there was desperate for them. He ended up invading Russia without suitable equipment and pointlessly declaring war on the United States of America. These were not the acts of a rational commander.

Mussolini was, in fact, a textbook example of the wrong personality for a war leader. Emotionally, he was far too insecure. He ranted against his enemies instead of appraising them objectively, and he did this because objective appraisement might come up with unwelcome information or conclusions. He feared and rejected information, always a dreadful symptom in a leader, and so failed to take normal precautions. Faced with manifest failures by naval intelligence, he did nothing until the

Germans complained. He resented and feared his allies, and most of his bad decisions were because of his desire to keep up with them. Like all bad generals and unlike all good ones, he threw his men into unnecessary campaigns and sacrificed their lives quite uselessly. Indeed, he despised his subordinates and above all his fellow-countrymen. With this outlook he was unlikely to rally the people with rousing speeches, and made remarkably few during the war. Mussolini even misread the political aspects of the war – whether Britain, Greece and Russia would resist, the nature of Hitler's ambitions in eastern Europe, the role of the United States of America. He knew a great deal less and had travelled far less, both physically and in the mind, than he needed. Perhaps the war came too late for him. Aged 57 in July 1940, he could no longer hear contrary views, master detail, seize opportunities or arouse enthusiasm.

Admittedly his military commanders let him down. There were too many of them (600 generals and 80 admirals in 1939), promoted largely on seniority and much given to squabbling among themselves. They disliked responsibility, they panicked easily, they had their own traditions and culture, and they had the king's support. They usually overestimated enemy strength – for example, Graziani in 1940 refused to advance on Egypt for fear of Weygand's phantom army in Syria – and this made them overcautious and defensive. The admirals never thought for one moment that they might defeat the Royal Navy. The top generals still thought in 1940 in terms of trench warfare, fought by mass immobile armies in the Alps; the First World War all over again. They had not drawn up detailed plans to attack Malta and Tunisia, or even Egypt and Greece. However, they were the men who controlled actual operations and they were not willing to be told what to do by an incompetent ex-corporal. After the fiascos in Greece and at Taranto Mussolini replaced virtually all the top military chiefs, including Badoglio, Graziani, Soddu and Admiral Cavagnari, but he then became the prisoner of the new ones and treated them with surprising deference, at least in public. Only they, or the Germans, could rescue him from humiliation. They failed to do so, although Cavallero was certainly an improvement on Badoglio as chief of general staff. But even on the rare occasions when the generals did urge an attack, as Cavallero did on Malta from late 1941 onwards, they received little support from Mussolini.

It is worth stressing that Mussolini set up no effective machinery to control the military or to ensure his orders were being implemented, or to allow them to influence him. Unlike Churchill, he had no trusted military adviser with the status to veto his more absurd ideas and the power to enforce his good ones. Mussolini himself was minister of all three services and also 'supreme commander' of operational forces. He met daily with the chief of general staff and occasionally with the service chiefs, but he convened them rarely as a group and only then to give instructions, not to debate strategy or coordinate plans. Indeed, he had no staff to do so and nor did the chief of general staff, although Cavallero built up something like a general staff after 1941. Even so, the three service chiefs largely ran their own show. They could by-pass Cavallero and see Mussolini directly. The *Duce* also chaired a number of special committees, e.g. on arms supply or economic autarchy, but again he made no effort to coordinate their work. The lack of routine high-level meetings was typical of Mussolini's style of government, and in military matters it proved disastrous. There was no consideration of alternatives and no coordination. The army in North Africa, for example, received little air support, since General Pricolo did not send the planes he had promised.[22]

The other government bodies were unable to fill the gap. The Grand Council did not meet between December 1939 and its final meeting on 24 July 1943. The Council of Ministers usually met monthly, but it did not debate war issues. It heard lengthy monologues from the *Duce*, and it nodded through technical legislation on domestic affairs; on 8 May 1941, for example, the only subject discussed was a proposal to change the title of the 'Chief of Police' to 'Director-General Chief of Police' (it was rejected).[23] There was certainly no British-type restricted 'War Cabinet' of senior politicians and military advisers, able to contain Mussolini's more fanciful ideas. Indeed, for several months in the first half of 1941 there was no government at all and no Cabinet meetings, because Mussolini sent most of his ministers off to fight in Greece or North Africa until the resulting chaos forced him to bring them back again. They returned well aware of the army's inadequacies, very unhappy at having been ordered off like junior recruits, and conscious that Mussolini had sent them away so as to be able to take all the decisions himself. Even Mussolini's son-in-law Galeazzo Ciano had no influence now. It was extraordinary that Mussolini kept him on as Foreign Minister, particularly as he was very unpopular with party, public and Germans. It is difficult to say which, in the *Duce*'s eyes, was Ciano's greater offence: to have been wrong about Greece, or to have been right about Hitler. Ciano spent most of his time writing his diary, trying to keep the Germans out of Croatia and openly criticising Mussolini as a pig-headed old fool. As for the other ministers, even when they were in Rome they counted for little and their views were not asked. Mussolini often appointed them at random. In February 1943 the new Minister of Corporations turned out to be in a mental hospital; the *Duce* had taken his name off some old list and given him the job because it was his turn.[24] Indeed, Mussolini now disliked seeing ministers at all. Instead of calling them in individually, he now expected them to send him their reports *in writing*; the documents would be returned with the simple message, 'yes' or 'no'.[25] So any collective decision-making was impossible. Furthermore, collective decision-making is designed not only to make better decisions, but to cement (and commit) the collectivity. Mussolini's method produced dreadful decisions and also alienated everybody else, leaving him dangerously alone. He was an erratic man and he needed calm professional advice, but he had made sure he did not receive it.

After mid-1941 the deficiencies of Italian decision-making had less military impact. The Germans had taken over effective command on all fronts. Mussolini was far too insecure to argue the Italian case strongly with Hitler, although he later admitted that Cavallero had been right in the spring of 1942 to press for an occupation of Malta instead of allowing Rommel to advance to Alamein.[26] Rommel's refusal even to meet the *Duce* in the summer of 1942 was symptomatic. Mussolini's quest for prestige had literally run into the sands. The Germans controlled the war and had little but contempt for their Italian subordinates. They distrusted them so much they would no longer pass on any information. Mussolini might still hope for victory as Hitler's ally but no longer as Hitler's equal, let alone as Hitler's mentor. He was left distraught and frustrated as his 'parallel war' vanished, and with it his role as war leader. Nobody – Germans, military chiefs, ordinary soldiers, ministers, even his son-in-law – now took him seriously. Mussolini's war had led only to humiliation. In August 1941 he suffered an even greater blow. His son Bruno, by now an experienced pilot who had served in both Ethiopia and Spain, was killed when his engines failed as he was landing at Pisa airport. Mussolini wrote a moving account of Bruno's life, as he had done about Arnaldo nearly 10 years earlier.[27] He had to cope now with his own personal grief as well as all the sorrows and bitterness of war.

Mussolini's relations with Hitler were as unproductive as ever. They wrote to each other regularly though formally (it was always *'Führer!'*, not *'Dear Adolf'*), but their meetings were infrequent (about twice a year) and increasingly farcical. They had no agenda, no analysis and no conclusions, and Mussolini disliked having to sit through an interminable, boring *Führer* monologue which he could barely understand. The two dictators could not have been more different, and their diverse experiences of war in 1940–1 widened the gap. Hitler talked about strategy and conquest in eastern Europe; Mussolini talked, when he talked at all, of a peace settlement and the need not to alienate the conquered, and of his 'claims' in the Mediterranean. Their trickiest meeting was in Florence in October 1940, just as Mussolini was beginning to invade Greece largely to spite Hitler and despite Hitler's strong advice and warnings (although the *Führer* accepted the fait accompli with surprising grace); their most friendly encounter was in spring 1942 at Salzburg, when Mussolini's cheerful zest and liveliness cheered Hitler up after a gloomy winter deep in the east Prussian forest. But they did not trust each other. One of Mussolini's motives for joining the war at all had been to avoid the Germans dominating Europe on their own, and in autumn 1939 the Italians had begun rebuilding their own 'Maginot line', i.e. their fortresses along the Austrian (now German) border – work that continued, quite deliberately, until 1942, although it proved useless when needed in August–September 1943. Mussolini even welcomed the early German reverses on the Russian front, as they would prevent the Germans being too overbearing. He respected Hitler's determination but resented his success and feared his fanaticism: 'his brain is abstruse. He has something of the sorcerer and of the saloon-bar philosopher. He has constructed for his own purposes a history, politics and geography of the world, and he only drinks from that well!'[28]

For his part, Hitler still felt grateful to Mussolini personally for his support in the past, which had enabled him to militarise the Rhineland, annex Austria and liquidate Czechoslovakia; even in June 1940 Italy had tied up French divisions in the Alps. He even regarded Mussolini as his one true soulmate. In August 1941 he took the *Duce* on a long tour of the eastern front, although to his dismay Mussolini insisted on piloting the plane. Certainly Mussolini was a far more reliable partner than Franco, who refused to allow the Germans to move through Spain and take Gibraltar. But Hitler did not trust Mussolini's strategic judgement nor his entourage, especially Ciano and the king. He thought Mussolini had been far too soft on the Establishment and had made far too many compromises. He also did not trust the Italian generals, not even with information. There was, in fact, no regular formal consultation between the two countries' general staffs: apart from Göring's occasional visits to Rome, the military chiefs met only when accompanying their leaders to their meetings.

The real obstacle to good German–Italian relations was that the Greek fiasco in 1940–1 ended all hope of an Italian 'parallel war' and permanently ruined Mussolini's standing in German eyes. In November 1940 Hitler wrote him a very sharp letter (a 'rap on the knuckles', Mussolini called it[29]) about the disastrous results of invading Greece. The next month the Italian ambassador in Berlin presented another list of Italian arms and raw material requirements, and was met only with exasperation.[30] The leaders' meetings thenceforth fell into an unwelcome pattern. Italy was always a supplicant for German assistance, and always kept coming back asking for more. Hitler agreed to send enough to keep the Italian show on the road but insisted on deciding how it was used. From the German viewpoint the Italians were hopeless allies. They had insisted on fighting their Greek campaign without telling anybody what they were up to, indeed against Hitler's express advice, and they had then needed to be rescued with massive arms support that the Germans needed elsewhere.[31] Hitler could not allow this to continue, and the Germans took over control both in North Africa and in Greece, despite having little interest in either. He was willing to save the *Duce*'s face, and did so in Yugoslavia in April 1941: instead of running matters overtly himself, he allowed Mussolini to continue to issue orders to Italian troops on the basis of 'recommendations and wishes' communicated secretly ('between the two of us') by the *Führer*.[32] But he was not willing to bail out Mussolini on every occasion and he was certainly not willing to fight Mussolini's war for him, nor to allow Mussolini to decide strategy. Mussolini had assumed that sending troops to Russia would give him a voice on strategy there, but by 1942 he had little say even in North Africa. He was left to nurse his resentment and to fight a 'subordinate war', pleading for anything the Germans might be willing to concede. For a man of his temperament it was an utter humiliation.

Arms and the Man

One of the main reasons for Italy's poor performance in the Second World War was her lack of up-to-date arms. Italy had spent huge sums on her military in the late 1930s, but the money had gone into Ethiopia or Spain rather than into modern equipment. Her soldiers carried the same rifle as in the First World War, indeed as in 1891. Her artillery, too, was 1915–18 vintage, often Austrian guns captured in 1918. Her tanks were too few, about 1,500 at most, and all but around seventy of them were 3-tonne 'sardine tins', too slow, too light and too badly armed – armoured cars rather than real tanks. The air force relied on obsolescent biplane fighters and two- or three-engined bombers with limited range that made nonsense of the belief that 'the bomber would always get through', or hit the target if it did. The navy was better equipped, with battleships and submarines; but it lacked aircraft carriers, anti-aircraft defence, radar, adequate firepower and fuel. After its early disasters it did little throughout the rest of the war except to provide convoy escorts for troops and munitions crossing to North Africa, and it was conspicuously unsuccessful even at that.[33] These weaknesses were evident before the war began, but did not matter much in a short war. In a long one they mattered a great deal.

To civilians, anti-aircraft defence was the most conspicuous failing. In 1940 Italy had two searchlights and 230 anti-aircraft batteries,[34] mostly protecting airfields and ports rather than towns. In Rome, the few anti-aircraft batteries were manned by the Fascist Militia and were affectionately known as 'Toscas', because they 'never harmed a living soul'. The city's air defence consisted essentially of the Pope, who persuaded the British not to bomb Rome in return for the Italians not bombing Cairo.[35] So Rome was not bombed for most of the war, but nonetheless Mussolini ordered the sirens to sound whenever there was a raid on Naples, over a hundred miles away. This was designed to toughen up the citizenry, but crying wolf so often led to many unnecessary deaths when Rome *was* finally bombed on 19 July 1943.

The equipment problem was, of course, not all Mussolini's fault. The senior officers had for years spent the available money on promotions and wages for themselves rather than on better guns or vehicles. But Mussolini, as minister of all three services since 1933, had connived at this. The politico-administrative system was such that if Mussolini did not ensure modern arms and vehicles were available in the right place at the right time, nobody else would. His generals, as usual, had prepared for the last war: a static slogging-match in the Alps, essentially defensive and won by the side with more troops and higher morale. Neither they nor Mussolini realised that serious long-term war preparation no longer meant boosting the birth rate and ordering more rifles and blankets. It meant industrial reconstruction, ensuring the capacity to produce more arms and vehicles by the million. Italy needed tanks, not bayonets; mines and torpedoes, not battleships that had to stay in port throughout the war. But she lacked both the raw materials and the industrial infrastructure. In 1939 she produced only just over 2 million tonnes of steel and 1.5 million tonnes of coal, and she had no oil. Her munitions industries produced a maximum of almost 250 aircraft a month by 1942, less than in the closing months of the First World War; they also managed 185 tanks a month, including 55 light ones, but by then only about 20 a month were reaching Libya. That was completely inadequate. Military spending pre-war should have gone into arms factories, not into generals' pockets or into Ethiopia and Spain. This is not hindsight. Even in 1935 there was much criticism of the battleship programme and of the lack of tanks,[36] and General Baistrocchi had warned Mussolini in 1936 to build up stocks of weapons and raw materials: 'otherwise, *Duce*, you will lose the empire that you have gained'.[37] But Mussolini had taken no notice. He seemed a man in denial, as Ciano observed: 'is he so afraid of the truth that he does not wish to hear it?'[38]

In fact, Mussolini knew perfectly well the true state of affairs, and had done for years. When he dismissed Balbo from the Aviation Ministry in 1933 he found that there were only 911 serviceable planes instead of the 3,125 that Balbo had claimed.[39] The air force continued to have problems counting its own planes, and in October 1939 Balbo's successor was dismissed for exactly the same reason.[40] So, too, was the under-secretary at the War Ministry. In any case, Mussolini himself had helped draw up the 'Cavallero memorandum' (see p. 247) in May 1939, explaining why Italy could not fight before 1942; and he had sent Hitler the huge list of needed materials in August 1939, to justify staying out of the war. The *Duce* received detailed monthly reports from all three services on arms, oil stocks, transport, ammunition, etc., and in the first months of 1940 Badoglio had stressed the complete inadequacy of equipment for a long war against Great Powers. The head of the Munitions Commissariat told him that even if the war industries worked two 10-hour shifts a day and could afford unlimited imports of materials, Italy would not be able to equip her army and navy until 1944, or face a year's war until 1949.[41] Even a few days before Italy joined the war Mussolini received another such report from Graziani and told its part-author Rossi that he had read it with interest, but 'if I had to wait until the army was ready it would be years before I could enter the war, whereas I have to join now. We will have to do the best we can.'[42] He did not, in June 1940, care about the condition of the armed forces but about the condition of France, and of Hitler.

Morale and the Home Front

During the whole war Mussolini visited the front, or fronts, only three times. He went to Albania in March 1941, hoping to supervise the defeat of Greece; to the Russian front in August 1941, as Hitler's guest; and to North Africa in July 1942, where he was snubbed by Rommel and acquired a nasty amoeba that laid him low for months. Indeed, on all three occasions disaster followed, so Mussolini became known as a man to avoid and his visits certainly did not improve the troops' morale. It had never been high. Even in August 1940, before any serious defeats, a police informer in Rome reported that in the barracks there was animated debate about why Italy was in the war at all: 'defeatism reigns supreme and people act as they did in the Dark Ages. There is no discipline and cowardice is almost general.'[43] Army officers had never been keen Fascists and they greatly resented the Militia. Until the Greek campaign they still had some respect for the *Duce*; but they had none after it, and the dismissal of Badoglio was a nasty shock. Naval officers were even more disaffected. They were often Anglophile, they realised Britain was far stronger at sea, and they knew the importance of Malta and of the Tunisian ports. They too had no respect for Mussolini personally: he was not a former naval person, he understood nothing about their activities and he had insulted the navy publicly in 1925 (see p. 99). They had not wanted war and Admiral Cavagnari had told Mussolini in April 1940 that Italy might arrive at the peace negotiations 'not only without her territorial claims but also without a navy or an air force'.[44] The air force was the most 'Fascist' of the services, but her pilots knew the planes were surprisingly slow and no use against serious opposition; some flatly refused to fly the Caproni 310.[45] Most of the pilots were reserve officers, who did the fighting in the air while the regulars stayed on the ground and were promoted. Neither navy nor air force had any intention of collaborating with each other or with the army, and there was no institutional mechanism forcing them to do so.

The experience of defeat naturally worsened matters. Most of the casualties in the initial Alpine campaign of June 1940 were from frostbite, and returned soldiers told of lack of mountain clothing or even food. But it was the Greek campaign of October–November 1940 that destroyed all Mussolini's pretensions to military expertise, and most of his prestige. By spring 1941 Greece had been followed by Graziani's defeat in North Africa, the loss of the empire in East Africa and by the naval disasters at Taranto and Matapan. Italy lost early and she lost consistently, and her forces naturally became demoralised. In any case, why were they fighting at all? They had no interest in a Mediterranean empire and detested their German allies. The expeditionary force in Russia was totally ill-equipped for the conditions and had no motive for being there. Furthermore, they could see how the Germans treated prisoners, civilians, and Jews. The slogan was still 'believe, obey, fight'; the troops obeyed and fought, but they no longer believed.

Civilian morale was considerably worse than that of the troops. By December 1940 the police spoke of 'very widespread lack of confidence and rising discontent'.[46] Similarly, in July 1941 the British ambassador in Lisbon reported, after talking to various American consuls who had just left Italy, that 'there was universal agreement that war weariness existed everywhere and that the people were only anxious for one thing, the speedy termination of the war. Mussolini was admitted by all the officials to have been losing his grip rapidly during recent months.'[47] The main popular grievance in the first two years of the war was about food shortages. Coffee, soap and heating oil were very scarce, and shoes were rationed to one pair a year. Some basic foods were rationed by 1941, but the rations were too low – 150g of bread a day by 1942, and a third of it made from maize. Farmers were compelled to sell their wheat to the state but received only 1,750 lire per tonne, which they claimed was less than the cost of production. So they stopped producing except for the black market, and bread shortages became even worse. So did meat shortages, because there was no animal feed. By 1942–3 adults were expected to survive on 1,100 calories a day (although manual workers received more). Food riots occurred sporadically, e.g. in Matera in March 1942, but this was rare. Food rationing was effective at preventing starvation and revolt, but it did not prevent food disappearing on to the black market amid wholesale accusations of corruption. The Mussolini family, of course, was all right: Rachele still kept chickens and pigs at villa Torlonia.

Italy not only lost the war, she lost the propaganda war as well. The great war propagandist and journalist of the First World War was now strangely silent. Not only did Mussolini rarely visit the front, he did not visit bombed-out city areas either, partly because they were mostly in northern industrial zones where both war and *Duce* were particularly unpopular. He made only four major public speeches during the war – his first in parliament was in June 1941, on the anniversary of Italy's entry – and he rarely appeared on his balcony. Everybody noticed that 28 October 1942, the twentieth anniversary of the March on Rome, passed without a speech from the *Duce*. He knew that thrusting out his jaw and rolling his eyes no longer impressed anybody, and he had little positive to say anyway. His only other speech to the Chamber, in December 1942, made no mention of the recent American landings in North Africa or the obvious threat to Libya. He did, however, advise people to evacuate the cities, which caused much panic especially as there was no planning or organisation to do it.[48] When he did speak he failed to impress: too much blaming others, too much self-pity, too much resentment.[49] Mussolini spent nearly all his time inside palazzo Venezia, immersed in bureaucratic routine; when ill, as in 1942–3, he went to his country retreat at Rocca delle Caminate.

Mussolini also made some basic political errors that lowered morale even further. Making Badoglio the scapegoat for the Greek campaign was a mistake, as it was seen as a victory for the Militia over the army, and anyway everybody knew Ciano was the man responsible for the fiasco. In August 1941 the *Duce* made himself thoroughly disliked in Sicily by ordering all Sicilian-born government employees on the island to be transferred to the mainland, for fear they might be disloyal if Sicily were invaded. In practice, only about a thousand officials were moved, because nobody else was willing to go there to replace them.[50] Police informers also reported much public concern about the fate of the Jews, who during the war *were* being seriously persecuted: by May 1942 (a year *before* the German takeover) 5,000 were doing forced labour.[51] Mussolini's coming out on to his balcony in December 1941 and declaring war on the United States of America was the final straw. It was an astonishingly foolish move that needlessly alienated millions of Italians with relatives in America, and of course it made the war unwinnable. No Italian supposed that Italy, or Germany, could defeat the United States of America. People realised that Mussolini had managed to lead a totally unprepared Italy into war against all three of the strongest powers in the world.[52]

By 1942 neither the Ministry of Popular Culture (Minculpop) nor the party could persuade anyone of anything. The ministry's propaganda stressed the Bolshevik crimes of the Russians and the imperialist greed and materialism of the British and Americans, but most Italians disliked the Germans even more and knew more about them. The troops on the eastern front sent letters home about the situation there, and there were also 200,000 Italian civilian workers in Germany, often working alongside concentration camp inmates. One of the ministry's bright ideas was to issue a compilation of false news stories put about by the enemy, but unfortunately everybody believed them.[53] The party was even less effective. After Starace's dismissal in 1939, it was run for a year each by Ettore Muti and then by Adelchi Serena; each of them appointed new federal secretaries in each province, so there was total instability. The party split into factions, fighting for spoils – literally so in Serena's case, for he had to be dismissed after a fist-fight with the Minister of Agriculture in Mussolini's ante-chamber. In December 1941 Mussolini therefore appointed yet another party secretary, the 26-year-old Aldo Vidussoni, who had been wounded in Spain and had won a gold medal for valour there. No doubt he incarnated the Fascist ideal of youth and courage, but he could not make a coherent speech nor organise a political party. The Fascist old guard resented having to take orders from a young upstart, and rightly saw his appointment as proof that the *Duce* did not trust them. The party had real tasks. It administered much of welfare, relief work, rationing, food prices and civil defence, but it had no competent officials.

It performed its functions very badly and aroused much popular resentment. It certainly did not boost morale, and had no idea how to do so.

Moreover, the Italian propaganda effort had rivals. People could listen to Radio Vatican and buy the Vatican newspaper, *L'Osservatore Romano*, which published more objective international news and whose circulation rose to 200,000. They could also listen to 'Colonel Stevens' of Radio London, as did Mussolini himself. Wireless sets, unlike newspapers, could not be censored, and the BBC's version of events was widely discussed in bars and cafés throughout the land. '*Radio Londra*' transmitted surprisingly reliable information, particularly on the Greek campaign, and its propaganda was well chosen and extremely appealing. The line was that Britain's enemy was Germany, not Italy. Italy had become involved only because of the idiocy of one man, who had imposed untold hardships on his people and who alone should take all the blame. This was not true (see p. 255), but it was just what the Italians wanted to hear.[54] Churchill put it most memorably in a radio broadcast of December 1940:

One man, and one man alone has ranged the Italian people in deadly struggle against the British empire, and has deprived Italy of the sympathy and intimacy of the United States of America. That he is a great man I do not deny, but that after eighteen years of unbridled power he has led your country to the horrid verge of ruin can be denied by none. It is one man who, against the Crown and Royal Family of Italy, against the Pope and all the authority of the Vatican and of the Roman Catholic Church, against the wishes of the Italian people, who had no lust for this war, has arrayed the trustees and inheritors of ancient Rome upon the side of the ferocious pagan barbarians.[55]

Even the best propaganda machine in the world could not have countered that.

However, until autumn 1942 Mussolini was still respected more than his regime and considerably more than Ciano (the 'one man' who took the blame for Greece). Morale even recovered somewhat in 1941–2 as the position in North Africa improved. But it remained fragile, and it collapsed after El Alamein in autumn 1942. In the winter of 1942–3 Axis forces began retreating everywhere, the Allies began serious bombing raids on both northern and southern cities, and an Allied invasion of Italy looked increasingly likely. Moreover, for several months after his visit to Libya in July 1942 Mussolini was seriously ill, although his doctors could not agree what was wrong – an amoeba? A revival of his gastric ulcer, so troublesome in 1925? Whatever it was, he was often in great pain and could hardly eat. He lost about a quarter of his weight, and his blood pressure became dangerously low. His doctors thought he was run down and recommended rest, but if he rested all government and military business stopped. Early in 1943 the pain died down and he began to put on weight, but in early summer it flared up again, now diagnosed as gastritis and a small duodenal ulcer. Perhaps for once the cause really was psychological: Mussolini's inner dejection, his anger and frustration, the loss of his son, his isolation, his awareness that he had failed.[56]

At any rate, Mussolini now personified defeat and became really unpopular. He made few appearances or speeches and he was clearly no longer a war leader in any meaningful sense. He looked much older and was said to spend all his time in bed with Claretta Petacci, while her relatives ruined the country – her brother was allegedly the richest man in Italy. Radio London made great play with the 'Petacci clan', and made sure the affair was widely known all over Italy. And why was the *Duce*'s son Vittorio not in the front line? Some of Mussolini's devoted admirers, like Bottai, now saw through him: 'The *Duce* has declined intellectually and physically. I am no longer susceptible to his charm (*fascino*). He is not strong-willed, he is just a man with ridiculous aspirations who wants to be adulated, flattered and deceived.'[57] Many people thought that the Allies would offer peace if Italy handed over the *Duce*, and this meant that the whole war was being fought to save his skin.[58] In Milan, a police agent reported that the name of the department store UPIM was said to signify *'Uniamoci per Impiccare Mussolini'* ('Let's Join Together to Hang Mussolini').[59]

Mussolini himself thought the Italians had let him down. He had given them a great opportunity for glory but despite all his efforts they had proved useless in war. Ciano regularly noted his comments on his fellow-citizens: 'a race of sheep'; 'they need the rod, the rod, the rod'; 'it is the raw material I lack. Even Michelangelo needed marble to carve his statues'; planting more trees on the Apennines would make for a colder climate, and toughen them up; a smaller bread ration would sort them out.[60] This theme became an obsession as the war went on. From 1935 to 1940 he had thought he really *had* transformed the Italians, but by 1941 it was clear that his life's work had failed. After El Alamein he told the Cabinet that the battle had been lost 'because of deficiencies in the race, and I could not change the race in twenty years'.[61] Some ministers noted a strange paradoxical calm and indifference in the face of disaster, a feature often associated with 'histrionic' personalities.[62] However, he continued to rant against the bourgeois. In 1942, just to annoy them, he abolished first-class seats and restaurant cars on the trains, but the move infuriated all the officers in his armed forces and also led to such a loss of revenue that it soon had to be rescinded. In similar vein the new party secretary Vidussoni threatened to ban golf, to Ciano's horror.

Mussolini consoled himself with Claretta, although even with her there were rows, temporary break-offs and one real crisis, in summer 1940, when she had an extra-uterine pregnancy and very nearly died. This drama, and the loss of their unborn child, brought them closer together, although he always had other lovers too. Most people around Mussolini disliked Claretta and thought she made him less responsible, but there was probably some envy in this judgement. He needed her company and affection, if only to relax from the stress of a losing war. Moreover, his wife Rachele was less supportive than previously, and began taking sides in political disputes among the *gerarchi*; her nagging and recriminations made matters even worse.

Decline and Fall of a Roman Empire

By winter 1942–3 the war was lost and everybody knew it. People spent their money quickly on the black market or on property, and hoped the Anglo-Americans would arrive before the Russians. In January 1943 Tripoli fell and the Libyan colony was no more. The Axis troops retreated to Tunisia, and so Mussolini failed to bring his army back from North Africa even though it was in a hopeless situation fighting on two fronts. Nor, of course, could he pull his troops back from the Balkans or Russia, where the battle of Stalingrad was lost at the end of January. In mid-May Tunis fell and a quarter of a million Axis troops surrendered – a loss comparable to Stalingrad in its political impact. Italy was now totally exposed to invasion from the south. Her remaining army was elsewhere, her navy was short of fuel and vessels, there was no air defence and there was no heavy artillery to repel invaders.

Mussolini's main response to the new situation was a government reshuffle, forced on him by the fact that most of his existing colleagues were no longer trustworthy. In February he dismissed 9 out of his 11 ministers, including Ciano who went to be ambassador to the Vatican; one of the two ministers to remain was the minister for Africa, although Italian Africa had been lost. He also soon replaced the chief of police and the chief of general staff; and Carlo Scorza, a tough ex-*squadrista*, took over from Vidussoni as party secretary. This was not so much a 'changing of the guard' as a Stalinist purge without the shootings. The previous ministers were not appointed to new jobs, or at least not to senior new jobs. They became even more disgruntled than previously. Effective power was slipping from Mussolini's hands. In Italian-occupied Croatia and Montenegro the military authorities and diplomats, sometimes with Mussolini's tacit support, sheltered Jewish refugees from Germans and German-backed *Ustasha* alike, and organised their transport to Italy. Moreover, the Italian army there allied with pro-Allied Serb monarchists (*Chetniks*) against the Communist partisans and even against the *Ustasha*, to German fury.[63] Similar policies were followed in the Italian-occupied zones of southern France and Greece, where Italian officials often tried to prevent mass deportation of Jews. In August 1942 Mussolini yielded to German pressure on this issue, but he soon told his officials to 'invent every excuse you like so as not to hand over a single Jew'; he knew about the German extermination programme from the horrified reports of his ambassador in Berlin.[64] The two allies quarrelled not only over Croatia and the Jews but also over the future of the South Tyrol, where the German-speakers realised that a weak Italy might be forced to yield to German pressure.

In the February 1943 reshuffle Mussolini became his own Foreign Minister again, with Bastianini as under-secretary. He knew he had to stay in the war, not only for reasons of honour but because, like Macbeth, he was

in blood
Stepp'd in so far that, should I wade no more,
Returning were as tedious as go o'er.[65]

But Italy could do very little on her own. His strategy now consisted, therefore, of persuading the Germans to rescue the Italians in Tunisia and above all to pull out of Russia, or at least to go on the defensive there. It was not much of a strategy, and although Göring was fairly sympathetic and the Japanese gave it cautious support, it was conspicuously unsuccessful. Mussolini sent a stream of messages and letters to Hitler on this theme, stressing that 'Russia is no longer a threat ... and it can never be conquered'.[66] He also, of course, continued to request German planes and munitions. Hitler sent some planes – in May he told Mussolini with some exasperation, in response to a further request, that he had already sent 574 in March[67] – but he was not going to leave Russia voluntarily, nor divert his forces. He had Stalingrad to avenge, and cared little for the Mediterranean. Moreover, he knew Stalin would never concede territory; he would just use an armistice to rebuild his war machine, and would attack again a few months later. In any case, the German war effort had come to depend on Russian coal and steel. In fact, Hitler's overall strategic view was the exact opposite of Mussolini's. He was still willing to come to terms with Britain and the United States of America, but not with Russia. German propaganda was now all about the need for western solidarity against the Bolshevik Slav-Asiatic hordes. Even the Japanese victories in the Far East dismayed the Germans, since they meant yellow Asiatics defeating white Aryans.[68] In these circumstances the *Duce* was helpless. In April he met Hitler at Salzburg and for once spoke quite firmly, but in vain.[69] His failure made him expendable. As long as people at home thought he might be able to influence Hitler in Italy's favour, Mussolini's own position was safe. After April 1943 and especially after his last futile meeting with the *Führer* in July, it became clear that he could not influence Hitler significantly and that the two Axis powers were at cross purposes.

Meanwhile Bastianini was pursuing a different track. Whereas Mussolini wished to stay in the war but limit it only to the west, Bastianini was hoping to pull out of the war altogether, by diplomatic agreement with Germany and her other allies. He thought only Mussolini might be able to achieve this, without risk of the Germans invading Italy. He even approached the British in Lisbon, apparently with Mussolini's approval. The new chief of staff, Ambrosio, also took this view, at least initially. Hitler, on the other hand, thought that only Mussolini could keep Italy *in* the war. Many senior Italian diplomats and military officers agreed with this, in a way: they thought Italy should pull out and that Mussolini was the greatest obstacle to her doing so. So, increasingly, did the top *gerarchi*. Some, including the king, went even further. They aimed not merely at neutrality but at switching sides, and Mussolini was certainly an obstacle to that. But Mussolini was not going to bow out. Even those who only wanted neutrality realised they would have to overthrow the *Duce* first.

By the spring of 1943 political intrigue was ubiquitous – within court and military circles, within embassies, within Fascism and even within anti-Fascism, both at home and abroad. The old leaders of the opposition parties were beginning to re-emerge. Ivanoe Bonomi, last prime minister but one, contacted the king and played bridge with Badoglio and with Orlando, last prime minister but four. Catholic Action had a million members and former Popular party leaders were resuming activities, e.g. producing a clandestine newspaper. The Communists – still, just about, an organised party in some regions – also published a paper and in March successfully fomented strikes in northern Italy. This was a huge blow to the regime's prestige.[70] There were at least six anti-Fascist groups: Communists, Socialists, Action Party (largely the old 'Justice and Liberty' movement renamed), Christian Democrats, Bonomians and Liberals. They were all at least semi-active, each with its own journal, each seeking supporters and finance. In April some of them agreed to found a United Freedom Front, although the Republicans and Action Party did not join because its strategy consisted essentially of waiting for the king to overthrow Fascism for them. Within the Fascist party similar dissidence and intrigue dominated, and some of the leaders put out feelers to the Allies via Lisbon, Switzerland or the Vatican. No wonder Mussolini dismissed most of his government in February; he could no longer trust them. But now they had even more time for intrigue.

Fascism was manifestly collapsing, like Mussolini's health and Italy's war. But one big question remained. As Monsignor Tardini wondered in the Vatican, 'How do you tell Mussolini to go away?'[71] Only the king – the other pole of the Fascist–monarchy 'dyarchy' – could do that, and he was understandably cautious. If he dismissed Mussolini, the Fascists might rise up to defend their *Duce*, and provoke a civil war; in any case the Germans would probably move in, occupy Italy and restore him. Besides, who would replace him? His successor's task would be to persuade Hitler to let Italy leave the war, but the only man with the slightest chance of doing that was Mussolini. Furthermore, the king's real aim was not an armistice but a change of sides, so that Italy might avoid the post-war fate of Germany. A successor would therefore have to be acceptable to the Allies as well as the Germans – and indeed to both of the western Allies, since Roosevelt favoured the 'democratic' republican émigrés like Sforza, whereas Churchill detested Sforza and favoured a monarchist general. So the king hesitated. However, he encouraged the minister of the Royal Household, Duke Acquarone, to talk to everybody and to ensure the compliance of army and police if he made a move. Meanwhile the Vatican warned the American State Department off the anti-clerical Sforza, and urged the Americans to let the king decide.[72] Eventually the White House, after 18 months of its usual rhetoric about the evils of militarism and the necessity of restoring democracy, agreed that the new post-Fascist government would be a non-elected military one imposed by the king.

However, the king still needed military and political cover if he were to act. Soon the war provided all the military cover required. In June the Allies took the Italian island of Pantelleria, off Sicily, meeting negligible resistance even though the island was well fortified. Mussolini himself authorised the island's commander to surrender. The contrast with Malta was obvious. To surrender Pantelleria without a fight was incomprehensible, and wrecked any efforts to resist elsewhere. Mussolini then made matters worse by trying, on 24 June, to imitate Churchill's famous speech in 1940 about fighting on the beaches. The Italians, he proclaimed, would throw back the invaders before they reached the 'high water mark' ('*bagnasciuga*'); but unfortunately the Italian word actually means a ship's water line. His ignorance of basic naval terms aroused great mirth and derision; it was the navy's revenge on the *Duce*.[73] On 10 July the Allies landed in Sicily, where the Italians had stationed only four divisions, and took the western half of the island within a week. Clearly they would soon be on the Italian mainland.

Pressed by the high command, Mussolini decided on a desperate last plea to Hitler. He wrote to him in surprisingly tough terms, calling for an urgent meeting and hinting at a pull-out: 'the sacrifice of my country cannot have as its main aim that of delaying a direct attack on Germany'.[74] On 19 July the two men met at Feltre, near Treviso in northern Italy. It was an even more ludicrous conference than usual. The Italian delegation wanted Mussolini to insist on a settlement with the USSR, or at the very least to secure German armoured divisions and 2,000 planes to defend Italy.[75] The Germans had their own preoccupations and had just lost the battle of Kursk; if they sent troops at all, they would be under German command, and they would 'protect', i.e. occupy, northern Italy while the Italians fought the Allies in the south. Hitler spoke for two hours without translators, while Mussolini made no pretence of listening and the other Italians present made no pretence of understanding. Evidently bored and ill, the *Duce* kept sighing and looking at his watch. In the middle of Hitler's harangue, Mussolini was told of a major American bombing raid on Rome that morning. It was the first serious raid on Rome during the war and it killed around 1,500 people, wrecking the central railway station and the basilica of San Lorenzo, the latter only about half a mile from villa Torlonia. Astonished, Mussolini gave out instructions while the *Führer* ranted on. The American bombs did at least give Mussolini an excuse to leave the conference early, and although Mussolini had lunch privately with Hitler and accompanied him back to Treviso by train, it is clear that he did not press his case seriously. He told the rest of his delegation later that Hitler had promised to send all assistance needed, within reason. They did not believe a word of it.

The main result of the Feltre conference, indeed, was that the Italian chief of staff Ambrosio finally lost patience with the *Duce*. He was furious at Mussolini's silence, virtually upbraided him for not responding to Hitler, and demanded that Italy should pull out of the war. Back in Rome, he told the king how hopelessly Mussolini had behaved. That, and the bombs on Rome, settled the issue. Everyone in Rome had assumed that Vatican influence would protect the city from bombing, but this was clearly no longer true and the whole city might soon be devastated. The bombs had a huge impact on morale.[76] The king could hesitate no longer.

Mussolini had to go, and go quickly; and it was the army and the king who would have to get rid of him.

The king's *political* cover came from an unexpected source. Back in April, shaken by the strikes in March, Farinacci had written to Mussolini asking him to rally the party against the defeatists: he should convene the Grand Council to help in this task.[77] He took this theme up in his newspaper, and party secretary Scorza agreed with him. The Grand Council had not met since 1939 but it was virtually the only 'constitutional' institution in the country, with semi-parliamentary status. Although it rarely voted and was only consultative, it permitted free debate and always had pretensions to be a genuinely collective body and the supreme focus of Fascism. Its members were mostly the Fascist 'old guard', loyal to the *Duce* but to Italy first. By July 1943 these men were disgruntled with Mussolini: he had not asked their opinion before entering the war nor about how it should be fought, and they could see that it was lost. They became more disgruntled still when Scorza, at Mussolini's suggestion, ordered 12 of them to go round the country making speeches to mobilise the people against the invaders. They knew exactly what sort of reception they would receive, and refused to go unless they knew what government policy actually was; so they joined the call for the Grand Council to meet. On 16 July 15 of them, including Scorza, called on Mussolini in a scene reminiscent of the 'movement of consuls' in 1924 (see p. 87).[78] They demanded a Grand Council meeting and more 'collegial' decision-making in future. A sick and contemptuous Mussolini agreed to the meeting. It was not, as yet, a direct challenge to his authority; on the contrary, Scorza and Farinacci wanted tougher discipline and a tougher line on the war. In any case, Mussolini despised his colleagues, had unpleasant information about all of them and thought he could always talk them round. Even so, his decision to convene the Grand Council illustrates how far he had lost his grip on power, and how resigned and war-weary he too had become. Dictators do not usually allow subordinates to question their policies. Certainly he knew the meeting would be difficult, and told Claretta so on 20 and 23 July: 'they will call me to account for all my activities'.[79]

This development gave the king his opportunity. In early June he had spoken to Dino Grandi, Speaker of the Chamber: 'trust your king and make his task easier by mobilising the legislative assembly or possibly even the Grand Council, as substitute for parliament'.[80] Now the Grand Council was about to meet, and Grandi – who had not been among those pressing for it – realised its potential. He drew up a resolution and circularised it round the members, lobbying for support. It urged that all state institutions – Crown, Grand Council, government, parliament and corporations – should resume their proper functions and responsibilities. It also called on the government to ask the king to 'assume with the effective command of the armed forces on land, sea and air, according to article 5 of the Constitution (*Statuto*), that supreme initiative of decision-making which our institutions attribute to him'. This was clearly *not* a demand for the war to be waged more energetically; nor for Mussolini himself to seek an armistice. It was, instead, an explicit disavowal of the way the Fascist regime had evolved, a virtual admission that Mussolini had failed as war leader, and a request that the king should replace him. Grandi thought that Mussolini, who knew the text of the resolution by 21 July, would react very strongly; he and Bottai both had hand grenades in their pockets during the meeting.[81]

In fact, Mussolini barely reacted at all. He had three days' notice before the meeting took place. He might have rallied the party faithful and the Militia, or arrested the dissidents. But he did almost nothing before the meeting, which finally assembled at 5.00 p.m. on Saturday 24 July – five hours earlier than usual, and without any of the usual publicity and ceremonial. During the meeting Mussolini still seemed lethargic and indecisive. He made a rambling speech, mostly about the war, and criticised everybody except himself. When asked what Hitler had promised at Feltre five days earlier, he could give no answer. Clearly he could find no political solution to the war, or at least none compatible with his sense of honour and with his anxiety not to betray. Mussolini did, however, make it clear that Grandi's motion was about far more than the king's role as supreme commander; if passed, it might lead to the fall of the regime. Perhaps he knew the game was up; perhaps he wanted to play his last great role: the tragic hero betrayed by lesser men. More probably he thought it did not matter too much what they said or how they voted. It was best to let them talk, since arresting most of Italy's most eminent office-holders would certainly have outraged the king. Still, he wanted to win the vote, because legitimation from the Grand Council would strengthen his hand with the king. It was Victor Emmanuel III, not the Grand Council, who would decide the outcome, and he thought (or hoped) that he still had the king's backing. Indeed, he told the meeting so: 'I have the entire confidence of the king, who will not approve your motion. And then, gentlemen, what sort of situation will you be in?'[82]

After a long, confused and tense debate that went on until about 2.30 a.m. on 25 July, Mussolini allowed a vote. The weary *gerarchi* approved Grandi's motion by 19 votes to 7. Many did so with great reluctance. After all, these men owed everything to Mussolini. They had supported him for 20 years, through all his triumphs and disasters. Now they were betraying him, and most of them knew it. The 'moderates' voted with Grandi, including Ciano himself, the most unkindest vote of all. It was a complete surrender, although Mussolini learned later that overnight one of the 19, the syndicalist leader Tullio Cianetti, had changed his mind and rescinded his vote, an act that saved his life in a few months' time. At 3.40 a.m. Mussolini rang Claretta to give her the news, and told her to go into hiding immediately: 'we have reached the epilogue, the greatest turnround in history . . . everything is finished'.[83] Clearly at this point he was in despair. Then he went back to villa Torlonia, and an anxious Rachele.

Nevertheless, by 8.00 a.m. he was at his desk in palazzo Venezia as usual. Despite his momentary panic in the night, Mussolini had worked out what to do. Perhaps the Grand Council vote could be used to advantage after all. It might improve his bargaining position with Hitler, who would now have to send more arms or risk losing an ally. He tried to contact the Anglophile Grandi to offer him the Foreign Ministry, in an effort to defuse any political threat from the vote and again to show Hitler that his war policy had to change. But Grandi was not to be found. After the meeting he had reported to Duke Acquarone what had happened, and had then wisely disappeared. Mussolini had to content himself with meeting the Japanese ambassador Hidaka instead. It was his last official act. He used it to reiterate a familiar theme. He himself, at Feltre, had failed to persuade Hitler to withdraw from Russia and seek a 'political solution'; perhaps the Japanese would be more successful. Otherwise Italy would shortly have to withdraw from the war.[84] Mussolini clearly assumed he was still Prime Minister and would carry on, albeit with a reshuffled government. At 11.00 a.m. his secretary rang the palace, to arrange for the *Duce* to see the king that afternoon (a Sunday) instead of at their normal Monday morning meeting as the king was expecting. Mussolini had to act fast, before the king lost patience. He had known all about the 'Fascist plot' and had ignored it; he knew he could not ignore the king.

At 5.00 p.m., against Rachele's strong advice, Mussolini reported to the king at villa Savoia. He told the king of his new plans. He would give up the three service ministries, appoint three new ministers there and also three new chiefs of staff. With a new Foreign Minister, he would initiate real, plain-speaking 'negotiations' with the Germans, especially with Göring who also wanted to pull out of Russia and who fortunately was about to visit Rome for Mussolini's sixtieth birthday on 29 July.[85] But then the king rather apologetically told the *Duce* of his decision. The Grand Council had given him the necessary 'constitutional' signal; the regime had collapsed; morale in the country was dreadful. Mussolini could no longer continue as Head of Government. The *Duce* was genuinely shocked: 'and what do I do now?' On the way out the crucial second phase of the royal–military plot began. Mussolini was hustled into an ambulance belonging to the *carabinieri* – not the ordinary police, who were not royalist enough – and taken off initially to Podgora barracks in Trastevere, later to the officer cadet barracks in via Legnano. He was once more in custody, 'for his own safety'. A few other top Fascists were arrested, and the *carabinieri* occupied some key sites – the Ministry of the Interior, the telephone exchange, the central post office, etc. There was remarkably little trouble from the Militia or the Fascists, few of whom had known about the Grand Council meeting let alone about the royal plot. The king appointed Marshal Badoglio to head a government of military leaders and top civil servants. At 10.45 p.m. the radio broadcast the news: the government had changed, but 'the war continues'. Nobody, least of all the Germans, believed this last message. Within a few days all the major Fascist institutions, including the party itself, had been dissolved. Fascism, like Mussolini, vanished overnight.

Notes

1 Mussolini to King Victor Emmanuel, 20 June 1940, in ACS, Carte della Valigia, b. 6, f. 36; Mussolini to Hitler, 22 June 1940, in *OO* xxx, pp. 4, 162; *DDI*, s. 9, v, no. 83. Cf. also R. De Felice, *Mussolini l'Alleato* (Turin, 1990–6), i, pp. 119–31; R. Rainero (ed.), *Mussolini e Pétain* (Rome, 1990–2).

2 C. De Risio, *Generali, Servizi Segreti e Fascismo* (Milan, 1978), pp. 33–4; D. Mack Smith, *Mussolini as a Military Leader* (Reading, 1974), pp. 26–7; G. Rochat, 'Mussolini as war leader', in *The Oxford Companion to the Second World War* (Oxford, 1995), pp. 766–71.

3 *Ciano's Diplomatic Papers* (London, 1948), p. 398; *OO* xxxv, pp. 177ff.; L. Ceva, *La Condotta Italiana della Guerra: Cavallero e il Comando Supremo 1941–2* (Milan, 1975), p. 48.

4 Mussolini to Hitler, 29 December 1941; *DDI*, s. 9, viii, pp. 71 and 160; *OO* xxxi, pp. 5–8; ACS, SPD, RSI, Fascicolo di Mussolini.

5 Hitler to Mussolini, 23 June 1942; *OO* xxxi, pp. 231–2.

6 See Ciano (from Berlin, after seeing Hitler) to Mussolini, 7 July 1940; *DDI*, s. 9, v, no. 200; also Alfieri (Italian ambassador in Berlin) to Ciano, 14, 17, 20 and 25 August 1940; nos 413, 431, 451 and 490.

7 The letter is in *OO* xxx, pp. 170–2; *DDI*, s. 9, v, no. 753.

8 G. Ciano, *Diario 1937–43* (Milan 1990 edn), 12 October 1940.

9 Meeting of 15 October 1940; *DDI*, s. 9, v, no. 728; *OO* xxx, pp. 18–25.

10 E. Grazzi, *L'Impresa di Grecia* (Rome, 1945), pp. 204, 218–22.

11 Ciano, *Diario* cit., 17 October 1940.

12 Meeting of 10 November 1940; *DDI*, s. 9, vi, no. 71.

13 *OO* xxx, p. 71.

14 E. Faldella, *L'Italia nella Seconda Guerra Mondiale* (Bologna, 1959), p. 343; M. Cervi, *Hollow Legions* (London, 1972), p. 196.

15 Speech to Chamber, 10 June 1941; *OO* xxx, pp. 90–101, at p. 93.

16 G. Gorla, *L'Italia nella Seconda Guerra Mondiale* (Milan, 1959), p. 217; F. Anfuso, *Da Palazzo Venezia al Lago di Garda* (Bologna, 1957), p. 205; ACS, Carte della Valigia, b. 1.

17 Hitler to Mussolini, 21 June 1941; ACS, Carte della Valigia, b. 2; Cavallero to Mussolini, 6 January 1942, in Ceva, *La Condotta Italiana* cit., pp. 196–7.

18 Ceva, *La Condotta Italiana* cit., pp. 84–118.

19 De Risio, *Generali* cit., pp. 144–7; MacGregor Knox, *Hitler's Italian Allies* (Cambridge, 2000), pp. 130–2.

20 MacGregor Knox, in A.R. Millett and W. Murray (eds), *Military Effectiveness* (Boston, Mass., 1988), iii, p. 142. On 4 October 1942 Mussolini belatedly said that aircraft carriers were 'the umbrellas of our naval forces', without which battle could not be joined: *OO* xxxi, p. 110.

21 Mussolini to Cavallero, 1 January 1941; *OO* xxx, p. 184; Cervi, *Hollow Legions* cit., pp. 199–200; cf. also Ceva, *La Condotta Italiana* cit., pp. 17–37.

22 Cavallero to Mussolini, 20 October 1941; ACS, SPD, c. ris., b. 60.

23 ACS, *Verbale Consiglio dei Ministri*, 8 May 1941.

24 U. Guspini, *L'Orecchio del Regime* (Milan, 1973), pp. 205–6; G. Giuriati, *La Parabola di Mussolini nei Ricordi di un Gerarca* (Bologna, 1981), p. 50.

25 T. Cianetti, *Memorie dal Carcere di Verona* (Milan, 1983), p. 345; De Felice, *Mussolini l'Alleato* cit., i, p. 998.

26 On 20 October 1942; U. Cavallero, *Diario 1940–3* (Rome, 1984 edn), p. 509. Cf. note 5 above.

27 'Parlo con Bruno'; *OO* xxxiv, no. 269.

28 N. D'Aroma, *Mussolini Segreto* (Bologna, 1958), p. 250 (April 1942).

29 Ciano, *Diario* cit., 22 November 1940; for Hitler's letter, see *OO* xxx, pp. 174–8; *DDI*, s. 9, vi, no. 140.

30 Alfieri to Ciano, 20 December 1940; *DDI*, s. 9, vi, no. 323.

31 De Felice, *Mussolini l'Alleato* cit., p. 363.

32 Hitler to Mussolini, 5 April 1941; *DDI*, s. 9, vi, no. 865.

33 Ceva, *La Condotta Italiana* cit., pp. 102–6, 199 (doc. 38); P. Puntoni, *Parla Vittorio Emanuele III* (Milan, 1958), pp. 94–8; C. Favagrossa, *Perchè Perdemmo la Guerra* (Milan, 1946); F. Minniti, 'Il problema degli armamenti nella preparazione militare italiana

1935–43', in *Storia Contemporanea* ix (1978), pp. 5–61; F. Minniti, 'L'industria degli armamenti dal 1940 al 1943', in V. Zamagni (ed.), *Come Perdere la Guerra e Vincere la Pace* (Bologna, 1997), pp. 55–148; E. Canevari, *La Guerra Italiana* (Rome, 1949), i, pp. 422–32.

34 W. Deakin, *The Brutal Friendship* (Harmondsworth, 1966 edn), p. 27.

35 *Actes et Documents du Saint Siège Relatifs à la Seconde Guerre Mondiale* (Rome, 1965–81), v, p. 307; O. Chadwick, *Britain and the Vatican during the Second World War* (Cambridge, 1986), p. 233.

36 ACS, Min. Int., Dir. Gen. P.S., Div. Pol. Pol., b. 191, f. 4 'Regia Marina'.

37 Faldella, *L'Italia* cit., p. 55.

38 Ciano, *Diario* cit., 2 May 1939.

39 ACS, SPD, c. ris., b. 278R, f. 'Balbo'; G. Bocca, *Storia d'Italia nella Guerra Fascista* (Bari, 1969), p. 110.

40 ACS, SPD, c. ris., b. 60, 'Valle' (Gen. Pricolo on Gen Valle, 16 April 1941).

41 Favagrossa, *Perchè Perdemmo la Guerra* cit., pp. 112–14, 246–53, 263–6.

42 F. Rossi, *Mussolini e lo Stato Maggiore* (Rome, 1951), pp. 14–15; Faldella, *L'Italia* cit., p. 59; cf. Ciano, *Diario* cit., 15 January 1940.

43 Report on Rome, 21 August 1940; ACS, Min. Int., Dir. Gen. P.S., Div. Pol. Pol., b. 213, f. 2.

44 De Felice, *Mussolini l'Alleato* cit., p. 1111; ACS, Min. Int., Dir. Gen. P.S., Pol. Pol., b. 213, f. 4 (navy) and b. 219 (army).

45 Report of Inspector Norcia, Bologna, 20 December 1940; ACS, Min. Int., Dir. Gen. P.S., Div. Pol. Pol., b. 213, f. 1 ('Aeronautica').

46 A. Imbriani, *Gli Italiani e il Duce* (Naples, 1992), pp. 105ff., 142–54; P. Cavallo, *Gli Italiani in Guerra* (Bologna, 1997), p. 57; Puntoni, *Parla* cit., p. 38.

47 Memo, 26 July 1941, Lisbon to Foreign Office, R 7402; PRO, FO, 371/22929.

48 Speech of 2 December 1942; *OO* xxxi, pp. 118–33.

49 G. Bottai, *Diario 1935–44* (Milan, 1989 edn), 9 May 1943. Mussolini's one rousing speech of the war was to provincial party leaders on 18 November 1940 (*OO* xxx, pp. 30–8).

50 Mussolini's order of 5 August 1941; *OO* xliii, p. 54; cf. also M. Salvati, *Il Regime e gli Impiegati* (Bari, 1992), p. 212.

51 ACS, Min. Int., Dir. Gen. P.S., Div. Pol. Pol., b. 219, f. 1.

52 Cavallo, *Gli Italiani in Guerra* cit., p. 98; Imbriani, *Gli Italiani e il Duce* cit., p. 153; S. Colarizi, *L'Opinione degli Italiani sotto il Regime* (Bari, 1991), pp. 339–410.

53 ACS, Min. Int., Dir. Gen. P.S., Div. Pol. Pol., b. 239, f. 2. Cf. also Mussolini's misguided attempts (e.g. on 2 December 1942, *OO* xxxi, pp. 118–33) to refute Churchill's claims, which simply gave them greater publicity.

54 ACS, SPD, *Bollettini e Informazioni*, b. 339, 'Radio Londra'.

55 W. Churchill, *Their Finest Hour* (London, 1949), p. 488.

56 See, esp., report of Dr Bianchini, 19–20 November 1942; ACS, SPD, b. 104, f. 6.

57 Bottai, *Diario* cit., 8 June 1943 (also 14 October 1941 and 7 October 1942).

58 Imbriani, *Gli Italiani e il Duce* cit., p. 185.

59 Colarizi, *L'Opinione* cit., p. 402.

60 Ciano, *Diario* cit., has multiple examples: 29 January 1940; 7 February 1940; 21 June 1940; 5 August 1940; 27 September 1941.

61 Bottai, *Diario* cit., 23 January 1943; Gorla, *L'Italia* cit., p. 378.

62 R.H. Woody (ed.), *Encyclopedia of Clinical Assessment* (San Francisco, 1980), i, p. 184.

63 Hitler to Mussolini, 16 February 1943, in *DDI*, s. 9, x, no. 31; Ribbentrop–Mussolini conversation, 26 February 1943, in *DDI*, s. 9, x, no. 61; J. Steinberg, *All or Nothing* (London, 1990), pp. 50–84; I. Herzer (ed.), *The Italian Refuge* (Washington, 1989), esp. chapters by Shelah and Bierman, pp. 205–17 and pp. 218–27.

64 De Felice, *Mussolini l'Alleato* cit., p. 413–16. For an example of Alfieri's reports from Berlin, see Alfieri to Ciano, 3 February 1943, in DDI, s. 9, ix, no. 578, which was seen by Mussolini.

65 W. Shakespeare, *Macbeth*, III iv 136–8.

66 Mussolini to Hitler, 26 March 1943; DDI, s. 9, x, no. 159. Cf. also his letter of 9 March, no. 95.

67 ACS, Carte della Valigia, b. 2; *DDI*, s. 9, x, no. 283.

68 Ciano, *Diario* cit., 10 March 1942 (Prince Urach's visit to Rome).

69 Deakin, *Brutal Friendship* cit., pp. 289–307; De Felice, *Mussolini l'Alleato* cit., pp. 1297–1301; G. Bastianini, *Uomini, Cose, Fatti* (Milan, 1959), pp. 92ff.

70 P. Spriano, *Storia del Partito Comunista Italiano* (Turin, 1967–75), iv, pp. 100ff., 168–96; V. Castronovo, *Giovanni Agnelli* (Turin, 1972), pp. 609ff.

71 On 31 May 1943; *Actes et Documents* cit., vii, p. 383.

72 Monsignor Tardini to Monsignor Ciccognani, 7 December 1942, in *Actes et Documents* cit., vii, pp. 131–2; Card. Maglione to Monsignor Ciccognani, 22 May 1943, ibid., p. 362.

73 Speech to PNF Directorate, 24 June 1943; *OO* xxxi, pp. 185–97; also in De Felice, *Mussolini l'Alleato* cit., Appendix 11, pp. 1466–79.

74 Mussolini to Hitler, 18 July 1943; *DDI*, s. 9, x, no. 528; *OO* xliii, pp. 78–9.

75 Ambrosio to Mussolini, 14 July 1943; ACS, SPD, RSI, *Fascicolo di Mussolini*, b. unica, f. 21; F.K. von Plehwe, *End of an Alliance* (Oxford, 1971), pp. 30–1. On the Feltre conference, see *DDI*, s. 9, x, nos 530–3; Deakin, *Brutal Friendship* cit., pp. 433–58; D. Alfieri, *Dictators Face to Face* (London, 1954), pp. 240ff.; on German aims, E. von Rintelen, *Mussolini als Bundesgenosse* (Tübingen, 1951), p. 212.

76 ACS, Min. Int., Dir. Gen. P.S., Div. Pol. Pol., b. 239, f. 2; Gorla, *L'Italia* cit., p. 427.

77 Farinacci's letter to Mussolini of 1 April 1943 is in Deakin, *Brutal Friendship* cit., pp. 253–4.

78 The best account of this meeting is in G. Bottai, *Diario* cit., pp. 393–8. For Mussolini's version, see *OO* xxxiv, pp. 288 and 292. See also Giuriati, *La Parabola* cit., p. 219.

79 Guspini, *L'Orecchio* cit., pp. 215–18.

80 ASAE, Carte Grandi, b. 151 sottof. 5 (diary entry, 4 June 1943).

81 G.B. Guerri, *Galeazzo Ciano* (Milan, 1979), pp. 586–7. On the Grand Council session of 24–5 July, see Deakin, *Brutal Friendship* cit., pp. 482–500; De Felice, *Mussolini l'Alleato* cit., pp. 1341ff.; L. Federzoni, *Italia di Ieri per la Storia di Domani* (Milan, 1967), pp. 192–221; G. Bottai, *Diario 1935–44* cit., pp. 405–21; ACS, SPD, c. ris., b. 30, sottof. 20.

82 G. Bottai, *Diario 1944–8* (Milan, 1988), p. 460; De Felice, *Mussolini l'Alleato* cit., p. 1377.

83 Guspini, *L'Orecchio* cit., p. 224.

84 *DDI*, s. 9, x, no. 551.

85 De Felice, *Mussolini l'Alleato* cit., pp. 1396–9.

Chapter 11

The Years of Captivity 1943–5

From Ponza to the Gran Sasso

The king and the military had planned Mussolini's arrest meticulously, but they had no idea what to do with him afterwards. At about 1.00 a.m. on 26 July the new Prime Minister, Marshal Badoglio, sent him a message regretting his arrest, 'done solely in your personal interest, detailed information having reached us from several quarters of a serious plot against your person',[1] and offering him safe conduct to wherever he chose. Mussolini replied instantly. He said he would like to go to the only house he owned, Rocca delle Caminate. Furthermore, he would 'cooperate in every possible way' with the new government: 'I welcome the decision to continue the war together with our allies, as the honour and interests of our country require at this time, and I hope that success will crown the heavy task which the Marshal has assumed by order of, and in the name of, His Majesty the King, whose loyal servant I have been for twenty-one years and remain. Long Live Italy!'[2] So he had heard, or more likely been told about, Badoglio's broadcast; and he did not expect a Fascist restoration. In that, at least, he was perfectly realistic. Although Manlio Morgagni, head of the *Stefani* press agency, shot himself when he heard the news, hardly any other Fascists reacted at all except to hide their black shirts and assure the Chief of Police of their loyalty to the new regime.[3] Indeed, celebrations continued all night and into the next day throughout the country, as people hoped for the end of the war.

However, Mussolini was not realistic if he expected to be left in peace at Rocca delle Caminate. The Prefect of Forlì could not guarantee to protect his safety; the government feared he might rally the Fascists against them; both Germans and Allies would probably try to seize him. The ex-*Duce* had to be taken somewhere safe and remote. Where better than that classic dumping ground for political prisoners, a southern island? So after 48 hours in the *carabinieri* barracks, Mussolini was dispatched from Rome (which he never saw again) to Gaeta, and thence to the islands. After a quick stop at Ventotene they took him to Ponza, where he stayed for the next 10 days and where he celebrated his sixtieth birthday on 29 July with four peaches, a gift from the local *carabiniere* sergeant. Göring sent him a friendly telegram, and Hitler thoughtfully sent a birthday present – the complete works of Friedrich Nietzsche in 24 volumes, in German; just the thing for an ex-dictator with time on his hands. Ironically, Mussolini on Ponza stayed in the 'house of the *ras*', as a cousin of the Ethiopian Emperor had been a recent guest. On 1 August a launch arrived with a letter from Rachele, some money and a change of clothes – welcome by this time, for he was still in the same clothes he had worn when arrested on 25 July. She also sent on a copy of Father Giuseppe Ricciotti's *Life of Jesus Christ*, which she had found on his desk at villa Torlonia; Mussolini underlined the passages about Jesus' betrayal and passed the book on to the local priest with a strong recommendation.[4] Mussolini had to be guarded from the other internees, most of them anti-Fascist political prisoners whom he had sent there himself and who had not yet been released. They included his old comrade Pietro Nenni, with whom he had shared imprisonment at Forlì 30 years earlier, and also Tito Zaniboni who had famously tried to shoot the *Duce* in November 1925 (see p. 94).

Word soon got round about Mussolini's whereabouts, and on 6 August he was transferred to villa Weber at La Maddalena, off the north-east coast of Sardinia. Here were more historical ironies. Garibaldi's home at Caprera was nearby; moreover, La Maddalena was the site of Napoleon Bonaparte's first (and unsuccessful) battle on Italian soil in 1793, and of Nelson's long wait for the French fleet in 1803–5. But it was not too secure either. It was a big naval base, and German ships were in harbour. Soon a German reconnaissance plane flew overhead, and so Mussolini had to be moved again. Early on 28 August he was flown off to Lake Bracciano and thence to Assergi, high up in the Gran Sasso mountains of Abruzzi near L'Aquila; after a few days he was taken to the Hotel Imperatore near the Gran Sasso summit, over 6,500 feet above sea level. Surely nobody would find him there?

They did, of course. Within a couple of days everyone in the province, including German secret agents, knew where the *Duce* was. He was sitting at the top of a mountain, helpless and withdrawn, wondering what had happened to his Fascists and waiting to see who would seize him first. On 8 September he was horrified to hear that the Badoglio government had signed an armistice with the Allies five days earlier. Furthermore, both government and king had fled from Rome to Pescara, and thence to Brindisi. They had saved their skins but betrayed their allies and the whole country. Rome herself was now left defenceless, and would be fought over by Allies and Germans. Mussolini also realised that the armistice terms with the Allies would probably include provision for him to be handed over (and in fact the more extensive 'long armistice' signed on 29 September did include such a clause). That was too humiliating for a man like Mussolini. Early in the morning of 12 September he cut his wrists with a razor blade, but his guards rushed in and staunched the blood.[5] It was a moment of despair, most uncharacteristic of the man.

It was true that both Germans and Allies wanted Mussolini, but the problem was: how to reach him? The hotel stood on a rough plateau, but there was no landing strip and in pre-helicopter days it could only be reached by cable car from the valley below, or on foot. Senior German officers – General Student and Major Mors of the parachutists, but not SS Captain Skorzeny, although he later claimed the credit – planned their move. At 2.00 p.m. on 12 September 12 gliders moved in, although only 9 landed safely, together with a light biplane. Fortunately, the Chief of Police in Rome had known they were coming and had rung up Mussolini's guards twice (the second time was half an hour before the gliders arrived) to urge 'maximum prudence'; i.e. not to shoot, either at the Germans or at the *Duce*.[6] The Germans had also brought an Italian general in full uniform along, to shout out the same message. So naturally nobody did shoot. The guards had grown to like Mussolini. They had gone for walks with him in the afternoons, and played cards with him in the evenings. They were Fascists themselves, and it was an honour to protect the *Duce*. Besides, it looked as if he might be coming back to power. Mussolini, ill, resigned and not too pleased to be rescued by Germans rather than by Italians, was taken off in the biplane (an extremely difficult take-off, since the heavy Skorzeny insisted on going with him) to nearby Pratica del Mare, and thence in a larger plane to Vienna. It was a spectacular rescue, well planned and brilliantly executed, and it was a huge propaganda triumph for the Germans. But it was a disaster for Mussolini. He had wanted only to go back to Rocca delle Caminate, to recuperate or die. Instead, by the evening of 12 September he was in Vienna, just as exhausted and in practice just as much a prisoner as he had been earlier.

These seven weeks at Ponza, La Maddalena and the Gran Sasso were, for Mussolini, a period of gradual recuperation and reflection. It was, indeed, the first time since his illness in 1925 that he had not been immersed in political activity. Now he had little interest in it, and did not even miss the newspapers. He knew that politically he was dead, and he did not wish to be resurrected. Physically he was very weak, and mentally he was depressed. He worried about his family, as until 19 August he had no news about his eldest son Vittorio, and he could not be sure the others were safe. He complained about his detention: he, the Fascist dictator, had never imprisoned his prime ministerial predecessors. He brooded on how he had been betrayed by his own disciples, like Jesus; his son-in-law had betrayed him too, not to mention his king and his army. Now these traitors might hand him over to the Allies for ignominious trial and execution. Worst of all was the destruction of his life's work. As he wrote in his diary at La Maddalena, 'it is impossible that everything should have collapsed. When I think back today on the tasks and achievement, the work and hopes of these twenty years, I ask myself: was I dreaming? Was it all illusion? Was it all superficial? Was there nothing profound?'[7] He consoled himself with thinking of Fascism's achievements in the great days: the Empire, the corporations, the social legislation. If only he had died in 1937!

Mussolini had never been a religious man and never became one, but he was isolated and very distressed, and he had reason to reflect on the meaning of life and the vanity of earthly ambition. At La Maddalena Mussolini talked several times with the local priest, Father Salvatore Capula, hoping that the priest's visits would help him recover from what he called his 'grave moral crisis, provoked by isolation more than anything else'. Father Capula, clearly a strong-minded man, was not having that. He told Mussolini, 'you have not always been great when fortune smiled; be great now in misfortune. This is how the world will judge you, from what you are from now on, much more than from what you were until yesterday.'[8] This forecast was more prescient than he knew. At any rate, Mussolini had to promise not to do anything contrary to religious principles in future, 'even if there occurred new strokes of fate'. A few days later, after leaving La Maddalena, he wrote to his pious sister Edvige, saying that after 40 years he had begun to become closer to religion, and telling her about Father Capula. He also claimed to have left a testament (written in May 1943) on his desk at palazzo Venezia: 'Born a Roman, apostolic Catholic, such I intend to die. I do not want funeral ceremonies or honours of any kind'.[9] This last request was certainly granted in full, but the rest is puzzling. Perhaps he was just writing to please his sister, but about such matters it is always difficult to judge. Mussolini's 'religious' perspective does not seem to have lasted long, but in many ways he became a better human being after July 1943. He was more reflective and less aggressive, and he postured far less. He recognised the change himself: 'If men are always placed upon the altar they end up believing they are supermen or divine beings. Falling down into the dust brings them back their humanity, the basic humanity we all share.'[10]

A Republic at Salò

On 13 September 1943 Mussolini was flown from Vienna to Munich, where he was reunited with his wife and children for the first time in seven weeks, and where he caught up with the news. The next day he was flown off again, to meet Hitler at Rastenburg. The *Führer* was pleased to see his old mentor but was in 'I told you so' mood. He criticised Mussolini harshly for having been too trusting towards the king and the generals. He was dismayed to find that Mussolini was *not* thirsting for revenge, not even on Ciano and the other traitors on the Grand Council. Hitler later told Goebbels that this 'showed his [Mussolini's] real limitations', and in his diary Goebbels commented that 'I have never before seen the *Führer* so disappointed in the *Duce* as this time ... he will never stage a come-back. It is certain that he has not lived up to political or personal expectations and has thereby spoiled his great chance for the future.'[11] Still, Hitler now needed Mussolini more than ever. Since 25 July he had been thinking of setting up a new Fascist regime in Italy, but there was no one to lead it; most of the Grand Council were traitors, and even Hitler could see that the strident and resentful Farinacci would not do. So he had pretended to believe that Badoglio would continue the war, and had quietly moved German troops into Italy. But after Badoglio's armistice with the Allies the Germans urgently needed a friendly Italian government. The only reliable Fascist with any prestige had to be restored to 'power' whether he wanted it or not, and whether he was fit for it or not.

Mussolini was certainly not fit for it, and initially did not want it. He felt like Lazarus, surprised to be alive at all. He was now thin and pale, and looked much older. His stomach pains had grown worse in captivity. He could not eat or sleep, and he feared he might have cancer. He knew that the Italians hated him, that Fascism was finished and that the war was lost. He soon realised that the Germans wanted a figurehead, not an ally. After the Grand Council's betrayal on 25 July and Badoglio's betrayal on 8 September, they did not trust Italians at all, and they thought Mussolini himself was far too soft on opponents and on Jews. They took over six north Italian provinces themselves on 10 September, sending in *Gauleiters* to run all Italy's First World War gains – the South Tyrol, Trentino, Trieste and Venezia Giulia – and parts of Venetia as well.

Croatia and Albania were given their 'independence'. Italian soldiers in the Balkans and elsewhere were interned in Germany. All this was not likely to encourage Mussolini to take on a Quisling role. However, eventually Hitler persuaded him to take the job. The *Führer* implied, although apparently did not specifically promise, that Italy would receive her northern territories back at the end of the war, but only if Mussolini accepted. Above all, he threatened that, if Mussolini did not accept, the Germans would treat treacherous Italy as she thoroughly deserved: not as a civilised Western state like France or Denmark with its own 'government', but like Poland or Serbia, under direct military rule.[12] Possibly she might be treated even worse, because the Italians had betrayed the cause and the Germans needed to deter others from taking the same path. Only Mussolini could prevent the Germans from wreaking a terrible revenge in northern Italy.

This was an all too plausible threat. Mussolini knew what the Germans had done, and were still doing, in central and eastern Europe. He knew, too, that the Germans in Rome would soon discover Bastianini's peace moves, which he himself had authorised (see p. 286). It would certainly be humiliating to be a puppet, particularly one who had lost much of his territory, but there was no option. Hitler had made him an offer he could not refuse. By agreeing, Mussolini might be able to win back Trent and Trieste; he might mitigate German vengeance; he might, indeed would, keep the Fascist hard men out of power; above all, he might do something to restore Italian honour – as always, the key motive for him and for many of his followers, also horrified by Badoglio's action and the king's flight. A new republic led by himself would surely be more attractive than a totally discredited Badoglio regime, which had betrayed its allies and its own soldiers, and had fled ignominiously from Rome. Note, incidentally, the choice facing Italians: Badoglio or Mussolini, both discredited; in the north, direct German rule or a regime of Fascist zealots, both horrendous. There was no partisan movement yet, let alone a 'civil war' between Fascists and resistance. Perhaps Mussolini thought Germany might yet become willing to negotiate an honourable peace, and that he might be able to mediate at last. And, of course, even shadow power would give him a role: the chance to strut once more upon the stage, to issue orders and be treated with deference; to become, once more, the *Duce*. In any case, Mussolini had never been good at arguing with Hitler even when he was fit; and, after all, Hitler had just rescued him from the Gran Sasso and probably from an Allied jail. So he agreed to Hitler's terms, although it was not a task he relished. However, he insisted that the new Italian state should be called the 'Italian Social

Republic', not 'Italian Fascist Republic' as Hitler preferred; even Mussolini now thought Fascism was outdated.

On 18 September, now back in Munich, Mussolini broadcast to Italy. He denounced the king's dual betrayal, of *Duce* and Fascism on 25 July and of the whole country and allies on 8 September. Here was his main theme, for the last 18 months of his life:

O, what a fall was there, my countrymen!
Then I, and you, and all of us fell down,
Whilst bloody treason flourish'd over us.[13]

He proclaimed a new state, the Italian Social Republic (*Repubblica Sociale Italiana*, RSI), which would resume the war and redeem Italy's honour.[14] The Fascist party was refounded as the 'Fascist Republican Party' (*Partito Fascista Repubblicano*, PFR), with the former Minister of Popular Culture Pavolini as secretary – not an obvious choice, since he was a friend of Ciano and his brother had a Jewish wife. Then the search began for ministers. For once, hardly anybody wanted a government job, but eventually Mussolini persuaded some of his old colleagues like Buffarini Guidi to return to government, a welcome change from the prison he had been in since 26 July. He offered his strong-minded former Interior undersecretary Arpinati his old job back, hoping he would be able to 'reconcile' anti-Fascists in Emilia-Romagna to the new regime, but Arpinati refused this hopeless task.[15] Mussolini's most prominent adherent was Marshal Graziani, who was a big catch – he might easily have joined the other side and become the Italian de Gaulle, but fortunately he detested Badoglio. The new government was, in fact, surprisingly 'moderate'; even Pavolini had been an open-minded intellectual in the past, although he soon proved otherwise in the RSI. Indeed, the problem was that the new 'social', 'republican' ministers looked remarkably like the same corrupt old gang as before; the 'intransigents' like Farinacci were still kept out, more disgruntled than ever. On 23 September Mussolini flew back to Italy, and on the 27th his new Cabinet met for the first time, at Rocca delle Caminate. The Germans would not allow him to set up his government in Rome, now officially an 'open city' run by technical commissars under German supervision, and this was obviously a huge blow to the new government's prestige.

The Germans, not the *Duce*, chose the site of government. By early October Mussolini was installed with his family in villa Feltrinelli, at Gargnano on the west bank of Lake Garda, although a month later he moved his daytime office to villa delle Orsoline, half a mile away. He had to pay 8,000 lire a month to the Feltrinelli family and so for the first time he took his ministerial salary, although he stopped it in January 1945 when the royalties from his memoirs came in. Claretta Petacci moved into the lodge of D'Annunzio's old house nearby, to Rachele's fury. The various ministries were scattered round northern Italy: Finance at Brescia, Public Works at Venice, Interior at Maderno, etc. In wartime conditions it was very difficult for ministers to travel to Gargnano to report or for Cabinet meetings to be held; even telephone links were tapped by the Germans or cut by the partisans. Inevitably, therefore, each minister pursued his own policy, sometimes successfully. The Finance Minister Pellegrini Giampietro was surprisingly good at maintaining the value of the RSI lira, and most of the civil administration and public services – schools, hospitals, food distribution, railways – of northern Italy continued to function somehow, even in the last few months of the war. Only the Ministry of Popular Culture was at Salò, also on Lake Garda, but as its communiqués began 'Salò communicates', the whole regime soon became known as the 'Republic of Salò'. Mussolini disliked being at Gargnano and kept sending his secretary off to reconnoitre other sites, but they were all even worse.

Mussolini was nominal Head of State and of Government, but there was little state or government for him to head. It was an improvised regime without frontiers, capital, army or (its worse failing) effective police, and it was dominated by its overbearing ally; but then, so was Badoglio's government in the south. Mussolini resented not being in Rome, not ruling the six northern provinces, and not having an army. His telephone was tapped, he was surrounded by 800 SS guards and he was not allowed to travel without German permission. Even his doctor was sent by Hitler and reported back to Germany. The *Duce* wrote constantly to Hitler, particularly about how strongly the German annexation of the Trieste and South Tyrol–Trentino zones was resented in Italy.[16] On 4 October 1943, for example, he asked Hitler to ensure that the German military authorities did not interfere in Italian civil or judicial matters; otherwise 'Italian and world opinion would judge the government as being incapable of functioning, and the government would fall into discredit or, worse, ridicule'.[17] He also wrote appraisals of the military situation, but neither Hitler nor Field Marshal Kesselring, commanding German forces in Italy, took any notice. In effect, he was a prisoner on the lake, cut off from the rest of Italy and from the war. The real rulers of northern Italy were the German ambassador, Rudolf von Rahn, who acted as Mussolini's 'political adviser' and could appoint 'civil advisers' to all the ministries, and Himmler's man in Italy, SS General Karl Wolff, who controlled the all-important police and security forces. These men were usually polite to the *Duce* but the fact remained that Mussolini himself had nothing to do, and as his health recovered in spring 1944 it became hugely frustrating. It was a classic case of post-retirement depression. He did not even have his own newspaper any more, since he had sold the *Popolo d'Italia* to a Milanese industrialist for 30 million Swiss francs, and had given most of the money to his children. He detested Lake Garda, which he regarded as too much a German holiday zone (*der Gardasee*). Indeed, he did not like lakes in general. They had no tides, no currents, no movement or vivacity. They were gloomy and utterly unFascist, a useless parliamentary compromise between river and sea.[18]

He settled back into his old routine: he met his officials and issued orders in the morning, read and wrote in the afternoon. In the early months he wrote a self-justifying account of the previous year, published by the *Corriere della Sera* in Milan and later in book form as *Storia di un Anno* (in English, *Memoirs 1942–3*), and this at least gave him something to do and cheered him up, but most of his activity was meaningless and he knew it.[19] Moreover, it was not only his political circumstances that were dire; his personal ones were even worse. Gargnano was a small place, and he was surrounded far too closely by his squabbling family. Bruno's widow Gina and her small daughter were at the villa Feltrinelli with him; Anna Maria was there too, although she spent some months in Germany having treatment for polio; Vittorio lived nearby with his children, but tried to take over the *Duce*'s secretariat and have real political influence. The great absentee was Edda and her children, living near Parma. Mussolini liked having children around, but all the adults except Gina proved very tiresome. His wife Rachele had apparently only found out about Claretta Petacci after 25 July. Now the mistress was living just down the road. This was a real insult to a tough woman like Rachele, and she made sure Mussolini knew it. Vittorio, insensitive and blundering as always, pleaded with his father to give Claretta up, and was put firmly in his place. Mussolini greatly respected his wife, who had given him constant support and was the mother of his children, but she was jealous and domineering; he needed some human affection and warmth too, and Claretta was the only one who gave it to him. In October 1944 Rachele went off to Claretta's villa and confronted her directly, only to be told to mind her own business. She went back home in a fury, and Mussolini had to cheer her up by reminiscences of their life together.[20] But he continued to visit Claretta, and was nagged mercilessly by Rachele on his return. So he infuriated his wife, completely alienated his eldest daughter (see below), and had to tolerate absurd intrigues by his eldest son. It was not a happy household, and he could not even take refuge in his work; there was none.

Mussolini's last 18 months at Gargnano were truly painful for a proud man like him, and might have meant the loss of all self-respect and dignity. They also destroyed what was left of his reputation, both at the time and in historical perspective. Yet at the personal level the effect was curiously benign. He was no longer the proud dictator. Indeed, he was subdued, thoughtful and approachable, and willing to talk on an equal basis even to anti-Fascists. He seemed grateful to his colleagues for still supporting him. So even Mussolini mellowed through suffering, or rather coped with suffering by becoming strangely detached, a sadder and a wiser man. He knew his life had been a failure and of course he still blamed and resented others, but he now recognised his own weakness and humanity too. His new ambassador in Berlin, greeting him in September 1943, was astonished when Mussolini actually shook hands and asked him to sit down for a chat.[21] True, he took few political initiatives and had little control of anything, but at least the peremptory arrogance of palazzo Venezia was no more.

The RSI was clearly not an effective regime but it appealed to some, not all of them Fascist zealots. Fascism had disappeared after 25 July 1943, but after 8 September it revived. There were many Italians who felt deeply ashamed that Italy had abandoned her allies by negotiating a secret armistice, and they were even more ashamed of the Badoglio government's flight from Rome. When Mussolini talked of Italian honour and the king's betrayal, his argument had real appeal. In addition, there were some youthful idealists, ex-syndicalists and Republicans, who thought the Republic might embody radical social ideals. Many people were unimpressed by all this but simply saw Mussolini as a lesser evil, a man who might contain the Germans and repress the Communist partisans. Even some older Socialists came round, including Carlo Silvestri, a courageous man who had been one of the *Duce*'s main opponents during the Matteotti crisis and had spent six years in Fascist prisons. Silvestri, like many others, wanted to avoid or mitigate the nascent civil war; he ran a surprisingly successful one-man 'Red Cross' for Socialists and Communists in trouble, secured Mussolini's support for it, and urged him to take a pacifying lead.[22] Another figure from the past who turned up at Salò was the appropriately named Nicola Bombacci, a friend of Mussolini back in 1902 at Gualtieri and a notorious Communist firebrand in 1919–20. Mussolini, who needed people to talk to, welcomed these uncompromising, adventurous men who had close ties to prominent anti-Fascists, and spent long hours reminiscing with them. He told the party secretary in Milan, 'I don't know how I would get through the evenings if I didn't often have Bombacci's company.'[23]

The Trial of Verona

However, most of the people who joined the new Fascist party had been in the old one, or at least on the fringes of it. Some *were* zealots, anxious for revenge on the traitors of 25 July. In November 1943 the PFR held its first (and last) congress, at Verona. It approved a manifesto of 18 points, drafted by Pavolini and amended by Mussolini with contributions from Bombacci and others. The manifesto promised a charter of citizens' rights and 'socialisation' of industrial management, but also promised a special tribunal and death for traitors. The Republic would try to bring about a federal European Community, based on the abolition of the capitalist system. All Jews were to be regarded as foreigners; in wartime, as enemy foreigners. The one demand the congress did *not* make was to fight the Allies. In mid-congress news came through that anti-Fascists had assassinated the Ferrara party secretary, and so some of the delegates dashed off there to avenge his murder. Mussolini did not attend. He told his secretary later that it had been 'a real shambles': too confused, too left-wing on the economy, too bent on vengeance.[24] Mussolini realised that reprisals were counter-productive, but he could not stop them. On this issue he was the prisoner not only of the Germans, but of his own hardliners. Indeed, he made some efforts to make his regime acceptable to its many opponents, via Arpinati, Silvestri and others. Fascist syndicalists at Ravenna met their Communist and Republican counterparts in autumn 1943, in an attempt to avoid civil strife, but there was too much bitterness between them and also too much commitment to opposing sides in the war.

The 'intransigent' Fascists hated anti-Fascists, partisans, Badoglio and the king. Most of all, they hated Galeazzo Ciano and those who had voted against the *Duce* on 25 July. Many of these 'traitors' had fled the country, or remained in hiding; but six were caught, including Ciano himself and also De Bono, one of the two surviving *Quadrumviri* of the March on Rome. None had been among the ringleaders but they had to be tried, and a special tribunal was set up in October. The Germans agreed, but deliberately exercised no pressure: it had to be an Italian decision. Mussolini himself was certainly not desperate to punish his former colleagues. He knew Ciano had not been one of the conspirators before 25 July. At Munich, in mid-September, the whole family had met amicably together, and Edda had seemed to succeed in reconciling her father and her husband. Moreover, the new Minister of Justice Pisenti thought there was no case against the accused. They had clearly *not* conspired with the army or king; they had merely exercised their vote in a normal way at a meeting called by Mussolini, at which he had allowed a free vote that in any case was not binding.[25] Mussolini agreed: the 'treason' had not been on 25 July but six weeks later, by Badoglio and the king, who had betrayed both the Germans and Italy.

However, the trial was not legal but political, like all war crimes trials. Mussolini kept out of the proceedings but this in itself was a political choice – he could have prevented the trial easily enough if he had wished. Politically, he needed to show the new regime was serious about redeeming Italy's honour, and about rooting out the 'traitors'. He also wanted to win back some status in German eyes and in Fascist ones. It was a test of his Fascist virility and of his devotion to the Axis cause. But it was also a family crisis, a real Greek drama in the House of Mussolini. His wife Rachele had never liked Ciano and she detested him even more now that he had betrayed her husband; she demanded his head. Meanwhile Mussolini's strong-willed daughter Edda was trying desperately to protect *her* husband. In September she made a passionate plea for Ciano's life to Hitler himself, and back in Italy she visited Gargnano regularly to implore mercy from her father and to row furiously with her mother. She moved her children to Switzerland and told Mussolini exactly what she thought of him, his allies, and his war.[26] She even tried to blackmail him, and Hitler. Ciano, while Foreign Minister, had kept a diary full of scabrous details about how decisions had really been made and what the leading figures really thought of each other. The Germans, in the classic Hollywood manner, planted a 22-year-old 'interpreter', 'Frau Beetz', on Ciano, hoping she would find the whereabouts of the diary; but unfortunately she was prey to the classic Hollywood weakness of female agents and seems to have fallen in love with him. The diary, in several copies, remained hidden in Rome, and Edda tried to swap them for Galeazzo's life. Even Himmler and the SS approved a plan to let Ciano escape to Turkey, in return for the diaries. But Hitler vetoed it, and Mussolini still did not intervene.

On 8 January 1944 the accused were brought to trial before the Special Tribunal at Verona. They were all condemned to death by firing squad, except for Cianetti who had withdrawn his Grand Council vote early on 25 July and was therefore given life imprisonment instead. The condemned men appealed to Mussolini for mercy. The prosecutors and the party secretary Pavolini then had to make sure that the appeal never reached him; nobody was sure Mussolini would bring himself to reject it, since that would be the equivalent of signing Ciano's death warrant. They also had to tour round northern Italy looking for someone else senior enough to reject it himself. Eventually, after several refusals, they prevailed upon the Republican Guard commander in Verona, and the five men were shot in the back as traitors on the morning of 11 January. Although the appeal did not formally reach Mussolini he had of course known about it, and had rung up General Wolff in the early hours of 11 January, apparently to find out what Himmler would think of him if he granted a reprieve.[27] Later on he reacted in the normal manner of guilt-ridden rulers: he blamed his subordinates. He tried to dismiss both Pavolini and Buffarini Guidi, but the Germans prevented him. As for Edda, she fled to Switzerland to join her children, and never saw her father again.

Mussolini's genius for melodrama had prevailed yet again. It is, after all, not every family where Grandpa ('*nonno Duce*', as the children called him) has Daddy shot, and is likely soon to be shot himself; and where Granny and Mummy fight furiously over whether Daddy should die – not to mention the fights between Grandpa and Granny over Grandpa's girlfriend down the road. Yet the really odd feature of this imbroglio is that Mussolini was one of the few people in Salò who did *not* want the 'traitors' shot. The German ambassador von Rahn even claimed later that he had had to talk the *Duce* out of publishing a laudatory obituary of Ciano in the next day's paper.[28] Mussolini was not a particularly bloodthirsty man for a politician, and he loved his daughter. True, he had always argued that the Italians were too sentimental and that war alone might make them tougher; but he had not expected to have to prove it in his own family. In any case, he himself had become noticeably less tough in the previous few months. Indeed, one of the main reasons Ciano and the others died was because Mussolini wanted to show that he had not become a weakling and that he was above family ties. Mussolini even thought that the executions might have been avoided altogether, if Ciano had not been the *Duce*'s son-in-law.[29] This is highly unlikely, given the inflamed state of Fascist opinion. Probably the victims would have been shot eventually anyway, by Fascists, Germans, Allies or partisans. However, Mussolini certainly *had* been weak, and had allowed others to act in his name. Perhaps he could not have saved Ciano in any case; but he did not even try.

Disillusion and Disorder

He tried rather harder with his scheme for 'socialisation' of industry, designed to appeal to the radical urban left. It was not clear what this meant, except that it was directed against the treacherous industrialists (who were now believed, often rightly, to be financing the partisans) and against the people who really controlled most of north Italian industry, the Germans. Mussolini needed a dynamic-sounding economic policy, since 'corporatism' had long since been discredited. So in February 1944 the government issued a law nationalising the basic industries like electricity, and also laying down that in the larger private firms with shareholders the management board should be elected by the workforce, from lists of candidates approved by the Fascist syndicates (i.e. no Communists); in private-capital firms with no shareholders half the board would be so elected. Profits were to be shared between owners, managers and staff, but the managing director would be chosen by the shareholders or by the Minister of Economics. Mussolini was proud of this legislation and told his Economics minister that he had wanted to bring it in since 1919.[30] No doubt he wanted to create an image of Fascist rule very different from that of 1926–43.

However, the German armaments minister Albert Speer and his representative in Italy, Hans Leyers of RUK (*Rüstung und Kriegsproduktion*), had no intention of sharing decision-making with any Italians, least of all workers or trade unionists. In practice, little happened. The new law came into force in June 1944 but applied only to the media, to publishing houses and newspapers, always the true preoccupation of the *Duce*. Certainly it did not apply to the arms firms, which the Germans were still trying to loot or even to transfer en bloc to Germany. Industrial workers were unimpressed, since clearly the war was lost and 'socialisation' would be a dead letter. They preferred to go on strike to secure better conditions immediately, and 200,000 workers in Milan and Turin downed tools for three to five days in March 1944. This was an unambiguous response to Mussolini's leftist schemes. Equally unambiguous responses came later on when factory elections to the new management bodies were held. Hardly anyone voted at all, and many of those that did put a blank paper in the ballot box, or one marked with obscenities (often about Claretta Petacci). At the main Fiat plant of Mirafiori in Turin there were 47 valid votes from a 14,000 workforce; at Lingotto, 9 from 4,000.[31] It seemed that 'socialisation' was, like 'Fascism', an idea whose time had gone, although actually the victorious resistance parties soon adopted rather similar schemes, derived not directly from Mussolini but from Catholic social thought and from the Gramscian origins of Italian Communism.

'Socialisation', therefore, was not a great success; but the real justification for the RSI lay elsewhere. If the Republic were to redeem Italy's honour, it would need an army and it would need to fight. Apart from some units in northern Italy, the Italian army had in effect disbanded after 8 September 1943, and within a few weeks around 600,000 ex-soldiers, mostly from the eastern front or the Balkans, were internees in

German camps. The Germans regarded them as 'Badoglio troops', traitors to the Axis cause, and treated them worse than prisoners of war, or at least than British or American prisoners of war. There were also 120,000–150,000 Italian civilians in Germany already, working in the arms factories or clearing up bomb rubble, and more were rounded up to work there later in dreadful conditions (about 50,000 of them died). Mussolini and Graziani wanted to recruit volunteers from among the Italian internees in Germany to form a new Italian army, but the Germans distrusted them as soldiers and preferred to keep them in Germany as cheap labour. Eventually it was agreed that the Italians might form four divisions from among the internees and also from recruits conscripted in Italy. But these troops would be trained in Germany, and would return to Italy only when the Germans decided that they were combat-ready and politically reliable. Graziani was horrified: he wanted his soldiers in Germany to be allowed back, not new ones to be sent there. In practice, few of the internees volunteered, except in the hope of being *eventually* sent back to Italy where they might easily desert.

In spring 1944, therefore, the Republic introduced conscription, but over 40 per cent of those called up failed to appear, and over 10 per cent deserted later.[32] The older recruits perfected the traditional way of avoiding conscription: bribe, or threaten, the medical officer. By autumn 1944 less than a quarter of the 30-year-olds were being passed as fit for military service.[33] In any case, even the reluctant conscripts who did enter the Republic's army were ill-trained and worse equipped, and were lucky to receive even food and clothing. Moreover, they had a fair chance of being sent off to Germany as industrial workers rather than soldiers. Conscription was the Republic's worst mistake, particularly as it was not just conscription but deportation. It alienated all the active young population and their families, and it gave them a big incentive to take to the hills and join the partisans – who became a serious force only after conscription started.

Thus a disciplined Fascist army was never a plausible hope. True, there were still many Italians who *did* want to fight for the Republic, but they usually had no wish to fight for the Germans, and in any case they preferred a 'people's army' formed from the old Militia and run by Fascist enthusiasts, not a conventional force run by Graziani. It was more exciting to serve in one of the several semi-private outfits or in Prince Valerio Borghese's '*Decima Mas*' (10th Torpedo-Boat Squadron), now mostly land-based. Borghese fought his own very dramatic commando war and had little respect for Graziani, the Germans, the navy, the Fascists or the *Duce*. Indeed, in January 1944 Borghese was arrested in

Mussolini's own ante-chamber and imprisoned at Brescia, although he soon had to be released when his men threatened to liberate both him and Mussolini. The *Duce*, sitting in Gargnano and looking out over his gloomy lake, could not understand all this. He thought it obvious that all true Italians would be desperate to fight in a disciplined manner for their country's honour; those, after all, were the values that Fascism had instilled. He blamed the Germans for not trusting Italian valour, and for using good fighting men for low-grade manual labour. How many divisions had the *Duce*? Four, with around 55,000 men, and they were not enough. Still, he did his best to keep his new troops Italian in spirit, and after visiting Hitler in April 1944 he went round Germany on a special train inspecting their training camps. The men gave him a very warm welcome and it was a big boost to morale, both theirs and his. In late summer they returned to Italy, although when Graziani visited them at Aosta he found morale low again: the food was lousy, the post never arrived and there were not even enough feathers for the *bersaglieri*'s hats.[34] Around 15–20 per cent of them soon deserted, and the Germans refused to use the rest against the Allies. So Italian honour was not redeemed after all.

What the RSI needed most was not an army but an effective police force. In spring 1944 the number of clandestine 'partisans' rapidly increased to around 70,000–80,000, boosted by deserters, escaped prisoners of war, urban evacuees and released political detainees – Badoglio's government had let out 3,000 Communists, who made a big difference in the next few months.[35] Regular troops were not much use against rural 'bandits' or urban terrorists, but the Republic's policemen were no good either. They could see who was going to win the war, and they wanted to remain on good terms with the victors. The Republic distrusted and disbanded the *carabinieri* because they were too monarchist and had carried out Mussolini's arrest in July 1943. Instead, it formed a 'Republican National Guard' (GNR), which necessarily included many former *carabinieri* but also ex-Militia members and ex-colonial police from Africa, as well as the older or less fit conscripts. It acted as the rural police and its main function was to fight the partisans, but neither the ex-*carabinieri* nor the conscripts showed great dedication to this task, nor indeed to the Republic. They, too, soon began to desert, taking their guns with them and leaving rural areas in partisan hands. As for the ex-African police, they flatly refused to leave Rome and go north. In the towns, the professional policemen of the former 'public security' forces continued to operate as previously, under Prefects and Interior Ministry; they, too, proved less than zealous in hunting down anti-Fascists and Jews.

By August 1944 the GNR had proved so ineffective that it was incorporated into the army. Mussolini now allowed the party to run its own 'Black Brigades', the aim being both to fight the partisans and to revive true *squadrismo*.[36] These 'Brigades' were very different bodies from the GNR or the Militia. They were real 'squads' with about 30,000 members in all, run locally by local men, undisciplined and not under Pavolini's or central party control. They were certainly zealous, but they proved a disastrous mistake. The party, as a coherent organisation, was replaced by a network of fiercely independent local bosses anxious to settle their own personal scores. The 'civil war' became fiercer, and impossible to contain. Moreover, just as the Republic had several private armies, so it also had several virtually private police forces run by freelance thugs like Pietro Koch or Francesco Colombo. These men gave Fascist policing an even worse name. They ran open extortion rackets, robbing banks and raiding houses with impunity, and kidnapping 'anti-Fascists', i.e. anyone rich enough to pay a ransom. By October 1944 Cardinal Schuster was complaining strongly to Mussolini about the situation in Milan,[37] and Mussolini did then manage to have Koch arrested and held in prison until the end of the war despite German wishes, but often both he and the Prefects were helpless. All Mussolini could do was issue circulars to the Prefects telling them not to permit arbitrary arrests ('harmful to the aims of national recovery, the supreme objective of all those Italians worthy of the name'), but the Prefects had no forces to prevent them. In December 1944 the Prefect of Bologna threatened to resign unless the local Black Brigade commanders were sacked.[38]

After spring 1944 the main task of all these bodies, and of the army, was to fight not the Allies but the 'bandits', the partisans. It was a fierce, unsuccessful struggle. Partisan numbers, around 80,000 in the summer, reached 110,000 by autumn 1944, then declined sharply but were boosted by thousands of 'last-minute partisans' in the last month of the war, from about 80,000 in March to 250,000 in April 1945.[39] But for every active partisan there were a dozen supporters, willing to give refuge or food both to partisans and to deserters or escaped prisoners of war. Partisan warfare was mobile, punitive and spontaneous. It was a war of sabotage, assassinations and surprise attacks. It relied on local knowledge and support, it often continued a local tradition of vendetta and banditry, and its essential motives were revenge and a desire to avoid conscription, at least as much as to overthrow the feeble Fascist regime or to fight the Germans. The nascent political parties tried to use the bands and sometimes helped to form them: six parties in search of a militia. They also formed shadow governments – Committees of National Liberation – locally and for the whole of northern Italy, but many people just joined the local band irrespective of party affiliation. The conflict was fairly vicious, on both sides: Pavone estimated 44,720 partisans were killed, along with almost 10,000 civilians (often hostages) from October 1943 to April 1945; so too were 5,000 Germans and an unknown number of 'Fascists' – at least 12,000 'Fascists' were also killed in the three months *after* the war.[40] In the towns, Communist-run and much smaller 'Groups of Patriotic Action' (GAP) terrorists killed Fascists and Germans alike, deliberately provoking German reprisals. The most notorious episode was not in the RSI but in Rome on 23 March 1944, when a GAP bomb killed 33 members of a German police battalion from the South Tyrol. The Germans responded by rounding up and killing 335 Italians, mostly political prisoners or Jews (including Aldo Finzi, Mussolini's first under-secretary at the Interior back in 1922–4), at the Fosse Ardeatine on the outskirts of the city. Another high-profile reprisal was in August 1944 in Milan, when 15 civilians were shot in piazzale Loreto – an episode that determined Mussolini's posthumous career. Although these urban massacres received the most publicity, most of the reprisal victims were in rural areas. The SS sometimes wiped out whole villages, e.g. Marzabutto in the province of Bologna, where 1,830 people, including women and children, were killed in August 1944.

This partisan warfare was completely unexpected, and had not been foreseen by anybody in September 1943, least of all Mussolini who told Hitler in November that it was no danger.[41] It might easily not have occurred. It came about because the army disintegrated, and with it the guards on prisons and prisoner-of-war camps; because the *carabinieri* were dissolved, and hence there was no policing in rural areas; because there were thousands of southern ex-soldiers caught in the north, unable to return home; because of the RSI's futile efforts at conscription and deportation, which generated more partisans than it did soldiers; and because the Allies bombed the northern cities heavily and forced people to flee to the countryside. The Allies also provided some support for partisan groups, with drops of food and weapons etc. It also came about by political choice, on both sides. Mussolini realised the need for 'reconciliation' early on, but his efforts were feeble and outweighed by Fascist thirst for revenge. In any case, Communist partisans deliberately wrecked them by a successful tactic of assassinating Fascist officials (including the party secretaries of both Milan and Bologna, as well as the philosopher Giovanni Gentile) and thereby ensuring Fascist reprisals.[42] Even so, the partisans were not all that numerous: until April 1945 there were always more police, GNR, Black Brigade members, etc., than there were partisans.

Nor, of course, did the partisans defeat the Germans; the Allies did that for them. The more politically sophisticated partisans were essentially fighting to establish their legitimacy in the post-war political world; they were also fighting for Italian honour, as Mussolini recognised.

The Germans had no answer to partisan violence except reprisals, which had a disastrous impact on morale and turned everyone against the RSI. Mussolini kept telling them so. After all, protecting Italy from savage occupation had been one of his main justifications for agreeing to head the new Salò government at all. He wrote often to von Rahn, linking humanitarian arguments and political ones, especially the need to give the RSI some independent credibility in civil matters.[43] For example, in August 1944 he wrote complaining about the Milan massacre: 'We must give the 22 million Italians in the Po valley the feeling that a Republic and a government exist, and that this government is considered an ally.'[44] A month later he went further, and threatened to resign: reprisals cause 'an increase in the number of partisans; a boost to enemy propaganda; sentiments of hatred among the population who have been so unjustly and cruelly punished. As a man and a Fascist I can no longer take responsibility, however indirect, for this massacre of women and children which is additional to those caused by enemy bombing and machine-gunning.'[45] His letters had some effect on von Rahn but little on the German military commanders and the SS, who were responsible for the massacres. Still, he probably avoided the worst; the Germans had to have some regard for his views. He managed to save some well-known anti-Fascist leaders like Parri, Roveda and Nenni from almost certain death, and in September 1944 he succeeded in preventing the Germans from executing 20 hostages held in Milan. He also helped to prevent industrial machinery (and therefore workers) from being transferred to Bavaria. Even so, there was a great deal he could not prevent. He was no longer the proud *Duce*, in command of events; he was merely a fairly minor actor in the vast tragedy of war.

Historians have argued a great deal about these events and their consequences. From the viewpoint of his later reputation, Mussolini was unlucky to be rescued from the Gran Sasso. If Badoglio had handed him over to the Allies, he would have been imprisoned, sent off to an island exile like Napoleon, or shot; and in all three cases it is unlikely that there would have been a 'Fascist regime' in northern Italy between 1943 and 1945. Certainly there had been no sign of one between 25 July and 12 September 1943. If no Fascist regime, then no civil war. There would still have been war, of course. Anti-Fascist partisans would still have fought against the Germans – but against the Germans, not against their

MUSSOLINI

fellow-Italians, apart from obvious collaborators. The 'civil war' aspect of the resistance, with all its legacy of bitterness and division in the future, might perhaps have been avoided. In that case Fascism would not have been tarnished by its own war crimes of 1943–5, or by its association with the far worse German reprisals. As it was, Mussolini and his regime came to share the blame, both at the time and later.[46]

They also came to share the blame, of course, for the fate of north Italian Jews. Here, too, the Italians were less extreme than the Germans, who rounded up over a thousand Jews in Rome in October 1943 and dispatched them to Auschwitz; 16 returned. But the RSI did pass its own anti-Semitic legislation in 1943–4. All Jews were interned in concentration camps; all their property was seized; people born of mixed marriages were subject to special surveillance. By March 1944 the most prominent Italian anti-Semite, Giovanni Preziosi, had been appointed Inspector of Race, charged with thinking up new persecutory schemes. The Jews were certainly persecuted far more under the Republic in 1943–5 than they had been in the previous five years. Until September 1943 Jews had not been deported from Italy to Germany; after 8 September 1943 at least 7,495 of them were, about 15 per cent of the Jewish population.[47] This was, of course, because the Germans took over much of the anti-Jewish drive themselves, particularly in Rome and central Italy, and because putting Jews in concentration camps made it far easier for the Germans to find them; but it was also because the Fascists of the Republic were more zealous and radical than their predecessors. Several hundred Jews were killed in Italy itself; at Trieste there was even a gas chamber. However, around 30,000 Jews survived: in Rome mostly by hiding in church buildings and monasteries; elsewhere relying on shelter often given by ordinary citizens at real danger to themselves.[48] Mussolini did little to encourage this persecution but he also did little to prevent it. It was the price of the German alliance. The new anti-Semitic legislation was drafted by others but he revised it personally, as he had done the original Racial Manifesto back in 1938. However, he rarely spoke or wrote publicly on the issue, and privately he condemned the Germans' insane zeal. It is striking that during these years, when he was blaming all and sundry for the betrayal of Fascism and of Italy, the one group he did not blame was the Jews.

The Last Months at Salò 1944–5

By the summer of 1944 Mussolini's health had recovered. Dr Zachariae, sent by Hitler, had diagnosed chronic atrophic gastritis and duodenal ulcer, with partial closure of the bile canal so that bile and gastric juices accumulated behind the ulcer, causing acute pain and stomach cramps after food. He also found secondary anaemia, low blood pressure (100/70) and enlargement of the liver. He put Mussolini, who had eaten little but milk and fruit for years, on a diet of meat and mineral water supplemented by urgently needed vitamins and hormones; milk was now banned.[49] The treatment worked. The stomach cramps vanished, and Mussolini was able to sleep at night. Once again he did his physical exercises every morning and played tennis in the afternoon. But his political prospects did not improve. On 4 June the Germans surrendered Rome, without fighting; Mussolini had not been consulted about the fate of his capital city. Two days later came the Normandy landings, seen in Italy as a sure sign that the war was nearly over. By the end of June the Allies occupied most of Tuscany.

It was time for an emergency consultation with Hitler. In July he went off to Germany again, once more visiting the training camps and once more being greeted with enthusiasm. On 20 July he moved on to Hitler's headquarters at Rastenburg. He had chosen the wrong day. As ever, Mussolini could not avoid high drama. A few miles from the Wolf's Lair his train halted; eventually it moved on slowly, but with blinds drawn and packed by SS guards. When it arrived, Hitler proffered his left hand and explained, '*Duce*, an infernal machine has just been let off at me.'[50] He had just escaped being blown up by Stauffenberg's bomb, which might well have killed the Italian delegation too. Mussolini congratulated the *Führer* but seems to have been secretly pleased that it was not only Italian generals who turned out to be traitors. The Germans feared that a coup might be taking place in Berlin, and they were far too distracted to discuss high strategy or anything else. Mussolini spoke only briefly to Hitler over tea, but he (or Graziani) secured a promise that the famous four divisions would soon be sent back to Italy and that conditions for the internees in Germany would improve. Then the *Duce*'s entourage moved off, after only three hours at *Führer* headquarters. Mussolini never saw Hitler again.

Meanwhile the war came nearer. Mussolini managed to visit his house at Rocca delle Caminate in August 1944, but the Allies took it a few weeks later. His regime grew steadily weaker, and the Germans less respectful. The *Duce*, revived in health, in turn became more aggressive; there was less to lose now. He insisted on his socialisation scheme despite strong German opposition, and he demanded that some of Fiat's lorries be used for food distribution. There were continuing rows with the Germans over the four Italian divisions, which the Germans would not use except against partisans.[51] Mussolini also tried yet again to persuade Hitler to resume the offensive in Italy, but as usual had no success. To console himself, and to get away from Salò, he decided on a surprise trip to Milan. On 16 December the old entertainer made positively his last public appearance at the Teatro Lirico.[52] He denounced the betrayal by king, generals, bourgeoisie, etc., and promised that Germany's 'secret weapons' would soon vanquish her enemies. He also claimed that the Allies would soon split up. This was true, but it did not happen in time to save Fascist Italy. As for weapons of mass destruction, they proved as elusive as usual; or rather, they did soon exist, but in other hands. Nonetheless, Mussolini's speech – or speeches, for he spoke twice more in Milan – went down very well. Here was the *Duce* in person, without a police escort, surrounded by cheering crowds, driving in an open car through the city and making speeches in public squares, while much of northern Italy was convulsed by civil war. Many people thought him much changed, and for the better. He was still the warrior hero but he had suffered and become more human. The visit brought him into touch with the masses and with events, and showed that many Italians still admired their *Duce*.

In January 1945 he managed another trip, this time to inspect a division in Emilia, and in March he spoke to ex-Militia officers at Brescia. Meanwhile Italo-German relations reached a new low. Mussolini dismissed Buffarini Guidi from his post as Interior under-secretary for being too subservient to the Germans; the Germans retaliated by arresting a Prefect and a member of Mussolini's personal secretariat. Once again the *Duce* threatened to resign: 'I intend to have satisfaction immediately. Otherwise it is better that the Germans should arrest me, dissolve the Republican government and transform this disguised and humiliating occupation into a real, open occupation.'[53] By now von Rahn and Wolff saw Mussolini rarely, and only at their request. When they did see him, they were met by a stream of complaints – South Tyrol, Trieste, the internees in Germany, reprisals, transfer of labour and machinery, not letting his four divisions fight; the list of Mussolini's grievances was as long as ever. By now he envied the partisans. It was the Fascists, he mused, who ought to be up in the hills fighting a spontaneous, courageous, *exciting* war against the corrupt Establishment and against their country's invaders. Indeed, if he had not been rescued from the Gran Sasso, they might have been.[54]

Yet he knew it was no good. The war was lost, and his life had ended in defeat. He told a visiting journalist in March, 'My star has set. I still work and make an effort, but I know it is only a farce . . . I await the end of the tragedy and I feel strangely detached from it all. I do not feel like an actor, but like the merest spectator.'[55] The tragedy was no longer *Coriolanus*, but *King Lear*: the old ruler, after making a disastrous decision and betraying his favourite daughter, wanders around the country consoled only by his Fool (Bombacci), and is quite unable to influence events. His only hope was to leave a legacy of patriotism and of his socialisation schemes, and to that end in the last months he allowed, even encouraged, Edmondo Cione to found a 'Republican Socialist Grouping', with its own journal: the *Duce's* loyal opposition, proposed by Mussolini himself. He was clearly trying to woo the Socialists, as he had done early in June 1924; no doubt he was relying on his old personal friendship with Pietro Nenni, whose life Mussolini had just saved by persuading a very reluctant Hitler to send Nenni back to Italy after the SS had arrested him in France. If Mussolini could manage to hand over his Social Republic peacefully to the Socialists and Republicans, then much of his achievement might survive after all, and there might even be some sort of post-war national reconciliation instead of continuing vendettas and recrimination.

Alternatively, he could follow Pavolini's suggestion, made in September 1944, of a last stand in an Alpine stronghold (*Ridotto Alpino Repubblicano*, RAR), independent of the Germans, invulnerable to attack, well supplied with food and arms, and guarded by elite troops. Mussolini had approved this idea and set up a commission to plan it in detail. But most of the Italian Alpine zones had been taken over by the Germans, and the areas west of South Tyrol by the partisans, so only the Valtellina, north of Lake Como, looked feasible and even that would need to be cleared of 'rebels' first. The Valtellina also had the great advantage of being near Switzerland. However, Marshal Graziani made it clear he would not go to the RAR; he would prefer to surrender, if necessary.[56] Moreover, when the RAR was needed in spring 1945, it turned out not to be available. No detailed planning had been done. There were no stores, arms or troops in the area, and it was full of well-armed partisans.

From Milan to Dongo, and Back

By April 1945 the war was nearly over, and there were several sets of clandestine negotiations among the various parties. Easily the most significant was 'Operation Sunrise', talks between SS General Wolff and Allied representatives in Switzerland over the surrender of the 20 German divisions in Italy.[57] Wolff also negotiated with the Committee of National Liberation for Northern Italy (CLNAI), hoping that the partisans would allow the German troops to return north of the Alps peacefully. The Germans deliberately left the Italian Fascists out of these negotiations; they were to be left to the mercy of the partisans, particularly if the Allies arrived late. Mussolini, too, encouraged his police chief Montagna to negotiate with the CLNAI, and hoped for a peaceful handover to the Socialists and Action party members on the committee. But the Socialists were not willing to ditch their colleagues in other parties, particularly the Communists; and the Communists were determined to call a general insurrection *against the Fascists* (not the Germans), to strengthen their hand in post-war political manoeuvres.[58] Mussolini also sent his son Vittorio to see Cardinal Schuster in Milan with proposals for the Allies. Mussolini assumed the Allies would welcome his help in preventing a Communist takeover, and again he was disappointed. He proposed that RSI forces should repress the Communists until the Allies arrived, and that the Allies should then take over the same task. This was not the Allies' intention, if they could avoid it.

On 18 April Mussolini decided to leave Gargnano and move the whole government to Milan, to find out exactly what was going on. He took a large number of documents with him, dating from throughout his career as Prime Minister, and took up residence in the Prefecture. He spent a week in Milan, seeking to hand over to the Socialists. Montagna continued to negotiate with the CLNAI and according to some versions actually reached a deal with them on 24 April for a peaceful handover, but it was superseded by a higher level meeting next day called by Cardinal Schuster. Mussolini still spoke of going to the Valtellina (a quite impracticable project by this time) and summoned thousands of his Fascist hardliners to Milan, presumably to escort their *Duce* there. He also asked his wife and the two youngest children to come to Como, which is on the way from Milan to the Valtellina, and they were there by the evening of 24 April. Certainly he did not try to escape while the going was relatively good, as he might easily have done – he could have flown to Spain, as Claretta Petacci's father and sister did on 22 April, but he refused.[59]

In the afternoon of 25 April Mussolini went to the Archbishop's palace to meet the CLNAI representatives. The other delegates were late, so while waiting he had an uneasy chat with Cardinal Schuster, who told him reassuringly that he would be remembered most for the 'reconciliation' with the Church. Mussolini, none too pleased by this, told the Cardinal that he intended to dissolve his army and go off to the Valtellina with his Fascists, but only for a short time until the Allies had taken over northern Italy; then he would surrender, to them. However, when the partisan leaders arrived they required immediate, unconditional surrender to themselves; the Fascists would be treated decently, as prisoners of war. It is possible that Mussolini might have accepted this outcome, but Marshal Graziani objected that to do so would be a betrayal of the Germans, all too similar to Badoglio's betrayal on 8 September 1943. Clearly Mussolini, who had spent five years avoiding any accusation of betraying his allies, could not do so now. However, the Archbishop's secretary incautiously revealed that the Germans were themselves negotiating a surrender to the Allies, again via Schuster, without having informed Mussolini and without making any provision for the Fascists.[60] So it was the Germans who had betrayed him, not the other way round. Furious, he walked out of the meeting, saying he would give the CLNAI his answer within an hour.

In fact, he decided to flee, although it is not clear where to, nor even exactly why. Despite his show of anger, he had known about the German–Allied negotiations for some time; General Wolff had discussed them with him on 15 April.[61] But he knew what a German 'unconditional surrender' to the Allies, by-passing both the Fascists and the CLNAI, would mean: unconditional surrender of himself. He would end up in Allied hands, facing an ignominious trial by the demo-plutocrats. Much better to be shot quickly, on Italian soil, by men he respected; or to take his chance and go to the hills, or to Switzerland. So he did not hole up in the Prefecture and wait for the Allies to arrive; at 8.00 p.m. he fled by car to Como, into partisan-controlled territory. But why Como? And why did he leave thousands of his most dedicated supporters – supposedly his escort to the Valtellina – behind, in Milan? It is perhaps typical of Mussolini's sense of drama, and his ambiguity, that nobody knows, just as nobody knows the details of the next (and last) three days of Mussolini's life, or what his intentions were. But one may guess that he went to Como, and then on the next day to Menaggio, in order to hand over documents to the Japanese embassy at nearby Cadenabbia; and/or because he intended to cross into Switzerland. Certainly he told his wife to take herself and the children across the border, although the Swiss would not let them in when they tried to cross at Chiasso in the early hours of 26 April. Nor, of course, would Mussolini have been allowed in either. In any case his SS guards had orders to take him to Germany and to shoot him if he tried to escape elsewhere. The Germans would not let him go; the Swiss would not let him in. Some versions of events on 26 April have him (accompanied now by Claretta Petacci) trying to cross into Switzerland several times, driving to Grandola near the frontier but giving up eventually and moving back to Menaggio.

By the early morning of 27 April he had realised he was not going to make it into Switzerland, and joined a large convoy of Luftwaffe personnel retreating northwards from Menaggio along the lakeside towards Germany. He still had a briefcase full of key justificatory documents with him, extraordinary baggage for a man fleeing for his life. Did he hope to use them to bargain with the Allies? To write his memoirs? To defend himself at a war tribunal? Probably he had no idea himself, but he knew they might come in useful whatever befell, and they might yet improve his image. The convoy was halted and searched by Communist partisans of the 52nd Garibaldi brigade at the appropriately named Musso, near Dongo. Mussolini was hastily moved into a German truck and a German greatcoat, but was recognised. He was held at Dongo for most of the day, but early in the morning of 28 April both he and Petacci were moved to Bonzanigo, into the house of a local farmer, Giacomo De Maria, probably to prevent the Allies finding him. From this point onwards Italian versions of events differ markedly. There were few witnesses, and those few usually had political or financial motives for their accounts. The traditional view, probably correct, is that Mussolini and Claretta Petacci were shot that afternoon at the gate of villa Belmonte outside Giulino di Mezzegra, near Dongo, by a group of Communist partisans led by Walter Audisio ('Colonel Valerio'), who had been sent from Milan that morning for the purpose. The group was clearly authorised by the Communist partisan command, but the CLNAI itself does not seem to have been consulted until later; Nenni might not have approved. Sixteen of Mussolini's most prominent followers, including Pavolini, Bombacci and Claretta's brother Marcello, were also killed at Dongo.[62]

Mussolini did not die a martyr's death, quite the contrary. Like the king whom he had so often denounced, he chose to flee rather than to fight, and he abandoned his loyal followers to their fate. He even abandoned his wife and children: Rachele was forced to go into hiding in Como, and heard of her husband's death on the radio. It was his mistress who accompanied him at the end, and who was shot by his side. Most symbolic of all, he put on German outer uniform and was captured wearing it. He died as he had lived in youth: wandering, ill-dressed and excluded from Switzerland. He might have fought to the death in a romantic last-ditch defence of Italian honour in the Alps. Instead, he was caught huddled in a German lorry, having tried and failed to flee to Switzerland with his money and his mistress.

Still greater humiliation was to come. Mussolini could not avoid melodrama even in death. The partisans took the bodies of Mussolini and Claretta back to Milan, and on the morning of 29 April hung them upside down for a few hours at a petrol station in piazzale Loreto, along-side the corpses of a few other leading *gerarchi,* while the crowd hurled abuse. The site was deliberately chosen: it was where the Germans had shot 15 Italians in a reprisal the previous August. Now the victims had been avenged. The real aim of the demonstration was to show that the *Duce* was dead and ignominiously dead, and that it was the anti-Fascists who had killed him. It was his last political message, to his last 'oceanic assembly', and it was one of his most powerful. Like a toppled statue, Mussolini could now at last be safely reviled. The great publicity genius, the astute manipulator of men's minds, in death became himself a massive political symbol manipulated by others; a demonstration of irreversible regime change.

Notes

1 B. Mussolini, *Storia di un Anno* (Milan, 1944); *OO* xxxiv, pp. 301–444, at p. 357; in English, *Memoirs 1942–3* (London, 1949), pp. 83–4.

2 *OO* xxxiv, p. 358; in English, *Memoirs* cit., pp. 84–5.

3 C. Senise, *Quando Ero Capo della Polizia* (Rome, 1946), pp. 206–7.

4 *OO* xxxi, p. 265.

5 R. De Felice, *Mussolini l'Alleato: la Guerra Civile* (Turin, 1997), p. 25.

6 Senise, *Quando Ero Capo* cit., pp. 256–9; J. Schroeder, 'La caduta di Mussolini e le contromisure tedesche', in R. De Felice (ed.), *L'Italia fra Alleati e Tedeschi* (Bologna, 1973), pp. 137–69, at pp.155ff.

7 'Pensieri pontini e sardi'; *OO* xxxiv, pp. 271–99, at p. 278.

8 Ibid., at p. 290.

9 *OO* xxxi, pp. 267–8.

10 'Pensieri pontini e sardi'; *OO* xxxiv, p. 287.

11 J. Goebbels, *The Goebbels Diaries* (London, 1948), pp. 378–9 (23 September 1943).

12 F.W. Deakin, *The Last Days of Mussolini* (Harmondsworth, 1966 edn), pp. 46–57; De Felice, *Guerra Civile* cit., pp. 45ff.; Mussolini, 'colloquio con Nicoletti', 18 April 1945, in *OO* xxxii, pp. 186–90; V. Costa, *L'Ultimo Federale* (Bologna, 1997), p. 125. It is, of course, possible that the Germans would have set up a 'collaborationist' government anyway, possibly under Graziani, but it would have had a great deal less prestige.

13 W. Shakespeare, *Julius Caesar*, III ii 190–2.

14 *OO* xxxii, p. 4.

15 V. Cattani, *Rappresaglia* (Venice, 1997), pp. 117–18; A. Turati, *Fuori dell' Ombra della Mia Vita* (Brescia, 1971), pp. 79–80.

16 For example, to von Rahn, 11 February 1944; ACS, SPD, RSI, c. ris., b. 16, f. 91/R.

17 Mussolini to Hitler, 4 October 1943; *OO* xxxii, pp. 205–7, at p. 207.

18 A. Mellini, *Guerra Diplomatica a Salò* (Bologna, 1949), p. 85.

19 L. Ganapini, *La Repubblica delle Camicie Nere* (Milan, 1999), pp. 453–71; interview with Mollier, *OO* xxxii, pp. 157–61.

20 Mussolini, *Memoirs 1942–3* cit., pp. 165–7; F. Bandini, *Claretta* (Milan, 1969), pp. 191–204.

21 F. Anfuso, *Da Palazzo Venezia al Lago di Garda* (Bologna, 1957), pp. 318, 332–5.

22 Dolfin to Silvestri, 2 February 1944, in ACS, SPD, RSI, c. ris., b. 7.

23 Costa, *L'Ultimo Federale* cit., p. 125. On Bombacci, cf. G. Salotti, *Nicola Bombacci da Mosca a Salò* (Rome, 1986).

24 E. Dolfin, *Con Mussolini nella Tragedia* (Milan, 1949), p. 97; Deakin, *The Last Days* cit., p. 126.

25 De Felice, *La Guerra Civile* cit., pp. 525–6. On the Verona trial, see transcript in G.F. Venè, *Il Processo di Verona* (Milan, 1963).

26 Edda Ciano, *My Truth* (London, 1976), pp. 226–7; Deakin, *The Last Days* cit., p. 144; A. Spinosa, *Edda: una Tragedia Italiana* (Milan, 1993), pp. 339ff.

27 R. Lazzero, *Il Sacco d'Italia* (Milan, 1994), pp. 22–3; P. Monelli, *Mussolini Piccolo Borghese* (Milan, 1950), pp. 350–3.

28 R. von Rahn, *Ruheloses Leben* (Düsseldorf, 1949), p. 251.

29 Colloquio, 14 February 1944, in ACS, Fondo Susmel, b. 8.

30 G. Bocca, *La Repubblica di Mussolini* (Bari, 1977), p. 159; cf. also Deakin, *The Last Days* cit., pp. 166–80; Ganapini, *La Repubblica* cit., ch. 5.

31 R. Luraghi, *Il Movimento Operaio Torinese durante la Resistenza* (Turin, 1958), pp. 268–9; Ganapini, *La Repubblica* cit., p. 434; A. Lepre, *La Storia della Repubblica di Mussolini* (Milan, 1999), p. 144.

32 Open letter to the *Duce*, 4 July 1944, in ACS, SPD, RSI, c. ris., b. 68; Lepre, *Storia della Repubblica* cit., p. 154; S. Bertoldi, *La Guerra Parallela* (Milan, 1966), p. 15; De Felice, *Guerra Civile* cit., pp. 301–19.

33 ACS, SPD, RSI, c. ris., b. 68, sottof. 7.

34 Ibid.

35 P. Spriano, *Storia del Partito Comunista Italiano* (Turin, 1967–75), iv, pp. 333–5.

36 Aldo Melchiorri to Mussolini, 15 June 1944; ACS, SPD, RSI, c. ris, b. 16. Cf. De Felice, *Guerra Civile* cit., p. 141.

37 'In the history of the Roman Empire there was a period of anarchy known as the time of the Thirty Tyrants. Make sure it does not come back, and abolish them.' Schuster to Mussolini, 30 October 1944: ACS, SPD, RSI, c. ris., b. 49.

38 G. Buffarini Guidi, *La Vera Verità* (Milan, 1970), p. 134. For Mussolini's circulars to Prefects ('Heads of Provinces') on 23 December 1943 and 9 June 1944, see ACS, SPD, RSI, c. ris., b. 26, f. 191R. Cf. also Bertoldi, *La Guerra Parallela* cit., pp. 205–14.

39 Spriano, *Storia del Partito Comunista* cit., v, p. 346; De Felice, *Guerra Civile* cit., pp. 161–4; G. Bocca, *Storia dell' Italia Partigiana* (Bari, 1966), p. 569.

40 C. Pavone, *Una Guerra Civile* (Turin, 1991), pp. 413, 511–12. On post-war deaths, cf. N.S. Onofrio, *Il Triangolo Rosso* (Rome, 1994); G. Oliva, *La Resa dei Conti* (Milan, 2000); G. Pansa, *Il Sangue dei Vinti* (Milan, 2003).

41 Mussolini to Hitler, 1 November 1943; *OO* xxxii, pp. 207–8.

42 Spriano, *Storia del Partito Comunista* cit., v, pp. 184ff.; Bocca, *La Repubblica di Mussolini* cit., pp. 75–6, 97ff.

43 ACS, SPD, RSI, c. ris., b. 16; Mellini, *Guerra Diplomatica* cit., pp. 71–2, 157–8.

44 Mussolini to von Rahn, 17 August 1944; *OO* xliii, pp. 161–6.

45 Mussolini to von Rahn, 15 September 1944; ACS, SPD, RSI, c. ris., b. 16.

46 R. De Felice, *Rosso e Nero* (Milan, 1995), pp. 109–10.

47 M. Michaelis, *Mussolini and the Jews* (Oxford, 1978), p. 392; R. De Felice, *Storia degli Ebrei Italiani sotto il Fascismo* (Turin, 1961), pp. 465ff. About 600 survived.

48 Michaelis, *Mussolini and the Jews* cit., pp. 365, 392–406; De Felice, *Storia degli Ebrei Italiani* cit., pp. 472ff. (on the role of Church organisations in Rome, pp. 476–83).

49 G. Zachariae, *Mussolini si Confessa* (Milan, 1950), pp. 9–13, 220; ACS, Fondo Susmel, b. 8.

50 Deakin, *The Last Days* cit., pp. 213–16; S. Bertoldi, *Soldati a Salò* (Milan, 1995), pp. 67–81.

51 On 20 January 1945 an RSI delegation went to see von Rahn; M. Viganò, *Il Ministero degli Affari Esteri della Repubblica di Salò* (Milan, 1991), pp. 568ff.; Deakin, *The Last Days* cit., pp. 244–5; Lepre, *Storia della Repubblica* cit., p. 282.

52 His speech is in *OO* xxxii, pp.126–39. Cf. Lepre, *Storia della Repubblica* cit., pp. 266–74.

53 Mussolini to Mellini, 17 February 1945; Mellini, *Guerra Diplomatica* cit, pp. 70–1.

54 Anfuso, *Da Palazzo Venezia* cit., p. 403.

55 *OO* xxxii, pp. 157–61.

56 ACS, Graziani papers, b. 71.

57 B. Smith and E. Aga Rossi, *Operation Sunrise* (London, 1979).

58 Spriano, *Storia del Partito Comunista Italiano* cit., v, pp. 538–9.

59 Bertoldi, *Guerra Parallela* cit., p. 57.

60 Deakin, *The Last Days* cit., pp. 316–20; I. Schuster, 'My last meeting with Mussolini', in Mussolini, *Memoirs 1942–3* cit. (English edn), pp. 254–60; also I. Schuster, *Gli Ultimi Tempi di un Regime* (Milan, 1960).

61 G. Contini, *La Valigia di Mussolini* (Milan, 1996), pp. 235–7.

62 G. Pisanò, *Gli Ultimi Cinque Secondi del Duce* (Milan, 1996), pp. 69ff.; F. Bandini, *Le Ultime 95 Ore di Mussolini* (Milan, 1972).

Conclusion

Debates Among Historians

The macabre scene at piazzale Loreto was not the end of the story. Mussolini's body was subject to a hasty autopsy at the forensic medicine institute and was then buried in Musocco cemetery in Milan. It soon became a political trophy, pursued by his devoted followers and concealed by the authorities. Only in 1957 was it restored to his family and finally buried at San Cassiano cemetery in Predappio.[1] Meanwhile many of his supporters were also being buried. At least 12,000 'Fascists' (many simply local landowners or officials, ex-Fascists or not), perhaps as many as 30,000, were killed in the summer of 1945, after the war had ended; the 'civil war' continued, particularly in Emilia-Romagna and Piedmont.[2] Anti-Fascism, at least in northern Italy, became far more widespread than it had been in July 1943, or even in 1943–5. Indeed, in these regions local government and public sector jobs were soon controlled by the resistance parties. The 'values of the resistance' became compulsory; even in 1975 a law on public order laid down severe penalties for anyone who dared to criticise them.[3] The resistance parties also brought in a new constitution in 1946–7, deliberately designed to disperse power and prevent any revival of one-man rule. Northern anti-Fascist coalitions ruled the country, on overtly northern anti-Fascist principles. But there had been little resistance in the south, and in any case the Cold War soon cooled down excesses of anti-Fascist ardour. By 1946 Fascist squads were active again in Rome and the south, tacitly condoned as a bulwark against a far more pressing Communist threat than had been evident in 1919–20.[4] A revived neo-Fascist party, the 'Italian Social Movement' (*Movimento Sociale Italiano*, MSI), arose and eventually became quite respectable, although it had no outstanding leader: there was no second *Duce*. In 1994, and again in 2001, it entered the government coalition.

Mussolini, therefore, left a legacy of both anti-Fascism and neo-Fascism, a rich source of conflict for years to come. He also left behind a defeated country, much of it rent by civil war. The new Christian

Democrat rulers of post-war Italy retained much of the Fascist welfare state and the various economic agencies, so Mussolini's corporatist, interventionist legacy lived on. However, the Christian Democrats also brought Italy into the Western fold. Italy had lost a world war, but the Allied occupation – never very stringent – soon ended, the country was not partitioned and the Marshall aid flowed in. The fall of Fascism and the military defeat proved much less damaging than they might have done, both for Italy and for Mussolini's surviving supporters. True, Italy lost her colonies and her Adriatic territories at the peace treaty of 1947, and her post-war politicians complained loudly about this 'mutilated defeat', but she retained Trieste and the South Tyrol and in general got away remarkably lightly. This was partly because the Badoglio government had managed to change sides in 1943–5 and partly because of the resistance, but mainly because of the Cold War, the Italian lobby in the United States of America, and the Church.

Mussolini's death also triggered a historical debate that has continued, particularly in Italy, to this day: how to make sense of Mussolini, and of Fascism? These arguments are not just about the past; they concern also the nature of the Italian state and of Italian national identity. As the historian Gioacchino Volpe wrote in 1945, 'we will rebuild the houses, we will repair the roads and the bridges, perhaps we will restore our industries and our agriculture; but what about our status in other countries? And our own self-confidence? And our work of civilisation in Africa? And our independence?'[5] Initially, it is true, most historical writers did not worry too much about such matters. Anti-Fascist sentiment was de rigueur, although within this framework opinions might differ widely. The liberal philosopher and historian Benedetto Croce, for example, dismissed Fascism as an unwelcome interlude – a '20 years' parenthesis' – in the long Whig advance of secular progress; Mussolini himself was best forgotten with a fastidious shudder.[6] More radical historians, especially those with connections to the Communist, Socialist or Action parties, were more astringent. The spirit of piazzale Loreto lived on. Fascism was seen as a cruel tyranny imposed on the Italian people, usually by the agrarian-capitalist class. Often it was virtually equated with Nazism, and always with war and defeat. Interestingly, these historians wrote a great deal about the Fascists' 'seizure of power' in 1919–25 and about the Republic of Salò and the resistance (1943–5), but relatively little about the main years of Fascist dominance from 1926 to 1943. In other words, they concentrated on periods when there *was* some evident opposition to Fascism. Historians shared the perspective of the general (northern) public and of the political parties, and contributed to it. The 'Fascist regime' was seen essentially in the light of Salò; 'anti-Fascism', too, meant the heroic, fighting resistance of 1943–5, not the long earlier years of squabbling exile and impotence. This perspective was, of course, convenient. It enabled many people who had collaborated without protest for years before 1943 to claim anti-Fascist credentials because of what they had done in 1944–5 or even, as was true of almost half the partisans, only in April 1945. Above all, the resistance, seen as a heroic national struggle, legitimised the post-war Republic and its ruling anti-Fascist parties.

In Anglo-Saxon countries this 'anti-Fascist' view also largely prevailed, being a continuation of wartime propaganda about Italy's woes having been caused by 'one man alone'. However, British and American historians tended to regard Mussolini and his regime more condescendingly. The *Duce* appeared as a ludicrous buffoon, a man who might have deceived simple-minded Italians but would never have been taken seriously in more sophisticated societies. The classic expression of this view is in Denis Mack Smith's biography and other works,[7] but it is worth also quoting A.J.P. Taylor's assessment of Fascism: 'Everything about Fascism was a fraud. The social peril from which it saved Italy was a fraud; the revolution by which it seized power was a fraud; the ability and policy of Mussolini were fraudulent. Fascist rule was corrupt, incompetent, empty; Mussolini himself a vain, blundering boaster without either ideas or aims.'[8] Well, yes; but that's politics, and not only in Italy.

As wartime memories faded, these views came to be challenged. Mussolini's own collected works were gradually published, eventually in 44 volumes of around 500 pages each.[9] The massive biography of Mussolini by Renzo De Felice – eight volumes, around 6,500 pages in all plus documentary appendices[10] – soon followed. So Mussolini was not only prolix in himself, but the cause that prolixity was in other men. De Felice provided an extremely well-documented account of a huge range of topics, some only loosely connected with Mussolini; his book notably lacked coherence. He clearly changed his mind about the *Duce* as he went along, not surprisingly since the biography took him 30 years and was left unfinished even then. Moreover, De Felice wrote with a lofty contempt for style, presentation or readers. However, he liked a good argument and so he also produced several lighter and more polemical pieces, usually based on interviews given to journalists and written up by them: his 'Interview on Fascism' of 1975, and his 'Red and Black' in 1995,[11] were far more accessible than the biography and reached a far larger audience.

De Felice's message may be summarised crudely as being 'anti-anti-Fascist'. In his view Mussolini, a man of his times, was not really a tyrant and indeed had many political virtues. He was a brilliant manoeuvrer and mediator who spotted his opportunity in 1920–2, put himself at the head of middle-class reaction to the trade unions and the (not serious) Bolshevik threat, then reached a viable compromise with the Establishment in the 1920s, ruled with consensus and considerable popular support for many years, and delighted the country by two outstanding achievements: 'reconciling' Church and state, and founding an empire. He had no great original ideas: 'corporatism' helped buy off discontent during the Depression, but it was no way to run an economy. However, Mussolini pushed through beneficial development schemes, particularly in the Pontine marshes, and was widely admired both at home and abroad. His regime was of course oppressive, *ma non troppo*; he sought Mediterranean glory on the cheap, but that was normal practice for Italian (and non-Italian) politicians. De Felice admitted that by the late 1930s the *Duce* and his regime were in decline. The 'reform of customs' was absurd and alienated many, as did the anti-Semitic laws. The war itself was a disaster, although Mussolini should not be blamed too much for joining it as there was no realistic alternative in June 1940. Nor was there any realistic alternative to his heading the Salò Republic in 1943, at a time when the Nazis were bent on revenge and no one predicted the northern civil war. De Felice regarded anti-Fascist sentiment as negligible between 1926 and 1943. The resistance itself was, in his view, morally questionable, restricted to a few regions, largely Communist and militarily ineffective. It was both divided and divisive, and certainly could not be regarded as the legitimating basis of the post-war Republic.

The influence of De Felice on my own book will be readily apparent, as it is on all contemporary work and debate about the Fascist period. But perhaps the real subject of De Felice's work was not so much Mussolini himself as the 'flankers' – the Establishment men, the conservative trimmers and office-holders who backed the *Duce* for good reasons in 1922 and curbed his excesses thereafter. Fascism had *not* been a 'parenthesis', nor even an imposition; it had been an imaginative response to particular circumstances, and it had relied on support from all the important groups in the country. If, as many Anglo-Saxon historians seem to believe, the true function of the historian is to name the guilty men, then in De Felice's view they were many, not just one.

Similar 'revisionist' views are found in other historians, including at least three recent British works by Richard Lamb, Jasper Ridley and Nicholas Farrell.[12] Most 'revisionists', less nuancés or perhaps less obscure than De Felice, praise Mussolini's domestic policies and in some cases even stress how Mussolini made the trains run on time[13] – not, of course, such a trivial achievement, as recent British experience shows. The *Duce* appears as the Italian Mrs Thatcher, rescuing his country from leftist shambles and acting as stern custodian of patriotic values. In extreme moments some of the 'revisionists' even defend the indefensible, Mussolini's foreign policy in the late 1930s; for them the villain was Eden, who obstinately rejected Italy's perfectly reasonable claims and forced poor Mussolini into Hitler's arms. No one, I think, has yet defended Mussolini's conduct of the war itself, but perhaps it is only a matter of time.

De Felice's work was a nasty shock to anti-Fascist historians. They could hardly deny De Felice's encyclopaedic knowledge of the archival sources, but they certainly questioned many of his conclusions. They insisted that the Fascist regime had never enjoyed popular support, that the regime *had* been oppressive and violent, that the methods (e.g. gas) used in *colonial* wars had been barbaric, above all that the resistance *had* been a victorious national struggle, not a fratricidal conflict between two sides and largely irrelevant to the German–Allied war. No consensus on these matters is yet in sight. Nonetheless, there were soon clear signs that the De Felice camp was winning the main arguments on domestic policy (not on colonial issues, where the anti-Fascist consensus remained as fashionable as ever). The collapse of the Communist regimes in eastern Europe in 1989, and the slightly later collapse of the anti-Fascist parties in Italy amid corruption scandals, further weakened the previous anti-Fascist ideological front. In 1991 even a well-known anti-Fascist historian like Claudio Pavone entitled a major work on the resistance *Una Guerra Civile*, 'A Civil War',[14] a title unthinkable a decade earlier as it implies two sides. Historians no longer felt the need to proclaim their anti-Fascist credentials, nor to fight yesterday's battles. On the contrary, now it became fashionable to criticise the left parties, especially the Communists, more freely. The moral guilt of Fascism was less heavy, or was at least shared with others. Anti-Fascist historians remained anti-Fascist, but became more moderate and more aware of regional complexities and differences. De Felice's opponents absorbed much from the master, while rejecting 'revisionism' overall. In France and Britain, two successful recent biographies by Pierre Milza and Richard Bosworth[15] have been not so much 'anti-Fascist' as 'anti-anti-anti-Fascist'. Further refinements will no doubt follow.

Another aspect of the debate has become more prominent recently. Since 1945 (or rather since 8 September 1943) the Italian state has had little real independence, its foreign and defence policies being controlled by foreigners. Its values and institutions have been imported too, usually from America, Russia or 'Europe'. All the dominant anti-Fascist groups belonged to international networks of some kind, and were cosmopolitan in outlook. However, as the Cold War ended and Yugoslavia imploded, it looked briefly as if Italy might have to stand on her own again, for the first time since the Second World War. Mussolini therefore came to be seen as the last independent Italian, indeed as the embodiment of Italian national identity. An excellent biography of him in the mid-1990s was entitled *Mussolini l'Italiano*, 'Mussolini the Italian'.[16] He was regarded either as an awful warning of the dangers of 'going it alone', or as a reminder that Italy had been an autonomous international actor in recent times and might become so again. Mussolini, like Haider or Le Pen, became a prominent spectre at the 'global' feast; a reminder that history was not dead yet and that prosperous, cosmopolitan society might have to contend with more than just *religious* fundamentalism.

In fact, however, Mussolini was fairly cosmopolitan too. He spoke French well, used German and English regularly, read widely in European culture and himself flirted with the idea of European union – to contain the Germans![17] His problem was not that he was excessively chauvinistic; it was the fact that he was so insecure, and therefore so competitive. The most important lesson of Mussolini's life is simply a very old-fashioned truism: character *is* destiny – although in politics character is always constrained by circumstance. Mussolini had great gifts; they brought him to power. He had great faults too; they determined how he used it, and brought about disaster. This is not all that unusual. Indeed, Mussolini's life and regime is a familiar story in the business world. A dynamic, ambitious new managing director comes in, sacks the incompetent and brings in new men and new ideas. The share price goes up, and the press is highly impressed. Then the manager becomes determined to make his company bigger, and to take over smaller rivals. He expands into foreign markets that he knows nothing about, and disaster follows. But it is all a familiar story in politics too. The qualities that help bring men into power, and even those required for initial success, are not the same as those needed to exercise it well in the long run. Very few people use power well, and the few who do are usually those who win wars and are then lucky enough to be dismissed (Churchill) or to die quickly (Cavour, Lincoln and F.D. Roosevelt).

Another obvious, indeed banal, lesson of Mussolini's career is that public debate, opposition and constitutional liberties *are* desirable, not just for the individual citizen but for good government – although admittedly this may only become apparent in the long run. Power always rests on opinion, but opinion needs to be easily expressed and alternatives need to be widely discussed, including among non-experts.

However, this is not exciting news. It is, I think, more interesting to stress that Mussolini's legacy *is* a real challenge to contemporary Italian and European society, because his values in general have become so politically incorrect but are still in fact widely shared. For his admirers, he is 'the Last Man in Europe', embodying the unfashionable masculine virtues – courage, forthrightness, initiative and a robust acceptance of risk. He believed in order and discipline, in rewarding the talented and punishing the guilty. He had no interest in money, nor in domestic comfort. He was not afraid to offend people, nor to fight for his beliefs. He found competition and exercise stimulating, he was genuinely patriotic and he had little patience for tedious debate or legal/bureaucratic conventions. Mussolini was undoubtedly a 'man of the people', one of the very few prominent Italian politicians without a conventional middle-class background or a law degree. He was clever, streetwise and attractively subversive of established pieties. He also took a firm line on women's rights, population issues and race relations. He was aggressively male, and both men and women admired him for it. As he said himself at the end of his life, 'I did not create Fascism; I drew it from the Italians' unconscious minds. If that had not been so, they would not all have followed me for 20 years – I repeat, all of them, because a tiny, really microscopic minority can have no weight.'[18] His views were widespread at the time and still are, although now they have become unacceptable in polite society. But not all society is polite.

Another aspect of Mussolini's personality has provided an even more significant legacy. His unabashed masculinity may now be unusual, but his 'histrionic personality' still seems relatively common. We live in a media-saturated age when political power rests on showmanship, and people of Mussolini's kind are the ones most likely to be successful. His regime was arguably the world's first true 'mediacracy': the rule of a journalist king where media control, propaganda and 'spin' were often the central activities of government. Mussolini replaced parliamentary government by 'the cult of personality', a curious mix of omniscience and posturing; a quasi-presidential government with no need for colleagues, merely for a few disposable, ever-changing technical assistants. Mussolini's regime also reduced local government to impotence, bureaucratised and centralised social welfare, tried to impose a 'corporatist' economy, and did impose grotesque over-regulation and an obvious 'democratic deficit'. In his later years the *Duce* also sought to change people's social habits and everyday behaviour, even to control their language and to make some things unsayable. None of this gave him real power, but it did give him the opportunity to posture and to interfere, and he made the most of it. Mussolini was never willing to mind his own business, and he was not alone in that. Most of his aspirations and innovations have been all too widely copied, and are indeed the basis of the modern European state. Furthermore, Mussolini's regime, like other people's, constantly sought prestige by foreign wars against apparently weak opponents, and ultimately collapsed as a result. Perhaps Mussolini was right after all. He had seen the future, although it doesn't work.

Notes

1 S. Luzzatto, *Il Corpo del Duce* (Turin, 1998).

2 G. Oliva, *La Resa dei Conti* (Milan, 1999), pp. 12, 115–17; G. Bocca, *La Repubblica di Mussolini* (Bari, 1977), p. 339.

3 Law 22 May 1976, no. 152 ('legge Reale'), art. 7.

4 M. Clark, 'Italian *squadrismo* and contemporary vigilantism', in *European History Quarterly* xviii (1988), pp. 33–49, at pp. 42–5; G. Salierno, *Autobiografia di un Picchiatore Fascista* (Turin, 1978); P. Murgia, *Il Vento del Nord* (Milan, 1975).

5 G. Volpe, *Storici e Maestri* (2nd edn, Florence, 1967), p. 285.

6 B. Croce, speech to parties of Committee of National Liberation, 28 January 1944; in *Per la Nuova Vita dell' Italia* (Naples, 1944), pp. 55–6.

7 D. Mack Smith, *Mussolini* (London, 1981); *Italy: A Modern History* (2nd edn, Ann Arbor, 1969); *Mussolini's Roman Empire* (Harmondsworth, 1976).

8 A.J.P. Taylor, *The Origins of the Second World War* (Harmondsworth, 1964), pp. 84–5.

9 B. Mussolini, *Opera Omnia* (vols 1–36, Florence, 1951–63; vols 37–44, Rome, 1978–81).

10 R. De Felice, *Mussolini il Rivoluzionario* (Turin, 1965); *Mussolini il Fascista*, 2 vols (Turin, 1966–8); *Mussolini il Duce*, 2 vols (Turin, 1974–81); *Mussolini l'Alleato*, 3 vols (Turin, 1990–7).

11 R. De Felice, *Intervista sul Fascismo* (Bari, 1975); *Rosso e Nero* (Milan, 1995).

12 R. Lamb, *Mussolini and the British* (London, 1997); J. Ridley, *Mussolini* (London, 1997); N. Farrell, *Mussolini: A New Life* (London, 2003).

13 Ridley, *Mussolini* cit., pp. 210–11.

14 C. Pavone, *Una Guerra Civile* (Turin, 1991).

15 P. Milza, *Mussolini* (Paris, 1999); R.J.B. Bosworth, *Mussolini* (London, 2002).

16 A. Lepre, *Mussolini l'Italiano* (Milan, 1995).

17 'Conversation with Maddalena Moulier', in *OO* xxxii, pp. 157–61, at p. 159.

18 'Soliloquy on Trimellone island', 20 March 1945, in *OO* xxxii, p. 170.

Chronology

1883	(29 July) Birth of Benito Mussolini near Predappio
1885	(January) Birth of Arnaldo (brother)
1888	(November) Birth of Edvige (sister)
1892–4	Attends school of Salesian friars at Faenza; expelled
1894–1901	Attends teacher-training school at Forlimpopoli
1896	(March) Battle of Adowa; Ethiopians defeat Italians
1902	(February–July) Temporary teacher at Gualtieri
1902–4	(July 1902–November 1904) In Switzerland, as manual worker and Socialist journalist
1905–6	(January 1905–September 1906) Military service in regiment of *bersaglieri*
1906–7	(November 1906–July 1907) Teaching job at Tolmezzo
1907	(November) Qualifies as secondary school teacher in French
1908	(March–July) Teaching job at Oneglia; edits *La Lima*
1909	(February–September) Secretary of Chamber of Labour in Trent; expelled from Austria
1909–12	(September 1909–November 1912) In Forlì, begins serious journalistic and political activity in Italian Socialist party Cohabits with Rachele Guidi; daughter Edda born 1910
1911	(September) Italy invades Libya; protest movements in Romagna
1911–12	(October 1911–March 1912) In Forlì prison for instigation to violence; writes autobiography
1912	(July) Triumphant speech at Socialist party congress in Reggio Emilia
1912–14	(November 1912–October 1914) In Milan, successful editor of Socialist party newspaper *Avanti!*
1914	(June) 'Red Week' (August) First World War begins. Italy remains neutral (October–November) Decides to support Italian entry into war; expelled from Socialist party; founds own newspaper *Il Popolo d'Italia*

1915	(May) Italy enters First World War on side of France, Britain and Russia
	(September 1915–February 1917) Serves in war with *bersaglieri*
	(November) Birth of Benito, son of Ida Dalser
	(December) Marries Rachele Guidi
1916	(September) Birth of eldest legitimate son, Vittorio
1917	(February) Badly wounded in artillery accident; in military hospitals until July
	(August 1917–November 1918) Journalist in Milan; prominent anti-defeatist campaigner
1917	(October) Battle of Caporetto; Germans and Austrians occupy much of Venetia
1918	(April) Birth of second legitimate son, Bruno
1918	(November) Italy and her allies win First World War
	(November 1918–October 1922) Journalist and political campaigner in Milan
1919	(23 March) Founds Fascist political movement, *Fasci di Combattimento*
	(June) Peace treaty signed at Versailles
	(September) D'Annunzio takes Fiume (Rijeka)
	(November) General election. Fascists do very badly
1920	(Autumn) Squad activities become prominent in Po valley and Tuscany
	(November) Treaty of Rapallo settles Italo-Yugoslav border disputes
	(December) Italian government ejects D'Annunzio from Fiume
1921	(May) Elected as deputy to Italian parliament
	(July) 'Pact of Pacification' between Fascists and Socialists
	(November) Fascist movement becomes 'Fascist National Party' (PNF)
1922	(28 October) 'March on Rome'
	(30 October) Appointed Prime Minister
	(December) Founds Grand Council and Militia (MVSN)
1923	(August) Corfu incident
1924	(April) Parliamentary elections give big majority to Fascists and allies
	(10 June) Abduction and murder of Giacomo Matteotti
1925	(3 January) Speech in Chamber of Deputies; end of 'Matteotti crisis'

(Spring) Ill with suspected ulcer

(February 1925–March 1926) Farinacci secretary of PNF

(May) Foundation of *Opera Nazionale Dopolavoro* (leisure activities)

(June) Second (and last) Congress of PNF

(June) Proclaims 'Battle for wheat'

(October) Locarno conference and treaty

(November) Assassination attempt by Zaniboni foiled by police; laws curbing press and banning secret associations (Freemasons)

1925–9 Campaign led by Prefect Mori against Mafia in Sicily

1926 (March 1926–October 1930) Augusto Turati party secretary

(April) Assassination attempt by Violet Gibson; law on labour relations (Rocco)

(July) Ministry of Corporations founded

(August) Speech on lira at Pesaro

(September) Assassination attempt by Lucetti

(October) Assassination attempt by Zamboni in Bologna

(November) Special Tribunal for Defence of State founded; internal exile (*confino*) introduced for political prisoners

1927 (April) Charter of Labour

(May) Ascension Day speech

(September) Birth of third legitimate son, Romano

1928 (November) National Confederation of Fascist Syndicates split up

(December) 'Mussolini law' on land improvement and reclamation

1929 (February) Lateran Pacts; 'Reconciliation' between Church and state

(March) New Chamber of Deputies elected on 'plebiscite' system

(September) Birth of second daughter, Anna Maria; Moves into villa Torlonia; moves office to palazzo Venezia; government reshuffle: Grandi Foreign Minister, Arpinati under-secretary of Interior

(October) Inauguration of Royal Italian Academy

1930 (April) Edda marries Galeazzo Ciano

(October 1930–December 1931) Giovanni Giuriati party secretary

1931	(September) Dispute over Catholic Action and youth clubs settled
	(December) Death of Arnaldo (brother)
	Starace becomes party secretary
1932	(July) Resumes Foreign Ministry; Grandi sent to be ambassador in London
1933	(January) Adolf Hitler becomes Chancellor of Germany
	(May) Arpinati dismissed as under-secretary of Interior; replaced by Buffarini Guidi
	(June) 'Four-Power Pact' signed in Rome
	(July) Balbo leads mass transatlantic flight to Chicago
1934	(January) Balbo sent to be Governor of Libya
	(February) 'Corporations' founded
	(July) Murder of Dollfuss; first Austrian crisis
1935	(January) 'Rome Accords' with France
	(April) Stresa conference
	(June) Ministry of Press and Propaganda founded, Galeazzo Ciano as minister
	(October 1935–May 1936) Italo-Ethiopian War
	(November) League of Nations imposes sanctions on Italy
	(December) 'Hoare–Laval Pact'
1936	(March) Germany moves troops into Rhineland 'demilitarised zone'
	(May) Italy defeats Ethiopia; King Victor Emmanuel III proclaimed Emperor
	(June) Galeazzo Ciano becomes Foreign Minister; Anna Maria contracts polio
	(July) German–Austrian 'modus vivendi'; sanctions on Italy lifted; Spanish Civil War begins
	(Autumn) Claretta Petacci becomes favourite mistress
	(November) Proclaims Rome–Berlin 'Axis'
1937	(March) Battle of Guadalajara
	(May) Ministry of Press and Propaganda becomes Ministry of Popular Culture
	(June) Murder of Rosselli brothers
	(September) Visits Berlin
1938	(March) Germany annexes Austria (*Anschluss*)
	(April) 'Easter Agreement' with Britain
	(May) Hitler visits Rome
	(September) Munich conference
	(October) Anti-Jewish laws

337

1938–9	Anti-bourgeois campaign; 'reform of customs'
1939	(January) 'Chamber of *Fasci* and Corporations' replaces Chamber of Deputies
	(March) Germany annexes whole of Czechoslovakia
	(April) Italy annexes Albania
	Franco wins Spanish Civil War
	(May) 'Pact of Steel', Italo-German military alliance, signed
	(August) Nazi–Soviet Pact between Germany and USSR
	(September) Germany and USSR invade Poland; Second World War begins. Italy remains neutral
	(October) Starace replaced as party secretary by Muti
1940	(May) Germany defeats French army
	(June) Italy joins war on German side; Franco–German armistice
	(October) Italy invades Greece; Serena replaces Muti as party secretary
	(November) British attack Italian fleet at Taranto
	(December) British defeat Italian troops in North Africa, take Cyrenaica and Tobruk
1941	(March) British naval victory at battle of Matapan
	(June) Germany invades USSR
	(August) Bruno killed in air crash at Pisa
	(December) Pearl Harbor; USA enters war; Vidussoni becomes party secretary
1942	(October–November) Battle of El Alamein
1943	(January) Russians defeat Germans at battle of Stalingrad
	Allies take Libya; Axis troops retreat to Tunisia
	(February) Government reshuffle; Ciano becomes ambassador to Vatican
	(April) Scorza becomes party secretary
	(May) Allies take Tunisia
	(July) Allies take Sicily; Feltre conference with Hitler
	(24–5 July) Meeting of Grand Council; dismissed by King Victor Emmanuel III
	(25 July–12 Sept) In custody at Ponza, La Maddalena and the Gran Sasso
	(12 Sept) Rescued from Gran Sasso
	(September–October) Installed at Gargnano as head of Italian Social Republic (RSI, 'Republic of Salò')

1944	(January) Ciano and four others shot at Verona
	(Spring) Partisans active against RSI and Germans in N. Italy
	(June) Allies occupy Rome; Normandy landings ('D-day')
	(July) Visits Hitler at Rastenburg
	(December) Visits and makes public speeches in Milan
1945	(18 April) Moves from Gargnano to Milan
	(25 April) Meeting in Milan with Cardinal Schuster and CLNAI leaders
	(25–7 April) Flees to Lake Como area; captured by partisans near Dongo
	(28 April) Shot by Communist partisans, as is Claretta Petacci
	(29 April) Body exhibited publicly at piazzale Loreto, Milan
1957	Buried at San Cassiano cemetery, Predappio

Index